ECONOMIC DEVELOPMENT

An Introduction

ECONOMIC DEVELOPMENT

An Introduction

Clarence Zuvekas, Jr.

ST. MARTIN'S PRESS · NEW YORK

54018

TO ANN

Library of Congress Catalog Card Number: 78–73035
Copyright © 1979 by St. Martin's Press, Inc.
All Rights Reserved.
Manufactured in the United States of America.
32109
fedcba
For information, write St. Martin's Press, Inc.,
175 Fifth Avenue, New York, N. Y. 10010

cover design: Janice Poretz
typography: Leon Bolognese

ISBN: 0–312–22806–6

Preface

This textbook treats economic development as an interdisciplinary subject and is designed specifically for courses in which many students may not be economics majors. Its focus thus differs from that of the several good-to-excellent texts aimed at advanced undergraduate and graduate students in economics. Still, it is written from an economist's perspective, with no attempt at any "grand synthesis" of the social sciences.

Coverage of the subject matter is fairly comprehensive but certainly not exhaustive. Space considerations dictate that some topics be treated only briefly, and this results inevitably in generalizations with which I myself am sometimes uncomfortable. However, students should not have to wade through qualifications and exceptions to every statement. For those who wish to explore certain topics in more detail, the annotated references at the end of each chapter provide a guide to studies that can be read without great difficulty. These references are selective because important works on the subject now run into the thousands. The compactness of the text should afford instructors considerable flexibility in assigning additional readings of particular interest to them.

Since I began teaching development economics in the early 1960s, this relatively new field has matured and changed significantly. Fifteen years ago, economists tended to devote much attention to abstract theories of development. There were several reasons for this, including (1) a natural tendency to try to bring order and simplicity to a new field of inquiry; (2) fascination with the new Keynesian growth theories; (3) lack of data, which restricted the opportunities for empirical research; and (4) limited experience with institutional environments and practical policy issues in a wide range of developing countries. More recently, greater availability of data and improved tools of analysis have stimulated a great deal of empirical research, much of which has caused economists to revise their notions about the development process. In addition, the firsthand experience acquired by many economists, a result of what might be called the "foreign aid boom" of the 1960s, has made them more concerned about development policy issues and more aware of the importance of political and other noneconomic factors in the development process.

My own classroom teaching has reflected these broad trends. Particularly since acquiring my own overseas experience, both as an academic researcher and as a government employee and consultant, I have placed less emphasis on theories of development and devoted increasing attention to policy issues and empirical findings. But theory cannot be neglected. Microeconomic theory can be used imaginatively to examine a variety of specific policy issues, and macroeconomic theory is necessary if we are to understand problems such as inflation and balance-of-payments deficits. I have no regrets, however, about abandoning the search for a comprehensive theory of development, or mentioning only briefly great debates such as the one over "balanced" versus "unbalanced" growth. Writings on these subjects have often been far removed from the arenas in which policy decisions are made. Graduate students in economics should become acquainted with them, but for undergraduates the priorities lie elsewhere.

In summary, I have tried to achieve a balance between theory and policy, leaving space also for historical interpretation, description, and empirical evidence. The analytical tools used are simple, but they do presume an acquaintance with basic macro and micro theory and with the specialized terminology of economics. Ideally, students should also be acquainted with the theory of comparative advantage in international trade, but for those who are not, a brief introduction is provided.

One of the early and great development economists, Nobel prize-winner Gunnar Myrdal, has advised his colleagues to say something about their values in their writings, since nothing is written from a perfectly value-free, or "objective," standpoint. The very choice of topics and relative emphasis given to each, for example, constitutes a value judgment. May I simply say that I share Myrdal's ideals of liberty and equality of opportunity, recognizing with him that these general terms have different policy implications in each country. It follows from this position, I think, that attitudes toward any particular government's development policy should be based not on what kind of hat the chief executive wears, or on what kind of "ism" he, she, or they *claim* to represent, but rather on what is being done to improve equality of opportunity and the quality of life for *all* of the country's population.

My opinions about the desirability of certain policy actions and the degree to which various governments have pursued them are expressed in this book only occasionally, and, I hope, without implying that they are the only reasonable opinions possible. The policy discussions in this text strive rather to emphasize the reporting of facts and empirical findings and a consideration of different viewpoints. A description and interpretation of events is also necessary to provide perspective, and here I strive to report what I think is happening, even if these perceived trends disappoint or displease me. Readers should not assume that I endorse every reported trend. Instead, they should make up their own minds about the merits of alternative policies regarding such issues as tariffs, land ownership, and population growth, based on their own values and an awareness of the implications of each alternative.

Readers may find it difficult to pin a label on me, for I do not claim to represent any particular "ism." These and similar labels have been so abused that they now have little meaning. Too often there is little connection between what a government actually does and what the stereotype of its label says it is doing, and it is the former that should concern us.

This book draws not only on published materials but also on my research and work experience, since 1965, in Argentina, Bolivia, Ecuador, Haiti, and eight island states in the eastern Caribbean. Each of these countries is unique, and outside of the Western Hemisphere the differences among countries are greater still. I am indebted to the participants in the U.S. Department of Labor's 1964 International Manpower Seminar, for which I served as Chief Rapporteur, for introducing me to some of the issues in their twenty-one countries, mainly in Africa and Asia. Without this experience, my selection of examples from outside Latin America and the Caribbean would have been less informed.

In preparing the final manuscript, I have benefited from critical comments by John Adams and several anonymous reviewers. I would also like to thank Jacques Defay for illuminating discussions of the absorptive capacity issue; Elizabeth Erickson for comments on the Physical Quality of Life Index and many stimulating conversations about development issues generally; and Ann Zuvekas for a valuable critical reading of the section on public health. Judith Cromwell deserves much credit for undertaking the typing of the manuscript and executing it so well on top of an already heavy workload. Valuable editorial assistance was provided by Bertrand W. Lummus and Carolyn Eggleston of St. Martin's Press. Finally, I wish to thank my children, Sam and Ann, for their patience.

Clarence Zuvekas, Jr.

Contents

Introduction

More than 4 billion people now inhabit the earth, and a majority live under conditions that make low-income groups in the United States seem wealthy by comparison. Most of us have seen, on television, the human suffering associated with malnutrition, hunger, and the lack of opportunity for individual or community advancement in some developing countries. Many seem to think that these conditions are inevitable in the early stages of development but gradually will improve as economic growth occurs and yields benefits that will "trickle down" to the poor. In the short run, they may conclude, there is little that can be done to alleviate world poverty, especially in areas such as South Asia and Africa which seem remote and plagued by problems that are too big and complex to solve.

Such attitudes, which combine resignation with complacency, may threaten world political order—and perhaps even the survival of the human race—if they continue to be widely held in the advanced industrial nations. Less industrialized countries (or *developing countries,* as they are now usually called) certainly see nothing inevitable about the present situation, and in the last few decades they have acquired the political power necessary to challenge it effectively. This power is increasingly being exercised in the world arena for the purpose of bringing about a redistribution of global resources and income. The industrial nations are now on the defensive, and if they do not respond to the challenge of the developing countries, the result could well be an increase in the use of economic boycotts, terrorism, and other forms of politically motivated violence. As developing countries acquire nuclear capabilities —as some of them now are doing—the potential results of their actions become frightening.

The very unequal distribution of world income and wealth is deeply rooted in history. The evolution of human society has proceeded at different rates in different geographic regions of the world. Civilization, or the culture of cities, developed first in the Near East and Mediterranean regions, as did the important invention of writing (which seems to have been invented contemporaneously in China). Because of population growth and climatic changes, among other factors, civilization and writing spread northward and westward into Europe, where further advances occurred. After a temporary pause during the so-called Dark Ages following the collapse of the Roman Empire in the fifth century A.D., the groundwork began to be laid in Europe for the scientific and technological revolution that burst forth in the seventeenth and eighteenth centuries.

Scientific and technological developments gave the Europeans not only a material advantage over peoples in other parts of the world but a political and military advantage as well. After Europeans began to cross the oceans in the fifteenth and sixteenth centuries, they were able to subjugate peoples on other continents and to keep for themselves a large share of the fruits of the economic growth they stimulated overseas. At the same time, many Europeans sincerely believed that they were helping to accelerate economic progress in these "heathen" or "barbarian" lands. And most economists (an easily identifiable breed only since the late nineteenth century) were convinced that economic progress in non-European lands would best be stimulated by worldwide application of the principles of free trade and *laissez faire*.

Some writers have attributed international inequality to an "international capitalist conspiracy"; but sophisticated critics of capitalism know that an unconspiratorial "invisible hand" can lead to the same result if capitalists have some form of monopoly power. Because such power did exist in the era of colonialism, international trade policies and the mechanics of colonial administration discriminated in several important respects against the developing countries. On the other hand, we should be careful not to place the entire blame for poverty in the developing countries on European colonists, Yankee imperialists, multinational corporations, or other foreign agents. An examination of the policies followed by independent governments in developing countries quickly reveals that these policies often have prevented economic growth or limited its benefits to a small segment of the popluation.

On the whole, however, governments in developing countries have been following policies in the last two or three decades which have increased domestic savings rates and rates of economic growth. Although this has not generally been accompanied by a more equal distribution of income, impressive gains have been made in many developing countries in nonmonetary dimensions of welfare, such as education, health, and access to transportation and communications facilities. These improvements—together with unprecedented rates of economic growth in the developing world as a whole—are often obscured by ill-informed media reports of "the rich countries getting richer and the poor countries getting poorer." Spokesmen for developing countries may also convey the impression of stagnation or retrogression by expressing disappointment that economic growth and welfare gains have fallen short of expectations. Finally, economists—including the writer of this text—may sometimes lead readers astray by emphasizing the shortcomings of policy making rather than the successes.

This is not say that recent trends in developing countries should be regarded with satisfaction. World Bank President Robert McNamara has estimated that about 40 percent of the developing world's population has not benefited at all from the growth of the last few decades.[1] Indeed, living standards for many persons in this group have declined. With developing countries' aspirations so much higher now than they were twenty to thirty years ago,[2] complacency about recent gains in the developing world—as we argued in our opening paragraphs—is an unhealthy attitude. In our view, it is in the interests of the industrialized countries to support the developing countries' call for more rapid rates of growth and a more widespread improvement of living standards. On equity grounds alone, of course, these are objectives with which many people are in accord. Others, however, see no need for special efforts to accelerate change in the developing world, arguing that the benefits of growth will be widespread in the long run and that tensions between developing countries and industrialized countries can be relieved without resort to violence on a global scale.

Before discussing briefly the organization of this text, it is useful to highlight several major themes that will appear frequently, either explicitly or implicitly. One is that there is no magic key, or surefire formula, for rapid economic development. When one considers the great diversity of resources and institutions in the developing countries, and the fact that they began or are beginning their processes of economic developments in very different historical contexts, it should not be surprising that attempts to construct a grand theory of development have been unsuccessful. A development strategy which works well for one country may fail for others, not just because of political, social, and cultural differences

1. Robert S. McNamara, *One Hundred Countries, Two Billion People: The Dimensions of Development* (New York: Praeger Publishers, 1973), p. 11.
2. The highly industrialized nations were never faced with a large gap between what they had and what they knew had been attained by other nations. The present wide gap has a profound effect on attitudes in the developing countries toward the highly industrialized nations.

but also because of radically different relative factor endowments. Country size is another important factor. Independent countries with populations of only a few hundred thousand or even a few million have domestic markets that are too small for significant economies of scale to be realized for a wide range of products. This fact, combined with a narrow resource base, makes their economic growth and development much more dependent on foreign trade than is the case for countries with large populations and a diversified resource base, such as China and India.

A second theme of this book is that development is more appropriately viewed as a complex, interdisciplinary "art" rather than a narrow branch of economic "science." Too often in the last few decades, economic advisors, donor governments, and international agencies have found that "obvious" solutions to development problems in a particular country turn out to be unrealistic because of social, cultural, and political realities or administrative limitations. And where reliance is placed on the market mechanism, it is sometimes naïvely assumed that markets function as efficiently in developing countries as they do in industrialized capitalist or socialist market economies. In fact, market participants in developing countries—both buyers and sellers—usually have considerably less information than participants in industrialized countries, thus making their responses slower and their risks higher. Many markets have strong elements of monopoly or monopsony (monopoly on the buying side of the market), and if these are ignored, a project may benefit not the intended beneficiaries but rather a privileged few. A project which seeks to increase wheat production among small farmers, for example, may fail to have a significant impact on their incomes if wheat marketing is controlled by a small number of buyers with market power.

Over time, foreign assistance agencies have come to realize that development projects are complex undertakings which must consider more than economic relationships. Project preparation teams now often include anthropologists or sociologists as well as economists, engineers, and other "technical" specialists. Many technocrats have become more flexible in their approaches to policy suggestions, considering the feasibility of their proposals in the light of the social, cultural, and political characteristics peculiar to each project. But despite this greater sensitivity to the complexity of development activities, many projects still are poorly conceived. This may occur because project designers are too inflexible; or because they fail to consult intended project beneficiaries, who even though illiterate may know more about local agronomic or sociological conditions than outside "experts"; or because they misjudge a government's commitment to the project. Whatever the reasons, the "science" of development is still a very imperfect one.

A third theme is that many development projects are undertaken not primarily for their economic benefits but rather for their political impact. The same applies to many development policies. There is nothing unusual about this: "pork barreling" is a common practice in industrialized countries, as are subsidy schemes which benefit influential voting constituencies and are paid for by society at large. To argue that political considerations should play no role in development is naïve; to ignore them is to present an incomplete analysis. Unfortunately, economists have had a difficult time bringing political and other noneconomic variables explicitly into their analyses of the benefits and costs of economic policies and projects.

Finally, we shall argue that the price mechanism is a powerful tool at the disposal of government policy makers. By manipulating relative prices in factor and product markets, policy makers can create incentives for action to achieve development objectives. But some price manipulations—e.g., price controls on retail food sales and public utility rates, or overvalued exchange rates which discourage exports and encourage the importation of capital-intensive technology—can actually retard development. We should make clear that emphasis on the power of the price mechanism does not imply advocacy of a capitalist market economy. Socialist economies, even those relying heavily on the command mechanism, also stand to gain from more judicious manipulation of relative prices.

A few words are now in order about how this book is organized. Chapter 1 attempts to clarify the subject matter of development by examining the semantics of some widely used terms in the field. Particularly important is the distinction between economic growth and economic development. We then consider, in chapters 2 and 3, various economic and noneconomic factors that are alleged to be obstacles to development. Chapter 4 discusses rapid population growth, also widely considered to be an obstacle to development. In chapter 5, we analyze the historical relationship between international trade and economic development, another alleged constraint hindering the progress of the developing countries.

The next ten chapters examine the responses of developing countries' public and private sectors to these constraints. Chapters 6 to 8 are concerned with the role of government in providing physical infrastructure, education, health care, and nutrition, and planning the development process itself. Chapters 9 and 10 examine the development problems of (and relationships between) agriculture and industry, the major production sectors of the economy. Chapters 11 and 12 discuss income distribution and employment, issues that became important in the 1970s because several decades of economic growth had not generally been accompanied by lower unemployment rates and more equal distributions of income. In chapters 13 and 14, we look at problems of mobilizing domestic and foreign savings to meet the investment requirements of rapid economic growth. Chapter 15 evaluates the results of the efforts developing countries have made in the last fifteen to twenty years to change the structure of international trade and finance to their advantage. Finally, in chapter 16, we consider the debate over the limits to world economic growth, focusing on such issues as environmental pollution, energy availabilities, and global food supplies in the context of rapid population growth.

1

Economic Growth and Economic Development
Meaning and Measurement

There is an important distinction between the terms *economic growth* and *economic development,* a distinction not always made clear in the literature on the world's materially poor countries. There are also subtle differences in meaning in the terms that have been used to describe these countries. Language tends to reflect attitudes, and in this particular case it is clear that attitudes have been changing rapidly in the last three decades.

WHAT'S IN A NAME?

Only since the early 1940s have economists given serious attention to the problems of the less affluent countries. In the United States, interest in Latin America was aroused during World War II by security considerations, which resulted in the provision of economic as well as military assistance to countries in that region. After the war, the decolonization movement in Africa and Asia stimulated economists and social scientists all over the world to become concerned with the fate of countries in these continents. At first, economists usually described them as *backward.* This term conjures up images of Rudyard Kipling and his "white man's burden"; or perhaps it reminds us of the views held by some colonial administrators and other Europeans and North Americans encountered in the novels of Joseph Conrad or Graham Greene. Such attitudes, in fact, were quite common at the time and reflected our failure to appreciate the capabilities of both the leaders and the masses in these emerging nations.

By the 1950s the term "backward," with its pejorative connotations, had been generally abandoned in favor of *underdeveloped,* which implied

7

the existence of a potential that could be realized and did not so directly suggest an attitude of cultural superiority on the part of the highly industrialized nations. In the 1960s we began to refer to these countries as *less developed,* an even more acceptable term ("the countries in question are developed, only less so than some others"). Still less of a value judgment, perhaps, was implied by the expression *Third World countries,* used to distinguish these nations from the industrialized Western ("capitalist") nations, on the one hand, and the Eastern ("socialist") nations, on the other.

In the 1970s several new terms came to be frequently employed. One is the expression *developing countries,* which seems to remove all implications of inferiority, since no country has completed the process of development. Another term is *Fourth World countries,* used to indicate the materially least fortunate countries in the old Third World. Alternatively, these very poor countries have been referred to as the *most seriously affected* (MSA) countries. A distinction has also been made between *oil-producing* and *non-oil-producing developing countries* (ODs and NODs). Finally, increasing concern with the preservation of scarce resources and their more equitable distribution among nations has led some writers to refer to the United States and other highly industrialized nations as *overdeveloped countries* (ODCs).

Not everyone is highly sensitive to the choice of terms (though few people would now consider "backward" to be in good taste). Indeed, some representatives of the Third and Fourth Worlds still describe their own countries, as "underdeveloped." The term "less developed countries" continues to be widely used, especially in acronym form (LDCs). But in this text, we shall acknowledge the shift in the literature, and in public forums, toward the term "developing countries."

GROWTH VERSUS DEVELOPMENT

The problems confronting today's developing countries are much different from those now facing the developed countries. We recognize this semantically by referring to the *economic development* problems of the former, while with the latter we are more likely to use the term *economic growth.* Unfortunately, many writers confuse the issue by using these two terms interchangeably. We should, however, make a distinction between them.

Economists generally use the term *economic growth* to refer to increases over time in a country's real output of goods and services—or, more appropriately, real output per capita. Output is conveniently measured by gross national product (GNP) or national income, though other measures could also be used. *Economic development* is a more comprehensive term. Some economists have defined it as growth accompanied by change—changes in the structure of the economy, in the country's social structure, and in its political structure.[1] Viewed in this way, economic development implies a decline in agriculture's share of the gross national product and a corresponding increase in the share of such sectors as manufacturing, utilities, financial institutions, construction, and government administration. Accompanying this shift in economic structure is a shift in the occupational structure of the labor force and an increase in the degree of education and training required of those who seek jobs. Not only do the types of jobs change, but so does their geographic distribution, with most new jobs found in urban areas.

As the population shifts to the cities, new social classes are created: manufacturing, commercial, and financial elites; "middle sectors" of civil servants, shopkeepers, lawyers, managers, students, and other groups who unite on some issues (e.g., education) but not on others (e.g., tax and trade policies); skilled (and often unionized) industrial workers; and, finally, the unskilled masses who exist at the margin of urban economic activity and whose material well-being may be no different from that of the rural poor. Historically, these economic and social changes have been accompanied by a shift in the locus of political power from the regional level, where the landed elite were dominant, to the national level, where the landed elite are forced to compete for power and share it with other socioeconomic interest groups.

Growth does not necessarily imply development. Indeed, a well-known book about an African country is entitled *Growth without Development*.[2] What this essentially means is that a country produces more of the same types of goods and services, to keep up with a growing population or send to overseas markets, while the benefits of this growth continue to go almost exclusively to a privileged elite and a small middle class; the vast majority of the country's people are completely unaffected.

One pattern of growth is sometimes referred to as *dualistic development* (but is more appropriately termed *dualistic growth*). Dualism in this context means that one sector or subsector of the economy experiences significant growth, while the rest of the economy does not. Economic growth in a dual economy often is centered on the production and export of one or a few primary products, the exploitation of which usu-

---

1. This definition is somewhat misleading, since growth is almost always accompanied by some change. It would be more appropriate to distinguish development from growth by focusing on the *types* of change occurring in the economic, social, and political spheres. For example, one might say that development occurs if, over time, a progressively higher percentage of the population shares the fruits of economic growth.

2. Robert Clower et al., *Growth without Development: An Economic Survey of Liberia* (Evanston, Ill.: Northwestern University Press, 1966).

ally can be traced to actions by European (and, later, North American) countries beginning in the sixteenth century.[3] Income generated by this economic growth was shared by representatives of the colonial powers and by a small segment of the indigenous population which benefited through the creation of service jobs. In some cases, workers directly employed in the production of primary products received higher incomes than those engaged in subsistence farming or producing food for the domestic market, as was the case in some of the so-called "banana republics" in the early twentieth century. On other occasions, however, living standards seemed to decline—e.g., for those engaged in gold and silver production under Spanish rulers in the Americas or in the production of spices under the Dutch in Indonesia.

Dualistic growth sometimes left completely untouched those areas and peoples who contributed nothing to the export economy; in the absence of any outside interference, these community-centered, subsistence societies changed very little. This variant of dualism has been referred to as the *enclave economy*. Often, however, the influence of the colonizers extended beyond the export trade.[4] In Latin America, for example, soldiers and religious institutions assumed control of land used to grow crops and raise livestock for domestic consumption. But little if any economic growth occurred in these rural areas; wealth was simply transferred to the new rulers from the indigenous population, whose living standards tended to decline.[5]

During the colonial period, considerations of political power and social status led those governing the destinies of dual economies to restrict educational opportunities to persons who could make some contribution to the export trade or who could occupy lower or middle-level civil service positions in the colonial administration (e.g., overseers, clerks, and accountants). This emergent indigenous middle class expanded as trade increased, but except in a few Latin American countries it was still very small as the world entered the twentieth century.

---

3. A dualistic pattern of growth can also result from inward-looking strategies based on import-substituting industrialization. Such strategies have often discriminated against rural areas (see chapter 10).

4. Some writers deny the existence of a dual economy. Marxist André Gunder Frank (see chapter 5) argues that the effects of external capitalist domination have reached to the farthest corners of the countries being dominated to create what he calls "underdevelopment." While this is a plausible interpretation of what happened in some countries, one can argue that the "enclave economy" model is more appropriate for others. For a review and critique of other meanings that have been given to the term *dual economy,* see Gerald M. Meier, *Leading Issues in Economic Development,* 3rd ed. (New York: Oxford University Press, 1976), pp. 125–165. We discuss dualism again in chapter 5.

5. For a brief interpretation of the colonial period in Latin America, see Celso Furtado, *Economic Development of Latin America: Historical Background and Contemporary Problems,* 2nd ed. (New York: Cambridge University Press, 1976), ch. 2.

Political colonialism has almost entirely disappeared; but because of the persistence of what has been called *economic colonialism,* many independent countries can still be characterized as dual economies. Even in those countries whose economies have become more diversified and less influenced by foreigners, rapid economic growth in the last few decades has bypassed large segments of the population. For developing countries as a group, as we noted in the Introduction, World Bank president Robert McNamara estimates that the poorest 40 percent of the population are not participating in the fruits of economic growth. This writer's experience supports the validity of this rough estimate.

Disappointment over the lack of widespread socioeconomic advances, even under conditions of very rapid economic growth, led in the 1970s to the widespread adoption of an alternative definition, or conception, of economic development. According to this new viewpoint, usually referred to as the *basic (human) needs* approach, economic development should be defined in terms of progress toward reducing the incidences of poverty, unemployment, and income inequalities.[6] For those whose living standards have not been rising, amelioration of those conditions—and not rising GNP per capita—is clearly the essence of development. This is the definition of development we shall adopt in our text. *Poverty,* it should be noted, is defined under the basic human needs approach not in terms of income but rather as the lack of good nutrition, good health, educational opportunities, and similar dimensions of welfare.

NOT BY ECONOMICS ALONE

What we are implying, of course, is that development is not just a matter of economics—a fact recognized explicitly by the University of Wisconsin in Madison, which offers an interdisciplinary Ph.D. in "Development" (not "Economic Development"). Economists who base their policy advice on growth models emphasizing capital formation take too many things for granted (or assume that "other things are equal," as we like to put it). And those who assume that everyone is a rational economic being who responds quickly and predictably to marginal price incentives ignore the very imperfect nature of factor and product markets in developing countries and the lack of information necessary for these markets to function smoothly.

It is difficult, for example, to speak of a rural land market in areas where land is held to maintain social status and political power and ownership rarely changes except through inheritance. With so little land

6. For a brief introduction to the basic needs concept, see Paul Streeten, "The Distinctive Features of a Basic Needs Approach to Development," *International Development Review,* 19 (1977/3), 8–16.

bought and sold in the marketplace, it becomes difficult to know what the true market price might be. Labor mobility is restricted by such phenomena as debt peonage, language barriers, and racial and class discrimination. Few capital markets exist in the early stages of development, and business firms tend to be family concerns whose expansion is limited by the availability of internal savings. Credit may be available only from commercial banks, and then only to a small, privileged clientele. Other financial intermediaries, such as stock and bond exchanges, life insurance companies, credit unions, and savings and loan associations, may be totally absent.

The element of risk is high in such an environment. For a farmer living close to the margin of existence, the prospect of achieving a 30 percent increase in income by switching to a cash crop may be unappealing if it means losing the relative food security that subsistence farming provides, planting an unfamiliar crop with greater risks, and going into debt. This is not to say that subsistence farmers in traditional societies are simply uninterested in change. There is enough accumulated evidence to reject this argument and to support the view that they will indeed respond to economic incentives when the perceived benefits *strongly* outweigh the costs after the benefits have been discounted for risks. It is important to note that the projected economic benefits must be substantial under such circumstances. It has been suggested, for example, that small farmers will not go into debt to purchase chemical fertilizers unless the perceived return on investment is on the order of 3 to 1. While this ratio is very likely an exaggeration, it seems clear that the behavior of the small farmer differs from that of the "marginal man" of traditional economics literature who switches out of treasury bills into other securities at the drop of a half-percentage point in yield.

Most development economists are now aware of these problems and recognize that it is important to take into account political realities, bureaucratic structures, land tenure systems, and a variety of social and cultural factors. Since these "institutional" factors vary so much from country to country, a general theory of economic development is very difficult to formulate. Indeed, no widely accepted general theory exists.

THE THEORY OF DEVELOPMENT AND THE DEVELOPMENT OF THEORY

Fifteen to twenty years ago, the search for a general theory of development was being widely pursued. The less ambitious were content with constructing partial theories explaining only certain aspects of the development process. Today, development economists are less concerned with theorizing about development. The controversies over "balanced" versus "unbalanced" growth (the details of which you will be spared) now seem like the debates of medieval theologians over how many angels could stand on the head of a pin.[7]

Why this declining interest in theorizing? One reason has already been given—the difficulty in finding, and incorporating into our theories and models, institutional or noneconomic phenomena common to more than 100 developing countries. In a different kind of world, economists might have devoted more attention to these knotty theoretical problems. But today's world differs radically from that of the 1940s and 1950s, and this leads us to the second reason for the decline of theorizing: the pressures by the developing countries—many of them newly independent and in control of their destinies for the first time—for immediate development results. What concerns them is not whether they are in Stage 2 or Stage 3 of the growth sequence described by economic historian W. W. Rostow (1971),[*] but rather what specific actions they can take to better feed their growing populations and increase educational opportunities. These are policy questions, and policy must deal with the unique situation of each country; what works in one country will not necessarily work in another. A third reason for the shift away from theorizing is that many economists now have extensive overseas experience as employees of or consultants to international development agencies. As such, they, too, have become concerned with policy, and with the costs and benefits of specific development projects in individual countries. Finally, the increased availablility of statistical data has enticed economists into directing their talents toward empirical studies of particular issues.

All of this is not to say that economic theory has been completely discarded. It is still most valuable in helping us deal with specific problems. In fact, one of the more recent developments in theory—the concept

---

7. The classic treatise on "unbalanced" growth is Albert O. Hirschman, *The Strategy of Economic Development* (New Haven: Yale University Press, 1958). Hirschman called for a development (growth) strategy emphasizing deliberate imbalances in factor and product markets, the rationale being that the existence of shortages (e.g., in electric power, skilled labor, and foreign exchange) would stimulate the investment required to relieve them. "Balanced" growth theories (criticized in Hirschman, pp. 50–61) stressed the need for the various sectors of the economy to grow in harmony with each other in order to minimize project delays and inefficiencies and to ensure the creation of a sufficiently large market for industrial and agricultural products. In general, balanced growth advocates stressed simultaneous expansion of all sectors of the economy, industrial production for the domestic market, and macroeconomic planning, and they were concerned primarily with demand problems. Those supporting unbalanced growth tended to favor specialization in production, orientation toward export markets, and reliance on the market mechanism; supply problems were more of a concern than demand problems. Actually, this neat dichotomy of viewpoints did not always characterize participants in the debate. Balanced growth, in particular, meant different things to different people, and the controversy ultimately became quite muddled.

[*] References cited in this manner are found in the Suggested Readings at the end of each chapter.

of human capital—has been of immense importance in helping to clear up some of our misconceptions about the development process. We now recognize, for example, that there is more to growth (not to speak of development) than capital formation. Skilled workers are needed to operate and repair machinery and equipment, and the productivity of capital will also depend on the quality of entrepreneurship and management. We also recognize that additional spending on food items by the poor often should be considered not as increased consumption, but as increased investment enabling workers to produce more by becoming healthier and stronger.

MEASURING ECONOMIC GROWTH

Economic growth is usually measured by increases in a country's per capita GNP. Fifteen or twenty years ago, few people in the United States questioned the desirability of economic growth, both generally and specifically in the United States. We needed it, it was argued, not only to provide more goods and services—and jobs—for the poorest segments of our population, but also to stay well ahead of the Soviet Union. The Soviet Union's interest in economic growth was probably even greater. Its leaders wanted to close the gap separating Soviet output from U.S. output, and they wanted to demonstrate to the newly independent nations of the developing world the superiority of the Soviet economic (and political) system.

Today, the desirability of growth has been widely questioned, as scientists from many disciplines have made us aware of the potentially serious adverse effects of growth on the environment. This subject will be discussed in detail in the concluding chapter of this book.

For now, let us assume that growth *is* desirable and deal with the ways in which it may be measured. Economists typically measure economic growth by increases in per capita GNP. Unfortunately, they sometimes also use per capita GNP figures, explicitly or implicitly, to rank countries according to their level of development. They do this not so much because they believe in the inherent theoretical and statistical accuracy of these figures as indicators of development, but rather because there is no clearly superior, widely accepted, and readily available alternative. Among the major—and widely admitted—deficiencies of the GNP indicator as a measure of welfare are the following:

1. The GNP figure tells us nothing about the *types* of goods and services produced or the amount of welfare derived from the use of these goods and services. It tells us nothing about the *costs* to society of increased environmental pollution, urbanization, or population growth. To use the United States as an illustration, why should we include in the

GNP money spent to build expressway networks in our major metropolitan areas, as well as the money spent on automobile operation and maintenance by commuters who jam these expressways to get to and from work? And why should we also include the money spent to clean up the environmental pollution caused by automobile traffic? Some economists suggest that we count such expenditures as costs and subtract them from the GNP. Another has suggested dividing GNP into two parts: government policy would seek to maximize that part produced with renewable resources and recyclable wastes, and to minimize that part based on the exhaustion of irreplaceable resources and production of indestructible wastes.[8]

2. Many goods and services not passing through the market are excluded from GNP estimates. In all countries, for example, unpaid housework and do-it-yourself repairs are not considered as production. But in the developing countries, failure to include nonmarket transactions distorts GNP figures more than in the highly industrialized countries because these transactions are relatively more important. Furthermore, even when estimates are made of the value of certain nonmarket transactions (particularly food produced and consumed on the farm), they are often biased on the downward side. Because of this problem, growth rates of developing countries may be overstated. What is recorded as increased output may simply reflect a *transfer* of production from the household or barter economy to the marketplace, where it will be recorded for the first time.

3. GNP tells us nothing about the *distribution* of income, a subject we shall discuss in detail in chapter 11. Output per capita may be growing by 2 percent annually, but only 20 percent of the population may be experiencing rising living standards. To call this "development" is questionable, and even to speak of growth of "the economy" is misleading.

4. Numerous other problems arise when we try to make comparisons of GNP per capita among countries. These comparisons are usually made by converting national currency values to their equivalent in U.S. dollars. If exchange rates are fixed, many currencies will be undervalued or overvalued. In the late 1960s, for example, the official exchange rate of the Japanese yen with the dollar was about Y360.00 = $1.00. A more realistic figure then was perhaps Y315.00.[9] Calculating the Japanese GNP per capita on the basis of the official exchange rate thus understated its dollar equivalent. Dividing a given yen figure by 315 instead of 360 would yield a dollar figure 14 percent higher. Even if exchange rates are not pegged but fluctuate (float) "cleanly" in foreign exchange markets,

8. Edwin G. Dolan, *TANSTAAFL: The Economic Strategy for Environmental Crisis* (New York: Holt, Rinehart and Winston, Inc., 1971), p. 10.
9. Fixed exchange rates were abandoned in early 1973, and by July 1978 the value of the U.S. dollar had fallen to less than Y200.00.

without Central Bank intervention, one has to choose among several possible ways to calculate an "average" exchange rate for a given year.

5. Another problem in making international comparisons concerns the great differences in domestic relative price structures among countries. In comparing China and the United States, for example, should we accept the reported GNP figures, which are based on Chinese price tags for Chinese goods and U.S. price tags for U.S. goods? Or should we use U.S. price tags for the output of both countries? Or Chinese price tags? Our choice of method can make a great deal of difference. Food prices in China are generally very low relative to those in the United States. Thus the average Chinese can manage to survive by spending less than $100 a year on food (converting yuan to dollars at some "official" exchange rate). In the United States $100 would buy much less food, and it is doubtful that many adults could survive on this amount for 365 days. Thus the purchasing power of a dollar in China—at least for food and other basic necessities—is much greater than in the United States, and reported GNP per capita figures for China are misleadingly low. While the World Bank reported a 1971 figure of $160, a reevaluation of Chinese output in terms of U.S. retail prices results in a figure of $451.[10] (We might note parenthetically that the prices of manufactured goods in many developing countries are often much higher than in the United States. But these products constitute such a small part of the GNP, and food and other necessities such a large part, that placing U.S. price tags on all output would still significantly raise its dollar value.)

6. Another problem in making international comparisons arises when we try to obtain dollar values for GNP in countries basing their output estimates on the procedures pioneered by the Soviet Union. Marxist theory defines production only in terms of goods, and estimating the value of services output of these countries is quite difficult. Furthermore, output estimates are made in terms of gross value, not value added, and they must be adjusted to avoid double counting. Finally, rent and interest were not recognized as true components of GNP until quite recently, and even now estimates of these items do not accurately reflect scarcity values.

7. Lastly, we must recognize that statistics in developing countries (and in some developed countries, too) are often quite poor for reasons other than those already discussed. These include lack of technical skills in data collection and processing, insufficient funds to conduct reasonably unbiased sample surveys, and deliberate falsification. The extent to which data inaccuracies can affect GNP estimates is vividly demon-

10. Colin Clark, "Economic Development in Communist China," *Journal of Political Economy*, 84 (April 1976), 239–264.

TABLE 1.1 (*Continued*)

	Amount (US $)	Real Growth Rate (%)	
		1960–1975	*1970–1975*
°Lebanon	1,070	n.a.	n.a.
Mexico	1,050	3.2	2.3
Brazil	1,030	4.3	6.2
Chile	990	1.3	−2.7
Costa Rica	960	3.4	3.7
China, Republic of	930	6.3	5.7
Turkey	900	4.0	4.9
Algeria	870	1.8	4.3
°Mongolia	860	1.0	2.3
°Cuba	800	−0.6	1.0
Malaysia	760	4.0	5.3
Peru	760	2.7	3.4
°Tunisia	730	4.1	6.9
Dominican Republic	720	3.4	6.6
Syrian Arab Republic	720	2.2	1.8
Nicaragua	700	2.4	2.5
Ghana	590	−0.2	−0.3
Ecuador	590	3.4	6.1
Colombia	580	2.7	3.9
Paraguay	580	2.0	3.3
Guatemala	570	2.4	2.8
Korea, Republic of	560	7.1	8.2
Rhodesia	550	2.4	2.8
Ivory Coast	540	3.5	1.9
Congo, People's Republic of	510	2.9	4.3
°Albania	510	4.5	3.8
Morocco	470	1.9	3.0
Papua New Guinea	470	3.8	2.3
Jordan	460	1.3	1.9
El Salvador	460	1.8	1.9
°Korea, Democratic People's Republic of	450	3.8	0.9
Zambia	420	2.0	0.9
Liberia	410	1.8	0.9
Philippines	380	2.5	3.7
°China, People's Republic of	380	5.2	5.3
°Angola	370	3.6	3.2
Bolivia	360	2.5	3.4
Honduras	360	1.5	0.8
Senegal	360	−0.7	−1.1
Thailand	350	4.6	3.6
Nigeria	340	3.4	5.3
Mauritania	320	3.8	2.6
Cameroon	280	3.0	0.5
°Sudan	270	0.1	3.8
Egypt, Arab Republic of	260	1.5	1.3
Togo	250	4.4	2.0
°Yemen, People's Democratic Republic of	250	−6.3	−5.8
Uganda	230	1.0	−4.5

Continued

TABLE 1.1 (*Continued*)

	Amount (US $)	Real Growth Rate (%)	
		1960–1975	1970–1975
Kenya	220	3.2	2.4
Indonesia	220	2.4	3.5
Central African Empire	220	0.4	−0.7
*Yemen Arab Republic	200	n.a.	5.8
*Sierra Leone	200	1.5	−0.5
Madagascar	200	0.1	−2.2
Sri Lanka	190	2.0	1.1
Haiti	190	0.0	1.5
*Mozambique	180	2.0	−2.6
*Tanzania	170	3.0	2.9
Pakistan	160	3.3	0.8
*Lesotho	160	4.6	7.3
Afghanistan	150	−0.2	2.1
India	140	1.3	0.5
Zaire	140	1.6	1.5
Guinea	130	0.2	1.3
Malawi	130	4.1	7.0
Niger	130	−1.3	−2.8
Benin	130	−0.3	−1.1
Chad	120	−1.1	−2.0
Burma	110	0.7	0.9
Burundi	110	2.7	−1.1
*Somalia	110	−0.3	−0.2
Upper Volta	110	0.7	1.1
Nepal	110	0.3	0.7
Rwanda	100	0.5	0.2
Ethiopia	100	2.0	0.4
Mali	90	0.9	−0.1
Bangladesh	90	−0.6	−2.3
*Lao People's Democratic Republic	90	n.a.	−15.9
*Bhutan	n.a.	n.a.	n.a.
Cambodia	n.a.	n.a.	n.a.
Viet Nam	n.a.	n.a.	n.a.

Source: World Bank Atlas 1977.

* See notes in the source.

be expected to widen for at least several decades. The absolute gap would narrow, of course, if growth were halted in the developed countries but continued in the developing countries. Many persons would favor such a situation on equity grounds. But apart from the political difficulties of getting the developed countries to agree to halt their growth, stagnation of economic activity in the developed countries would seriously threaten the growth prospects of the developing countries. This will become clear in the ensuing chapters, and a final statement about international *inter*dependence will be made in the last chapter.

Those who favor a narrowing gap, while possibly having to wait several decades to see a realization of their goal, can at least be encouraged by recent developments in comparative growth rates between developed and developing countries (see Table 1.2). During the 1970s, for the first time, per capita growth rates in the developing countries exceeded those in the developed countries.[12] While a continuation of this trend would still result in a widening gap for a number of years, a narrowing of the gap is now mathematically possible at some time in the future.

Not everyone, however, is willing to wait for existing mathematical trends to take their course. Developing countries have acquired the political power to challenge international inequities, and this power—as we shall see in chapter 15—has been effectively used in the last ten to fifteen years. But the developed countries still have considerably more power, and most of their citizens are strongly opposed to a "no-growth" society. They are also opposed to massive international migration of labor, which could be another means of reducing international inequali-

TABLE 1.2
**Average Annual Rates of Growth of GNP Per Capita,
Developing and Industrial Countries, 1961–1975**
(percent)

	1961–1965	1966–1971	1971–1974	1975[a]
Developing Countries	3.3	3.6	4.3	0.1
Africa South of the Sahara	1.4	2.8	2.1	0.2
East Asia and Pacific	2.7	4.6	4.9	1.6
Latin America and the Caribbean	2.4	2.9	3.9	0.0
North Africa and the Middle East	3.8	5.0	9.4	−2.8
South Asia	1.3	1.8	−1.0	1.9
More Advanced Mediterranean Countries	5.8	5.1	5.2	1.0
Industrialized Countries	4.0	3.6	3.0	−2.0

Source: International Bank for Reconstruction and Development (World Bank), *Annual Report 1976*, Statistical Annex, Table 1, pp. 96–97.
[a] Preliminary.

12. This is attributable in part to the much higher foreign exchange earnings of petroleum-exporting countries beginning in 1974; but many other developing countries also experienced more rapid growth during 1970–1975. The absolute income gap actually narrowed in 1975, but this was a short-term phenomenon caused by the world recession. Per capita output in the developed countries declined, while a slight increase was recorded in the developing countries. The absolute income gap again widened in 1976.

ties.[13] Unless attitudes in the developed countries change much more rapidly, or the international balance of political power shifts even faster to the developing countries, we can expect the absolute income gap to continue widening, at least for some time. Nevertheless, the narrowing of power inequalities may have been great enough to permit the developing countries to maintain the faster rates of economic growth, relative to the developed countries, that they achieved during the 1970s.[14]

MEASURING ECONOMIC DEVELOPMENT

It is difficult enough to determine levels of output and rates of economic growth. Measuring economic development is an even more demanding task. If we assume that the concept of development is related to personal and community welfare, we must first obtain agreement on the various dimensions of welfare. Quite likely, these would include items such as consumption of basic necessities, equity in the distribution of income and wealth, literacy, health, and employment.[15] Each of these indicators of welfare is measured in a different way, and combining them (along with others) into a simple measure of development is akin to adding apples, oranges, pineapples, and grapes. The problem, however, is not insurmountable, and the reward for such efforts could well be a more meaningful indicator of economic welfare than GNP per capita.

A number of attempts have been made to assign weights to various indicators and combine them into a single index of development. The variables used in three such efforts are indicated in Table 1.3. Interest-

TABLE 1.3
Items Included in Three Comprehensive Indicators of Development

Items	Hagen (1962)	Niewiaroski (1966)	UNRISD (1970)
Durable Goods-Clothing-Housing			
Vehicles per capita	x	x	
Radios per capita	x	x	
Fiber consumption per capita		x	
Persons per room			x
			Continued

13. International migration tends to lower the average product of labor in the country receiving it, thus depressing wage rates (or causing them to rise more slowly), while in the labor-surplus country of origin the average product of labor tends to rise.

14. While it may appear that only petroleum-producing developing countries, and perhaps a few others, have gained international political power in recent years, the fact that developing countries have been able to unite in pushing for changes in the structure of international trade and finance (see chapter 15) has raised the relative power of developing countries generally.

15. Ideally, both the quantity and *quality* of employment would be taken into account (see chapter 12).

TABLE 1.3 (*Continued*)

Items	Hagen (1962)	Niewiaroski (1966)	UNRISD (1970)
Communications-Services			
Telephones per capita	x	x	
Newspaper circulation per capita	x	x	x
Energy consumption per capita	x	x	x^a
Basic Industrial Products			
Steel consumption per capita		x	x
Cement consumption per capita		x	
Health and Nutrition			
Doctors per capita	x	x	
Life expectancy at birth			x
Protein consumption		x	x^b
Education			
Literacy rate	x	x	
Primary school enrollment rate	x		x^c
Postprimary enrollment rate		x	x^c
Vocational school enrollment rate			x
Employment			
Percent of labor force not in agriculture or services	x		
Percent of economically active population in agriculture		x	x^d
Percent of economically active population in public utilities			x
Wage and salary workers as a percent of the economically active population			x
Other			
GNP per capita	x		
Manufacturing's share of GDP			x
Agricultural production per male agricultural worker			x
Exports per capita		x	x^e
Percent of population in urban areas	x^f		x^g

Sources: Data from Everett E. Hagen, "A Framework for Analyzing Economic and Political Development," in *Development of the Emerging Countries*, ed. Robert E. Asher (Washington, D.C.: Brookings Institution, 1962): 1–38; Donald H. Niewiaroski, "The Level of Living of Nations: Meaning and Measurement," *Estadística: Journal of the Inter-America Statistical Institute* (March 1965): 3–31; United Nations Research Institute for Social Development, *Contents and Measurement of Social Economic Development*, Report No. 70.10 (Geneva, 1970).

[a] Separate categories for electricity and other energy.

[b] Animal protein.

[c] Primary and secondary enrollment rates combined.

[d] Adult male workers.

[e] Foreign trade.

[f] Cities with more than 100,000 people.

[g] Cities with more than 20,000 people.

ingly, these combined indices, each with eleven to eighteen separate items, have only two indicators in common: newspaper circulation and energy consumption. Other indicators may seem similar, but these apparent similarities sometimes mask major disagreements, such as that concerning the relative importance of primary versus postprimary education. Note also that the UNRISD index assigns less importance to the consumption of durable and nondurable goods than the other two indicators. On the other hand, all three indices stress the importance of health, nutrition, and education as welfare indicators.

These are not the only comprehensive indices of development that have been devised. Irma Adelman and Cynthia Taft Morris examined forty-one variables, many of them of a social or political nature, in seeking to measure development performance. Harbison, Maruhnic, and Resnick used forty variables, emphasizing human resources development, in formulating their indicators of development and modernization.[16] Morris D. Morris has prepared a "Physical Quality of Life Index," stressing health and education indicators, which we shall examine in chapter 7. Generally, the comprehensive indicators show less international inequality than per capita GNP.[17]

While this approach is commendable, its limitations should be carefully considered. First, existing data for most of these indicators are just as inaccurate as GNP data, and sometimes even more so (e.g., literacy rates). Second, many indicators can be questioned on conceptual grounds. Why, for example, should folk medicine be ignored in the health statistics? Should we not adjust fiber consumption for differences in climatic conditions which affect clothing needs? And should we not adjust nutrition data to reflect physical stature, climate, and the age structure of the population?

16. Irma Adelman and Cynthia Taft Morris, *Society, Politics and Economic Development* (Baltimore: The Johns Hopkins Press, 1967); Frederick H. Harbison, Joan Maruhnic, and Jane R. Resnick, *Quantitative Analysis of Modernization and Development* (Princeton, N.J.: Industrial Relations Section, Department of Economics, Princeton University, 1970). These and other studies are summarized in chapter 1 of the book edited by Nancy Baster (1972) and listed in the Suggested Readings at the end of this chapter.

17. For example, differences between per capita GNP and the Niewiaroski index (see Table 1.3) for the late 1950s were as follows, using the United States as a base (= 100):

Region	Per Capita Income Index	Niewiaroski Index
Latin America	11	26
Southern Europe	11	24
Western Europe	39	61
Asia (except Japan)	5	12
Africa	5	12
Middle East	6	16
Socialist Countries	24	46

On the other hand, use of a comprehensive development index has several advantages. First, many of the individual components are more direct measures of human welfare than is income; and improvement of human welfare, after all, is the ultimate objective of development. Second, individual countries can each choose their own list of development indicators, and assign weights to them, in accordance with their own value systems. This might annoy economists looking for a uniform measure of development with which to make international comparisons, but this problem is not insoluble. More importantly, one must raise the question of who, within each country, should choose and assign weights to the indicators.[18] This philosophical issue aside, there is little doubt that values differ significantly from country to country, and a meaningful index for one country may be less so for another.

In the future, it is possible to foresee a time when each country has its own index of development. It is also likely that enough similarities in values exist among countries so that nations can agree on one or more alternative indices for purposes of making international comparisons. First, however, formidable statistical and conceptual problems will have to be solved. So will the problem of assigning weights to the various components of the index (or indices) on which agreement has been reached. Meanwhile, GNP per capita will continue to be widely used—rightly or wrongly—to measure development as well as growth.

DEVELOPMENT VERSUS LIBERATION

Some writers have not only rejected the focus on economic growth but have also attacked the concept of economic development. What is really important for developing countries, they say, is their liberation from economic dependence on other countries and from the poverty which "development" policies have done little to eliminate. This position, which has been argued forcefully by "theology of liberation" writers in Latin American Roman Catholic circles and by social critic Denis Goulet (1971), has considerable merit and deserves careful consideration. Those of us who have worked in the Third and Fourth Worlds can attest to the strength of feelings about national and personal liberation. It is difficult to deny that welfare and self-esteem improve, other things being equal, when nations become politically independent, foreign enterprises are nationalized, civil services are "Africanized," or poor farmers receive title to their land.

But in rejecting "developmentalism," liberationists sometimes have a

---

18. Who chose GNP? Alas, it seems that we economists are responsible for this measure, and it is doubtful that "the people" gave us the authority to impose the values implicit in this indicator.

tendency to throw out the baby of development with the bathwater of growth. So much attention is focused on the process of attaining liberation that the problem of improving welfare after liberation has been achieved is slighted. A sustained increase in living standards is not automatic; it requires conscious policy actions that attack poverty, unemployment, and extreme inequalities in the distribution of income and wealth. What the liberationists are really criticizing, of course, is not really development, but growth policies masquerading under the name of development. Redefining the concept of development, rather than attacking it, would seem to be a better approach.

The dangers of placing too much emphasis on liberation are vividly illustrated by the case of Indonesia, whose postindependence (1949) leaders drove foreigners (Dutch, Chinese, British, Americans) out of industrial and commercial activities and led the public to believe that this would automatically ensure prosperity. But since indigenous private entrepreneurial activity was also stifled and the government failed to fill the void by assuming creative leadership in the development process, per capita output stagnated through the mid-1960s and development indicators suggested little improvement, if any, in overall well-being.

Liberation theorists point to Cuba as an example of successful liberation; and while Cuba is a controversial case, this writer would support their position, despite the negative per capita growth rate reported in Table 1.1. Income inequalities in Cuba have been reduced since 1959, and education and health care services are more equitably distributed than before.[19] Despite the much-talked-about food lines and other discomforts, the poorer segments of Cuban society seem to feel "liberated" in a very real way from their pre-1959 situation. And while Cuba is economically dependent upon the Soviet Union, it is questionable that this relationship is stronger than was dependence on the United States before the revolution. Nevertheless, the country's leaders have been disappointed with the economy's performance, and the language of liberation seems to be giving way to the language of development.

SUMMARY

Economic growth in the developing countries has been faster since 1960 than at any time in the past. Per capita income growth rates also exceed those achieved by today's developed countries in their early years of

---

19. See Roberto E. Hernández and Carmelo Mesa-Lago, "Labor Organization and Wages in Cuba," in *Revolutionary Change in Cuba*, ed. Carmelo Mesa-Lago (Pittsburgh: University of Pittsburgh Press, 1971), pp. 209–249; and Archibald R. M. Ritter, *The Economic Development of Revolutionary Cuba: Strategy and Performance* (New York: Praeger Publishers, 1974).

development. Nevertheless, it may seem to the average newspaper reader or TV watcher in the developed world that developing countries are increasingly discontented with their economic performance.

It is not difficult to understand why this is so. First, growth of the developed countries has also been rapid by historical standards. Until the 1970s, it equaled or exceeded that of the developing countries, thus tending to widen international inequalities. Second, improved communications have made more people in developing countries aware of the great gap in living standards among nations. Third, political independence has given to leaders of developing countries new forums—notably the United Nations and its specialized agencies—in which their views can be expressed and in which they can exercise their newly acquired political power. We thus read and hear a lot more about the discontent which was present long before independence.

Finally, economic growth, even when very rapid, has often bypassed the majority of a country's population. As former Brazilian president Emilio Garrastazu Medici (1969–1974) admitted about his country, "the economy is doing well, but the people fare badly." The masses, however, are gaining political power as a result of better communications channels, gains in education, and urbanization. Some political leaders believe that the best way to improve the living standards of the increasingly restless masses (and thus contain them politically) is to have even faster growth. Many economists also argue that faster growth is a better way to raise living standards than redistribution of existing income and wealth.

While growthmanship games continue to be played—as evidenced by the considerable attention given even in the developing countries to the widening income gap—there is increasing awareness among economists that true *development* is more properly measured by indicators other than GNP. There is also a greater realization that earlier faith in the widespread "trickling down" of growth benefits was misplaced. Development, it is now apparent, requires programs designed to benefit lower income groups directly; otherwise the living standards of some people may actually fall with economic growth.[20] International assistance agencies are designing an increasing proportion of their loans and grants in this way, but their actions alone will have little effect on rates of development unless governments in developing countries are prepared to alter significantly the allocation of their own budget resources to provide more direct benefits to the poor.

---

20. Historically, this has been the pattern. See Irma Adelman and Cynthia Taft Morris, "A Typology of Poverty in 1850," in *Essays in Economic Development and Cultural Change in Honor of Bert Hoselitz*, ed. Manning Nash, *Supplement to Economic Development and Cultural Change*, 25 (1977), 314–343.

Suggested Readings

Baran, Paul A. *The Political Economy of Growth*. New York: Monthly Review Press, 1957.

A Marxist interpretation of how capitalist economic institutions in developing countries, by unequally distributing the fruits of economic growth, limit the amount of growth that can occur. Though weak on documentation of its theses, this influential book is well argued.

Baster, Nancy, ed. *Measuring Development: The Role and Adequacy of Development Indicators*. London: Frank Cass and Co., Ltd., 1972. Also published as a special issue of the *Journal of Development Studies*, 8 (April 1972).

The contributors to this volume agree that GNP is an unsatifactory measure of development. A number of ideas are presented for using social, political, and other noneconomic variables as development indicators. The theoretical problems discussed are often thorny ones, but none of the articles requires any mathematics beyond simple arithmetic.

Goulet, Denis. *The Cruel Choice: A New Concept in the Theory of Development*. New York: Atheneum, 1971.

A forceful critic of "growthmanship," Goulet emphasizes—from an ethical standpoint—the importance of freedom, not just from political and social oppression, but also from the oppression of poverty.

Haq, Mahbub ul. *The Poverty Curtain: Choices for the Third World*. New York: Columbia University Press, 1976.

Mahbub ul Haq, formerly Chief Economist of the Pakistan Planning Commission, is now Director of the World Bank's Policy Planning and Program Review Department. He has become one of the most influential spokesmen for the interests of the developing countries. Haq argues calmly but forcefully and convincingly that serious international inequalities, like those within nations, are in the interests of neither the poor nor the rich.

Kuznets, Simon S. *Economic Growth of Nations: Total Output and Production Structure*. Cambridge, Mass.: The Belknap Press of the Harvard University Press, 1971.

Kuznets' pioneer work in national income accounting, and his herculean efforts to collect and analyze historical statistics for a wide range of developed and developing countries, were rewarded with a Nobel Prize. This book, which brings together only a small part of his work, is concerned mainly with the historical experiences of the developed countries. Undergraduates may have difficulty coping with the detailed evaluations of the quality of the statistical evidence, but the broad conclusions can be understood without great difficulty.

Rostow, W. W. *The Stages of Economic Growth: A Non-Communist Manifesto*. Cambridge, Eng.: Cambridge University Press, 1960; 2nd ed., 1971.

The first ninety-two pages of this short book present a theory of economic growth which argues that countries pass sequentially through a series of five stages: (1) traditional society; (2) preconditions for takeoff; (3) takeoff; (4) the drive to maturity; and (5) high mass consumption. Stage theories are easily criticized, but Rostow's very readable presentation has been an excellent stimulus to debate on the historical aspects of growth and development. The second half of the book compares economic growth in the United States and the Soviet Union. Rostow's viewpoints tend to be "hawkish," and not everyone will agree with them, but he argues his case well. He served as President Lyndon B. Johnson's national security advisor.

2

Economic Obstacles to Growth and Development
Natural Resource and Capital Constraints

Widespread poverty in the developing nations has sometimes been attributed to hostile climate, lack of fertile soils, rugged terrain, or the absence of industrial raw materials. Other things being equal, a country with abundant natural resources clearly has an advantage in the process of growth or development. However, countries do not develop by natural resources alone, and some economists would argue that natural resource endowments are not even of primary importance.

In the 1940s and 1950s, most economists regarded the shortage of capital as the principal obstacle to economic growth. (Economic development, as defined in chapter 1, was usually a secondary concern if it was discussed at all.) Indeed, some theories of growth seemed to regard capital as the *only* missing ingredient.

Economists now have a more balanced view of the processes of growth and development. In particular, we now appreciate the influential role of human elements, a subject to be discussed in chapter 3. But first, we need to evaluate the importance of natural resources and capital, factors which have sometimes been ignored by "human capital" theories overreacting to the older emphasis on physical capital.

CLIMATE, SOILS, AND TERRAIN

Since the developed countries are concentrated in temperate climates and the developing countries in tropical and subtropical zones, some observers have concluded that climate plays a major role in the processes of economic growth and development. One theory, popular several decades ago, argued that human energy and achievement are limited in tropical climates by heat, humidity, and the lack of a challenge to human ingenuity which a variable climate provides. There is little empirical support, however, for this rather crude theory of geographic determinism. Indeed, some studies have cast doubt on the notion that climate significantly affects attitudes toward work and leisure.[1]

Attempts to draw conclusions about the observed relationship between climate and economic development can easily ignore other possible causes of low per capita income. Furthermore, this relationship has been viewed with historical blinders. The emergence of *homo sapiens,* we now believe, occurred in the not-so-temperate climate of East Africa. Agriculture, metal working, writing, and other technological and cultural achievements flourished first in the Near East, Northern Africa, China, and the Indus Valley; the temperate zones of 2000 B.C. were the less developed regions of their day. They may well occupy the same position sometime in the future.

While broad generalizations linking climate to economic performance can be viewed with skepticism, the picture changes when we examine in detail the effects of climate on agriculture in the tropics. World Bank economist Andrew Kamarck (1976) has recently revived interest in research on climatic factors in development, after years of neglect by economists rejecting geographical determinism. Kamarck is careful not to regard climate as an absolute obstacle to development, or even as the most important obstacle; but he clearly demonstrates that countries in the tropics face development problems different from those in the temperate zones. Problems in agricultural production, minerals exploration, and health cannot be dealt with by simple transfer of technology from the developed countries.

Because of heat, torrential rains, and other factors, most tropical soils are poor, containing little organic matter. If ground cover is removed, the thin layer of humus will soon be washed away—a sobering thought for those who think the Amazon basin is the next great breadbasket of the world. The low-protein foods produced by tropical soils contribute to both physical and mental retardation. Droughts often occur at the worst possible time, when temperatures and wind velocities are highest; this results in a high rate of water loss through evaporation and transpiration. The tropics are also fertile breeding grounds for a variety of agricultural pests and diseases.

Diseases and pests directly attacking humans also thrive in tropical environments. We have all heard of malaria, yellow fever, hookworm, and leprosy, but there are other major diseases whose names may be un-

---

1. For a review of theories of geographical determinism, and evidence casting doubt on their validity, see Kamarck (1976: Ch. 1).

familiar—bilharzia and filariasis, for example, each of which affects about 200 million people, reducing their capacity to work. More than a billion people are weakened by intestinal parasites. Fertile land will not be cultivated where the incidence of malaria, river blindness, or other debilitating diseases is too high. The presence of the tsetse fly and its transmission of a disease called nagana prohibits the keeping of cattle for food or work in much of tropical Africa. If nagana were controlled, cattle could replace human effort for soil preparation, and manure would be available to fertilize crops. Pests and diseases are not unknown in the temperate zones, but the variable temperatures and the presence of frost there act as checks on their development. We shall return to the subject of health in chapter 7.

Although most developing countries in the tropics are at a disadvantage in terms of climate and soils, these are not insurmountable difficulties; they can be overcome with the aid of the other factors of production —capital and human skills—and with advances in technology. Irrigation projects can make unproductive land fertile, and malaria eradication programs can make already fertile lands hospitable for settlement and cultivation. These are investment projects, and investment requires savings, either from within the economy or from abroad. Human skills are also needed, and initially many of these skills will have to be imported. Most developing countries will find it difficult to undertake such projects without foreign assistance.

This is not to say that capital and human skills are the only missing ingredients; in many cases, what is lacking is an appropriate technology for dealing with problems peculiar to the tropics. Developed countries have spent billions of dollars on research on temperate agriculture, but only in the last three decades have significant efforts been devoted to research on crop and livestock production in the tropics. Even now, though, there is much that we do not know or cannot anticipate, such as the unexpected appearance of new pests and diseases when a crop is introduced into an area for the first time. The new "miracle" rice seeds have been particularly vulnerable to disease. In Senegal, a rice-growing project has been plagued by attacks from weaverbirds. Cattle and small livestock are susceptible to both temperate-zone diseases and to diseases peculiar to the tropics. Many years of research will be required before these problems are controlled to the same extent that similar problems in temperate zones have been checked.

The application of technology, capital, and human skills can also help overcome geographic obstacles in the form of rugged terrain. Europeans in North Africa, for example, settled and crossed the Appalachians and harnessed their water resources. For those who are tempted to dismiss the Appalachians as mere "hills," consider the case of Switzerland, a much more mountainous country, whose per capita GNP now exceeds that of the United States. Consider, too, the fact that level terrain does not guarantee economic growth. Some countries in Africa and Asia with large expanses of flat land have per capita incomes of less than $200.

Other things being equal, of course, countries with mountainous terrain are at a disadvantage with respect to transportation and communications costs. Road construction is more expensive than on the plains, and the frequent occurrence of landslides requires heavy maintenance expenditures if traffic delays and road deterioration are to be avoided. But terrain is just one of many important factors in growth and development, and the disadvantages of mountain ranges can be offset by advantages in other factors of production.

INDUSTRIAL RAW MATERIALS

Lack of industrial raw materials—e.g., coal, iron ore, copper, cement, natural gas, and petroleum—has also been considered a major obstacle to development. Shortages of these materials can sometimes be overcome more easily than the climatic obstacles. Raw materials can be imported for local processing, or—and this is often the less costly alternative— processed raw materials such as steel bars and sheets can be imported and fabricated locally into finished products. Imports, of course, require foreign exchange; but most developing countries have the potential significantly to increase foreign exchange availabilities by expanding or initiating the production and export of those products in which they have a comparative advantage,[2] and by increasing domestic agricultural production to reduce food imports.

The United Kingdom and Japan illustrate clearly that lack of industrial raw materials need not be an obstacle to growth. Both countries have developed into major industrial powers despite the fact that they must import a large proportion of their industrial raw materials. Japan, the most extreme case, imports 100 percent of its bauxite, 99 percent of its iron ore and petroleum, 90 percent of its copper, and 72 percent of its coal.[3] Yet it has had one of the fastest-growing economies in the world in the last three decades, and its level of development is now close to the European average. By the same token, the mere presence of industrial raw materials is no guarantee of growth and development, as attested to

2. According to the theory of comparative advantage, world output will be maximized if each nation specializes in the production of commodities and services which it can produce relatively cheaply. The policy implications of this theory for developing countries will be discussed in chapter 5.

3. *IMF Survey* (April 19, 1976), p. 128.

by the relatively low level of development in countries such as Bolivia, China, and Liberia.

All of this is not to say that possessing industrial raw materials gives a country no special advantage. Other things being equal, it is clearly beneficial, as demonstrated by the position of the petroleum-producing countries today. However, other things are not in fact equal, and countries cannot develop by petroleum alone. To begin with, other factors of production are needed simply to get petroleum out of the ground. One of these factors is capital.

CAPITAL AND GROWTH

There is no doubt that capital formation is a major determinant of economic growth. Labor is clearly more productive the more machinery and equipment it has to work with. In the United States, we are all familiar with the wonders of automated assembly lines, high-speed computers, and mechanized agriculture. (Sometimes, however, we forget about the education, research and development, and management skills that made these highly productive capital goods possible.)

While developing countries would be well advised to increase their rates of capital formation in order to stimulate economic growth and development, indiscriminate purchase of capital goods can be very wasteful if no provision is made for repairs, spare parts, and efficiently combining capital with other factors of production. Even relatively advanced industrial nations are not immune to these problems. As this chapter was being written, a newscast reported that thousands of tractors and other agricultural machines in the Soviet Union were idle for lack of rubber tires or spare parts, thus threatening the success of the current wheat harvest. Other things being equal, economic growth will be faster the greater is the share of output devoted to capital formation. But as can be seen in Figure 2.1, which provides data for twenty-six developing countries, the relationship is not as close as might be expected. This is due in large part to differences among countries in the rate of growth of complementary factors of production, including skilled labor and management.[4]

If developing countries have sometimes placed too much faith in capital goods relative to complementary factors of production, they may be forgiven for taking faulty advice from economists fascinated by the post-Keynesian growth theories developed shortly after World War II,

4. Other explanations for this relatively weak relationship will be explained below. The twenty-six countries in Figure 2.1 are all developing countries with a population of at least 10 million in 1975 for which the United Nations *Yearbook of National Accounts Statistics* provides both GDP and investment data.

Figure 2.1
Relationship between Gross Fixed Capital Formation as a Percentage of GDP,
1969–73 Average,[a] and Rate of Growth of Aggregate GDP,[b] 1970–74[a], for 26
Developing Countries

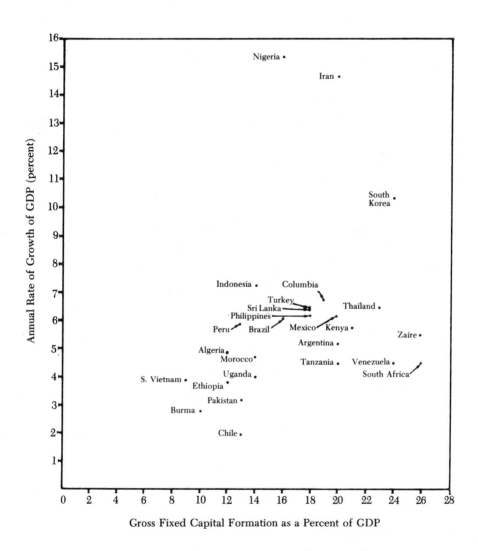

Gross Fixed Capital Formation as a Percent of GDP

Source: United Nations, *Yearbook of National Accounts Statistics 1975.*

[a] Or most recent five-year period for which data are available.

[b] Gross Domestic Product (GDP) equals GNP plus net factor payments abroad.

particularly those of Roy F. Harrod and Evsey D. Domar.[5] These theories have been quite useful in explaining the optimum growth rate of productive capacity in the developed countries (i.e., the growth rate that matches that of aggregate demand). But when economists applied these analytical tools to the developing countries, their conclusions were sometimes very misleading.

One of the key analytical concepts in post-Keynesian growth theory is the *capital-output (K/O) ratio*. This is simply the relationship between the value of a country's capital stock in a given year (net of depreciation, and regardless of the year in which the capital was created) and output in that year (net national product). This relationship was found to be quite stable in the developed countries, so that the marginal K/O ratio could be assumed to be equal to the average K/O ratio. For planning purposes, of course, what really counts is the *marginal* ratio—i.e., the ratio between additional capital formation and additional output—and there are some very good reasons why we might expect it to differ from the average ratio in the developing countries.

Before further exploring this problem, let us see how K/O ratios can be used for macroeconomic planning in developing countries.[6] Assume that in Year 0 the capital stock in country X is $300 and output (NNP) is $100. The country has a target growth rate of real output of 5 percent, 2.5 percent to match population growth and 2.5 percent to raise output per capita. If we assume that the marginal K/O ratio, like the average ratio, is 3:1, then the capital stock must also grow by 5 percent. Net capital formation, therefore, must be $15 ($300 × .05), which means that net savings in the economy must be 15 percent of NNP ($15/$100).

The relationship between the growth of output, the capital-output ratio, and the rate of savings may be expressed in equation form as follows:

$$\frac{dY}{Y} = \frac{s}{k}$$

where $\frac{dY}{Y}$ = target rate of growth of output (in percent)

k = the capital-output ratio

s = the required rate of net savings ($=$ net investment) (percent)

5. See Roy F. Harrod, *Towards a Dynamic Economics* (London: Macmillan & Co. Ltd., 1948), and Evsey D. Domar, "Expansion and Employment," *American Economic Review*, 37 (March 1947), 34–35. The two models are not identical, but they are similar enough that economists often refer to the "Harrod-Domar model." Students interested in a brief explanation of the model(s) may consult a textbook on macroeconomic theory.

6. In chapter 8 we define development planning as "the use by government of a coordinated set of policy instruments to achieve national or regional economic objectives."

Given the desired dY/Y, and the assumed figure for k, policy makers solve for s and attempt to use the policy tools at their disposal (see chapters 13 and 14) to achieve this rate of savings. In the example above, to repeat, the required rate of savings is 15 percent:

$$2.5 + 2.5 = 5.0 = \frac{s}{3}; s = 15$$

Note, however, that the savings rate required to achieve a 2.5 percent rate growth in *per capita* output is very much influenced by the rate of population growth. If the population is stable, total output need grow only by 2.5 percent, and the required savings rate is just 7.5 percent:

$$2.5 + 0.0 = 2.5 = \frac{s}{3}; s = 7.5$$

If population is growing by 1 percent annually, the required savings rate is 10.5 percent:

$$2.5 + 1.0 = 3.5 = \frac{s}{3}; s = 10.5$$

In the developed countries, K/O ratios are reasonably stable in the short run (and even medium run) because the complementary factors of production, including skilled labor and management, are already present or can be increased quickly in response to a growing demand. Furthermore, technological change is not going to cause the K/O to change dramatically in just a few years. In the developing countries, however, the situation is often quite different. Skilled labor and managerial personnel may not be available and cannot be trained quickly. If more capital is used by industries facing these bottlenecks, that capital is not likely to be very productive. In other words, the marginal K/O ratio in that industry is likely to be rather high. It will take more capital than planned to achieve a given output—or, looking at it the other way, the same amount of capital will yield a lower than expected output. Using the original example above, and assuming that the savings/investment target of 15 percent is met, output will grow by only 3.75 percent—not 5.0 percent—if the capital-output ratio turns out to be 4:1 instead of 3:1:

$$\frac{dY}{Y} = \frac{15}{4} = 3.75$$

If a country attempts to industrialize rapidly on the basis of highly capital-intensive techniques, the introduction of advanced technology into an economy where prevailing techniques are quite primitive can significantly affect the overall level of technology in just a few years. This will tend to increase the average K/O ratio, especially if there is a high rate of unused capacity, as is not uncommon.[7]

So far, we have casually assumed that capital is capital and have paid little attention to the sector of the economy (or specific industry) into which it is placed. This is a mistake many developing countries have made. Actually, it makes a great deal of difference where the capital goes. If, for example, capital formation emphasizes highways, dams, power facilities, water and sewage systems, and other forms of what is called "social overhead capital" (see chapter 6), the K/O ratio is likely to be very high in the short run, since these projects generally take a number of years to complete and the benefits may be indirect and spread-out over a number of years. Over the long run, however, the availability of social overhead capital will tend to lower K/O ratios for direct capital formation in agriculture or manufacturing. On the other hand, if capital formation concentrates on agriculture, the short-run K/O ratio is likely to be relatively low; but long-term economic growth elsewhere in the economy may be hindered by the lack of social overhead capital.

In contrast to the situation in the developed countries, new capital formation in the developing countries is likely to be unbalanced, weighted heavily at any given time toward one sector of the economy or another. This tendency, combined with a lack of attention to complementary factors of production, means that marginal K/O ratios will be quite unpredictable. Furthermore, many capital goods will be used inefficiently or simply be idle.

It should now be clear why there is so much variation in the marginal capital-output ratios derived from Figure 2.1, where the period of time covered by the data (five years) corresponds to that of a typical medium-term development plan. The extreme cases also illustrate several other factors which significantly affect short-run capital-output ratios. In Nigeria and Iran, the relatively low ratio is explained not only by new petroleum production resulting from *prior* investment but also by the sharply higher petroleum prices charged by exporting nations beginning in late 1973. (Similarly, other things being equal, a decline in a country's export prices will raise its capital-output ratio.) The relatively high ratio for Chile is explained largely by the political and economic turmoil surrounding the rise and fall of the Allende government (1970–1973).

---

7. Data for five Latin American countries in the 1950s and early 1960s show that unused capacity in some industries reached as high as 50 to 75 percent. In Chile (1957) and Ecuador (1959 and 1961) idle capacity for the industrial sector as a whole was about 40 percent. See United Nations Economic Commission for Latin America, *The Process of Industrial Development in Latin America* (New York, 1966), pp. 72–73.

Post-Keynesian growth theories utilizing capital-output ratios are not the only theories which regard lack of capital as the major obstacle to growth. In the remainder of this chapter, we shall examine two other theories, the "vicious circle of poverty" and the "big push," which were widely discussed in the late 1950s and early 1960s and still are sometimes used as explanations for lack of growth. We shall show that these theories, too, tend to ignore important noneconomic factors affecting economic growth.

THE VICIOUS CIRCLE OF POVERTY

The vicious circle of poverty is one of the most widely known theories based on the notion that a lack of capital is the key factor preventing growth and development. As the name implies, it is a theory explaining economic stagnation at very low levels of per capita output. At the time it was formulated, in the early 1950s, the model seemed to be an accurate description of conditions in many countries. Since then, however, most developing countries have achieved higher per capita GNPs and improvements in other socioeconomic indicators, and there is nothing in the vicious circle model to indicate why this growth and development have occurred.

The model is presented in Figure 2.2, which shows that there are actually two circles, one reflecting supply conditions and the other the

Figure 2.2
The Vicious Circles of Poverty

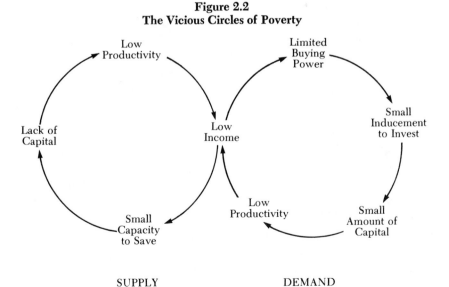

SUPPLY   DEMAND

forces of demand. On the supply side, low income means a small capacity to save, and this, in turn, results in little investment (capital formation). Lack of capital means that productivity is low, resulting in low income and thus completing the circle. On the demand side, low income means limited buying power and therefore a small inducement to invest. Accordingly, there will be little capital used in production, productivity will be low, and so will income; again the circle is complete.

As Bauer and Yamey have pointed out,[8] the model confuses low *levels* of development with low (or zero) *rates of change* in output. Equally important, there is a confusion between levels of savings and rates of savings. It is the latter that really counts. Absolute levels of per capita savings in developing countries will be low for many years even after savings rates begin to rise; but the rise in savings rates, other things being equal, will result in economic growth.

Low rates of savings should not really be attributed to poverty (i.e., low incomes) but rather to social, political, and other institutional factors. Even the poorest people in the poorest societies manage to set aside money for religious or secular festivals or for the purchase of alcoholic beverages, coca leaves, opium, or other drugs. Surely, then, the very poor have some capacity to save. What they lack is an incentive to save. If the social structure is rigid and denies them a reasonable chance for material advancement, savings cannot be channeled into productive investments. Producing more food with improved technology, for example, will not help the farmer who owns no land and who finds that his rent increases or the landowner's share of the crop rises, thus depriving him of his production gains. Even if he owns his own land, production increases may lead to falling prices for his crops. Under these circumstances, spending money on festive occasions—and even drinking or drug taking— may be very rational behavior. Once the social structure begins to break down, and farmers begin to have access to land and other productive resources previously denied them, incentives for the poor to save will increase. The problem then becomes one of mobilizing these potential savings.

While the poor constitute the vast majority of the population in developing countries, the 5 to 10 percent or so who are relatively if not absolutely wealthy may receive about 40 percent of the national income, and clearly there is savings potential here. Part of the income of the wealthy, however, is likely to be sent overseas; and part may be channeled into the building of elaborate sports stadiums and other monuments, the support of an elaborate religious establishment, the mainte-

8. P. T. Bauer and B. S. Yamey, "Underdeveloped Economies," *Science*, 130 (November 20, 1959), 1383–1387.

nance of hordes of personal retainers, or other forms of conspicuous consumption. If this wealthy segment of the population could cut its consumption by 15 percent (which by no means would leave it destitute), the national savings rate could rise by enough to transform a zero rate of per capita growth into a growth rate of perhaps 2 percent. Table 2.1 provides a hypothetical example, self-explanatory, to illustrate this point. Getting the rich to save more, however, is a difficult task, and financial institutions will have to be developed to channel the increased savings into productive investment (see chapters 3 and 13).

Another major problem with the vicious circle model is that it does not allow for foreign savings—in the form of direct investment, public and private lending, or foreign aid—as a means of increasing investment and thus initiating economic growth. This has been a major stimulus to

TABLE 2.1
Savings by the Rich and Economic Growth:
A Hypothetical Example

Assumptions
Zero rate of growth of population
No change in natural resource endowments
No change in the quality of the labor force
Stable capital-output ratio of 3:1
No change in the savings rate of the poor
Rich constitute 10% of the population and have 40% of the income
Poor constitute 90% of the population and have 60% of the income
6% of GNP needed to replace worn-out capital

	Example A: Conspicuous Consumption by the Rich	*Example B: Productive Investment by the Rich*[a]
Gross Savings as a % of GNP		
Rich	6	20
Poor	6	6
National Average	6	12
Net Savings as a % of GNP		
Rich	0	14
Poor	0	0
National Average	0	6
Rate of Growth of GNP (= GNP per capita) (%)	0	2

[a] Assumes a 15 percent cut in consumption by the rich—i.e., from 94 percent of their income to 80 percent—thus increasing their gross investment rate from 6 to 20 percent and their net investment rate from 0 to 14 percent.

growth in some developing countries, but such growth has not always been accompanied by development.[9]

Notwithstanding these criticisms, there is no denying that the vast majority of the population in the developing countries finds it difficult to save. And where population growth is rapid, a relatively high rate of savings is necessary just to keep per capita income constant. Chapters 13 and 14 describe the actions governments can take to mobilize potential savings, both within their borders and from abroad.

THE THEORY OF THE BIG PUSH

Another theory that assigns to capital the central role in the process of economic growth and development is the theory of the big push. Its origin can be traced to an article by Paul Rosenstein-Rodan, published in 1943.[10] In Rosenstein-Rodan's view, industrialization "is *the* way of achieving a more equal distribution of income between different areas of the world by raising incomes in depressed areas at a higher rate than in rich areas" (emphasis in original). Industrialization was defined as the increased use of capital by labor, both in agriculture and in nonagricultural production.

A big push, it was argued, was needed because industrial firms in the twentieth century were larger and more capital-intensive than those in the nineteenth. Entrepreneurs thus risked larger amounts of fixed capital, and they needed to mobilize larger amounts of savings in an environment where formal capital markets might not even exist. Sizable markets for their products, therefore, had to be developed to ensure favorable rates of return. Social overhead capital, too, had to be provided on a larger scale. On the demand side, low and often stagnant incomes—and the relatively small number of people whose incomes are in cash—limit the demand for industrial products. For example, if a new shoe factory were established in a stagnant economy, additional demand for shoes would be limited to the small number of previously unemployed workers now receiving cash wages from the new factory. With so limited a demand, the shoe factory would not be viable in a capitalist economy.[11]

9. Foreign savings have not been ignored—Nurkse (1953) and others have recognized it as a means of "breaking" the vicious circles—but the foreign sector of the economy is not explicitly incorporated into the model.

10. Paul N. Rosenstein-Rodan, "Problems of Industrialization of Eastern and Southeastern Europe," *Economic Journal*, 53 (June–September 1943), 202–211.

11. In a socialist economy, though, a single, state-owned factory like this could be built because its establishment would not depend on prospects for its profitability. The objective of providing a basic consumption good to more people could be sufficient motivation for establishing the factory and selling its product at a subsidized price.

The same would be true for factories producing any other product. However, if a large number of factories, each producing a different product, could be established simultaneously, the total market for each product—encompassing *all* factory workers as well as the initial buyers—would be large enough to make all firms profitable.

An additional advantage of a big push, it is argued, is that it would create external economies, i.e., cost reductions to an individual firm made possible by the proximity of large numbers of firms. An agglomeration of industrial activities encourages, for example, the establishment of specialized firms which can be contracted to provide services such as warehousing, deliveries, cleaning, and security. If each firm has to provide its own services, buildings, equipment, and manpower will be idle for much of the time (unless the firm is very large) and costs will be higher. Another example of an external economy would be the establishment of a government technical school in response to industrial demand for large numbers of skilled workers. This reduces the firms' on-the-job training costs.

A modified version of Rosenstein-Rodan's shoe-factory example is presented in Table 2.2 and illustrated diagrammatically in Figure 2.3. We assume, first of all, that to begin with our hypothetical developing country has no modern manufacturing industries, only artisan industries. Manufactured goods desired by upper and middle-income groups, and which artisans cannot supply, must be imported. Now, assume that the government is willing to provide some infant industry protection to firms in newly established industries, provided that the plants to be built operate at some minimum acceptable level of technical efficiency.[12] We can assume, arbitrarily, that this means an average total cost (ATC) at capacity that is no more than 20 percent greater than the ATC-at-capacity of the optimum-size plant (i.e., the size of the plant with the lowest ATC curve given prevailing technology). The ATC and marginal cost (MC) curves for such a plant in the shoe industry are indicated in Figure 2.3.

Now that we have considered supply factors, demand may be brought into the picture. Let us assume an initial (prefactory) quantity demanded of 20,000 pairs of shoes at P_L, the lowest possible price compatible with this size plant.[13] To simplify the analysis, assume that the demand sched-

---

12. The infant industry argument for tariffs, considered by most economists to be a valid one, is reviewed in chapter 5.

13. Actually, no profit-maximizing, unregulated monopoly—for that is what we have here—would charge only P_L, where profits as defined by economists are zero and as defined in the business world are only "normal" (and included in the ATC curve). The monopolist's price and output will be determined by the intersection of the marginal cost and marginal revenue schedules. A government-owned firm, of course, or a regulated monopoly, could charge a price as low as P_L.

TABLE 2.2
The Rationale for a Big Push: A Hypothetical Example

	Shoes (pairs)	Cloth (yards)	Pasta (pounds)	Beer (quarts)	Small Tools (units)	Concrete Blocks (tons)
Capacity of a plant with a minimum acceptable efficiency[a]	40,000	100,000	1,200,000	900,000	30,000	10,000
Preindustrialization quantity demanded at lowest price compatible with this size plant[b]	20,000	50,000	600,000	450,000	15,000	5,000
Quantity demanded by workers in new industries:						
Shoes	5,000	12,500	150,000	112,500	3,750	1,250
Cloth	5,000	12,500	150,000	112,500	3,750	1,250
Pasta	5,000	12,500	150,000	112,500	3,750	1,250
Beer	5,000	12,500	150,000	112,500	3,750	1,250
Small Tools	5,000	12,500	150,000	112,500	3,750	1,250
Concrete Blocks	5,000	12,500	150,000	112,500	3,750	1,250
Total quantity demanded at lowest possible price	50,000	125,000	1,500,000	1,125,000	37,500	12,500

[a] *Capacity* refers to the lowest point on the average total cost (ATC) curve. *Minimum acceptable efficiency* may be defined, arbitrarily, as an ATC-at-capacity no more than, say, 20 percent greater than the ATC-at-capacity of the optimum-size plant (i.e., the size of plant with the lowest ATC curve given prevailing technology).

[b] In the absence of subsidies, this price would be equal to ATC at capacity. Actually, since the firm in each industry is a monopoly, the price (unless regulated) will be higher than this, as determined by the intersection of the marginal cost and marginal revenue curves.

Figure 2.3
**The Big Push: The Unprofitability of a Single Firm Established in Isolation
and Its Profitability when Many Firms in Different Industries Are
Simultaneously Established**

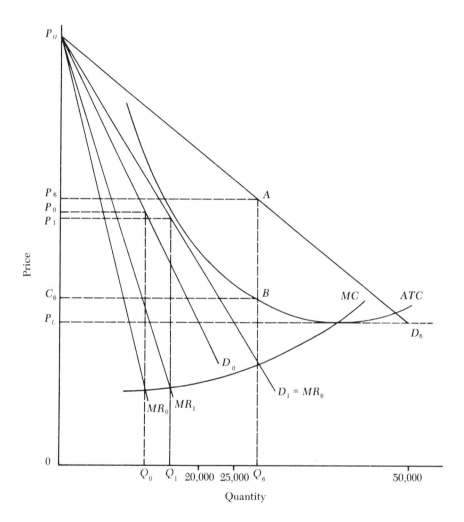

ule is linear $(P_H D_0)$. The marginal revenue schedule is thus $P_H MR_0$,
which bisects the angle $P_L P_H D_0$. To maximize profits, a single (monopoly) shoe firm would operate where $MC = MR$. With quantity demanded
so low, however, the optimum price (P_0) and quantity (Q_0) only minimize losses. In other words, the factory is not economically viable. Even
if we add to the original demand schedule the demand for shoes by the

shoe-factory workers (5,000 pairs, as shown in Table 2.2), the firm still cannot make a profit, as we can tell from the price (P_1) and quantity (Q_1) resulting from the intersection of MC and MR_1. The same would be true for any other single firm, in any other industry, if that firm were the *only one* established.

However, if a number of different industries are established simultaneously, *all* of them will be profitable. The monopoly solution for the shoe factory under such circumstances is indicated by P_6 and Q_6, as determined by the intersection of MC and MR_6. (The subscript "6" represents the cumulated demand of workers in the six industries established plus the initial, preindustrialization demand.) The shoe firm is making handsome profits of C_6P_6AB, which, with the economy now growing, may encourage a second firm to enter the industry.

What the big push calls for, of course, is a sudden, sharp increase in the rate of investment—i.e., capital formation. This could be done by mobilizing domestic savings; but a rapid rise in the investment rate would require strong action on the part of the government, since no individual entrepreneur, acting in isolation, would find it profitable to establish an industrial firm. The Soviet Union is the outstanding example of an internally financed big push that succeeded in rapidly raising the investment rate. But there have also been failures, most notably China's "Great Leap Forward" beginning in 1958. An alternative to the mobilization of domestic savings is to seek savings from abroad in the form of private foreign investment or government aid. This approach, too, has seen both success and failure.[14]

The notion that a big push is required to overcome the capital shortage bottleneck is open to question. In the twentieth century, as in the nineteenth, countries have experienced growth and development with *gradually* rising investment rates.[15] Although industry generally is much more capital-intensive than in the nineteenth century, and significant economies of scale exist in many industries, scale economies are relatively minor in food processing and textiles, typically the most important indus-

---

14. I have described the failure of one such effort in "Argentine Economic Policy, 1958–1962: The Frondizi Government's Development Plan," *Inter-American Economic Affairs*, 22, No. 1 (Summer 1968), 45–73. Frondizi explicitly referred to his strategy as a big push (49, fn. 24).

15. W. W. Rostow's stages-of-growth theory (see chapter 1) has been criticized for its argument that a rapidly rising investment rate is necessary to achieve economic "takeoff"—an argument similar to that of the big push theory. Most historical evidence suggests that investment rates have not risen as sharply as Rostow assumed. For a collection of papers in which Rostow's theory is debated, see W. W. Rostow et al., *The Economics of Take-Off into Sustained Economic Growth* (London: Macmillan & Co., Ltd., 1964).

try groups in the early stages of growth and development. Almost all developing countries have enough high- and moderate-income recipients to support small but technically efficient industrial establishments in these and other industry groups. Also, the incomes of those demanding industrial products are not always stagnant. Generally they can be expected to rise because of increased agricultural or mineral exports, tourism, or emigrants' remittances. Thus domestic demand for industrial goods can grow gradually and provide an incentive for new firms and industries to become established without the need for a big push. As the domestic market expands in size, greater economies of scale and external economies can be realized. Developing countries can also take advantage of opportunities in foreign markets (see chapter 10). Finally, not all social overhead capital is highly indivisible. Electric power, for example, can be provided initially by small generators, with massive hydroelectric projects coming later.

Some proponents of a big push might concede these points but argue that gradual growth does nothing to narrow income differentials between developing and developed countries. There is much merit to this argument. But note that the case for a big push is still based on the presumption that what is needed to accelerate economic growth is a rise in the rate of investment. Little if any attention is given to the development of human capital, or to measures to increase the efficiency of investment (lower the capital-output ratio) through improved administration, management, or technology.

SUMMARY

It is difficult to judge the effects of climate on economic growth, but broad theories centering on effort and achievement have not been verified. Climatic factors do affect agricultural productivity and the incidence of pests and diseases, but in the long run they may affect the composition of output more than its level.

Countries with abundant natural resources have an advantage over those that do not; but resource abundance is no guarantee of growth or development. By the same token, countries with relatively poor natural resource endowments have managed to become industrial powers, importing what they lack within their own borders.

Lack of capital is a more serious obstacle to growth and development. Low rates of capital formation are not so much a function of poverty as of the social, political, and other noneconomic forces characterizing low-income countries. These obstacles—and the important role of "human capital"—are the subject of the next chapter.

Suggested Readings

Hagen, Everett E. *On the Theory of Social Change: How Economic Growth Begins*. Homewood, Ill.: The Dorsey Press, Inc., 1962.
> Chapter 3 is a critique of economic growth theories focusing on the lack of capital as the major obstacle to be overcome.

Kamarck, Andrew M. *The Tropics and Economic Development: A Provocative Inquiry into the Poverty of Nations*. Foreword by Paul Streeten. Baltimore: The Johns Hopkins University Press for the World Bank, 1976.
> Written for a nonspecialized audience, this book is certain to awaken interest in the role of climate in the process of economic development. Kamarck shows how a tropical environment has adverse effects on a variety of factors ranging from human and animal health to minerals exploration. A short article based on this book appears in *Finance and Development*, 10 (June 1973), 2–8.

Lewis, W. Arthur. *The Theory of Economic Growth*. London: George Allen and Unwin Ltd., 1955; New York: Harper & Row, Publishers, 1970 (paperback ed.).
> Capital formation, in Lewis' view, plays the central role in the process of economic growth. But Lewis is also keenly aware that noneconomic factors play an important role in keeping savings rates low in developing countries. The title notwithstanding, this classic early text is concerned with development as well as growth.

Nurske, Ragnar. *Problems of Capital Formation in Underdeveloped Countries*. New York: Oxford University Press, 1953.
> This book contains the classic statement of the vicious circle of poverty, a theory very much in vogue during the 1950s, when little or no economic growth was evident in many developing countries.

3

Noneconomic Obstacles to Growth and Development

Two decades ago, economist Everett Hagen undertook a detailed study to answer the question, "Why have the people of some societies entered upon technological progress sooner or more effectively than others?" Hagen believed that "the differences were due only in very minor degree to economic obstacles, lack of information, or lack of training." This led him to seek explanations in the fields of anthropology, sociology, and psychology. In the book based on this research, *On the Theory of Social Change* (1962), Hagen assigned a central role to personality formation in the processes of economic growth and development.

This may seem a rather startling conclusion for an economist based at the mathematically sophisticated Massachusetts Institute of Technology. Today, however, few development economists would deny the importance of noneconomic factors in growth and development, even though they might disagree strongly with some of Hagen's specific conclusions. In this chapter, we shall examine some of the psychological, social, cultural (including religious), and political factors alleged to be obstacles to growth and development. Economic theorists and policy makers need to be aware of these factors, though it would be a mistake to assume that they are the only things that count. To do so would be to adopt a position just as extreme—and incomplete—as that of the economists and policy makers who have viewed the dynamics of growth only in terms of capital-output ratios.

We should point out that this chapter does not attempt to provide a complete inventory of noneconomic "obstacle theories," only a sample of those that have received a fair amount of attention in the development literature. Likewise, no effort is made to cover the vast literature on development by social scientists whose writings cannot be classified as obstacle theories but who instead explore various interrelationships between economic and noneconomic factors—e.g., the political determinants of economic policy formation or the effects of class conflict on income distribution. What we hope to do is provide enough examples of these interrelationships to show why they are important for understanding and analyzing development problems and devising strategies for solving them.

SOME ALLEGED NONECONOMIC OBSTACLES

Traditional Society: Resistance to Change

Societies which have never experienced significant economic growth may be characterized as *traditional*—i.e., they seek to preserve their *institutions*, or ways of doing things.[1] All societies, of course, attempt to hold on to some of their institutions, and it is by no means necessary or desirable that all traditional institutions be given up in order that growth and development might occur. But when we apply the term *traditional* to an entire society, we mean that it resists virtually all attempts to alter established patterns. This is not to say that everyone in a traditional society wants to preserve the status quo. In small, relatively democratic, communal societies (what Marx called "tribalism" or "primitive communism") this may be the case; but in large, authoritarian societies (e.g., the Egyptian or Inca empires) those outside the ruling classes are not necessarily satisfied with their lot in life. Nevertheless, prevailing institutions will be passively accepted if challenges to the existing order are seen to have little chance of success and may invite harsh reprisals. Moreover, even in authoritarian societies, serfs or slaves may recognize that the existing order—while by no means the best of all conceivable situations—at least affords some security and protection against outsiders.

At the risk of continuing to overgeneralize, let us examine some of the other characteristics of the traditional society. One of the more important ones is that individuals believe that they have no ability to change their environment fundamentally. Once they have adapted to it in a manner satisfactory to the community at large (or at least to those who exercise power), religious beliefs and other elements of the culture reinforce the behavior patterns that have been established. For example,

---

1. The term *society* is used loosely in this chapter; it can refer either to a tribe of several dozen individuals or to an empire of millions. Basically, it refers to a group of people with a large number of common values and institutions (including language and political institutions). While some empires have been culturally homogeneous societies, others are more appropriately called federations or confederations of distinct societies.

social, political, and economic relationships are said to be the will of God, or whatever the local deity or deities might be called. Religious authorities in medieval Europe, who were part of the ruling elite, told serfs to accept the lot ordained for them and to prepare for something better in the next life. Sermons on this theme continue to be preached in some parts of Latin America where conditions similar to serfdom still prevail. In Asia, Hinduism has particularly strong elements of fatalism and otherworldliness. If the ruling elite face few internal or external threats and continue in power for generations or centuries, fatalism will be deeply entrenched in the rest of the population.

A traditional society views new ideas with suspicion because they threaten the social order. Dissent is discouraged by social ostracism and other penalties, including frequently the ultimate penalty. If nature and neighbors leave a society alone, its way of life can persist for centuries. Stone age societies, such as that of the Tasaday in the Philippines or those of numerous communities in the Amazon basin, survive to this day.

Status and occupation in a traditional society are determined by ascription (inheritance), not by ability and achievement. Since traditions are not easily changed after economic growth begins,[2] persons who assume leadership roles (especially when we are talking about growth without development) are not necessarily those with the best managerial, administrative, innovative, and policymaking skills. Rather, they are individuals whose assumption of new roles can be traced to membership in traditional elite groups which are seeking to turn new circumstances to their advantage. If the political and economic leadership does not consist of those with the best talents for promoting growth and development, it should hardly be surprising that economic growth in such an environment is likely to be slow and characterized by inefficiency in both private and public decision making. Even those with greater talents in these areas would make many mistakes at first, but their learning process would be quicker. Such individuals, however, do not have an equal opportunity to compete for top leadership positions. Still, the fact that growth has begun creates some opportunities for them where none previously existed.

An institution characteristic of many traditional societies is the *extended family*, which is distinguished from the nuclear family of mother, father, and children by also including grandparents, sisters and brothers of the parents, or other relatives. It has frequently been argued that the extended family is an obstacle to economic growth and develop-

---

2. Let us not be concerned, for the moment, with how economic growth begins, except to point out that it is quite likely to come about accidentally rather than by the conscious decision of a traditional elite.

ment, but this contention is open to question. The most frequent charge against the extended family is that it stifles initiative. Why should a person work hard and try to increase output if the fruits of his or her labor must be shared with grandparents, siblings, and other relatives? And why should a person migrate and seek new opportunities in unfamiliar surroundings when the extended family provides insurance against unemployment, disability, and old age? In answer to these charges, it can be argued that the extended family permits the cultivation of more land without hired labor and allows for more specialization and division of labor than does the nuclear family. Also, feelings of responsibility toward family members may neutralize presumed disincentives.[3] Finally, the extended family does not seem to have been a barrier to rural-urban migration. Indeed, it offers some protection to the potential migrant by providing a home in the event that life in the urban area proves to be unsatisfactory.

The extended family is perhaps more a symptom of a low level of development and lack of opportunity than an obstacle to development. It is a means of providing food, clothing, and shelter to economically inactive members of the population who have no access to a government social security system—if indeed such a system exists. It can also serve as financial institution, providing funds for the education and training of its most talented members, who will repay their relatives with the fruits of this investment. Historically, as growth and development have occurred and the population has shifted toward urban areas, the extended family has tended to break up, though in the short run its size and strength have sometimes increased.[4] The eventual weakening of the extended family —which many observers lament—seems to be fundamentally a result of development (or at least urbanization). Factors contributing to the decline of the extended family include (1) the geographic separation of migrants from relatives who remain in rural areas, (2) the separation of the home from the place of work in the city, (3) an increase in impersonal relationships, (4) the higher cost of feeding marginally productive persons in urban areas, compared with the countryside, and, later in time, (5) the increased availability of retirement benefits which permit older

---

3. See Robert R. Kerton, "An Economic Analysis of the Extended Family in the West Indies," *Journal of Development Studies,* 7 (July 1971), 423–434. Kerton found that Jamaicans were willing to add poorer relations to the extended family as their incomes increased, with no negative effects, and perhaps even positive effects, on work incentives. He also cites evidence that this occurred earlier in the United States, where the extended family remained strong in some areas until well into the twentieth century.

4. Ibid. Kerton admits, though, that the extended family is likely to weaken in the long run.

persons to survive (barely, in many cases) outside the homes of their children.[5]

Community attitudes toward individual advancement constitute another aspect of traditional societies which appears to be an obstacle to economic growth and development. While the person who goes from rags to riches may be widely admired in the United States, efforts at self-improvement are often met with disapproval in developing countries. Perhaps the lack of change in a particular community leads its members to conclude that one person's advancement implies losses for others. Moritz Thomsen (1969), a perceptive former Peace Corps volunteer in Ecuador, reports that an individual in the community where he worked abandoned a successful new project because of peer pressures resulting precisely from that personal success. The problem, again, was not that community members were happy with things as they were. Rather, they felt that improvements in living standards should be shared by the entire community, and they were not convinced that they would be equally successful in similar ventures.

Traditional societies are not always static. They must be concerned about developments which affect their physical security, and they must react to new events over which they have no control. Historian Arnold Toynbee has described the process of socioeconomic change as one of "challenge and response." The challenges take the form of outside events, such as invasions by other societies and changes in temperature, rainfall, or the course of a river. If people are forced to leave their homeland for such a reason, and settle elsewhere, new institutions will have to be developed. If those moving into new areas have to compete with other groups for land and food supply, a "dovish" code of intercommunity relationships may have to be replaced by a "hawkish" one. Nomadic hunters and gatherers may become settled agriculturalists or turn to fishing. Mountains and rivers with religious significance must be left behind, and different religious institutions will have to be developed in the area of resettlement. Societies which do not meet the challenge of new events will disappear, being absorbed or decimated by more powerful societies or in some cases falling victim to starvation or disease. Those which survive do so because the creative response demanded of them has been forthcoming. If the response is sufficiently creative, economic advancement will occur.

---

5. The breakup of the extended family is not necessarily peculiar to capitalist development. In China, it would appear that the extended family is being weakened by official discouragement of the veneration of ancestors and of the traditional acceptance of age as a badge of authority, as well as by efforts to promote loyalty to production teams, brigades, and communes in agriculture (see chapter 9) and similar new institutions in urban centers.

Economic historian W. W. Rostow has argued that growth often begins in a traditional society as a reaction to actual or threatened intrusion by outside forces. If the ruling elite fail to respond adequately to the threat, their control over the social order will weaken. Others with a relatively high degree of status and power will then move to seize the reins of government and promote economic growth as a means of bolstering national defense. A classic example is the Meiji Revolution in Japan in 1868, prompted by growing foreign influence in nearby China and by Commodore Perry's appearance in Japanese waters in 1853 (see Hagen, 1962: Ch. 14).

Although Japanese society in the mid-1880s was by no means totally stagnant, it could still be described then as fundamentally traditional, as could the Japanese government. Today, few national governments could be characterized as traditional; all but a handful could be called "modernizing" to one degree or another.[6] Still, the central sociopolitical unit for the majority of the population in many developing countries is not the nation but the village. Many villagers, in fact, have difficulty understanding the concept of the "nation" in which they are told they live. The forces of tradition are still very powerful in the villages and on isolated farms. Introducing change into such an environment is no easy matter. This is *not*—as we have emphasized several times already—because people in poor communities are content with their poverty. Rather, it is because they fear the unknown and things over which they have no direct control. Moreover, they distrust outsiders, since outside intervention in the past has usually meant exploitation.

Psychological Obstacles: Personality Traits

Psychological factors are sometimes alleged to be major obstacles to economic growth and development. It has been claimed, for example, that certain nations have remained very poor because their citizens are too emotional, unstable, paranoid, fatalistic, or just plain lazy. These terms have even been applied to entire countries, whose "national character" is said to be inimical to development. (They have also been applied, as we know, to minority groups in developed countries.) Attempts to explain such personality traits—and just how they hinder development—are usually superficial, if made at all.

Another simplistic explanation of the role of psychological factors in development is the so-called "great man" theory of history, which attributes social change to the forceful and dominating personality of a single individual. Twentieth-century candidates for great men whose energies

---

6. Modernization will be discussed in a separate section later in this chapter.

have been directed toward national economic development include such diverse figures as Kemal Ataturk in Turkey, Lenin and Stalin in the Soviet Union, Mao Tse-Tung in China, Fidel Castro in Cuba, and Julius Nyerere in Tanzania. These individuals, many believe, have really made a difference in the development of their respective countries (though Marxist theory would emphasize the class struggle and not the role of individuals). But without denying the accomplishments of these men, we must ask *why* they have achieved such dominance. Others with equally strong personalities and visions have not had the same impact. Clearly, social, political, and economic conditions must be "right" in a country for such individuals to achieve positions of power. These conditions will vary from country to country, and we need not be concerned here with specific examples. It is sufficient to point out that a single man (or woman) cannot cause social change without the support or acquiescence of those who desire or tolerate it. It is then necessary to ask how many people fall into these categories, why they are there, and what resources they have at their disposal.

More important contributions to our understanding of the role of psychological factors in development have been made by economist Everett Hagen (1962) and social psychologist David McClelland (1961; 1969), whose research on entrepreneurship will be discussed below. It is also useful to comment briefly on Hagen's theory of personality change and how it affects economic growth and development.

Hagen argues that personality changes can be traced to alterations in the childhood environment which create new tensions, anxieties, and rage for which traditional society provides no relief or outlet. In a hierarchical social structure, anxiety is avoided by submitting to authority, and rage is vented against those below one in the social structure. These patterns of behavior, learned in childhood, persist in later life. If for some reason the social environment changes, psychologically satisfying solutions to normal anxieties may no longer be present. Adults become confused, and their erratic behavior in turn affects their children, who will be unable to find much order in the changed social structure.

Change may occur for a number of reasons, one of the most common of which has been the forcible displacement of a traditional elite, either by a group from within the society or by outsiders. The displaced elite suffer what Hagen calls "withdrawal of status respect," or lack of respect for the purposes and values in life which had been developed since childhood. The stage is thus set for a chain of events which may (or may not) lead—over several generations—to the appearance of innovative personality traits in a significant minority of the population.

Before this happens, however, the society may go through several generations in which the dominant personality trait is "retreatism," as exemplified by native Americans living listlessly on reservations, trying to cling to their societies' past glories, slipping into alcoholism, and having no clearly defined goals in life. In essence, Hagen says, these people learned as children that adult life was painful, and they dealt with the problem by suppressing their zeal for life, thus avoiding pain.

Over a period of several generations, Hagen argues, the adult personality gradually changes as individuals become more self-conscious about their situation, instead of passively accepting it. Innovative personality can emerge out of this situation via several routes, with the father either demanding achievement (to assuage his guilt about not being able to change his lot in life) or not standing in the way of achievement. The mother often plays a strong supporting role in the development of innovative personality.

An individual with an innovative personality views his[7] environment as amenable to logical analysis; the environment is also seen to value him as an individual. In psychological terms, he has high need autonomy, need achievement, need order, need succorance, and need nurturance. His need dependence and need submission-dominance, on the other hand, are low.

This is all very interesting, the reader might say, but what implications does it have for development policy? One implication is very disturbing: that colonialism, in the long run, has stimulated economic growth and development by withdrawing status respect from traditional elites and setting in motion the long process of personality change. Hagen and most other development economists today would reject colonialism as a policy prescription. Besides, there are virtually no societies remaining in which this phenomenon has not already occurred. There is another implication of the Hagen thesis, however, that is more widely accepted: namely, that identifying and giving assistance to persons with strong innovative personalities can constitute an investment in "human capital" with a potentially high payoff. We shall return to this subject later in this chapter.

Lack of Entrepreneurship

The importance of entrepreneurship was stressed by Joseph Schumpeter, whose influential book, *The Theory of Economic Development,* was first published in German in 1911. Since then, many economists have considered it to be a fourth factor of production, joining the traditional

---

7. As Hagen points out, women have not generally played leading roles in the process of social change. This is not to say that they are incapable of doing so, but rather that the social structure has denied them an opportunity.

factors of land, labor, and capital. Entrepreneurs are not just ordinary businessmen or businesswomen. They can be regarded as persons combining the traits of the visionary, the wheeler-dealer, and the empire builder. Entrepreneurs are willing to take great risks if they perceive high potential rewards. Most of those engaged in business, by contrast, are very concerned with security and have rather modest personal ambitions.

Entrepreneurs are not necessarily inventors, though inventors sometimes assume entrepreneurial roles, as in the case of Henry Ford. Entrepreneurs are more appropriately considered as innovators, combining existing factors of producton in new and more efficient ways or adapting a new invention for sale in the marketplace.

Some societies seem better endowed with entrepreneurship than others, and this naturally leads one to ask why this is so. In traditional societies, where social structures are rigid and change is regarded with suspicion, entrepreneurial activity is an example of what psychologists and sociologists would call "deviant behavior" that challenges existing social norms. Relatively few people are willing to suffer the slings and arrows (often literally) that their "outrageous fortunes" bring upon them. Some will succeed; but others who "don't know their place" may be put back there against their wills, and many will not try to leave again. In some traditional societies, even the ordinary business person may have rather low social status.

Still, political leaders have occasional need for entrepreneurial talents, in which case such activity will be tolerated or even encouraged. In medieval Europe, for example, rulers attempting to form or consolidate what we now call nation-states frequently needed financial assistance to pay mercenaries or to purchase military goods. This type of assistance was difficult to obtain because the wealth of the upper classes was primarily in the form of land. Furthermore, some landowners might have been reluctant to lend any money they had because the Christian religious authorities said that it was not right to charge interest on loans. It is questionable, though, that the prohibition of usury was very effective in limiting the supply of borrowed funds from this source.[8] In any event, money could also be borrowed from the Jewish community, for whom the antiusury injunction in Exodus 22:25 no longer held much authority. Some of the Jewish financiers during this period could be considered true

---

8. The Christian prohibition of usury, based on Luke 6:35, was originally applied only to the clergy. At the Lateran Council of 1179, and in subsequent decrees, it was applied to the laity as well. But as the demand for borrowed funds increased, the Church's prohibition of both the charging and paying of interest was increasingly ignored by secular society. Religious authorities accommodated this trend by granting various exceptions to the no-usury rule. See Eric Roll, *A History of Economic Thought,* rev. and enl. ed. (London: Faber and Faber Ltd., 1961), pp. 47–51.

entrepreneurs. Though "deviant" in a social sense, the Jews were tolerated under controlled conditions, and they were willing to perform useful economic functions which the mainstream of society relegated to a low status.

The Jews were able to exercise entrepreneurial talents because changes were occurring in Western Europe which the existing social order could not easily accommodate. As the pace of change increased and new social classes appeared (particularly as a result of urbanization), the old social order began to crumble and latent entrepreneurial talents in the society could be exercised with fewer threats of reprisal. The entrepreneurial drive was present not just in obvious groups of "outsiders" like the Jews but also in people closer to the mainstream of society (if not in it) who saw for the first time opportunities to increase their power and welfare.

A good deal of entrepreneurial activity was evident in Great Britain and elsewhere in Western Europe during the so-called Industrial Revolution of the eighteenth century. One of the pioneers of sociology, Max Weber, and the English economic historian R. H. Tawney, argued that this expansion of entrepreneurial activity was closely related to the rise of Protestant religious groups, particularly those based on the teachings of John Calvin, who stressed such capitalist virtues as hard work and thrift ($=$ savings $=$ investment).[9] Calvinist teachings contrasted with those of the Roman Catholic Church (and only slightly fallen Catholics, like the Anglicans), whose attitudes toward business activity were rather cool. Everett Hagen (1962: Ch. 13) found that the Protestant "noncomformists" in England, Scotland, and Wales did indeed contribute to entrepreneurial activity far out of proportion to their numbers. He attributed this activity, though, not to their religion but to personality traits which led them to be nonconformist in all aspects of their lives. Hagen's view is more plausible than extreme versions of the "Protestant ethic" theory (Weber and Tawney themselves acknowledged that capitalist behavior existed long before Calvinism), particularly when it is realized that entrepreneurial activity elsewhere in the world has been dominated by Jews, Moslems, Shintoists, Buddhists, Roman Catholics, Hindus, and other non-Protestant groups.

The personality or psychological theory of entrepreneurial orgins has also been stressed by David McClelland, whose book *The Achieving Society* (1961) argued that "a particular psychological factor—the need for Achievement (n-Ach)—is responsible for economic growth and de-

9. Max Weber, *The Protestant Ethic and the Spirit of Capitalism* (orginally published in German in 1904–1905), and R. H. Tawney, *Religion and the Rise of Capitalism* (originally published in 1926).

cline." Societies differ widely in their n-Ach levels, but even in those with low n-Ach levels there are some people with high n-Ach. Moreover, McClelland has argued, motivation training for business operators can increase their n-Ach levels. A subsequent book, *Motivating Economic Achievement* (1969), reported the results of such training in India and other countries, usually in connection with supervised credit programs which gave potential entrepreneurs the means to expand their activities.

Just how serious an obstacle to growth is the lack of entrepreneurial talent? Quite possibly it is only a minor one. The problem may really be that growth is held back by a political leadership strong enough to maintain the existing social order and to deny to those with entrepreneurial potential an opportunity to exercise their talents. Once internal or external events cause a traditional society to break up, those with entrepreneurial talents will seize opportunities to utilize their skills. Entrepreneurial activity can also be encouraged by government policy, as in Japan after the 1868 revolution and Turkey under Kemal Ataturk. In such cases, governments themselves are really performing entrepreneurial functions—usually because they represent interest groups newly risen to the top after the breakup of the old order. In addition to stimulating private business activity, governments can act as entrepreneurs by directly investing in and operating new activities.

All of this is not to say that the demand for entrepreneurship automatically and quickly brings forth the necessary skills. Those who have the potential will at first make many mistakes because of their inexperience in production layout, marketing, use of credit, cost accounting, and other aspects of their new activities. Without government assistance, they will improve their skills on the job, through trial and error. Many will fail. Government policy can speed up the development of entrepreneurial skills by providing motivation training and credit to carefully selected business operators, as McClelland has suggested. It can also provide incentives to encourage innovative behavior in the public sector. Such outlays can have high payoffs in terms of future output and income.

Political Obstacles

Some social scientists (including some economists) believe that the major obstacles to economic growth and development are political. Specific factors that have been identified include colonialism, neocolonialism, political instability, authoritarianism, lack of authoritarianism, and sheer incompetence. Let us briefly examine each of these alleged obstacles.

It seems fair to say that colonial administrations in Africa, the Americas, Asia, and other parts of the world were more interested in procuring raw materials for the mother countries than in promoting development in the colonies themselves. Educational opportunities in the colonies were restricted to a small fraction of the population, and jobs for those who finished this schooling were limited to relatively minor civil service posts and other white-collar positions. Nevertheless, the argument that colonialism has been an obstacle to economic growth and development encounters a major snag. It fails to demonstrate satisfactorily that growth and development would have been faster in the absence of foreign intervention (unless one assumes that intervention could have been much more enlightened). There are good reasons, in fact, for believing that growth and development would have been slower. When the colonial powers first attempted to assume political control in other lands, they encountered, for the most part, traditional societies with little capacity for resistance. In the absence of colonialism or some other outside influence, these societies probably would have changed more slowly in subsequent generations. In most (but not all) cases, colonialism at least provided for some growth, however limited, and this laid the groundwork for the eventual undermining of colonialism and the more rapid growth achieved by many of these countries since independence.

It is more difficult to dismiss the neocolonialist, or "external dependence" explanations of low levels of development. Briefly stated, these theories argue that economic growth and development have been restricted by the international division of labor resulting from the international trade policies promoted and controlled by the developed countries since the nineteenth century (see chapter 5). Relatively free trade and the international movement of capital, it is argued, forced the developing countries to specialize in the production of primary products whose prices fluctuate wildly and in the long run have declined relative to the prices of manufactured goods. Moreover, it is alleged that foreign governments and multinational corporations use various forms of bribery to maintain conservative governments in power or to overthrow modernizing governments interested in both growth and development.

In chapter 5, we shall see that dependence on primary products has not been as inimical to economic growth as is sometimes supposed. Though, for specific countries and for specific periods of time (e.g., the Great Depression), dependence on primary products has been especially harmful, in other cases (e.g., the oil-exporting countries), primary product specialization facilitated by foreign investment has clearly been beneficial. True, foreigners may sometimes earn unusually high rates of return on these activities, and nationalization might increase a country's rate of growth (provided that the gains are not offset by losses of managerial, technical, and entrepreneurial skills). But without the foreign investment to begin with, the country's level of development might have been significantly lower.

To the extent that external dependence does hold back economic growth and development—and we should not pretend that this never happens—it should be recognized that the dependency relationship is sustained by an alliance between foreign interests and domestic elite groups. While all dependency theorists make this point, many seem to overemphasize the role of foreigners and give insufficient attention to the discretionary powers of domestic elites to accept or reject foreign investment and to control the terms under which it is allowed.

The relationship between political instability and economic growth is not easy to determine. If by instability we mean frequent and irregular changes in the chief executive, then there seems to be little correlation between instability and growth rates. There are both fast- and slow-growth countries with high instability, and the same can be said for the stable countries. The world *instability* has also been used to describe a situation in which there is a persistent high degree of social unrest. This can be measured by counting numbers of strikes, numbers of major riots or demonstrations, man-hours lost because of such protests, or numbers of persons killed and wounded in civil disorders. Some observers have suggested that social unrest is inimical to growth because it hinders private investment and takes people away from their jobs and into the streets. But others have argued that this kind of instability is often a symptom of growth rather than an obstacle to growth, and that social protest of this nature can even lead to reforms that result in genuine development. Their reasoning is that people are more likely to participate in protest movements when there is some hope for material advancement (and economic growth generates hope) than when the situation seems hopeless (economic stagnation). Again, when we examine the relationship between this type of instability and economic growth, the correlation seems to be quite low.

What of the relationship between form of government and economic growth? If we look at per capita income tables, the incidence of political democracy seems to increase as income levels rise. However, this is likely to be a result of economic growth rather than a cause. In the early stages of growth, effective political democracy is difficult to reconcile with a largely illiterate population and a rigid social structure. Indeed, some social scientists have suggested that growth is more easily achieved under an authoritarian regime, citing such diverse examples as Brazil, China, South Korea, Taiwan, the Soviet Union, and Yugoslavia. Countries with more open political systems but dominated by a single party also have often had high growth rates; Israel, Japan, and Mexico are examples. On the other hand, authoritarian government has sometimes been accompanied by poor or mediocre growth rates, as in Burma, Ghana, Haiti, and Paraguay. Countries with relatively democratic forms of government have also had varying growth performances.

One recent study of fifty-eight developing countries found no statistical support for the hypothesis that authoritarian government is more favorable to economic growth than nonauthoritarian government; in fact, there was a slight tendency for the reverse to be true.[10] This study, however, did not examine other possible influences on the growth rates of these countries (e.g., price trends in the countries' major exports). More research is needed to clarify the relationship between authoritarianism and growth (development).

Finally, poor growth performance has sometimes been attributed to incompetent public administration or to economic policies born of ignorance. Tax collections may lag behind expectations, monetary policy may stifle growth, and ambitious industrialization programs may drain a country's scarce foreign exchange reserves. Technical advice on economic policy and public administration is available from abroad, sometimes free, sometimes at a price; but if political leaders do not even know what questions to ask, or if they cannot comprehend the answers, technical expertise cannot be tapped. While there seems to be some merit to the incompetence argument, its importance as an obstacle to growth would be very difficult to judge.

THE "MODERNIZATION" CONTROVERSY

If traditional attitudes and institutions can be viewed as obstacles to economic development, it would seem to follow that "modern" attitudes and institutions can facilitate development. The deliberate introduction of modernity—particularly in rural communities—might thus appear to be an appropriate strategy for national governments interested in accelerating economic development and social change. However, one must also consider the possibility that modernity is a result, not a cause, of development. Recent writings on the subject of modernity and modernization indicate that there is still a great deal of controversy over this issue (Nash, ed., 1977). Even within the same study, one can find conflicting statements concerning the direction of causation. For example, Inkeles and Smith (1974: 6) state that "men become modern through the particular life experiences they undergo"; but three pages later they write: "a nation is not modern unless its people are modern. . . . [W]e doubt that its economy can be highly productive, or its political and administrative institutions very effective, unless . . . people . . . have attained some degree of modernity." In effect, the authors are taking the not unreasonable position that the arrows linking modernity and development run in both directions. But we are left with considerable uncertainty about the relative strengths of the two arrows. Moreover, theoretical statements of this kind

10. G. William Dick, "Authoritarian versus Nonauthoritarian Approaches to Economic Development," *Journal of Political Economy*, 82 (July/August 1974), 817–827.

tell us little about which aspects of modernity should be encouraged, and how.

At this point, some clarifications are in order about the meaning of modernity and modernization. Again, we can find considerable disagreement. Some writers define modernization in terms of changing institutions; others stress changes in individual attitudes; still others emphasize group attitudes. Frequently, modernity has been equated with the attitudes and institutions of capitalist Western countries: a strong personal work ethic, individualism, entrepreneurship, materialism, optimism, and a government structure encouraging these attitudes and institutions. There is growing dissatisfaction, however, with ethnocentric definitions, and broader definitions of modernity have been sought which could encompass community- as well as individual-centered change, and noncapitalist as well as capitalist institutions. Manning Nash (Nash, ed., 1977: 21) defines modernity as "the social, cultural, and psychological framework which facilitates the application of tested knowledge to all phases and branches of production. Modernization is the process of transformation toward the establishment and institutionalization of modernity."

A similar definition is that of Wilbert Moore (Nash, ed., 1977: 33), who refers to modernization as "the rationalization of social behavior and social organization."[11] Both of these definitions emphasize that modernity is not a sharply defined set of attitudes and institutions that can be contrasted with an equally rigid "traditional" set. Nash and Moore also stress that modernization, as a process of *becoming,* or process of social change, has taken different forms in societies with different institutional backgrounds. While the *areas* in which rationalization takes place are essentially the same for all societies—Moore lists (1) monetization and commercialization, (2) technification of production and distribution, (3) education, (4) bureaucratization, (5) demographic rationalization, and (6) secularization—the particular institutions through which rationalization is achieved can be very different.

The study by Inkeles and Smith, cited above, is an interesting attempt to define modernity as a syndrome of individual attitudes that could be expected to be common to all societies. Specifically, the authors

> propose to classify as modern those personal qualities which are likely to be inculcated by participation in large-scale modern productive enterprises such as the factory, and perhaps more crucial, which may be required of the workers and the staff if the factory is to operate efficiently and effectively (p. 19).

11. The term *rationalization,* unfortunately, implies that individual behavior in traditional societies is irrational in terms of a person's own interests. Actually, taking into account the limits to decision making imposed by lack of technical information and a rigid social structure, individual decisions in traditional societies seem to be no less rational than they are in developed societies. This is illustrated in the following section.

The research design, which is too complicated to explain fully here,[12] involved comparisons among a number of different groups ranging from traditional farmers to skilled factory workers with long experience in urban areas. Research was conducted in six developing countries, three with very low incomes—East Pakistan (now Bangladesh), India, and Nigeria—and three whose development is well above average for developing countries—Argentina, Chile, and Israel.

Inkeles and Smith began by identifying fourteen personal attributes of modernity, including openness to new experiences, efficacy (the belief that one can exercise considerable control over one's environment), understanding of productive processes, placing a high value on technical skills, and acceptance of skill as a valid basis for distributing rewards. In addition, they looked at modernity from a "topical" perspective (e.g., attitudes toward family, family size, religion, politics, consumption) and a "behavioral" perspective, which involved psychological testing and interviews to determine political, religious, and other activity. Finally, a fourth perspective was obtained by devising several Overall Modernity (OM) scales combining elements of the other three perspectives (see Table 3.1 for a list of the areas covered in their most frequently used scale). Inkeles and Smith conclude (p. 290) that

> modern man's character . . . may be summed up under four major headings. He is an informed participant citizen; he has a marked sense of personal efficacy; he is highly independent and autonomous in his relation to traditional sources of influence, especially when he is making basic decisions about how to conduct his personal affairs; and he is ready for new experiences and ideas, that is, he is relatively open-minded and cognitively flexible.

As the authors expected, modernity scores tended to be highest for experienced factory workers and lowest for those with little or no factory experience.

The OM scale has been frequently criticized for being biased in favor of Western values, capitalist economic systems, and Western political institutions. Although some of the criticisms go too far, with some writers rejecting modernity as a peculiarly Western concept and not admitting the universality of some of its technological components, Inkeles and Smith's defense of their scale is not convincing on all points. In particular, there is indeed a bias toward individualism to the neglect of

---

12. The design of the study has been widely criticized on methodological grounds. See, for example, the review by Alejandro Portes in *Latin American Research Review*, 11 (1976/1), 213–221. Also discussed in this review, in a more favorable light, is the book by Oxall, Barnett, and Booth (1975) listed in the Suggested Readings.

TABLE 3.1
Subject Areas Covered in the Inkeles-Smith OM-500 Scale[a]

Active Public Participation
Aspirations (Educational and Occupational)
Aging and the Aged
Calculability
Change Orientation
Citizenship
Consumption Attitudes
Dignity
Efficacy
Family Size
Growth of Opinion
Identification with Nation
Information
Kinship Obligations
Mass Media
New Experience
Optimism
Particularism
Planning
Religion
Social-Class Stratification
Time Valuation
Technical-Skill Valuation
Understanding
Work Commitment
Women's Rights

Source: Inkeles and Smith (1974: 320, 345).
[a] The OM–500 scale contains a total of 100 questions.

attitudes toward community, cooperation, and communalism. Furthermore, attitudes which may be effective for increasing industrial productivity may differ in some important respects from those which will help raise productivity in the agricultural sector, where most workers in developing countries live and where often they are more likely to be proprietors than employees.

Finally, Inkeles and Smith do not satisfactorily resolve the imporant question of causation. To the extent that individuals become modern *because of* their experience in a modern enterprise, there would seem to be little scope for government to speed up economic growth and development through education, community development or other programs designed to affect attitudes directly. Modernization, conceived as a change in individual attitudes, thus would occur simply as a result of economic development (or simply growth). The problem then becomes one of explaining how growth or development is initiated in the first place.

On the other hand, to the extent that modernity facilitates development —as Inkeles and Smith maintain it does—an important role for government is implied. The Inkeles-Smith findings suggest that two of the most powerful tools that government can use to introduce modernity are education and control of (or influence over) mass media.[13] Psychologist David McClelland, as we noted above, argues that government can facilitate modernization and development by identifying, training, and providing credit to those with entrepreneurial skills.

STIMULATING CHANGE: A PREVIEW OF POLICY AND STRATEGY ISSUES

Promoting change in a developing country is no easy task, even for a government genuinely committed to economic development. In the following paragraphs, we shall discuss some of the problems that governments will encounter and some of the mistakes they are likely to make. We shall also speculate on the kinds of broad strategies which are likely to be most effective in stimulating development.

The literature on development abounds with stories of the frustrations of agricultural extension agents and other workers trying to promote change in a traditional environment. Extension agents who are unaware of local peculiarities in land tenure arrangements, water rights customs, religious beliefs, and other local traditions will find their advice ignored for reasons that may not be clearly articulated. Sometimes, of course, the advice is rejected because traditional farmers know more about local soils, rainfall patterns, pests, and diseases than the visiting "expert." But even if the extension agent knows his technical facts and successfully shows on a demonstration plot that crop yields could be tripled, his work may be regarded as a kind of magic, successful only on the agent's special land. The chances that the new techniques will be adopted will be better if the agent can demonstrate their productivity on the land of a respected member of the community. This requires some protection for that person against crop loss due to adverse weather or an unsuspected crop disease.

Extension agents will also find that the decision-making capabilities of many poor farmers are limited. Farmers may function rationally within their traditional technology, but they may have difficulty seeing

13. Interestingly, neither religion nor ethnic origin were found to be significant factors influencing modernization. Nor was the city found to be a significant influence, which suggests that individual modernization can occur just as well under a rural-based development strategy as under an urban-based strategy. Inkeles and Smith themselves provide evidence on this point by commenting on the high modernity scores of farmers in the Comilla cooperatives in what is now Bangladesh.

cause and effect relationships with new methods of production. They may not realize, for example, the importance of proper timing of fertilizer applications. Farmers who have just escaped from quasifeudal situations as a result of land reform usually have little confidence in their ability to solve their own problems. They have not been allowed to make major decisions before and might even have been told, in effect, that they were subhuman and therefore incapable of making their own decisions.

This is not to say that farmers in a traditional environment are always unable to evaluate new technology correctly. In fact, it is often the extension agent who is ignorant and the traditional farmer who is wise. The agent may not realize, for example, that the farmer places a high value on food security, which can be provided by interplanting a variety of subsistence crops on one or more small plots. Concentration on a single cash crop, which the extension agent might recommend, can force the farmer to go into debt and to face an uncertain market (and price) for his or her product. In the event of crop failure, the farmer is left with an insufficient supply of home-grown food and few resources to purchase food in the marketplace. Unless the potential gains from the cash crop more than offset the risks of low market prices and the probability of crop failure, it is perfectly rational for the farmer to reject cash crops and the new technology associated with them. In this situation, the extension agent who thinks that interplanting is always a bad practice is the real obstacle to change.

When a subsistence farmer sees that the potential gains from new crops or techniques outweigh the risks, tradition per se is not likely to be a major stumbling block.[14] Tradition can, however, keep the gains from outweighing the risks. If a farmer does not own the land, for example, any increase in his or her production is likely to be appropriated by the landowner, so there is little incentive to adopt new techniques. Even for the landowner, opportunities for economic betterment may be limited if the economy is stagnant, the market for cash crops is not growing, or oligopsony in the purchase of farm products channels the benefits of increased output to intermediaries rather than producers.

At the community level, change is most likely to occur in areas which have had long and frequent contacts with their national governments and with other aspects of the modern world, and whose residents are thus psychologically more prepared for change than those in isolated communities. After the Bolivian revolution of 1952, for example, peasants in the Lower Cochabamba Valley who were suddenly transformed from

14. Ten or fifteen years ago, such a statement would have been quite controversial. But evidence from around the world on farmers' decision-making processes has led to widespread agreement among social scientists on the "economic rationality" of traditional farmers.

serfs into landowners quickly switched from subsistence crops to cash crops, significantly raising their incomes in the process. Though they received almost no credit and little technical assistance from the government, they were able, by themselves, to take advantage of their favorable location with respect to urban markets. Before 1952, this area was already one of the (relatively) prosperous parts of the country; ties with major urban centers were strong, and peasants were not only exposed to new ideas but also organized. In the more remote parts of highland Bolivia, on the other hand, economic change has been slower and traditional institutions have undergone less change.[15]

In isolated areas such as these, the obstacles to change are not easily overcome, even if individuals with strong leadership and decision-making capabilities are present. For one thing, distance from the national capital makes it more difficult for the government to control the actions of locally powerful traditional elites, even if it is genuinely interested in doing so. Lack of roads limits marketing opportunities and the mobility of government extension workers. Communities in these areas may have little hope of receiving agricultural credit, extension services, roads, or educational facilities unless they are organized sufficiently to exercise power in their dealings with government authorities, who already have to face more claims on revenues than available funds can satisfy.

Organizations which can effectively exercise power include credit unions, cooperatives, and peasant leagues working through political channels. Formation of such groups usually requires outside assistance, either from foreign organizations, such as the U.S. Peace Corps and various United Nations agencies, or from domestic groups, such as political parties seeking to broaden their constituencies. In Venezuela, for example, Acción Democrática, one of the two major parties, began to provide assistance to peasant organizations during the 1930s, when a harsh military regime ruled the country and farm income had long been depressed because of a fall in cacao prices since the early 1920s and, later, the effects of the Great Depression. Governments, of course, do not always look favorably upon organization of the peasantry, and a strong regime unwilling to see political power shared more widely may take measures to suppress such activities (e.g., Brazil after 1964).

A widely adopted strategy for promoting social change and economic development in rural areas has been the formation of production and/or marketing cooperatives, a strategy we shall discuss in more detail in chapter 9. Cooperatives seem particularly attractive where farms are

---

15. I have described changes in rural Bolivia in considerable detail in a series of survey papers (on income, employment, production technology, and marketing) prepared for U.S. AID in 1977.

so small that it is uneconomic for any one individual to buy modern implements for use only on his or her land. They have also been seen as desirable for breaking the power of marketing intermediaries. Finally, administrative costs of credit and technical assistance are much cheaper per farmer if provided through a cooperative instead of to individual farmers.[16]

The formation of a production cooperative does not necessarily imply the abolition of private landholdings and the establishment of a Soviet-type *kolkhoz* or an Israeli-type *kibbutz*. A production cooperative can also be based on individual private plots, with the cooperative members jointly owning machinery, implements, and irrigation systems and buying their inputs as a group to obtain quantity discounts. The cooperative may also market its members' produce to have more marketing power and thus provide each member with a higher income. The Israeli *moshav* is one such model.

Efforts to organize cooperatives in developing countries have had mixed results. In many parts of the world, small farmers attach such significance to individual enterprise that communal farming will not be willingly accepted, and even more limited forms of cooperation will be viewed with suspicion. Distrust of one's neighbor in financial matters is often a powerful obstacle to cooperation. Even where cooperative traditions appear to exist, they may not be as strong as presumed by those trying to organize the peasantry. In Bolivia and Haiti, for example, anthropological fieldwork has shown that traditional forms of cooperative labor are generally restricted to members of an extended family or to a limited number of production tasks; permanent, formal institutions do not really exist. The government of Tanzania has been surprised by the considerable resistance to its policy of regrouping peasants into villages and organizing production predominantly along communal lines. Historical experience with village living and cooperative work effort suggested that such a program would be more acceptable. Tanzania now seems to have decided that private plots must play a more important role in rural development than originally anticipated.[17]

Given these kinds of difficulties, policies and programs designed to promote social change and economic development in traditional societies

---

16. An extreme example of the high costs of dealing with individual small farmers is that of a small rural credit agency in Haiti, whose administrative costs in the early 1970s were estimated to have been $17 (!) for every $1 lent. See Francis J. LeBeau, *Rural Sector Assessment of the Republic of Haiti* (Port-au-Prince: U.S. AID, 1974), p. 48.

17. See Richard N. Blue and James H. Weaver, "A Critical Assessment of the Tanzanian Model of Development," DSP Occasional Paper No. 1 (Washington, D.C.: U.S. AID, 1977). Also available as "Agricultural Development Council Reprint No. 30 (July 1977).

must adopt a long-term perspective. Since available resources for this task are limited, it is unfortunately doubtful that a significant impact can be made on the adult populations of communities with little or no exposure to twentieth-century technology and ideas. Scarce financial and human resources are likely to have higher payoffs in terms of either growth or development if priority is given not to the poorest of the poor but rather to communities and individuals who are psychologically more able to accept change. This may seem a callous statement, but it should be remembered that (1) few countries are likely to have the means and the political will to attempt to improve living standards for the entire population and (2) the ready-for-change communities, too, will be very poor by any standard. Even in these communities, change will not be easy—a ten-to-twenty-year planning horizon is probably called for, while for the poorest and most traditional communities it may be a matter of several generations.

This suggested order of priorities is not meant to preclude *all* forms of assistance to the very poorest communities. A strong humanitarian case can still be made for providing food and medical assistance to those threatened with starvation or epidemic diseases. But it is important to recognize that such assistance constitutes relief, the basic purpose of which is to prevent a situation from getting worse. The promotion of development requires a long-term outlook which must confront the issue of allocating scarce resources among competing groups of poor citizens.[18]

An important component of a long-term strategy for social change— and one which offers perhaps the best hope for the poorest of the poor— is education (see also chapter 7). Children are generally able to accept new ideas more readily than adults; but the transmission of change via the schools is likely to cause severe conflicts at home, and the resulting effects on children's personality may at first have quite ambiguous consequences for development. Using education to bring about social change does not just mean building schools where none previously existed. Attention must also be paid to the content of educational programs, with increased emphasis given to applications of knowledge to rural development problems. Educational programs based on this philosophy have a better chance of reaching adults, too, than programs with a more traditional basis. Countries wishing to promote rapid social change would do well to study the educational system of China, where education has been integrated with practical experience in farming and farm-related light industry.

18. The difference between relief and development is well summarized in the oft-quoted proverb, "Give a man a fish and he will eat for a day; teach a man to fish and he will eat for a lifetime."

SUMMARY

In this and the preceding chapter, we have examined numerous possible obstacles to economic growth and development. It should be clear by now that economic and noneconomic obstacles are closely interrelated, and that it is not always easy to distinguish cause from effect. Under these circumstances, and given the very different situations in individual countries, it is difficult to formulate a general strategy for overcoming obstacles to economic growth and development. A strategy based on physical capital formation may work well in some countries, but in others the emphasis would be better placed on the development of human capital. In some cases, it is tempting to argue that the best hopes for growth and development lie in military assistance to revolutionary movements.

Given our incomplete understanding of the relationships between economic and noneconomic variables, disagreements among economists over development strategies will persist. But we have learned to be wary of single-obstacle theories and to pay closer attention to the institutional frameworks in which economic policy decisions must be made. In our studies of the developing countries, the old name of our discipline, "political economy," is appropriately being revived.

Suggested Readings

Dalton, George, comp. *Economic Development and Social Change: The Modernization of Village Communities.* Garden City, N.Y.: Natural History Press for the American Museum of Natural History, 1971.

> The readings in this anthology are grouped under three topics: primitive and peasant economies before modernization; the short-run and long-run effects of colonialism; and theories and case studies of modernization and development. Dalton, an economic anthropologist, argues that multidisciplinary research is necessary for understanding the process of economic development.

Hagen, Everett E. *On the Theory of Social Change: How Economic Growth Begins.* Homewood, Ill.: The Dorsey Press, 1962.

> Hagen illustrates his thesis, described in this chapter, with case studies of England, Japan, Colombia, Indonesia, Burma, and Native Americans (Reservation Sioux).

Ilchman, Warren F., and Norman Thomas Uphoff. *The Political Economy of Change.* Berkeley: University of California Press, 1969.

> A valuable book on government decision making in developing countries and how it affects development. Though writing primarily from a political science framework, the authors in fact are examining development from an integrated social science perspective.

Inkeles, Alex and David M. Smith. *Becoming Modern: Individual Change in Six Developing Countries.* Cambridge, Mass.: Harvard University Press, 1974.
This is an important, controversial study of the relationships between modernization, defined in terms of changes in certain aspects of individual behavior, and economic development. The authors argue that causation runs in both directions, but it is not clear which directional flow is considered the strongest. Critics charge that the authors' measures of modernity are biased in favor of Western values and political institutions and capitalist economic systems.

McClelland, David C. *The Achieving Society.* Princeton, N.J.: D. Van Nostrand Co., Inc., 1961.
McClelland attributes differences in economic growth and development among nations primarily to differences in the incidence and level of the need for achievement (n Ach). N Ach is quantified for a number of societies, both by direct testing of individual subjects and by analyzing the n Ach content of stories in children's readers.

McClelland, David C., and David G. Winter. *Motivating Economic Achievement.* New York: The Free Press, 1969.
The authors developed a series of hypotheses about how achievement motivation training can stimulate entrepreneurial activity in businessmen in India. They report a statistically significant increase in business activity following training.

Myrdal, Gunnar. *Asian Drama: An Inquiry into the Poverty of Nations.* New York: Pantheon, 1968.
A monumental (2,284-page) study of South Asia directed by a Nobel prizewinning economist whose *Rich Lands and Poor* (1957) was one of the most influential books on economic development written in the 1950s. Myrdal stresses the interrelationship of economic and noneconomic variables and argues that Western models are inappropriate for understanding and prescribing for the economies of South Asia.

Nash, Manning, ed. *Essays in Economic Development and Cultural Change in Honor of Bert F. Hoselitz.* Supplement to *Economic Development and Cultural Change,* 25 (1977).
A collection of twenty-five essays by twenty-seven leading development economists, who present provocative ideas and empirical findings on the relationship of economic to noneconomic factors. Some of the essays also contain good succinct reviews and insights on the literature concerning specific issues.

Oxall, Ivar, Tony Barnett, and David Booth, eds. *Beyond the Sociology of Development: Economy and Society in Latin America and Africa.* Boston: Routledge and Kegan Paul, 1975.
The authors of the twelve stimulating papers in this volume reject the concept of modernity as a Western notion inappropriately applied to developing countries. Writing from what is sometimes called a "neo-Marxist" perspective, stressing external dependency, they nevertheless provide a good critique of the various strands of dependency theory.

Thomsen, Mortiz. *Living Poor: A Peace Corps Chronicle*. Seattle: University of Washington Press, 1969.

A moving, perceptive account of one volunteer's efforts to promote development in a poor village in coastal Ecuador and the numerous obstacles to change he encountered. Not exactly pessimistic, the author leaves the reader with a sense of sadness at the enormity of the task and the odds against success.

4

Population Growth and Urbanization

Sometime during 1976, the world's population passed the 4 billion mark. Most projections in the early 1970s showed that it would reach 6.3 to 6.5 billion by the year 2000 and as high as 16 to 17 billion by 2050. Many scientists and lay persons have long been concerned about the environmental effects of the "population explosion," and novelists like Anthony Burgess *(The Wanting Seed)* have given us grim pictures of life in a future world of tens of billions.

In the 1950s economists saw several reasons to become concerned about population trends, particularly in the developing countries. First, it was thought that rapid population growth might have adverse effects on the growth of per capita income. Second, there was concern about the possibility of increased unemployment and underemployment and other adverse effects on development (as opposed to growth). Third, there was doubt about the ability of the earth's resources to provide food for many more people. Fourth, more people—especially if their living standards were rising—would cause more environmental pollution, unless there were major advances in pollution-control technology. Finally, rapid population growth, combined with limited employment opportunities in agriculture, had created a demographic explosion in cities throughout the world, thus exacerbating urban social problems.

WORLD POPULATION IN HISTORICAL PERSPECTIVE

The rapid growth of the world's population is a recent phenomenon. Two thousand years ago, there were only 200 to 300 million people on the earth. By 1650 the figure had reached about 550 million, which implies an annual growth rate of well under one-tenth of 1 percent. Subsequently, population grew at increasingly faster rates (see Figure 4.1), reaching 1 billion in 1800 and 2.5 billion by 1950. Since 1950 the population explosion has been dramatic, with the rate of growth having reached 1.9 percent between 1950 and 1970 (compared with 0.8 percent in the previous fifty years) before declining to an estimated 1.64 percent in 1975.

What has caused the world's population to increase so rapidly in the twentieth century? By far the most important reason has been the lowering of death rates following the widespread introduction of public health measures; better medical care and improved nutrition have been contributing factors in some countries. Epidemic diseases like plague and smallpox are no longer major problems, and the incidence of malaria and other diseases has been drastically reduced. Infant mortality rates have fallen sharply in some countries. The Latin American average, for example, is now about 65 per 1,000 live births, compared with 100 to 200 for the very poorest developing countries, which except for Haiti are all in Africa and Asia.

Figure 4.2 illustrates diagrammatically the different patterns of demographic transition undergone by the developed countries and now being experienced by the developing countries. When the developed countries of Western Europe began their process of modern economic growth in the late eighteenth and early nineteenth centuries, the crude

Figure 4.1
Growth of the World's Population, 1650–2000

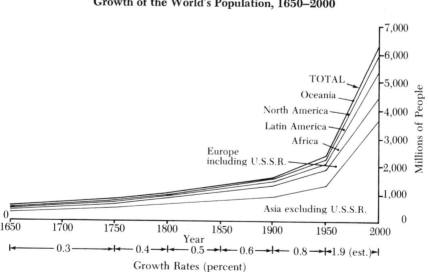

Source: Ian Bowen, " 'Nature's Feast' Today," *Finance and Development*, 10, No. 4 (December 1973), 16.

Figure 4.2
The Demographic Transition in Developed and Developing Countries

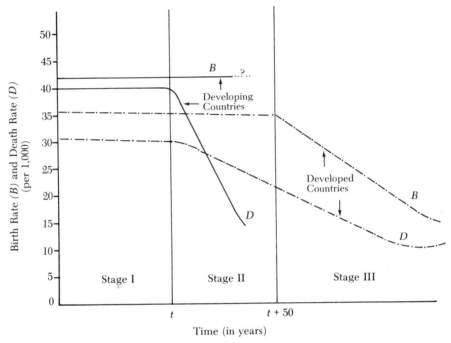

birth rate (number of births per 1,000 inhabitants) was perhaps 35/1000, while the death rate was approximately 30/1000. These figures had changed very slowly in the previous few centuries, a period indicated in Figure 4.2 as Stage I. As nutrition improved with economic growth and investments were made in better sanitation and other public health measures, death rates began to fall, albeit gradually, while birth rates remained virtually unchanged for perhaps two generations. The population growth rate increased to about 1 percent or slightly more. This is illustrated by Stage II in Figure 4.2. Stage III began when birth rates started to decline. This trend continued for several generations before leveling off—a process that has not been completed in all countries. Meanwhile, the death rate kept falling until it, too, leveled off (or actually rose slightly as populations became older). Birth and death rates, once again, were very close to each other and population growth was again slow.

For the developing countries the demographic transition has been very different. To begin with, both birth and death rates were typically higher than they were 150 to 200 years ago in the now-developed countries. They were also closer together. We illustrate this in Figure 4.2 by assigning our hypothetical developing country a birth rate of 42/1000 and a death rate of 40/1000. In Stage II, which for most developing countries did not start until the 1940s or later,[1] the death rate declined much faster than in the developed countries. In some cases it fell by 10 per 1,000 or more in only a decade, thus adding one full percentage point to the population growth rate, since birth rates were unchanged. If birth rates remain at the same level for two generations or so, a developing country can experience population growth rates of 2.5 to 3.5 percent a year for several decades. At 3.5 percent a year, a country's population will double in approximately twenty years.[2] This is the situation now faced by Mexico, a relatively high-income developing country whose 1975 population of 58 million is projected to reach 137 million by the year 2000 if there is no significant change in the birth rate.

DECLINING BIRTH RATES IN THE DEMOGRAPHIC TRANSITION

Since birth rates in Western Europe began to fall centuries ago, it is clearly wrong to attribute this trend to the development of modern methods of birth control such as the pill, the intrauterine device (IUD), and the vasectomy. Other methods—including abstention, *coitus interruptus,* delayed marriage, and abortion—have long been practiced, not only in Western Europe but in various other parts of the world. Centuries ago, these methods were usually employed in response to what was perceived as a long-term imbalance between population and food supply. Even as recently as the mid-nineteenth century, Irish society apparently adopted delayed marriage as a response to the potato famine during which an estimated 750,000 persons died. But generally, in the last few centuries, birth control measures have been adopted while the per capita food supply was expanding. Therefore, other reasons must be sought to explain their adoption.

There is disagreement among demographers and other social scientists concerning the relative importance of various possible explanations of falling birth rates, but many believe that a large part of the answer lies in what may be called the *urbanization-industrialization-modernization complex.* In urban areas, children often have fewer opportunities to contribute to the family income than they do on the farm, and feeding and clothing them is more expensive. The disadvantages of not going to school are greater in urban areas than in rural areas, so parents

1. In many Latin American countries, however, the transition was earlier.
2. A simple procedure, the so-called "Rule of 70," can be used to calculate the approximate length of time it takes a population (or anything else) to double. If the population growth rate, for example, is 3.5 percent, one simply divides 70 by 3.5 and obtains 20, which is quite close to the exact figure of 20.15.

are more willing to send their children to school, thus incurring another economic burden (which must, however, be compared with future family benefits in the form of the higher income that a more skilled job provides). More educational opportunities, more nonhousehold employment opportunities for women, and, in recent decades, the availability of birth control information (and devices) in urban areas may also contribute to lower birth rates.

Another possible reason for lower birth rates is simply lower death rates. When it is realized that a higher percentage of children survives to adulthood, there is less need to have large families to ensure succession of the family line and to provide financial assistance when the parents are forced by age to leave the labor force. It may take several generations, however, for societies to realize that death rates are falling, and the experience of the developed countries suggests that the resulting decline in birth rates is likely to be gradual rather than sudden.

Several generations may also be needed to overcome cultural obstacles to smaller families. In a low-income society with high death rates, the demographic requirement for families to have many children, just to keep the population stable, becomes institutionalized as a desirable or even obligatory aspect of the culture, necessary for the preservation of the society. Religious authorities are likely to favor large families, and many religions other than Roman Catholicism have opposed efforts to limit family size. Changes in demographic and economic conditions, however, will affect attitudes toward family size, and eventually this will be reflected in the culture. The official position of the Roman Catholic Church on birth control, in the opinion of many observers, is becoming increasingly untenable in view of the growing use of proscribed practices by Roman Catholics all over the world, and a change in Roman Catholic teachings in the next few decades would not be surprising. The change in attitudes toward birth control is likely to occur among women earlier than among men. In Latin America, in particular, fathering many children is considered a sign of virility, a "virtue" not easily given up.

We shall return, later in this chapter, to a consideration of policies for limiting population growth. For the present, let us look at the geographic distribution of world population and the prospects for reducing its growth, and then examine the widespread view that rapid population growth hinders development.

THE GEOGRAPHIC DISTRIBUTION
OF POPULATION

Table 4.1 shows that 57 percent of the world's population in 1970 lived in Asia and Oceania, nearly 10 percent in Africa, and close to 8 percent in Latin America. In other words, almost three-quarters of the world's

TABLE 4.1
World Population by Region, 1970 and Projections for 2000
(*millions; percentage distribution*)

Region	1970		2000-A[a]		2000-B[b]	
	Popula-tion	*Per-centage*	*Popula-tion*	*Per-centage*	*Popula-tion*	*Per-centage*
Asia and Oceania	2,051	56.8	3,968	60.7	3,583	60.1
Africa	346	9.6	783	12.0	677	11.4
Europe and the U.S.S.R.	704	19.5	854	13.1	843	14.1
North America	226	6.3	297	4.5	288	4.8
Latin America	280	7.8	635	9.7	567	9.5
World Total	3,607	100.0	6,536	100.0	5,958	100.0

Source: Joseph E. Gholl and K. C. Zachariah, "Toward the Year 2000," *Finance and Development*, 10, No. 4 (December 1973), 23.
[a] Assumes a moderate decline in fertility.
[b] Assumes a rapid decline in fertility.

population was located in the three regions where the developing countries are concentrated. Even after subtracting the few developed countries in these regions (Japan is the only one with a sizable population), we are left with approximately 70 percent of the world's population in the developing countries, not counting the inhabitants of several countries in Southern and Eastern Europe, which some economists would add to the list.[3]

Since the developing countries have experienced more rapid population growth (2.5 percent) than the developed countries (1.0 percent), their share of the world's population has been rising. By the year 2000, with a moderate decline in fertility, the shares of Asia and Oceania, Africa, and Latin America would rise to 61 percent, 12 percent, and 10 percent, respectively. Even with a more rapid decline in fertility—which, as we shall see below, now seems to be occurring—these figures would be only slightly lower. Europe and the Soviet Union, meanwhile, would have only 13 to 14 percent of the world's population, while North America would have less than 5 percent.

Table 4.2 presents data on total population in 1975 and population growth rates for 1960–1975 and 1970–1975, for all countries with more

3. We include, however, the oil-exporting nations of the Middle East. The status of some of them as "developing" countries may be questioned on the basis of their high per capita incomes, but if we use other indicators of development the designation still may be appropriate. Moreover, in international forums where reforms in international trade and finance have been discussed since the mid-1960s, Middle Eastern oil-exporting nations have usually sided with the developing nations of Africa, Asia, and Latin America.

25

TABLE 4.2

Population, 1975, and Population Growth Rates, 1960–1975 and 1970–1975, Countries with a Population of One Million or More

	Population (thousands)	Growth Rate (%) 1960–1975	Growth Rate (%) 1970–1975
China, People's Republic of	822,800	1.6	1.7
India	608,072	2.3	2.1
U.S.S.R.	254,393	1.1	0.9
United States	213,540	1.1	0.8
Indonesia	132,122	2.2	2.4
Japan	111,570	1.1	1.3
Brazil	106,996	2.9	2.9
Bangladesh	78,600	2.5	2.0
Nigeria	75,023	2.5	2.5
Pakistan	69,229	2.9	3.0
Germany, Federal Republic of	61,830	0.8	0.2
Mexico	59,928	3.5	3.5
United Kingdom	55,960	0.4	0.2
Italy	55,810	0.7	0.8
France	52,790	0.9	0.8
Vietnam[a]	47,600	n.a.	n.a.
Philippines	42,231	3.0	2.8
Thailand	41,870	3.1	2.9
Turkey	40,198	2.6	2.5
Egypt	37,230	2.5	2.2
Spain	35,348	1.1	1.0
Korea, Republic of	35,280	2.3	1.8
Poland	34,022	0.9	0.9
Iran	33,390	2.9	0.8
Burma	30,170	2.2	2.2
Ethiopia	27,950	2.3	2.6
South Africa	25,470	3.1	2.6
Argentina	25,383	1.4	1.3
Zaire	24,721	2.7	2.7
Colombia	23,576	2.8	2.8
Canada	22,830	1.6	1.4
Yugoslavia	21,350	1.0	0.9
Romania	21,245	1.0	0.9
German Democratic Republic of	16,850	0.0	−0.3
Morocco	16,680	2.4	2.4
China, Republic of	16,000	2.8	2.0
Korea, Democratic People's Republic of	15,848	2.8	2.7
Algeria	15,747	3.2	3.2
Sudan	15,550	2.2	2.1
Peru	15,387	2.9	2.9
Czechoslovakia	14,802	0.5	0.7
Tanzania[b]	14,738	2.9	2.7
Afghanistan	13,700	2.2	2.2
Netherlands	13,650	1.2	0.9
Sri Lanka	13,603	2.2	1.7
Australia	13,500	1.9	1.5
Kenya	13,350	3.2	3.5

Continued

TABLE 4.2 (*Continued*)

	Population (thousands)	Growth Rate (%) 1960–1975	1970–1975
Nepal	12,587	2.1	2.1
Malaysia	12,308	2.8	2.7
Venezuela	11,993	3.3	3.1
Uganda	11,556	2.9	3.3
Iraq	11,120	3.3	3.3
Hungary	10,541	0.3	0.4
Chile	10,253	2.0	1.8
Ghana	9,870	2.6	2.7
Belgium	9,799	0.5	0.3
Portugal	9,577	0.2	0.8
Cuba	9,332	2.0	1.8
Mozambique	9,240	2.1	2.4
Greece	9,101	0.6	0.7
Madagascar	8,833	2.7	3.1
Bulgaria	8,722	0.7	0.5
Saudi Arabia	8,296	1.8	2.4
Sweden	8,200	0.7	0.4
Austria	7,520	0.5	0.4
Cameroon	7,435	2.0	1.9
Syrian Arab Republic	7,410	3.4	3.3
Ecuador	7,069	3.3	3.5
Ivory Coast	6,700	3.7	4.2
Switzerland	6,400	1.2	0.8
Rhodesia	6,310	3.4	3.5
Guatemala	6,275	3.2	3.2
Upper Volta	6,032	2.1	2.3
Yemen Arab Republic	5,936	n.a.	1.9
Mali	5,697	2.2	2.5
Bolivia	5,634	2.6	2.7
Tunisia	5,594	2.2	2.3
Guinea	5,540	2.8	2.8
Angola	5,470	1.2	0.1
Denmark	5,060	0.7	0.5
Malawi	5,044	2.5	2.3
Senegal	5,000	2.6	2.7
Zambia	4,920	2.9	2.9
Finland	4,710	0.4	0.5
Dominican Republic	4,695	2.9	2.9
Niger	4,592	2.7	2.7
Haiti	4,584	1.6	1.6
Hong Kong	4,367	2.2	1.9
Rwanda	4,137	3.2	2.3
Chad	4,035	1.9	2.1
Norway	4,010	0.8	0.7
El Salvador	4,006	3.4	3.1
Burundi	3,732	2.0	2.1
Israel	3,469	3.3	3.3
Lao People's Democratic Republic	3,200	2.4	2.5
Somalia	3,180	2.4	2.4

Continued

TABLE 4.2 (*Continued*)

	Population (thousands)	Growth Rate (%)	
		1960–1975	*1970–1975*
Lebanon	3,164	2.7	3.0
Ireland	3,130	0.7	1.2
Benin	3,110	2.7	2.7
Puerto Rico	3,090	1.7	2.7
New Zealand	3,070	1.6	1.8
Sierra Leone	2,982	2.2	2.5
Honduras	2,890	2.7	2.7
Uruguay	2,764	0.5	0.4
Papua New Guinea	2,756	2.4	2.6
Jordan	2,700	3.3	3.2
Paraguay	2,553	2.6	2.7
Libya	2,442	4.1	4.2
Albania	2,404	2.7	2.4
Nicaragua	2,261	3.2	3.3
Singapore	2,250	2.0	1.7
Togo	2,220	2.7	2.6
Jamaica	2,042	1.7	1.8
Costa Rica	1,965	3.1	2.5
Central African Empire	1,787	2.2	2.2
Yemen, People's Democratic Republic of	1,677	3.2	2.7
Panama	1,668	3.1	3.1
Liberia	1,549	3.3	3.3
Mongolia	1,446	2.8	3.0
Congo, People's Republic of the	1,329	2.4	2.2
Mauritania	1,322	2.2	2.7
Lesotho	1,217	2.2	2.2
Bhutan	1,176	2.3	2.3
Trinidad and Tobago	1,082	1.5	1.1
Kuwait	1,005	8.6	6.2
Cambodia	n.a.	n.a.	n.a.

Source: World Bank Atlas, 1977.
ᵃ Population estimate is for 1976.
ᵇ Mainland Tanzania only.

than 1 million inhabitants. Seven of the ten most populous countries are in the developing world, including China and India, which rank first and second, respectively; the others are Indonesia, Brazil, Bangladesh, Nigeria, and Pakistan. Twenty-three developing countries have sustained a population growth rate of 3 percent a year or more since 1960, and in thirty-one others the growth rate has been between 2.5 and 2.9 percent.

THE ARITHMETIC OF
ZERO POPULATION GROWTH

There is ample reason to be concerned about the effects of rapid population growth on the future of humanity, a subject which we shall examine in detail in chapter 16. This concern has stimulated an interest in zero population growth (ZPG) as a policy objective for both developed and developing countries. Some of the more fanatical proponents of ZPG seem to think that we should try to stabilize world population by next Tuesday. This is an exaggeration, of course, but the point is that many persons do not realize how long it would take for the world population to stop growing, even under unrealistically optimistic assumptions about birth rates.

The principal reason for this continued growth momentum is that a rapidly increasing population is more heavily weighted toward the child-bearing age groups than a stable population. Even if, by next Tuesday, fertility rates were to drop to replacement levels—a net reproduction (NRR) of 1.00, or an average of 2.1 to 2.5 children per family, depending on mortality rates—the population in the typical developing country would continue to increase for approximately seventy years before stabilizing. For the world as a whole, if an NRR of 1.00 had been achieved by 1970–1975, population would have continued to grow well into the middle third of the twenty-first century, leveling off at 5.7 billion. That, of course, did not happen. Nor is an NRR of 1.00 likely by 1980–1985, in which case world population eventually would stabilize at 6.4 billion. If an NRR of 1.00 is not reached until 2040–2045, world population would climb to 15.2 billion.[4]

Few serious observers expect that the world's population will actually reach 15 billion. Even with optimistic assumptions about the wonders of technology, it is questionable that the planet could support that many people. But it is very likely that the figure will be at least 7 billion, which implies achievement of NRR of 1.0 by about 1990. Wars, diseases, and famines could of course intervene to keep the figure lower; but in the absence of these "Malthusian checks" (see below), the goals of the more radical ZPG proponents cannot be achieved.

POPULATION GROWTH AS AN OBSTACLE TO DEVELOPMENT

The Malthusian Theory

Thomas Robert Malthus' *Essay on the Principle of Population* (1798) is an important work in the history of economic thought, and its influence

---

4. Thomas Frejka, *The Future of Population Growth: Alternative Paths to Equilibrium* (New York: The Population Council, 1973), as reported in U.S. Department of State, *World Population Conference/World Population Year, August 1974,* Department of State Publication 8749, International Organization and Conference Series 110 (Washington, D.C., January 1974), Table 1.

on other economists was one reason why the Scottish historian Thomas Carlyle referred to economics as "the dismal science." Malthus' theory, which underwent a number of revisions in subsequent editions, may be summarized as follows: Rising per capita income will result in better health and nutrition, causing death rates to fall. Population will thus increase, but the food supply will not be able to keep pace because of the limited land resources. Incomes will thus fall back to the subsistence level, and population will be held in check—i.e., kept in balance with available food supplies—through wars, epidemics, plagues. Only by exercising "moral restraint"—i.e., delayed marriage and abstention— could these grim population checks be avoided. Even then, living standards would remain at the subsistence level over the long run.

Malthus' model was flawed in several respects that are not obvious from this brief summary, but it is easy enough to see two of the major reasons why his predictions have not come about. First, Malthus did not foresee the decline in birth rates that historically has followed falling death rates after a lag of several generations. Declining birth rates have occurred for reasons other than the kind of moral restraint Malthus preached about (literally: he was not only an academician but also a clergyman). A second major shortcoming was Malthus' underestimate of the amount of land available for cultivation, and, even more importantly, the degree to which technology would overcome diminishing returns to land and permit the food supply to grow in the long run at a faster rate than population.

The "Population Trap"

The Malthusian theory, for all its imperfections, has had a remarkable ability to continue attracting adherents. It received a good deal of attention in the 1950s, when the theory of the "population trap," or "low-level equilibrium trap," was used by neo-Malthusians to explain why developing countries seemed to have stagnant per capita incomes (see Figure 4.3).[5] This model assumes that the population growth rate is positively related to levels of per capita income; that is, it tends to rise as the level of per capita income increases, reaching 3 percent or more before leveling off (curve P in Figure 4.3). The rate of growth of aggregate income is also assumed to accelerate as per capita income levels rise, mainly because the savings rate will rise with income, thus permitting a higher rate of investment (curve Y). However, beyond a certain level of

5. As an explanation of economic stagnation, this theory can be considered as an alternative to the vicious circle of poverty, which was developed at roughly the same time (see chapter 2).

Figure 4.3
The Population Trap

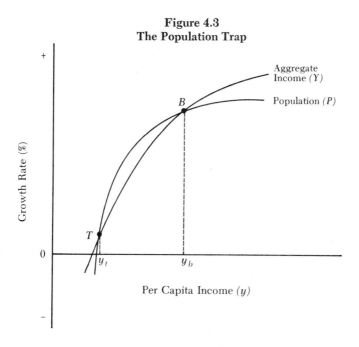

Per Capita Income (*y*)

very low per capita income (y_t), there is a problem: population growth tends to rise faster than aggregate income ($=$ aggregate output, half or more of which consists of food production). This means that any temporary increase in per capita income would be reversed, since $P > Y$. The "trapped" level of per capita income is a stable one, since $Y > P$ to the left of y_t.

In the absence of measures to reduce the population growth rate, the only way out of the trap is said to be the kind of "big push" described in chapter 2: a massive investment program—usually requiring foreign assistance—to raise per capita income so much that it will permanently grow faster than population. This is represented in Figure 4.3 by point B, which is associated with a per capita income level of y_b. Unlike point T, B is an *unstable* equilibrium: to the right, increases in y will not be reversed, while to the left a decrease in y will be cumulative, pushing the economy back to T.

Like Malthus' original theory, the theory of the population trap underestimates the degree to which technological change can accelerate the rate of growth of food production (or output generally). In terms of Figure 4.3, this would mean an upward shift in curve Y so that it is always above curve P. Moreover, the direct correlation postulated between income levels and per capita growth is not supported by empirical evidence, which shows no clear relationship between these variables. The population trap, like the vicious circle of poverty, is now out of vogue. But the belief is still widespread that rapid population growth is an obstacle to economic growth and development.

The Dependency Burden

In chapter 2, we saw that the faster population grows, the higher is the savings rate required to maintain a given rate of increase of per capita income. At the same time, it would appear that saving is more difficult—especially for low income families—the more children there are to feed, clothe, and send to school. Large families, combined with a rapid population growth rate, result in an age structure of the population heavily weighted toward the dependent, or non-labor force, age groups. In developing countries with rapidly growing populations, 45 percent of the population may be less than fifteen years old, compared with only 28 percent in the United States and even less in some European countries. Although the typical developed country has a higher percentage of the population sixty-five and older (10 percent) than the typical developing country (only 3 to 4 percent), the proportion of the population in all dependent age groups is still about eight percentage points higher in the developing countries than in the developed countries.

The relationship between the dependent and nondependent (i.e., labor force) age groups is sometimes referred to as the *dependency* burden or *dependency ratio*. Expressing the dependent population as a percentage of the nondependent, we obtain the ratios in Table 4.3 for developed and developing countries in the years 1950, 1960, and 1970. In the developed countries, every 100 members of the labor force age groups (15 to 64) had to support 57 young and old dependents in 1970. In the developing countries, eighty-one had to be supported, the great majority of them in the younger age groups.

TABLE 4.3
Population Dependency Ratios for Developed and Developing Countries, 1950, 1960, and 1970

	1950	1960	1970
Developed countries—Total	55.0	59.0	57.4
0–14 age groups	43.3	45.6	42.3
65+ age group	11.7	13.4	15.1
Developing countries—Total	78.7	81.4	80.8
0–14 age groups	72.4	75.5	74.8
65+ age group	6.4	5.8	6.0

Source: King (1974: Annex Table 8, p. 174.)

One of the major services provided to this young dependent population is education. Table 4.4 illustrates the effects on the quantity and quality of education of an age structure heavily weighted toward the younger ages. Country A and Country B are assumed to have identical populations and identical GNPs for the current year. Country A's population is growing rapidly, and 45 percent is under age fifteen. Country B, on the other hand, has a more slowly growing population, and only 30 percent is under age fifteen.

Given identical total budgets for education, and assuming for the moment that all primary school-age children are in school, Country B can spend 50 percent more per pupil than Country A. Alternatively, we can assume that children in both countries receive the same quality of education (indicated by equal spending per pupil). In this case, Country B can provide all its children an education of the quality available for $83.33 per pupil, while in Country A the budget would be exhausted after only two-thirds of the children received that level of education. If either the quantity or the quality of education suffers in Country A, its future growth will be affected because its labor force will be less well trained than that of Country B.

The dependency ratio, while useful in identifying a problem common to most developing countries, should be used with caution when applied to any particular country. First of all, the percentage of the fifteen to sixty-four age groups actually in the labor force will vary among countries, particularly because of differences in the labor force participation rates of women. Secondly, it is a mistake to think of those in the zero to fourteen and sixty-five plus age groups only as financial burdens. Children and older citizens also work, and the amount and productivity of

TABLE 4.4
Age Structure and Educational Spending: A Hypothetical Example

	Country A	Country B
Population	5,000,000	5,000,000
Population under 15	2,250,000	1,500,000
School-age population		
(50 percent of those under 15)	1,125,000	750,000
GNP	$2,500 million	$2,500 million
Government budget		
(20 percent of GNP)	500 million	500 million
Education budget		
(25 percent of total budget)	125 million	125 million
Primary education budget		
(50 percent of education budget)	62.5 million	62.5 million
Spending per primary school-age child	$55.56	$83.33

their efforts will vary from country to country. Particularly in the least developed countries, and among the poorest segments of the population, they can make important contributions to family welfare and GNP by assisting in agricultural field work, fetching the family's water requirements, helping with other household tasks, and doing part-time or temporary work for pay. In other words, they help produce goods and services, not just consume them.

The Demands of Urbanization

If rapid population growth is accompanied by migration from rural to urban areas, pressures on the government will be strong to expand or provide water supply systems, sewer systems, paved streets, street lights, and other services, These services either are not needed in rural areas or, since they are demanded by a dispersed population with little political power, they are easier for governments to ignore than similar demands in urban areas. Investment in these services may well have a positive rate of return (see chapter 6), but their effects on per capita income are likely to be felt in the long run rather than the short run. In the language of chapter 2, the short-run capital-output ratio is high; and to the extent that scarce resources could have been used instead for other activities with lower ratios, per capita GNP will suffer in the short run.

Statistical Evidence

Given the above considerations, one would expect to find that countries with rapid population growth tend to have lower rates of growth of per capita GNP than those with slowly rising populations. However, statistical evidence shows no such correlation. A comparison of the per capita GNP growth rates in Table 1.1 with the population growth rates in Table 4.2 yields the relationships shown in Table 4.5 for the period 1960–1975:

TABLE 4.5
Relationships between Population Growth Rates and Per Capita GNP
Growth Rates, 1960–1975

| Population Growth Rate | Number of Countries with Per Capita GNP Growth Rate That Is: | | |
	Low (<2.0%)	Moderate (2.0–2.9%)	High (3.0% +)
High (2.5% +)	20	12	22
Moderate (1.5–2.4%)	15	8	16
Low (<1.5%)	1	4	24

Of those countries with a high population growth rate (2.5 percent or more), the number with high rates of per capita GNP growth actually exceeded slightly the number of slow-growth countries; there was also a sizable number of countries whose income growth was moderate. If we leave out the developed countries, most of which are in the lower right hand corner of the above array, the lack of correlation is even more striking.

This does not necessarily mean that rapid population growth has no effect on the growth of per capita income. It is possible, for example, that negative effects are present, but that they are offset in the high-income-growth developing countries by special factors—e.g., unused arable land, petroleum reserves, or enlightened political leadership—not present in the low-income-growth countries. This is true to a certain extent, but one could just as well argue on the other side that the low-income-growth countries have been unusually plagued by war (including civil war).[6]

A recent review of the literature (Cassen, 1976) tends to support the view that rapid population growth has negative effects on development. However, the evidence on a number of issues is conflicting. For example, the hypothesis that people will work longer and harder the more children they have, thus increasing output, income, and the capacity for savings, is supported by evidence on the extended family cited in chapter 3. On the other hand, a recent statistical study of thirty-four developing countries found that higher dependency ratios were associated with *lower* female and total labor force participation rates.[7] Additional research is needed to clarify this issue. There is also a need to test the hypothesis that rapid population growth forces a government to increase its rate of investment in infrastructure in response to the demands of a growing population.

STRATEGIES FOR SLOWING POPULATION GROWTH

There is considerable disagreement among economists and other social scientists concerning the most effective way of slowing population growth (assuming that this is a desirable objective, which not everyone accepts).

6. Of the twenty countries in the rapid-population-growth, low-income-growth category, at least seven (Algeria, Bangladesh, Egypt, Jordan, Laos, the People's Democratic Republic of Yemen, and Zaire) have experienced serious disruptions since 1960 because of prolonged armed conflict.

7. R. E. Bilsborrow, "Effects of Economic Dependency on Labor Force Participation Rates in Less Developed Countries," *Oxford Economic Papers*, 29 (March 1977), 61–83.

One group argues that investment in family planning programs has a higher rate of return than any alternative strategy. Others question the results of studies used to support this position and argue that little money should be spent on programs directly aimed at limiting births. Instead, they recommend that priority be given to economic development programs that accelerate the urbanization-industrialization-modernization process, and thus hasten the "automatic" fall in birth rates which ushers in Stage III of the demographic transition. In particular, they emphasize programs which seek to improve living conditions for the poorer segments of the population.

Investing in Family Planning Programs

In an influential article written in 1966, the late Stephen Enke argued that "if economic resources of given value were devoted to retarding population growth, rather than accelerating production growth, the former resources could be 100 or more times as effective in raising *per capita* incomes in many LDCs."[8] An effective program, he maintained, might cost as little as 10 cents per capita. Given the very high estimated social (i.e., economywide) benefits from investment in family planning, subsidies could be justified for families whose economic calculations would not otherwise lead them to limit family size. Suppose, for example, that the present value of benefits to society from a prevented birth is $40,[9] while the medical and overhead costs of preventing a birth amount to $10. If a subsidy of $20 could induce a family not to have another child, program costs would rise to $30 per prevented birth, but the net gain to society would still be $10.

Simulation models developed by Enke and other economists attribute per capita income gains from family planning programs mainly to (1) an increase in the capital-labor ratio, because of the slower rate of growth of the labor force, and (2) a lower dependency ratio (Keeley, 1976: 42). One of Enke's later models (reprinted in Keeley, 1976) shows per capita income in a hypothetical developing country rising from $200 in 1970 to $293 in 2000 under conditions of high fertility; with low fertility, however, per capita income in 2000 would reach $419.

If these figures are accepted, they constitute a very strong case for investment in family planning programs. However, the evidence we reviewed in the previous section casts doubt on the hypothesis that a higher

8. Stephen Enke, "The Economic Aspects of Slowing Population Growth," *Economic Journal*, 76 (March 1966), 56.
9. The present value of benefits to society may be thought of as the saved costs of hospital and medical charges, food, education, etc., *minus* the present value of the expected income (a contribution to national output) of the individual whose birth was prevented (Morgan, 1975: 235–237).

GNP growth rate necessarily follows from a slower population growth rate.

The presumed benefits of a more slowly growing population, of course, must be compared with the costs of lowering the population growth rate. Morgan (1975: Ch. 12) has summarized the results of several studies which have attempted to put a price tag on family planning programs. Costs were found to vary considerably according to the type of birth control method employed and the range of services provided.

First, let us consider costs by method, using the mid-1960s figures reported by Morgan.

1. *Contraceptive pills,* which are nearly 100 percent effective if taken on schedule, cost approximately $4 to $7 a year. If we assume that births normally occur once in three years, this means a cost per birth prevented of $12 to $21. However, some women have serious undesirable side effects from using the pill, and so medical examinations in conjunction with their use are desirable. These costs—and the costs of treating the side effects—do not appear to be included in the figures cited by Morgan.

2. *Intrauterine devices (IUDs)* cost only a few cents and usually are reported to be more than 95 percent effective. They must be inserted by medical personnel, and when all expenses are considered the cost of a prevented birth is estimated to be $4 to $6. Many women, however, find the IUD uncomfortable and remove it within a few years after insertion.

3. *Condoms, diaphragms, and spermicides* cost less than $5 annually, but they are not as effective as the pill or the IUD. Taking into account failures, estimated costs of a prevented birth are from $8 to $20. To the extent that there are overhead costs for providing information on the use of these methods, these figures would be higher.

4. *Sterilization* of men has become a widely used contraceptive method in the developed countries and has been used in India, where an attempt to make it compulsory under certain circumstances helped defeat the government of Prime Minister Indira Gandhi. The attraction of male sterilization is that it is relatively inexpensive—an estimated $5 per prevented birth in India. However, because reversal is difficult and sometimes not possible, emotions can run high if men have second thoughts after the fact, or if they feel coerced to use this particular method of contraception. Sterilization of women is a more difficult and expensive procedure, and it is a relatively unimportant method of birth control.[10]

10. Still, as with male sterilization, it has caused considerable controversy. Allegations of forced sterilization led to the expulsion of the U.S. Peace Corps from Bolivia. And in the United States, it was revealed several years ago that some minority-group women, under a government-funded program, had been sterilized either without consent or without having been made fully aware of the implications of the procedure. While some observers have made charges of government-sponsored "genocide," a much more likely explanation is that such incidents, to the extent that they have occurred, represent aberrant behavior by individuals and not official policy.

5. *Abortion* is an ancient and widespread method of birth control. The International Planned Parenthood Federation estimates that there were 55 million abortions worldwide in 1971—a ratio of 4 for every 10 live births (King, 1974: 72). Of the world's population in 1971, 38 percent lived in countries where legal abortions could be obtained, and by 1976 the figure had jumped to 64 percent (Brown, 1976: 8). Even in some nominally Roman Catholic countries where this method is illegal, the number of abortions is thought to approximate the number of live births. The costs of an abortion under hygienic conditions is estimated to be $30 to $80 in developing countries, an extremely heavy financial burden for most families. Many abortions will thus be performed under less desirable conditions.

If we consider just the contraceptive methods of birth control (all of the above except abortion) and include overhead costs (estimated to be 15 to 40 percent), the estimated total cost of a prevented birth ranges from $4.50 to $30.

Most countries with family planning programs use a combination of approaches and methods. Morgan (1975) reports that India, South Korea, Pakistan, and Chile in the late 1960s had costs per couple-year of protection of $2.50 to $12 (in 1974 or 1975 dollars). Costs per prevented birth ranged from $7.50 to $72 assuming (1) that births normally occur once every three years and (2) a 50 to 100 percent effectiveness range. Another study projected that the costs per prevented birth in three countries would range from $20 to $99, depending on how comprehensive a program were adopted. In comparing these data with the net benefits of preventing a birth, Morgan calculates that a $1 investment in family planning programs will return benefits ranging from $2.12 to $507.50, depending upon the assumptions used. A $1 investment to raise GNP, on the other hand, would return only $0.29, assuming a marginal capital-output ratio of 3.5 to 1, though this is just the return in the first year. Morgan concludes that there is little doubt that family planning programs have a payoff much higher than investment to raise the level of GNP.

Not everyone, however, would agree that the payoffs are obviously high. There are a number of reasons why the above figure may be questioned.

1. Many of the prevented births attributed to investment in family planning programs would have occurred even without these programs through the use of traditional methods of birth control. In other words, for many persons who are recipients of family planning information and/or contraceptive devices, the effect is simply to switch the method of birth control or to improve the effectiveness of methods already being used. Only the *net* additions to the ranks of those practicing birth control

should be counted. Admittedly, these numbers are not easy to determine.

2. While there is some evidence of economies of scale in family planning programs, costs per prevented birth can be expected to rise as programs begin to reach out to remote areas and to families who have more resistance to suggestions that they limit the size of their families.

3. Overhead costs might well be underestimated. This is just a suspicion, but the experience of countries other than those cited above suggests that this possibility should be investigated.

4. In calculating the net benefits of a prevented birth to society (i.e., costs saved), Morgan includes the costs of nine years of education. However, only a small percentage of the population in the typical developing country attends school for that long, and in some countries, a high proportion does not attend school at all. Governments, then, do not really save the costs of nine years of education; in most cases, the probable number of years in school for a newborn child is much lower.

5. In Morgan's calculations, the present value of future earnings— a loss to society if a birth is prevented—is based on income earned between the ages of thirteen and sixty. Particularly in rural areas, however, children are productive members of the labor force well before the age of thirteen. At planting or harvest time, their presence reduces the need for hired labor. Since these contributions to output are excluded, the costs to society of a prevented birth are underestimated.

In summary, there is reason to be skeptical about the high rates of return to investment reported for family planning programs. Apart from the reasons just cited, the available data show wide variations in some cost or benefit estimates, suggesting the need for additional studies to clarify the uncertainties. Nevertheless, the figures presented by the advocates of family planning programs, even taking into account the above comments, are impressive enough to continue justifying expenditures on these programs—though not necessarily in all countries—until such time (if ever) that evidence to the contrary clearly indicates otherwise.[11]

Promoting Economic Development

Some economists believe that policies to slow population growth should not rely so much on family planning programs as on the promotion of economic *development*. (The word "development" is stressed here, for such a strategy does *not* focus on GNP). Michael Todaro, Deputy Direc-

---

11. Todaro (1977: 161) reports that resources devoted to family planning and other population programs in the developing countries rose from a mere $2 million in 1960 to nearly $3,000 million by the mid-1970s, as international agencies sharply increased their assistance in this field.

tor of the Population Council's Center for Policy Studies, makes the following comment on resources devoted to family planning programs (1977: 161):

It is a moot point . . . whether such resources (especially those allocated to premature family planning programs) might not have been more effectively used to achieve their fertility goals had they instead been devoted directly to assisting LDCs to raise the levels of living of their poorest peoples. . . . *[I]t is of little value to have sophisticated family planning programs where the people are not motivated to reduce family size* (emphasis added).

What factors cause people consciously to plan for fewer children than prevailing social norms suggest they should have? Earlier, we stated that part of the answer seems to lie in what we termed the urbanization-industrialization-modernization complex. Recent research on the economics of fertility decisions—a part of what has been termed the *new home economics*—has shed some light on some of the various possible determinants of fertility. This research views children as both consumption and investment goods, with the quantity demanded being a function of the costs and benefits attributable to children. While economists have had some difficulty in measuring the value of the social and psychological benefits of having children (e.g., preservation of the family line, extension of the self), information about the "economic" variables—those that can be related easily to monetary costs and benefits—has been quite revealing.

In summarizing this research, Anne Williams (in Keeley, 1976) reports a consensus on the following points:

1. *Education* is one of the most important factors affecting fertility. As women become more educated, they can contribute more to family income. Work and child rearing are to a certain extent competing activities, and the more education a woman has, the greater tends to be the income foregone by caring for children instead of working. Fertility rates thus tend to decline as the educational level of the female population increases.

2. *Female labor force participation*, determined in part by education (at least in urban areas), is negatively associated with fertility. The greater are the possibilities for employment outside the home, the lower is fertility.

3. *Child mortality rates* have a strong influence on fertility, which declines, after a lag, following a fall in mortality rates. Apparently there is reason to believe that the lag may be shorter now than in the past.

4. *Income* is *not* an important determinant of fertility when other

factors are held constant. Economic theory suggests that the demand for children will increase as income rises, but it appears that the relative price (opportunity cost) of children is increasing, particularly in urban areas, causing a substitution of goods and services for children.

5. *Urbanization, modernization, and migration,* holding other factors constant, appear to have little effect on fertility. This may seem to contradict what we said earlier about the urbanization-industrialization-modernization complex. However, it should be noted that items (1) to (3) above are closely related to the various elements in this complex.

One other factor has been found to be related to lower fertility:

6. *Income distribution.* A study in the early 1970s found that developing countries experiencing sharp reductions in birth rates had one common characteristic: "These are the countries in which the population as a whole has shared in the economic and social benefits of progress to a far greater degree than in most LDCs—and far more so than in Western countries during their comparable period of development."[12] Subsequent research has tended to confirm this relationship. In Taiwan, where rapid growth has been accompanied by development, the birth rate fell from 45 per 1,000 in 1953 to 24 in 1972.[13]

The policy implications of these findings are clear: programs which promote greater equality of opportunity for both men and women,[14] greater equality in the provision of public health and nutrition services, and greater equality of money incomes constitute an alternative to family planning programs for lowering the population growth rate. In a sense, one could argue that the reduction in fertility is a costless by-product of a strategy that is widely considered desirable in itself from a social standpoint. This is not to say that there is no place for family planning programs under such a strategy. Indeed, these programs can be quite effective in such an environment, since persons desiring fewer children are seeking information on effective means. But most of those who want fewer children probably make their decision without being influenced by family planning programs; they simply have economic incentives to have fewer children.

12. William Rich, "Smaller Families through Jobs and Justice," *International Development Review,* 14 (1972/3), 10.

13. Reported in Bruce F. Johnston and Anthony J. Meyer, "Nutrition, Health, and Population Strategies for Rural Development," *Economic Development and Cultural Change,* 26 (October 1977), 4.

14. Such programs would include legislation to provide civil rights and other protection to women and minority groups, thus helping to free them from the traditional roles to which they have been confined. Legislation alone, of course, does not automatically provide freedom. Overcoming racial, sexual, and caste barriers also requires long years of consciousness-raising, a process in which both private citizens and governments can play important roles.

Still, the issue cannot be considered settled. Proponents of both the family planning and social justice approaches, as we have seen, have good arguments. Perhaps the recent fertility declines in many countries can indeed be attributed to family planning programs. Future research by the new home economists should take this into account as an independent variable in their equations.

Recent Population Policies in Developing Countries

It would be misleading to say that government population policies in developing countries are of recent vintage, since even ignoring an issue is a policy decision to let it be resolved by the private sector. What is new is that in the last fifteen years or so, many governments have for the first time adopted conscious policies designed to slow population growth. Approximately sixty developing countries, with 87 percent of the developing world's population, now have government-sponsored or -supported family planning programs (Todaro, 1977: 158).[15]

Other countries, however, continue to reject the argument that rapid population growth poses a threat not only to their own economic development but also to the well-being of the entire planet. Countries with both rapid population growth and a rapidly rising per capita GNP find it difficult to see what the fuss is all about. Resistance to family planning is based on many factors, among which the following are probably the most important: (1) the political risks of challenging a strong, pronatalist religious establishment; (2) the belief that rapid population growth is an asset to development if vast land areas are available for settlement (e.g., Brazil); (3) the desire to settle more people in border areas thought to be coveted by neighboring countries; (4) the belief that a larger population will result in economies of scale in industry, thus lowering production costs; and (5) the view that developed-country proponents of population control are practicing a subtle form of genocide against nonwhite peoples.

Mexico, a large developing country whose per capita GNP as well as population has been growing rapidly, did not adopt a family planning program until 1972. The government was finally motivated to act by growing popular dissatisfaction with the failure of the country's rapidly growing economy to do much for the poorer segments of society, who were experiencing higher rates of unemployment and underemployment. Though Mexico's decision was a significant one, its family planning efforts remain modest. Brazil, the most populous country in Latin America, still has no family planning program. The inconclusive results of the United

15. For a brief summary of some of these programs, see Morgan (1975: 241–244).

Nations World Population Conference, held in Bucharest, Rumania, in 1974, demonstrated that other countries, too, were unwilling to adopt family planning programs.

India, with 610 million people in 1975, has long had a family planning program, but its modest achievements have been well below expectations. Growing concern about future population growth in India led to the adoption in 1976 of compulsory sterilization measures by some of the states. While this met with a great deal of resistance and was reversed after Prime Minister Gandhi's defeat in 1977, it should not be assumed that the issue is dead, either in India or in other countries. Where food supplies have difficulty keeping up with population growth (some observers believe that large-scale famine is inevitable in South Asia sometime in the next few decades), there will be growing pressure on governments to impose legal maximums on family size, levy heavy fines on offenders, or force them to undergo sterilization. Such measures may seem unpalatable, but so is mass starvation.[16]

China, as we have already noted, appears to have had considerable success in reducing birth rates, not only by making available contraceptive devices and abortion services but also by encouraging postponement of marriage, to about age twenty-eight for males and twenty-five for females. But few governments possess the ability of the Chinese government to manipulate peer pressure and other factors to make such a policy work. If they do, however, such "social consciousness-raising" is a most effective means of slowing population growth.[17] It is also a relatively inexpensive one, at least in economic terms.

Thus far, we have discussed only the family planning approach to reducing fertility. What is recent experience with the other approach, which is based on education, health, equality of opportunity for men and

16. If widespread famine occurs in South Asia, it now seems more likely to be in Bangladesh than in India, which after three good monsoons in a row has accumulated grain reserves of 25 million tons. Moreover, recent developments in Indian agriculture have brightened food production prospects (see *The Economist*, May 13, 1978, pp. 107–112). However, this promising future is by no means assured. And for developing countries as a whole, as we shall see in chapter 9, the growth of agricultural production since the mid-1960s has been discouraging, doing no better than just matching population growth. The nutritional status of most residents of the developing world remains well below recommended standards (see chapter 7).

17. The Chinese have also used "social consciousness raising" to promote new patterns of rural development (see chapter 9). Some observers object to such methods as "brainwashing by Big Brother." Supporters of these efforts would argue that they foster cooperation and concern for others while discouraging selfish behavior. They might also note that social structures dominated by private institutions can also engage in subtle forms of "brainwashing." For a sympathetic view by a U.S. economist of Chinese efforts to influence attitudes, see John Gurley, "Maoist Economic Development: The New Man in the New China," *The Center Magazine*, 3 (May 1970), 25–33.

women, and a redistribution of income and wealth? The area in which the most has been done probably is education, though educational policies have rarely made an explicit connection between education and fertility. Health programs continue to lower infant mortality rates, but in many countries improved nutrition can have an even greater impact on infant mortality. Food production trends in developing countries, though, have not been encouraging. Income distribution has become a widely discussed topic in the developing world, but income inequalities remain high in many countries and are even increasing in some. To summarize, what we have called the urbanization-industrialization-modernization complex can be expected to continue to push birth rates downward; but few countries, as we shall see in subsequent chapters, are doing much to accelerate this trend by more widely distributing the benefits of growth.

Apart from the two broad strategies discussed above, governments can influence family size by manipulating a variety of policy tools. In many countries, workers are paid wage supplements which increase with family size. Eliminating these schemes would increase the cost of having children. Improved social security benefits, and expanded coverage, would weaken the security motive for having large families. Tax deductions or tax credits could be limited to two or three children. Tuition charges could be introduced at the secondary school level for a family's third or fourth child and for subsequent children. This list could go on for several pages—and extending it on your own would be a good exercise—but suffice it to say that many of these possible actions would encounter stiff public resistance. This would be especially true if their immediate effect (and possibly long-run effect as well) is to hurt the poor more than the rich, as would be the case if family allowances for wage workers were eliminated. Governments with shaky political bases are unlikely to propose many of these changes. If they do, no single measure will likely have much effect on fertility; but the combined effect of a number of new incentives could be significant.

THE RECENT DECLINE IN POPULATION GROWTH RATES

As we noted briefly at the beginning of this chapter, there appears to have been a significant recent drop in the rate of growth of world population, from 1.90 percent in 1970 to 1.64 percent in 1975. One cannot be certain yet that the decline has in fact been this great, since much of it is attributable to trends in China, where population statistics have long been the subject of great controversy. Nevertheless, the trend is evident in all other areas of the world except for Africa, where most countries entered Stage II of the demographic transition only a few decades ago, and Eastern Europe, which has a low population growth rate but has been encouraging population growth in recent years (see Table 4.6).

TABLE 4.6
Demographic Changes, by Region, 1970–1975

Region	Crude Birth Rates (per 1,000 inhabitants)	Crude Death Rates	Natural Increase (percent)[a]	Population (millions)	Annual Natural Increase (millions)
North America					
1970	18.2	9.2	.90	226	2.04
1975	14.8	8.8	.60	236	1.42
Western Europe					
1970	16.2	10.6	.56	333	1.89
1975	13.7	10.5	.32	343	1.12
Eastern Europe					
1970	17.4	9.1	.84	368	3.14
1975	18.0	9.4	.86	384	3.31
East Asia					
1970	30.6	12.1	1.85	941	17.43
1975	19.6	7.8	1.18	1,005	11.91
Southeast Asia					
1970	42.1	15.5	2.66	278	7.40
1975	38.6	15.3	2.33	317	7.37
South Asia					
1970	40.8	15.9	2.48	709	17.57
1975	37.1	15.8	2.13	791	16.89
Middle East					
1970	44.3	15.5	2.88	136	3.91
1975	41.7	14.5	2.72	155	4.22
Africa					
1970	47.1	21.0	2.61	312	8.16
1975	47.1	20.0	2.71	355	9.65
Latin America					
1970	37.4	9.7	2.77	276	7.64
1975	35.5	9.0	2.65	317	8.39
Oceania					
1970	20.9	9.0	1.19	15	.18
1975	17.4	8.1	.93	17	.16
World Total					
1970	32.2	13.2	1.90	3,594	69.36
1975	28.3	11.9	1.64	3,920	64.44

Source: Brown (1976: 33).

[a] Does not include net interregional migration.

The apparent decline in the population growth rate since 1970 significantly alters earlier population projections for the year 2000 and beyond. Had the 1970 population growth rate of 1.90 percent continued through the rest of the century, the world's population would have reached 6,310 million in the year 2000. But if we apply the 1.64 percent figure to the new population estimate for 1975, the world's population at the end of the century would reach only 5,890 million—a difference of 420 million. Note that the revised figure for the year 2000 is slightly less than the rapid-fertility-decline figure shown in Table 4.1, which is based on earlier estimates. If, as now seems likely, the world population growth rate continues to decline, there will be even fewer people in the year 2000.

Both birth rates and death rates have declined during the 1970s. For the world as a whole, the death rate fell from 13.2/1000 to 11.9/1000, while the birth rate dropped from 32.2/1000 to 28.3/1000. In both cases the most spectacular decline was in China, which accounts for most of the population in the East Asia region in Table 4.6. The estimated drop in the Chinese birth rate, from 32/1000 to 19/1000, is the fastest ever reported for a five-year period (Brown, 1976: 9), though many observers regard these figures with skepticism. Whatever the true decline, the urbanization-industrialization-modernization complex may explain part of it, but most seems attributable to a conscious government policy of limiting population growth rates. Family planning information and services (including abortion), as we have pointed out, have been widely disseminated, and the country's well-organized political machinery has been used to encourage delayed marriage and fewer children.

Elsewhere in the developing world, birth rates fell by 2.6 to 3.7 points in South and Southeast Asia and in the Middle East, and by 1.9 points in Latin America. In Africa, however, the birth rate stayed at 47.1/1000, higher than in any other region. For most regions the decline in the death rate was modest. In fact, the death rate rose in countries plagued by drought or other natural disasters—e.g., Ethiopia, the Sahelian (sub-Saharan) countries, and Bangladesh.

In the developed world, there was a significant decline in the birth rate in all regions except Eastern Europe, where there was a small rise in response to government incentives to increase family size. Death rates fell only slightly, and in Eastern Europe they actually rose, reflecting a shift toward an older population. In four countries—East Germany, West Germany, Luxembourg, and Austria—the birth rate was in balance with the death rate (or slightly below), and Belgium and the United Kingdom were on the verge of joining these ranks (Brown, 1976: 11–12). Of the total increase in the world's population between 1970 and 1975, 326 million, the developed countries accounted for only 38 million, or 12 percent.

URBANIZATION

Accompanying rapid population growth in the developing countries has been a shift of population from rural to urban areas. Some people have been "pushed" off the land because of the limited job opportunities provided by slowly expanding farm sectors, the shortage of land available to growing numbers of low-income farmers, and the adoption of capital-intensive methods of production by larger-scale farm operators (see chapter 9). Others have been "pulled" to the cities by the prospects for higher-paying jobs, better educational opportunities for their children, or greater individual freedom in their daily lives.

Whether push or pull factors predominate in any particular country, the decision to migrate is largely an economic one. Michael Todaro (1977: 194–196 and 201–203) has devised a model which has been useful in explaining the migration process in these terms. The model states that the decision to migrate is based on a comparison of *expected* incomes in rural and urban areas. Wage rates for urban occupations to which a rural resident might reasonably aspire may be considerably higher than earnings in rural areas. But this differential alone will not guarantee migration, though traditional microeconomic theory says that is what should occur.[18] Traditional theory assumes full employment, and that is not what we generally find in developing countries, particularly in urban areas. The existence of high urban unemployment rates (see chapter 12) means that the probability of securing a job is well below 100 percent, compared with reasonably secure employment prospects in the countryside. If urban wages are twice as high as rural wages (or earnings from farming), the decision to migrate is not rational when the probability of securing the desired urban job (inversely proportional to the unemployment rate) is less than 50 percent. When it is greater than 50 percent, though, migration will occur, even though the unemployment rate is relatively high. This is not to say that migration decisions are motivated only by such considerations (the availability of better educational, health, and other services in urban areas are also important factors), nor that migrants make their calculations the same way economists do. Also, as Todaro recognizes, the costs of migration must be taken into account. Still, the Todaro model, and its refinements by other economists, explain a sizable proportion of rural-urban migration, and it is particularly illuminating in showing why rapid migration continues despite high and sometimes rising rates of urban unemployment.

---

18. Traditional theory also says that migration will equalize wages in rural and urban areas. But urban labor markets are imperfect, and substantial rural-urban wage differentials can persist (see chapter 12).

The population of urban areas in the developing countries is expected to grow by about 4 percent annually between 1975 and 2000, raising their share of the total population from 28 to 42 percent (Cohen, 1976). In the developing countries, 90 cities had populations of more than 1 million in 1975, and by 2000 there may be close to 300. According to United Nations projections, 5 urban areas in the developing countries will have populations of at least 20 million (!) by the end of the century (see Table 4.7).

Populations of this magnitude in fact may never be reached. As more and more people flock to urban areas, cities are being confronted with increasing demands for educational facilities, sewer and water systems, housing, and other urban services. In many large cities in the developing world, 25 to 50 percent of the population now live in what are commonly called slums (deteriorating older housing), but what more appropriately are termed "squatter settlements,"[19] where housing tends to be new construction, out of whatever scraps of material are available, by migrants

TABLE 4.7
Populations of Selected Urban Areas,
1950, 1975, and 2000
(millions of inhabitants)

Urban Area	1950	1975[a]	2000[b]
Bogotá	0.7	3.4	9.5
Bombay	2.9	7.1	19.8
Buenos Aires	4.5	9.3	13.7
Cairo	2.4	6.9	16.9
Calcutta	4.5	8.1	20.4
Jakarta	1.6	5.6	17.8
Karachi	1.0	4.5	16.6
Kinshasa	0.2	2.0	7.8
Lagos	0.3	2.1	9.4
Manila	1.5	4.4	12.8
Mexico City	2.9	10.9	31.5
Peking	2.2	8.9	22.0
Rio de Janeiro	2.9	8.3	19.3
São Paulo	2.5	9.9	26.0
Seoul	1.0	7.3	18.7
Shanghai	5.8	11.5	22.1

Source: Cohen (1976).
[a] Estimated.
[b] UN projections.

19. The difference between slums and squatter settlements is emphasized in William Mangin, "Latin American Squatter Settlements: A Problem and a Solution," *Latin American Research Review*, 2 (Summer 1967), 65–98.

from rural areas and smaller urban centers. Estimates for the late 1960s of the percentage of the population living under such conditions in nine major metropolitan centers are as follows (cited in Perlman, 1976: 12):

Istanbul	12
Singapore	15
Lima	25
Santiago	25
Rio de Janeiro	33
Caracas	35
Ankara	45
Mexico City	45
Algiers	65

In some cities, many people have no access even to the ramshackle housing that some new migrants are able to build for themselves. Perhaps half a million of Calcutta's 8.1 million residents in 1975 slept in the streets.

Until recently, it was widely believed that new arrivals to major metropolitan centers were characterized by psychological alienation, very high rates of unemployment, political apathy (except for a few radicals), and social disorganization (as evidenced by high rates of crime, prostitution, and random violence). The new urban masses were often described as *marginalized* from the mainstream of society—which, it was said, would accept them if only they would adopt mainstream norms and values. In effect, the poor were being blamed for their own poverty. Other observers, using the term *marginalization* in a somewhat different sense, placed the blame on a social and economic structure which denied opportunities to urban migrants.

The concept of marginality is similar to the dual economy models we discussed in chapter 1 and will refer to again in chapter 5. Indeed, the marginality hypothesis can be thought of as a dual society model. As such, it has been criticized by both radical and moderate observers for the same reasons that dual economy models have been criticized. As Janice Perlman (1976: 245) has put it, in very effectively criticizing what she calls "the myth of marginality," residents of squatter settlements do not live in a separate world of their own but rather constitute "exploited groups . . . very much integrated into the system."[20]

In studying squatter settlements in Rio de Janeiro, Perlman found what other researchers had begun to discern in Latin American cities since the mid-1960s—namely, that migrants have a relatively high degree of social organization and cohesiveness; experience no greater unemploy-

20. Compare this with André Gunder Frank's criticism of the dual economy, discussed in chapter 5.

ment problems than nonmigrants; are integrated with, not marginal to, mainstream economic activity; accept middle-class values and norms; and politically are neither radical nor apathetic. Studies have consistently shown that migrants tend to be among the better educated, more skilled, and more ambitious members of the communities from which they come. They value hard work, and as their incomes rise over time they will begin to make improvements to their houses, converting them into more permanent structures.[21]

Nevertheless, migrants do not have an equal opportunity to improve their welfare. In Brazil, Perlman (1976: 243) found that many lacked a birth certificate and therefore could not obtain the official work permits which would enable them to enjoy such benefits as minimum wages and social security. Thus migrants are concentrated in low-paying jobs unattractive in other respects as well. While sheer numbers give them some power, especially where they have meaningful voting privileges, attempts to demonstrate this power too vociferously (e.g., in seeking to obtain water, electricity, and other services) have often been met with repressive acts, including eviction and the razing of their homes by bulldozers. To the extent that such discrimination exists, it is still possible to use the term *dual society* or *marginalization* in some meaningful sense, albeit different from the one Perlman criticizes.

One wonders how far the process of urbanization can proceed, particularly where squatter settlements account for an increasing share of the metropolitan population, before social tensions increase and erupt into widespread destructive behavior. If reasonably productive jobs fail to increase as fast as urban populations, food does not reach the cities in sufficient quantities, and urban fiscal systems do not meet the demands placed on them, there may be limits to city size beyond which serious rioting or other forms of violence will be constant threats. This could have serious adverse consequences for both economic growth and economic development.

One possible way to deal with the problem of rapid urbanization is to use government policy to redirect migrants to smaller urban centers whose growth would cause fewer social problems than continued expansion of the larger cities. However, most major new business ventures are likely to resist locating in smaller cities because large cities offer too many attractions: a large pool of skilled labor; the availability of banking, insurance, and other financial services; relatively good transportation and communications facilities; and proximity to government offices. These advantages are so great that developing countries have had rather little success in inducing firms to locate in smaller cities by offering tax con-

21. See the studies and review articles cited in Perlman (1976: 244 and passim.).

cessions and other incentives. Greater subsidies might be given, but this would add to government's fiscal burdens in the short run, thus making it a politically difficult step to take. Where the government itself is a major owner of business enterprise, a policy of geographic dispersion has a better chance to succeed.[22]

Another action which governments might consider is to limit city size by law and/or force. China has had some success with this policy, and the new governments in Cambodia and Vietnam have sent hundreds of thousands of urban dwellers back to the countryside, though particularly in Cambodia this has been accomplished at a great cost in human suffering and loss of lives. Not many governments have the desire or the power to limit freedom of individual location decisions. But if large urban centers continue to grow rapidly, governments in developing countries might be confronted with a serious dilemma which makes them damned if they do and damned if they do not take such actions.

SUMMARY

It is not clear that rapid population growth has been a major obstacle to economic growth in the developing countries generally, as economic theory suggests it would be. Nevertheless, in countries where population densities are high and there is little unused arable land, economic growth may well have been slowed and is likely to be affected even more in the future as population continues to increase. The rapid growth of urban areas and the associated increase in social problems is also cause for concern.

While economic growth may not yet have suffered much because of rapid population increases, it is very likely that economic *development* already has been affected significantly in the form of growing inequalities in the distribution of income and higher rates of unemployment and/or underemployment. Recent studies suggest that measures to reduce these and other social inequities can create the conditions under which individuals are motivated to reduce family size. Family planning programs, especially in an environment where incentives to have fewer children already exist, also show promise of effectively lowering fertility, at favorable rates of return on investment.

---

22. A policy of geographic dispersion of government activities deserves serious consideration. While private, profit-maximizing firms must make their location decisions on the basis of *financial* costs and benefits, governments should allocate their resources on the basis of *social* costs and benefits, which include noncash items as well as indirect effects on other economic activities (see chapter 6). Using this investment criterion, geographic dispersion of public-sector activity might well be justified in many cases.

Suggested Readings

Brown, Lester R. *World Population Trends: Signs of Hope, Signs of Stress.* Worldwatch Paper No. 8. Washington, D.C.: Worldwatch Institute, October 1976.
A good, short (forty-page) summary of population trends and population policies, in both developing and developed countries, between 1970 and 1975. Brown argues that the world's population cannot reach the 10 to 16 billion ultimately projected by United Nations demographers because ecological and social systems cannot support that many people.

Cassen, Robert H. "Population and Development: A Survey" [with a comment by Michael S. Teitelbaum]. *World Development,* 4 (October–November 1976), 785–830 and 831–835.
The author's review of the literature convinces him that rapid population growth slows the improvement in living standards. A role is seen for both family planning and socioeconomic change in reducing birth rates, with the latter considered the more important.

Cohen, Michael A. "Cities in Developing Countries." *Finance and Development,* 13, No. 1 (March 1976), 12–15.
A short survey of urban population projections, based on a longer study prepared by the World Bank.

Keeley, Michael C., ed. *Population, Public Policy, and Economic Development.* Foreword by Mark Perlman. New York: Praeger Publishers, 1976.
This volume contains eight papers examining the causes of rapid population growth, its long-run economic implications, and the policy choices available to decision makers. Several papers are quite technical, but others, including a survey of the literature, can be read without great difficulty by undergraduates. Two of the papers are authored or coauthored by the late Stephen Enke, whose work has strongly influenced the other writers. Enke maintains that declining fertility has a strong positive effect on per capita income.

King, Timothy, coord. *Population Policies and Economic Development.* A World Bank Staff Report. Baltimore: The Johns Hopkins University Press for the World Bank, 1974.
Discusses recent demographic trends and prospects, reviews the evidence relating population growth and economic development, and explains the rationale for the World Bank's significantly increased lending for projects designed to slow population growth. Contains many useful statistical tables.

Latin American Urban Research. Beverly Hills, Calif.: Sage Publications, Inc., annual.
The volumes in this valuable series bring together studies by specialists representing the various social science disciplines. Each volume is devoted to a particular issue, such as the concept of urban marginality and the interrelationships between urban and national politics.

Morgan, Theodore. *Economic Development: Concepts and Strategy.* New York: Harper & Row, Publishers, 1975.

Chapter 12 reviews research findings which show that investment in family planning can have very high payoffs. Morgan strongly supports this position.

Perlman, Janice. *The Myth of Marginality: Urban Poverty and Politics in Rio de Janiero.* Berkeley: University of California Press, 1976.

This detailed study of squatter settlements in a large metropolitan area challenges the view that squatters are psychologically alienated, economically parasitic, politically apathetic, and socially disorganized. Perlman finds that they are socially well organized and cohesive; integrated with, not marginal to, urban economic activity; inclined toward middle-class values and norms; and politically neither apathetic nor radical. She also finds, though, that they are repressed and exploited.

Ridker, Ronald, ed. *Population and Development: The Search for Selective Interventions.* Baltimore: The Johns Hopkins University Press for Resources for the Future, 1976.

The authors of the twelve papers in this volume review the linkages between fertility and the determinants of fertility, and they assess the feasibility of policies for manipulating the latter in order to reduce fertility rates. The topics range from the economic value of children in peasant agriculture to reducing fertility through the use of mass media and modern consumer goods.

Todaro, Michael P. *Economic Development in the Third World.* New York: Longman, Inc., 1977.

Todaro, Deputy Director of the Population Council's Center for Policy Studies, devotes two chapters of his textbook to the population problem. He argues that economic policies promoting greater equality in the distribution of income and in levels of living can play a significant role in lowering birth rates. There is also a chapter on rural-urban migration, a subject on which Todaro has been a pioneer contributor.

5

International Trade and Economic Development

Developing countries have had an ambivalent attitude toward international trade as a means of stimulating economic growth and development. On the one hand, their policymakers have been skeptical of a trade-oriented strategy because it appears to be associated historically with colonialist domination, unstable export prices, dualistic patterns of economic growth, and an emphasis on nonindustrial production. On the other hand, developing countries wishing to become less dependent on the developed countries still have a need for foreign exchange to finance the importation of industrial raw materials, intermediate goods, and capital goods not available locally. When prices for their exports are favorable and world market demand is strong, trade seems clearly beneficial to growth and development. Accordingly, developing countries are motivated to seek ways of keeping export prices high and expanding the market for their products.

From the onset of the Great Depression until the early 1960s, anti-trade attitudes were dominant in most of Latin America and in many African countries which had attained independence (or were about to do so) toward the end of this period. Asian countries, on the whole, were more favorably disposed toward trade. But among the larger countries, the commitment was relatively weak in India and Pakistan, while Indonesia's policies discouraged trade. This is not to say that countries where antitrade attitudes prevailed wanted to dispense with international trade altogether. Rather, what they sought was to lessen the importance of trade in their economies and to rely on import-substituting industrialization as the major stimulus to growth.

These attitudes toward trade began to change in the early 1960s, largely because the strategy of import-substituting industrialization (see chapter 10) had not resulted in the expected degree of economic independence from the developed world. By the mid-1960s, protrade attitudes were dominant in most countries. To say this may seem odd in view of the frequent negative comments one hears from developing country leaders on the subjects of external dependence, multinational corporations, and sharply fluctuating prices for primary products. However, what seems on the surface to be a growing sentiment against trade has been more than offset since the early 1960s by vigorous efforts to increase export earnings. The most striking manifestation of protrade sentiment— though it has not usually been expressed in those terms—has been the action taken by the Organization of Petroleum Exporting Countries (OPEC) to increase petroleum prices sharply; but, as we shall see in chapter 15, this is by no means an isolated incident.

In this chapter, we shall concentrate on the negative attitudes toward trade—i.e., those which regard heavy dependence on trade as an obstacle to growth and development. These attitudes are in large part a reaction to the theory of comparative advantage and the free trade doctrine derived from it. Special attention will be given to the developing countries' terms of trade (the relationship between export prices and import prices) and to the problem of export price instability. Finally, we shall consider theories of external dependence, which maintain that participation in a relatively free-trade international economy not only has negative economic effects on developing countries but also creates undesirable social and political relationships.

THE THEORY OF COMPARATIVE ADVANTAGE AND THE TRADE-BASED STRATEGY OF DEVELOPMENT

The theory of comparative advantage says that world economic output— and, by implication, economic growth—will be maximized if each nation specializes in the production of those commodities and services which it can produce relatively cheaply. The foreign exchange earned from exporting competitive items can then be used to import products in which other countries have a comparative advantage. Since labor is usually the abundant and therefore inexpensive factor of production in the developing countries, economists and political leaders in the developed countries argued throughout the nineteenth century and much of the twentieth that the developing countries should concentrate on the production of foodstuffs, minerals, and other primary products, while manufactured products should be imported from the developed countries, which could produce them more cheaply. In colonial North America (relegated by the British to developing country status by the standards of the time), the

British actually forbade the production of a wide range of manufactured goods. As someone once said, this kind of thinking forever condemned the developing countries to be "hewers of wood and drawers of water."

Let us examine in more detail the simple, classical version of the theory of comparative advantage and see why it implies that a trade-based strategy of development is optimal. The key assumptions of the theory are as follows:[1]

1. Labor is the only factor of production explicitly taken into account. (However, other factors of production can be allowed for and expressed as labor-time equivalents.)
2. The cost of one hour of labor time is always the same *within* a country (but not between countries). This implies that labor is homogeneous (i.e., all workers have the same skills) and that the labor market is perfectly competitive.
3. Competition in all markets assures that product prices are equal to production costs (including a normal rate of return to the owners of capital).
4. Technology is constant.
5. There are constant returns to scale.
6. For each commodity, quality is identical in all countries producing that commodity.
7. The factors of production are perfectly mobile internally (hence the uniform cost of labor) but perfectly immobile internationally.
8. Trade is free, unhindered by tariffs, quotas, or other nontariff barriers to trade.
9. There are no transportation costs.

Given these assumptions, a simple model may be constructed to illustrate the advantages of a trade-based strategy of development.[2] In this model, illustrated in Figure 5.1, the world consists of two countries, Alpha and Beta, each of which produces just two commodities, wheat and cloth. The labor forces of the two countries are identical in size, supplying 120,000 days of work annually. Because of different endowments of other factors (not explicitly taken into account by the model), the production possibilities curves of the two countries have very differ-

1. It may be objected, and rightly so, that the classical theory of comparative advantage is not the most realistic version of the theory. Modern theory, beginning with the Heckscher-Ohlin two-factor model, and incorporating dynamic as well as static elements, is more realistic. But it is also more complex, and the case for trade is more easily grasped if the simple, classical model is used. In any event, most of the developing countries' criticisms of comparative advantage models apply to modern theory as much as to classical theory.
2. This model is adapted from Kenen and Lubitz (1971: 9–13).

Figure 5.1
The Gains from Trade: An Illustration

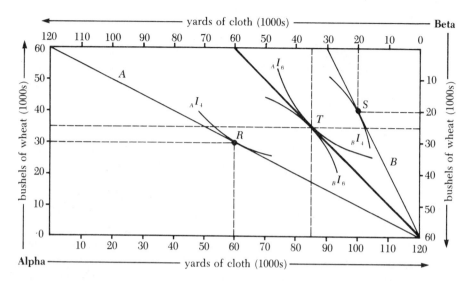

	Alpha		Beta	
	Cloth	*Wheat*	*Cloth*	*Wheat*
Before Trade				
Production	60,000	30,000	20,000	20,000
Consumption	60,000	30,000	20,000	20,000
After Trade				
Production	120,000	0	0	60,000
Consumption	85,000	35,000	35,000	25,000
Exports	35,000	0	0	35,000
Imports	0	35,000	35,000	0

ent shapes. In Alpha, 120,000 yards of cloth could be produced in a year if all labor time were devoted to cloth production. Alternatively, if all labor time were spent on wheat production, Alpha could produce 60,000 bushels of wheat. If we assume constant costs of production, the production possibilities curve is a straight line (line A in Figure 5.1). This means that production of an extra yard of cloth always involves the sacrifice of a fixed amount of wheat. If one work day of labor can produce either 1 yard of cloth (120,000 yds. ÷ 120,000 work days) or ½ bushel of wheat (60,000 bushels ÷ 120,000 work days), and labor is the only cost of production, we can say that 1 yard of cloth in Alpha costs ½ bushel of wheat. (This is the familiar concept of *opportunity cost*, or production foregone.)

In Beta, we assume that maximum cloth production with 120,000 work days of labor is only 30,000 yards, while maximum wheat production, as in Alpha, is 60,000 bushels. In this case, the cost of 1 yard of cloth is 2 bushels of wheat: to produce this 1 yard requires four work days of labor, and if that amount of labor is taken away from wheat production, output will fall by 2 bushels. The production possibilities curve in Beta is illustrated by line *B*. Note that the origin for Beta is in the upper-right-hand corner of Figure 5.1; the cloth production axis reads from right to left, and the wheat production axis reads from top to bottom.

On the surface, it might seem that there is no reason for the two countries to engage in trade. Alpha has a clear absolute advantage in cloth production and can produce just as much wheat as Beta. However, comparatively (or relatively) speaking, Beta does better in wheat production, and this *comparative advantage* constitutes the basis for trade between the two countries. It is clear in our example that Beta would like to send wheat to Alpha and buy cloth there at the prevailing price (½ bushel of wheat, compared with 2 bushels back home in Beta). At this price, Alpha would neither gain nor lose by buying wheat from Beta, rather than supplying its own wheat, and for noneconomic reasons we might presume that under these circumstances it would favor its own producers. However, if Alpha could buy wheat from Beta at the price prevailing in Beta (½ yard of cloth, compared with 2 yards of cloth in Alpha), this would clearly be advantageous, though Beta would not gain (or lose) anything from this transaction.

It can be demonstrated that at *any* international price between the two national prices, *both* countries stand to gain from trade because their consumption possibilities frontiers would be extended beyond their production possibilities frontiers. Before trade begins, let us assume that Alpha produces 60,000 yards of cloth and 30,000 bushels of wheat, because this is the combination of cloth and wheat yielding the maximum total utility consistent with production possibilities. This is illustrated by point *R* on indifference curve $_AI_4$, the highest indifference curve that Alpha is capable of reaching without trade.[3] Similarly, Beta produces 20,000 yards of cloth and 20,000 bushels of wheat, as illustrated by point *S* on indifference curve $_BI_4$.

Now assume that trade is established between the two countries at a price of 1 yard of cloth for 1 bushel of wheat. Alpha produces only cloth, in which it has a comparative advantage, and Beta produces only wheat.

3. Readers are asked to assume that there really are such things as national indifference curves, and to forget that their shape would depend on such factors as the distribution of income. Those not familiar with indifference curve analysis should get the point without having to find out what it is all about.

Total production of both commodities, it is clear, has increased, as has each country's consumption of both commodities; trade, in other words, enables them to reach higher indifference curves ($_AI_6$ and $_BI_6$, intersecting at point T). In our model, 35,000 yards of cloth are exchanged for 35,000 bushels of wheat. Alpha now consumes 85,000 yards of cloth and 35,000 bushels of wheat, while Beta's consumption has increased to 35,000 yards of cloth and 25,000 bushels of wheat.

THE COMPARATIVE ADVANTAGE ASSUMPTIONS: HOW REALISTIC?

Criticisms of the theory of comparative advantage are basically of two kinds: first, that its assumptions are unrealistic; and second, that it ignores the social and political relationships likely to prevail if trade policy is based on its principles. We shall consider the latter toward the end of this chapter in connection with theories of external dependence. For now, let us examine the realism of the assumptions on which the theory of comparative advantage, in its simplest form, is based. Let us also see what issues the theory sweeps under the carpet.

A quick review of the major assumptions makes it easy to see why they have been criticized. On closer examination, however, they are not quite so unrealistic as they seem to be—at least for the time and place in which the theory was developed. When David Ricardo presented a lucid explanation of the theory in early-nineteenth-century England, labor was by far the most important factor in the production of most goods and services. Moreover, most labor had few specialized skills; workers leaving the countryside for the mines or factories could be given what little skill they needed in a short period of time on the job. Thus the assumptions that labor was the only factor of production and that its wage was uniform within a country were useful simplifications that did not seem to be gross distortions of reality. The constant technology assumption was not unreasonable in a world where change was much slower than it is today, and it is doubtful that significant increasing or decreasing returns to scale existed in many industries. The assumption that trade is free was essential for showing why there is an underlying basis for trade.

Over time, however, most of the assumptions became less realistic. Capital became more important relative to labor, and labor became highly differentiated according to skill. Technology changed more rapidly, and industries typically were characterized by firms using different "vintages" of technology. Increasing returns to scale seemed to characterize some industries. Firms—and countries—competed increasingly in quality as well as price for a wide range of commodities. Both capital and labor became more mobile internationally after the mid-nineteenth century (though labor mobility is not as great now as it was before World War I).

What are the implications of these changes for the theory of comparative advantage? Actually, the theory can accommodate many of these real-world deviations from the initial assumptions, and it can deal with the problem of transportation costs, which are less important now than in the nineteenth century. Admittedly, it does so only by becoming more complex mathematically. But even on an intuitive level, the case for international specialization, division of labor, and free trade remains powerful despite recognition that the initial assumptions do not accurately describe the real world. Stated very simply, why should a country produce steel if it can buy steel abroad for fewer bushels of wheat than it costs domestically?

There are, in fact, a number of reasons why a country would indeed want to produce its own steel under such circumstances. First of all, it may fear that trade will be disrupted by wars or depressions abroad (as it was during much of the period from 1914 to 1945), even if it is not directly involved in the hostilities. Second, a steel industry may be deemed necessary for national defense. Third, it may be valued as a symbol of national pride and economic independence. The theory of comparative advantage —even in its modern form—blithely ignores these motivations, though clearly they involve elements of national welfare. In effect, the theory of comparative advantage assumes that the world is perpetually at peace and that such things as national pride are unworthy of measurement.

But even if we stick to "purely economic relationships," as some economists might put it, other "errors of omission" can be found, especially in the classical theory. A serious flaw in the reasoning behind the free trade policy implicitly recommended by the theory is that the model usually is presented only in static terms. It thus fails to account for the fact that a country can acquire comparative advantage over time. This can happen, for example, if the labor force (including managers and entrepreneurs) becomes more skilled, a cheaper source of power becomes available, or domestic markets become larger, thus permitting firms to enjoy economies of large-scale production. New industries attempting to get established because of these developments, however, will not always be immediately competitive with imports. Deliveries from suppliers will be irregular at first; labor and management lack the skills that only experience can bring; service to customers is not an established tradition, as it may be with importers of competing products; and product quality is likely to be uneven. These and other problems can be overcome with the passage of time, but meanwhile, firms in such industries need protection if they are to survive competition with imports.

What we have just done, of course, is to present the familiar *infant industry argument* for temporary tariffs during an industry's formative years. While this rationale for tariffs can be abused, to justify subsidizing industries that have little chance of becoming competitive, it is perfectly compatible with a *dynamic* theory of comparative advantage—one that allows for changes in comparative advantage over time.[4] Interestingly, one of the most notable challenges to the static theory of comparative advantage was made by the United States, which early in the nineteenth century adopted Alexander Hamilton's strategy of imposing protective tariffs on its fledgling industries. Some of these industries—which the static theory of comparative advantage said should not have been started in the first place—eventually became competitive enough to participate successfully in export markets.

The belief that developing countries can profit by a trade-based strategy of growth and development implicitly assumes that the developed countries will play by the rules of the game—i.e., will permit the developing countries to realize their comparative advantage. In fact, however, developed countries impose tariffs and nontariff barriers on imports. These restrictions often affect imports from developing countries more than imports from other developed countries. The United States, for example, imposes quotas (euphemistically called "orderly marketing agreements") on shoes, textiles, and other products for which comparative advantage has been shifting to developing countries. What this means, of course, is that a trade-based strategy of growth and development offers no garantee of success. The developed countries must cooperate if comparative advantage is to be realized.

Just how important is this objection to a trade-based strategy of growth and development? In general, the answer seems to be that trade restrictions have not been as important a deterrent to exports as many developing countries believe. Despite the existence of tariffs and nontariff barriers to trade, exports of manufactured products from the developing countries to the developed countries have increased rapidly in the last two decades (see chapter 15). For many products, entry into the

---

4. In benefit-cost terms, tariff protection is justified if the present value of the costs of protection (mainly higher prices paid by consumers) is more than outweighed by the present value of future benefits (lower consumer prices and, in some cases, participation in export markets). Actually, if capital markets were perfect, tariff protection should not be needed when the expected rate of return on an investment, over its lifetime, exceeds the social rate of return or the opportunity cost of capital (measures of the value of the investment to the economy as a whole, as described in chapter 6), to which the market rate of interest would be equal. But since capital markets in developing countries are far from perfect (see chapter 13), the market rate can exceed the social rate of return. If the rate of return on an investment is higher than the social rate but lower than the market rate of interest, tariff protection can be justified.

markets of the developed countries has been easy. Tariffs in the developed countries have declined significantly since World War II and now average only about 10 percent.[5] Opportunities for exporting, in other words, have been expanding rapidly, and countries like Hong Kong, South Korea, Singapore, and Taiwan have benefited greatly by taking advantage of them.

Several other objections to a trade-based strategy of growth and development remain to be discussed. One of these challenges the assumption that freer trade always brings about net welfare gains, and notes that even when it does, some groups in society may suffer permanent losses. A movement toward freer trade, of course, has two opposing effects within a country. Exports of some products will expand, but other industries will be forced out of existence by competition from imports. The comparative advantage model shows, though, that labor will shift out of declining industries into export industries. It also points out that the net gains from trade make it theoretically possible for the winners to fully compensate the losers and still have a net increase in welfare. As far as the model is concerned, nothing more need be said. Reality, however, can be very different. For example, textile and shoe workers in the United States could not easily find jobs in industries with export potential; they lack the necessary skills, and retraining (and probably also relocation) would be expensive. In the Andean countries of South America, free trade in grains would deprive tens of thousands of poor, illiterate, Quechua-speaking farmers of their livelihood, and few alternative occupations would be available to them. Thus one may question the assumption that a movement toward freer trade will always result in net welfare gains. Even if there are net gains from trade, there is no guarantee that those who lose their jobs will in fact be compensated. Without serious attention to this problem, freer trade could very easily have the effect of widening inequalities in the distribution of income and wealth. In other words, it can result in growth without development.

Two other objections to a trade-based strategy of development— declining terms of trade for developing countries and export price instability—are important enough to warrant special attention. Let us look first at the terms-of-trade problem.

THE TERMS OF TRADE

One of the developing countries' major objections to the structure of international trade is what they perceive to be a long-run tendency for the

5. Much less has been done, though, to decrease the use of quotas and other non-tariff barriers to trade.

terms of trade to turn against them. The terms of trade is an index relating a country's export prices to the prices it must pay for imports.[6] Symbolically, it may be written as $P_x/P_m \times 100$, where P_x and P_m are, respectively, a country's export and import price indices, having a common base year. It is the international equivalent of the "parity ratio" used to describe price relationships in U.S. agriculture. If export prices have increased relative to import prices, we say that the terms of trade have "improved"; if they experience a relative decline, we speak of a "deterioration."

Let us assume that export prices for Country A have risen by 150 percent from 1960 to 1975, while import prices have increased by 200 percent. Putting these data into price index form, we can show that the terms of trade have declined from 100 in the base year (1960) to 83 in 1975 (see Table 5.1).

The argument that the developing countries' terms of trade were destined to suffer a long-run decline was explained in detail in two influential articles published in 1950. The authors were Raúl Prebisch, an Argentine economist who was then Secretary General of the United Nations Economic Commission for Latin America, and Hans Singer, also of the United Nations (see the Suggested Readings at the end of this chapter). The Prebisch-Singer thesis is based on two major arguments. One involves differences between the "center" (developed countries) and "periphery" (developing countries) in the factors affecting the supply, demand, and price of labor. The other relates to differences between the developed and developing countries in supply and demand conditions for primary products and manufactured goods.

In the developing countries, it was argued, the supply of labor available for new jobs was abundant because of rapid population growth,

TABLE 5.1
The Terms of Trade: An Illustration

	Export Prices	Import Prices	Terms of Trade
1960	100	100	100*
1975	250	300	83*

$$*\frac{100}{100} = 1 \times 100 = 100; \quad \frac{250}{300} = .83 \times 100 = 83.$$

6. Actually, there are several different ways to measure the terms of trade. The index used in our example is referred to as the *commodity terms of trade* or *net barter terms of trade.*

labor-saving technological change in export activities, and restrictions in the developed countries on immigration from the developing countries. The demand for labor, meanwhile, was growing slowly because economic growth rates were low and little industrialization was occurring. These factors tended to keep wage rates (a major component of total production costs) near the subsistence level. Even if productivity increases in export commodities sometimes led to higher profits and wages, such increases were likely to be temporary since the competitive nature of primary product markets would force producers to pass the benefits of productivity increases on to consumers in the form of lower prices, not to owners and workers as higher profits and wages. The situation in the developed countries, on the other hand, was quite different. Labor there was relatively scarce, and it also had market power. Furthermore, labor was increasingly employed by large manufacturing firms which had the power to influence prices in product markets. Accordingly, there was a tendency in the developed countries for productivity gains to be passed on in the form of higher profits and wages, not lower prices. The prices of manufactured goods (developing country imports) thus rose relative to the price of primary products (developing country exports).

Supply and demand factors for these two types of goods also seemed to turn the terms of trade against the developing countries. Competition among the developing countries often led to overproduction of primary products, while demand for such products in the developed countries grew rather slowly because of low income elasticity of demand (YED)[7] for foodstuffs, the declining raw material content of finished products, and the substitution of synthetics—e.g., polyester fibers, nylon, and plastics—for such products as cotton, wool, rubber, and some metals. Meanwhile, demand by the developing countries for manufactured products tended to rise faster than their income (YED > 1). Since domestic investment in manufacturing was slow to develop, and foreign investors were interested in little besides primary product extraction, a large share of manufactured products had to be imported.

The Prebisch-Singer thesis has been subjected to considerable criticism. Prebisch supported his argument by reporting trends in the (reciprocal of the) British terms of trade from 1876 to 1938. These data suggest that the terms of trade for primary products suffered a decline of 36 per-

7. Income elasticity demand (YED) is the percentage change in quantity demanded divided by the percentage change in income. If, for any given product, the quantity demanded grows more slowly than income, we say that demand is *inelastic*, and YED is less than 1.0. For example, if the quantity of coffee demanded increases by only 2.5 percent when aggregate income rises by 5 percent, then YED = 2.5/5.0 = 0.5. When quantity demanded grows faster than income, YED >1 and demand is said to be *elastic*.

cent over this period. But the British data are not necessarily representative of trends in developed countries generally. The data are also distorted by the failure to consider the effects of declining transport costs.[8] Moreover, the time span ends in the middle of an unprecedented depression, when primary product prices dropped precipitously—but temporarily. (Extending the analysis by ten years would have radically altered the picture.) It has also been pointed out that quality improvements occurred in manufactured goods, and new and highly beneficial products were developed over this period (automobiles, radios, antibiotics), while there was little difference between an 1876 banana and a 1938 banana. Another problem is that many primary product imports came not from developing countries but from other developed countries. These and other criticisms are well taken. On the other hand, it is difficult to escape the conclusion that for some countries and for some products, price trends have been adverse for long periods of time.

In the first two decades after World War II, whether or not the terms of trade actually had been declining over the long run was irrelevant from a policy standpoint. What was important was that many governments in the developing countries believed that the terms of trade were deteriorating for them, and they sought to reduce their dependence on primary product exports by following a strategy of import-substituting industrialization. As we shall see in chapter 10, this strategy was not always successful in achieving greater economic independence.

Recent trends in the terms of trade are shown in Table 5.2, which presents data for the period 1953 to 1974. Immediately prior to this period, primary product prices generally had been rising because of the demand increases resulting from the post-World War II recovery in Europe and the so-called "Korean War boom" in the United States. Primary product prices continued to increase in 1954 but then began a relatively slow decline that lasted until the early 1960s. The total decline over the period was 13 percent, relatively modest in comparison with those experienced on some occasions during the period reviewed by Prebisch.[9] From the early 1960s to the early 1970s, the terms of trade for developing

8. Transportation costs as a percentage of export values fell considerably during this period. Since the British import price figures (assumed to represent developing countries' export prices) were reported on a CIF basis (cost + insurance + freight), a decline in transport costs will be incorrectly equated with falling primary product prices. Meanwhile, British export prices (assumed to represent developing countries' import prices) were reported on an FOB basis (free on board), and thus declining transport costs for developing countries' imports were not taken into account. See P. T. Ellsworth, "The Terms of Trade Between Primary Producing and Industrial Countries," *Inter-American Economic Affairs*, 10 (Summer 1956), 47–65.

9. See Ellsworth, op cit., Table 1, p. 50.

TABLE 5.2
Commodity Terms of Trade, Developing and
Developed Market Economies, 1953–1974[a]
(1970 = 100)

Year	Developing Market Economies	Developed Market Economies
1953	105	91
1954	111	89
1955	110	89
1956	106	90
1957	102	89
1958	102	93
1959	101	95
1960	101	96
1961	99	97
1962	97	98
1963	99	97
1964	100	98
1965	99	98
1966	100	98
1967	99	99
1968	100	99
1969	101	99
1970	100	100
1971	101	99
1972	101	100
1973	111	99
1974	156	87

Source: United Nations, *Yearbook of International Trade Statistics,* 1964, 1974, and 1975.

[a] Based on a linking of indices from the source volumes, where the base years used are 1958, 1963, and 1970, respectively.

countries as a group was remarkably stable. Then from 1972 to 1974 they suddenly rose by 55 percent.

Aggregate data like these, of course, hide a great deal. First, the significant improvement between 1972 and 1974 is attributable largely to the sharp increase in petroleum prices that occurred at that time. Second, these data fail to show sharp fluctuations or long-term declines in the terms of trade for individual countries. Table 5.3 presents some examples to illustrate this point. Note particularly the sharp swings in the Philippines and the long-term deterioration of 63 percent in Sri Lanka between 1958 and 1975. Other things equal, developing countries importing significant quantities of petroleum suffered a sharp deterioration in their terms of trade after 1973.

TABLE 5.3
Commodity Terms of Trade, Selected Developing Countries,
1958, 1963, and 1968–1975
(1970 = 100)

Year	Brazil	Kenya	Panama	Philippines	Sri Lanka	Thailand
1958	115	107	74	101	146	90
1963	80	103	64	92	122	97
1968	86	94	101	94	110	108
1969	90	91	100	94	103	114
1970	100	100	100	100	100	100
1971	93	88	99	85	93	91
1972	98	88	99	71	88	90
1973	108	86	97	101	78	117
1974	93	75	80	97	69	101
1975	86	73	72	65	55	91

Source: United Nations, *Statistical Yearbook,* 1976.

EXPORT PRICE INSTABILITY

Even if the terms of trade are not deteriorating for the developing countries in the long run, the fact that primary products are subject to much sharper price fluctuations than manufactured goods is cause for concern. Particularly if a developing country is heavily dependent on one or two primary exports (see Table 5.4 for data on export concentration in Latin American and Caribbean countries), its foreign exchange availabilities from year to year will be uncertain, and this can have adverse effects on its industrialization efforts. One of the classic examples is that of Colombia, which in the early 1950s was dependent on coffee for about 80 percent of its export earnings. Favorable trends in coffee prices after World War II had provided rapidly rising foreign exchange earnings which were used to import raw materials, intermediate goods, and capital goods for manufacturing and for the expansion of transport systems and utilities. GNP per capita increased by almost 4 percent annually from 1945 to 1954. But then the coffee price situation suddenly changed; from an average of nearly 80 cents a pound in 1954, prices fell to 45 cents by the end of 1958. Some industrial projects under construction could not be completed because foreign exchange had to be rationed, and already built factories operated at less than full capacity because of the restrictions on the importation of raw materials and intermediate products. Output grew much more slowly than in the years prior to 1954.

Until the 1960s there were few efforts to study systematically the effects of primary product price instability on long-run economic growth. While there is little doubt that falling prices could slow economic growth

TABLE 5.4

Export Concentration in Latin American and Caribbean Countries, 1975

Country	Major Export, 1975	Major Export, 1975, as a Percentage of Total Exports
Argentina	corn	17
Bolivia	tin	39
Brazil	soybeans	15
Chile	copper	57
Colombia	coffee	46
Costa Rica	bananas	29
Cuba	sugar	>75
Dominican Republic	sugar	65
Ecuador	petroleum	57
El Salvador	coffee	33
Guatemala	coffee	26
Haiti	coffee	26
Honduras	bananas	21
Jamaica	alumina	49
Mexico	petroleum	16
Nicaragua	cotton	25
Panama	refined petroleum	45
Paraguay	meat	18
Peru	sugar	22
Trinidad & Tobago	petroleum	88
Uruguay	wool	23
Venezuela	petroleum	95

Sources: International Monetary Fund, International Financial Statistics, and, for Cuba, Fidel Castro, "El desarrollo económico de Cuba (1959–1975)," Comercio Exterior (México), 26 (January 1976), 88–89.

in the short run, it seems possible that these negative effects might be offset by positive effects during periods of rapidly rising prices. Several studies during the 1960s, notably that of Alasdair MacBean (1966), suggested that this was in essence the case for developing countries as a group, even though examples could be found of countries whose long-run growth was affected adversely by export price instability. MacBean concluded that export instability in the developing countries differed little from that in the developed countries. Moreover, he found that instability was attributable not only to price changes but also to fluctuations in export volume. No relationship was found between export instability and economic growth. Subsequent research on export instability—some of which has criticized MacBean's methodology—has been conflicting, with some economists supporting his conclusions but others finding contrary results. Most studies show that export instability is indeed greater in the developing countries, but there is less of a consensus that it affects long-run growth adversely. There is general agreement that the degree of instability for both developed and developing countries declined between the 1950s and the 1960s. Most research has concluded that export concentration does not significantly affect the stability of export earnings.[10]

More research is needed on the instability issue before it can be considered settled. Meanwhile, few economists would deny that export instability has been harmful to growth in some countries. Policy makers in developing countries continue to feel strongly that export instability is undesirable, and several of the trade reforms they have been seeking are designed to stabilize either export prices or foreign exchange availability (see chapter 15).

THEORIES OF EXTERNAL DEPENDENCE

An influential group of writers has attributed the slowness of economic growth and development in the developing countries to their dependent relationships with the developed countries. International trade patterns are said to play a major role in determining these relationships. The dependency literature, already discussed briefly in chapters 1 and 3, is based mainly on the Latin American experience, and it has been clearly identifiable as a mode of analysis (in English, at any rate) only since the mid-1960s. It has roots not only in the Prebisch-Singer thesis but also in Marx, who did not discuss the subject in much detail, and in the more developed theories of imperialism of Lenin, Rosa Luxemburg, and J. A. Hobson.

One should be careful, however, in pinning labels on the dependency theorists. While some, like André Gunder Frank (1969), consider themselves Marxist revolutionaries, others, including Celso Furtado (1964) and Osvaldo Sunkel (1969), cannot be neatly placed in any ideological boxes. Dependency theorists disagree on nonideological matters as well, but there are enough common bonds among them to assume for most purposes that there is an agreed-upon framework of analysis. Bath and James (1976: 5) identify the unifying elements as follows: (1) identification of underdevelopment with the expansion of industrial capitalist countries; (2) the view that development and underdevelopment are parts of a unified system; (3) the view that underdevelopment is a persistent,

---

10. For a review of a number of studies of export instability, see Leslie Stein, "Export Instability and Development: A Review of Some Recent Findings," *Banca Nazionale del Lavoro Quarterly Review*, No. 122 (September 1977), 279–290. A recent study of export concentration, not included in Stein's review, is Jerry L. Kingston, "Export Concentration and Export Performance in Developing Countries, 1954–67," *Journal of Development Studies*, 12 (July 1976), 311–319.

natural condition, not a temporary, precapitalist, stage; and (4) agreement that dependence affects internal politics, society and culture.[11]

The following definition of external dependence is representative:

> By dependence we mean a situation in which the economy of certain countries is conditioned by the development and expansion of another economy to which the former is subjected. The relation of interdependence between two or more economies, and between these and world trade, assumes the form of dependence when some countries (the dominant ones) can expand and be self-sustaining, while other countries (the dependent ones) can do this only as a reflection of that expansion, which can have either a positive or a negative effect on their immediate development.[12]

In many cases, this dependence resulted from political subjugation by empire-building colonial powers, which controlled overseas trade in their colonies and sometimes instituted slavery or serfdom there. Imperialism is viewed by Marxists as the last phase of capitalism, made necessary after capitalists had exhausted their opportunities to exploit domestic markets.[13] Note that dependency theory admits that economic growth can occur in a dependent economy. This growth is sometimes referred to as *dependent development*, but dependency theorists do not mean development in the sense that we have been using this term.

One does not have to accept the Marxist stage theory of history to recognize that imperialist policies limited both the scope and direction of economic growth in the developing countries. Specifically, it can be argued that the colonial powers often created what in chapter 1 was referred to as a dual economy: a "modern" sector producing primary products for export with relatively advanced technology, skilled labor, and a supporting cast of teachers, clerks, customs officials, and other white-collar workers; and a "traditional" sector, comprising the vast majority of the population, whose welfare was virtually ignored by the colonial powers because they could make no contribution to exports. Since the traditional sector was denied the ability to initiate development policies on its own, it remained in a state of underdevelopment. Even in the modern sector, opportunities for the indigenous population to advance

11. For another review of the dependency literature, see the chapter by Philip J. O'Brien in Oxall, Barnett, and Booth (1975), listed in the Suggested Readings for chapter 3.

12. Theotonio Dos Santos, "The Structure of Dependence," *American Economic Review, Papers and Proceedings,* 60 (May 1970), 231.

13. The term *exploitation* need not be thought of as a "buzzword." If we define it as the exercise of monopoly power, it has a well-understood analytical meaning in economics.

were limited by the colonial powers' policy of keeping top managerial and administrative positions in the hands of their own nationals. Educational systems were thus limited, providing only (1) the lower- and middle-level manpower needed for positions not reserved for foreigners and (2) opportunities for the domestic elites who were the colonialists' allies. Road and railway networks were designed to serve the modern sector, linking export-producing areas with seaports but not joining major population centers within the country in order to expand the market for domestic-consumption goods. Indeed, this market was considered unimportant, and little effort was made by the colonial powers to invest in domestic manufacturing enterprises, either to produce for the local market or to transform raw materials into finished or semifinished products for export. Industrial activity, rather, was retained as a prerogative of the colonial powers.

The developed countries sometimes were able to establish dependent relationships with developing countries without having to reduce them to the political status of colonies. The United States, for example, allied itself with elites in independent Latin American countries who benefited from the export of primary products: the term *banana republics* accurately describes the attitudes of many North Americans toward these countries: their job was to grow bananas (or sugar, as in Cuba and the Dominican Republic). Threats to these economic relationships were sometimes dealt with by dispatching the Marines to "maintain order." Often, however, regular supplies of military and economic assistance were sufficient to prevent significant changes in the status quo.

Not all dependency theorists accept the dual economy model. Frank (1969) says that he rejects it, and instead argues that capitalism created a worldwide hierarchical system under which the entire economy of a developing country is influenced by events in the developed world. Economic growth (not development) in a developing country may well be concentrated geographically, as in the dual economy model—e.g., São Paulo, Brazil—but this is said to make other regions of the country "internal colonial satellites," whose development possibilities are restricted by the demands of international capitalism and its domestic allies. Readers may be excused for failing to see how this theoretical framework really differs from that of the dual economy.

Some of the dependency theorists' arguments are drawn from Prebisch (1950) and Singer (1950), who pointed out that specialization in primary products limits the scope for technical progress in the developing countries because the industries supplying them with machinery and other inputs, and transforming their raw materials, are almost all in the developed countries. Thus the developing countries cannot easily develop a diversity of labor and managerial skills, making it difficult for them to initiate the production of manufactured goods in which they are potentially competitive.

Even when industrialization does occur in the developing countries, it is often dominated by foreign firms which "jump" tariff walls to compete in protected markets. These firms often charge high fees for technology transfer, and their actual profit rates are sometimes considerably higher than their book profits. This occurs because they pay artificially high prices for inputs imported directly from the parent company, which manipulates intrafirm prices to minimize worldwide tax obligations or maximize post-tax profits[14] (see chapter 14). Frank (1969) argues that industrial growth under these circumstances historically has been slower than during periods when developing countries had weaker ties with the developed countries (e.g., the two world wars and the Great Depression). This argument, however, is based on a selective interpretation of the facts. Moreover, Frank would have a difficult time explaining the rapid growth that occurred in the 1970s in many Latin American countries.

One of the more simplistic arguments made by some dependency theorists is that private foreign investment in the developing countries results in a net drain of their foreign exchange reserves. More is taken out in a given year as profit remittances, technology transfer fees, etc., than is brought in as new direct investment. There are at least two major flaws in this argument. First, profit remittances (and total profit rates) should be related to cumulative investment in the past, not to new invesment in the same year. Second, the argument ignores the contributions of foreign firms to export earnings, much of which would not have been realized without foreign investment and the technology associated with it.

A more valid objection to private foreign investment on balance-of-payments grounds is that a sudden decline in new foreign investment can make it difficult for a country to meet its foreign exchange obligations to foreign industrialists—and to public and private creditors—unless imports for its development program are curtailed. Why might foreign investment decline? Those who think in terms of conspiracies would argue that withholding foreign investment (and encouraging international lending agencies to curtail their lending) is a powerful tool that capitalists can use to bring recalcitrant governments of developing countries to heel —or to throw them out, as with the Allende government in Chile in the early 1970s. Conspiratorial behavior sometimes does occur, but much of the instability of new foreign investment can be explained in other ways. All we have to do is make the assumption that capitalist firms behave normally and cut back on investment whenever profit prospects decline,

14. Dos Santos (ibid., p. 232) refers to this as the *technological-industrial* stage of external dependence.

for whatever reason. In any event, foreign investment instability is similar in its effects to instability of export earnings, and dependency theorists are correct in saying that developing countries have had little control over fluctuations in either type of foreign exchange inflow. The implication is that these kinds of problems can be avoided if there is little or no foreign investment.

Dependency theorists may be criticized on several other grounds. For example, the dependence of Eastern European countries and Cuba on trade with the Soviet Union suggests that the real culprit may not be capitalism but rather the unequal distribution of political power. Also, most dependency theorists have not been very specific about alternatives to a strategy of development based on external dependence. If the term *dependence* is to have any analytical meaning, alternative strategies would seem to imply some form of autarky, which has obvious limitations particularly for small countries lacking industrial raw materials.

The presumption that dependence on foreign trade is bound to be inimical to development becomes difficult to support when we examine trade data for some of the wealthy European countries. With the exception of a few small nations in the Middle East, Sweden and Switzerland have the highest GNP per capita in the world; yet exports in 1972–1974 averaged 28 and 34 percent, respectively, of their GNP (compared with 7 percent in the United States). In the Netherlands (No. 11 in GNP per capita) the export share was 51 percent. These export shares are higher than one usually finds in the developing world, except in some of the petroleum-producing countries—and these particular examples do not help the dependency theorists' case.

These criticisms notwithstanding, dependency theories should not be dismissed as mere rhetoric presented by ideologues. Exploitation of the developing countries has been great on a number of occasions. Economic growth in Indonesia, for example, did little to benefit native Indonesians during the Dutch colonial period. And the foreign-dominated growth in Mexico under Porfirio Díaz (1876–1911) actually resulted in a decline in the living standards of the rural masses and helped lead to a revolution, at the cost of a prolonged civil war which began in 1910. A recent study shows no relationship between increases in GNP and increases in the export share of relatively poor developing countries.[15]

---

15. For eighteen developing countries with a per capita GNP of less than $300, the Spearman rank correlation coefficient was actually negative (-0.04), though statistically insignificant. On the other hand, for twenty-three countries with a per capita income of more than $300, growth in GNP was positively (.523) and significantly correlated with growth in the export share. See Michael Michaely, "Exports and Growth: An Empirical Investigation," *Journal of Development Economics,* 4 (March 1977), 49–53.

Finally, it should be pointed out that dependency analysis has made some major contributions to our understanding of how foreign trade and investment help determine patterns of political, social, and cultural behavior in developing countries, often in undesirable ways.

While it may be granted that dependence on foreign trade and investment can have strong negative effects, there are times when it appears to be very beneficial. Consider for example, where Libya, Saudi Arabia, and Venezuela would be today without foreign investment in petroleum.

SUMMARY

Unless a country has a sizable domestic market and a diversity of natural resources within its borders, a strategy of economic growth and development based on autarky will have serious limitations. International trade in geographically large and populous countries such as the United States, the Soviet Union, and China may constitute a relatively small percentage of the GNP, but each of these countries is still dependent on the outside world for certain productive factors deemed necessary to satisfy growth and development objectives. The latter two countries, in fact, have made no secret of their belief that rapidly increased trade can benefit them.

This does not mean, however, that international trade always increases a country's welfare. Nor does it mean that steps in the direction of self-sufficiency are always undesirable. Each proposal for import substitution should be decided on its own merits on the basis of a dynamic view of comparative advantage. Noneconomic criteria, such as satisfaction of nationalist sentiments, should also be important inputs in the decision-making process; but governments should be aware of the economic costs of meeting these kinds of objectives.

A good case can be made that international trade patterns have discriminated against the developing countries and have often widened inequalities in the distribution of income among nations. Before 1960, many developing countries reacted to this situation by attempting to become less dependent on trade; the results of these efforts, however, were generally disappointing. Since then, developing countries have emphasized international action which would increase the rate of growth of their export earnings and provide greater stability in foreign exchange availabilities. This strategy and its results will be the subject of chapter 15.

Suggested Readings

Bath, C. Richard, and Dilmus D. James. "Dependency Analysis of Latin America." *Latin American Research Review*, 11 (1976/3), 3–54.

The authors, a political scientist and an economist, identify common strands in the dependency literature; classify dependency theorists into "conservative," "moderate," and "radical" groups; critically evaluate the literature on the political as well as economic aspects of dependency relationships; and offer suggestions for strengthening the analytical tools used in dependency analysis. They argue that dependency theory would be improved if the approaches of political science and economics were better integrated.

Cohen, Benjamin. *The Question of Imperialism: The Political Economy of Dominance and Dependence.* New York: Basic Books, 1973.

This book critically examines a number of theories of imperialism, from early-twentieth-century works such as those of Hobson and Lenin to recent "neo-imperialist" theories which have sought to adapt Marxist thought to the contemporary environment. Marxist and neo-Marxist theories argue that the motives for imperialism are exclusively economic, or at least predominantly so. Cohen provides evidence challenging these theories' assertions that capitalism depends on imperialism for survival. He also outlines an alternative theory of imperialism based essentially on power politics, not economics.

Frank André Gunder. *Latin America: Underdevelopment or Revolution.* New York: Monthly Review Press, 1969.

One of the most influential of the dependency theorists, Frank writes from a Marxist perspective. He attributes underdevelopment to the "historical process of capitalist development."

Furtado, Celso. *Development and Underdevelopment.* Berkeley: University of California Press, 1964. (Original Portuguese edition, 1961.)

An insightful analysis of the nature of underdevelopment by a Brazilian economist who is one of the more moderate dependency theorists.

Kenen, Peter B., and Raymond Lubitz. *International Economics,* 3rd ed. Englewood Cliffs, N.J.: Prentice-Hall, Inc., 1971.

An excellent, concise (127-page) introduction to theory and policy in the fields of international trade and international finance.

MacBean, Alasdair J. *Export Instability and Economic Development.* Foreword by Edward S. Mason. Cambridge, Mass.: Harvard University Press, 1966.

MacBean's detailed research challenges the conventional wisdom that developing countries' export earnings are more unstable than those of developed countries. Subsequent researchers have both confirmed and questioned MacBean's findings, leaving this an unsettled issue. Undergraduates may have some trouble understanding the research methodology, but the five country case studies and the policy chapters present no great difficulty.

Prebisch, Raul. *The Economic Development of Latin America and Its Principal Problems.* New York: United Nations Economic Commission for Latin America, 1950. Reprinted in *Economic Bulletin for Latin America,* 7 (February 1962), 1–22.

This study argued both with theory and empirical evidence that the terms of trade were declining for developing countries. It had a strong influence on many Latin American (and other developing) countries, whose governments attempted to escape this form of external dependence through a strategy of import-substituting industrialization (see chapter 10).

Singer, Hans B. "The Distribution of Gains between Borrowing and Investing Countries." *American Economic Review*, 40 (May 1950), 473–485.

This article complements that by Prebisch, written at about the same time. Singer also argues that foreign investment in developing countries, by concentrating on primary product extraction, offers little scope for technical progress or for the external economies that result from the development of an industrial base.

Sunkel, Osvaldo. "National Development Policy and External Dependence in Latin America." *Journal of Development Studies*, 6 (October 1969), 23–48.

A short statement on dependency theory by perhaps its most capable exponent.

6

The Role of
Government
Social Overhead Capital

Even the most ardent advocates of free markets have always admitted that the provision of social overhead capital (SOC) is a legitimate role for government in the process of economic growth and development. Social overhead capital—or infrastructure, as it is sometimes called— may be defined as capital goods used directly or indirectly in the production of goods and services generally (i.e., not tied to the production of a specific good or service). Examples are roads and highways, railroads, communications networks, electric power systems, multiple-purpose river projects, and water and sewer systems. Capital spending on education and health has also been regarded as SOC, but it is useful to consider these activities separately, as we shall do in chapter 7.

Improved transportation and communications networks stimulate economic growth by making product and factor markets function more efficiently—or, in the case of a planned economy, by providing better and quicker information flows between various levels of the planning hierarchy. Labor and other factors of production become more mobile; farmers spend less time and money in marketing their produce and can choose from a wider range of potential buyers; and traditional obstacles to both growth and development are broken down as individuals and communities are more exposed to different ideas and institutions and become aware of possibilities for social change. The extent to which transportation and communications projects contribute to economic development is often difficult to determine. Some roads are built primarily to facilitate contact between mining companies or large plantations and the export markets for which they produce. A relatively small number of poor rural residents along these mine- or plantation-to-port roads may benefit from the transportation services provided, but the distribution of benefits may favor the wealthy overwhelmingly. On the other hand, roads which improve contacts between different regions of a country may have benefits that are widely distributed.[1]

The provision of electricity, potable water, and waste disposal systems can have an even greater impact on development than transportation and communications projects, for they not only facilitate agricultural, industrial, and other economic activity but also provide important direct consumption benefits. Public utilities traditionally have received relatively little attention in the literature on developing countries. But as economists increasingly are adopting a definition of development which emphasizes the provision of basic human needs (rather than income), more attention is being paid to these types of SOC projects and to the distribution of their benefits among urban and rural residents.

CHARACTERISTICS OF SOCIAL OVERHEAD CAPITAL

SOC has several characteristics which make government involvement necessary. First, these capital goods are to one degree or another "public goods," which means that consumers' preferences for them will not be revealed accurately through market processes. This is best illustrated by considering the extreme case of a "pure public good," which has two distinguishing characteristics: (1) if the good is available in the economy, no one can be effectively excluded from consuming it, and (2) one person's consumption leaves others no worse off. A classic example is national defense. If, for some reason, national defense were to be provided in the marketplace, the rational individual's *expressed* demand for it would be zero, even though he or she does in fact want this kind of protection. If the good were bought by others, no one could stop any individual from consuming it, and his or her consumption would not take away from the amount available for others. Also, the failure of just one individual to purchase national defense goods would have no effect on national security. If all individuals were rational, of course, no national defense at all would be provided in the marketplace. In other words, the market mechanism breaks down for pure (and impure) public goods, and the command mechanism must be used if the society's true demands are to be met.

---

1. This will not always be the case. For example, in areas where small farmers do not have secure land tenure, they may be evicted by more powerful individuals wishing to profit from the rising land values and greater market opportunities resulting from road construction.

None of the examples of SOC given above could be termed a "pure" public good, but each is a public good to some extent. Most if not all residents of a country will benefit from such things as better sanitation, a more highly skilled labor force, and lower transportation costs for food, even if they make no payments for the SOC benefiting them. These capital goods could be provided through the marketplace, but the amounts so provided would be far less than actual demand for them. Public financing, through the tax mechanism, is thus justified.

Another characteristic of some (but not all) SOC is that it is "lumpy"; that is, if the project is to be economically justifiable, it must be a large one. As one writer has said, there is no such thing as half a transcontinental railroad. The purpose of such a project is to link two major market areas, and going from New York to San Francisco in stages makes no sense if Stage 1 ends in the middle of the Nebraska sandhills pending the mobilization of additional funds to bring the line out to the Utah desert, with completion of the project requiring twenty-five years. Similarly, a dam must go all the way across a river; going one-eighth of the way across is useless. Vast projects like these require the mobilization of substantial sums of money, something very difficult to do in the private sector if financial markets are weak.

Even if such large sums could be mobilized, private investors would be reluctant to put their funds into SOC projects whose payoff period is very long and whose benefits go in large part to "free riders" whom it would be almost impossible to charge. While there may be a high social rate of return on such investments—i.e., the rate of return for the economy as a whole—the private rate may be low or even negative.

Perhaps the best way to illustrate the importance of government in providing SOC is to review its role in the early stages of development in the United States, a country in which "free enterprise" is erroneously believed by some to have reigned supreme during the nineteenth century. A close examination of United States history reveals that government played a major role in the country's development well before the 1930s. The following are only some of the many examples that could be cited:

1. Construction of the National Road from Cumberland, Maryland, to Vandalia, Illinois, to facilitate westward expansion.
2. Land grants to private companies to build railroads which otherwise would not have been built.
3. Floating of bond issues by state governments to finance the construction of canals.
4. Provision of free public education.
5. Establishment of the land-grant colleges and universities, which among other things conducted agricultural research and provided technical assistance at no direct cost to farmers.

When examples such as these are combined with other government activities such as passage of the Homestead Acts and tariff protection to industry, it becomes quite clear that government in the United States was far from being a passive part of the nineteenth-century economic environment.

FINANCING SOCIAL OVERHEAD CAPITAL PROJECTS

Investment in SOC constitutes a relatively high share of the budgets of most developing countries. SOC projects often require heavy expenditures on imports—e.g., for road machinery, electric generators, structural steel, and cement—and this is one reason why much of the investment in SOC is financed by foreign exchange borrowed from international lending agencies. The long payoff period for SOC investments is another reason why developing countries seek international financial assistance.

The principal source of loan funds for SOC is the World Bank (formally the International Bank for Reconstruction and Development, or IBRD) and its affiliate, the International Development Association (IDA). During fiscal years 1974–1976, the IBRD-IDA lent an average of more than $2,500 million annually for SOC projects, distributed as follows (millions of dollars):

Education	$ 232.7
Electric power	740.8
Telecommunications	123.7
Transportation	1,105.3
Water supply and sewerage	217.8
Other urban infrastructure	95.2
TOTAL	$2,515.5

In addition, a substantial (but difficult to determine) percentage of IBRD-IDA lending for agriculture was destined for the construction of irrigation and other rural infrastructure facilities. In summary, more than half the IBRD-IDA loan commitments during 1974–1976 (which averaged $5,614 million a year) were made for SOC projects.

Other major sources of international assistance for SOC projects include the U.S. Agency for International Development (AID) and, in Latin America, the Inter-American Development Bank (IDB). In addition, developing countries sometimes finance SOC projects by borrowing from private banks or by obtaining suppliers' credits from the firms selling the items they are importing. Interest rates on these private loans and credits are almost always higher than those charged by public international development agencies, and repayment periods are not as long. But private financing is sometimes attractive for developing country governments if a project is considered to be of high priority by the country but not by the public lending agencies. Frequently—but by no means always —privately financed projects are of dubious economic merit and are undertaken to achieve political objectives. Sometimes they are undertaken simply because there are opportunities for developing country officials to receive kickbacks. Lest anyone construe these remarks as condescending toward developing countries, this writer hastens to point out that these same motives sometimes determine the decisions to undertake SOC projects in the United States and other developed countries.

TRANSPORTATION

An exchange economy is possible only if a community has access to goods and services from other communities. The better a country's transport system, the greater is the scope for internal specialization and division of labor, and the lower is the retail price of food and other items produced for the domestic market.

Transportation costs are also crucial for determining the ability of a country to sell primary products in world markets. It is not unusual for these costs to account for as much as 50 percent of the receipts from export sales (IBRD, 1972: 144), and if the market for a particular export commodity is reasonably competitive, a country with high transport costs can enter that market only if production costs are relatively low. Landlocked countries are at a particular disadvantage, especially if lack of direct access to the sea is compounded by great distances from major markets and geographic barriers such as mountain ranges.[2] A good example is Bolivia, whose extensive subtropical and tropical eastern lowlands have excellent agricultural potential for a variety of crops. To get products to Peruvian or Chilean ports to the west, the formidable Andes mountains must be crossed by truck and products then transferred to rail lines. The high transport costs severely limit export possibilities via this route. To the east, potentially important markets in Argentina and Brazil are far away. The recent completion of rail links with these countries, however, has enabled some of this potential to be realized. Even so, Bolivia will continue to be at a competitive disdvantage in the North American and European markets. Fortunately, the country also produces

2. Of the twenty-five least developed countries in the world in March 1975, fourteen were landlocked. See Martin Ira Glassner, "Land-Locked Nations and Development," *International Development Review*, 19, No. 2 (1977), 19–23.

petroleum, tin, and other minerals for which world markets are less competitive. Moreover, most of the minerals are found in the highlands, and rail lines to the Pacific coast only have to go down the Andes—not up and then down.

The demand for transport services is a derived demand, determined by the demand for the commodities transported and for personal travel. Since transport costs are usually a much higher proportion of final product prices in developing countries than in developed countries, the price elasticity of demand of the former tends to be higher. In other words, a 25 percent reduction in transport costs is likely to have a much greater effect on transport demand in a developing country, because the effect on final product prices will be proportionately greater. Table 6.1 illustrates this point. In our hypothetical example, a 25 percent reduction in transport costs lowers final product prices by 8 percent in the developing country, compared with only 2 percent in the developed country.

Investment in transportation, of course, does not automatically bring forth large increases in the production of goods and services. The areas opened up by new transport facilities must have something to offer in the way of productive resources, and other government support, such as agricultural credit and favorable agricultural price policies, is also necessary (Wilson et al., 1966). Investment in transport frequently is delayed until bottlenecks become obvious. This is a "safe" investment strategy, which the World Bank (1972: 146) admits it usually follows; but the Bank also admits that it is dealing with a "chicken-and-egg" situation in which "promotional transportation investments can be the agent of important economic developments." Supporting government services are particularly important when transportation investments are made to stimulate economic growth rather than to respond to it.

Geographers identify five modes of transport—roads, railways, waterways, airways, and pipelines. Road and rail facilities are by far the most

TABLE 6.1
Transport Cost Reductions and Final Price:
A Hypothetical Example

	Initial Assumptions			25% Transport Cost Reduction		
	Final Product Price	Transport Cost Component	Other Costs	Final Product Price	Transport Cost Component	Other Costs
Developed Country	100	8	92	98	6	92
Developing Country	100	32	68	92	24	68

important types of SOC in the transport sector of most economies. It is useful to comment briefly on these two modes of transport.

Railroads

Students of United States history are well aware of the importance of railroads in the country's economic growth, even before the construction of rail lines to the Pacific coast. In the view of economic historian W. W. Rostow (1960), the railroad was the "leading sector" in the economic "takeoff" of not just the United States but also of Canada, France, Germany, and Russia. Even those who question Rostow's theory of the takeoff[3] cannot deny that the railroad was an important stimulus to economic growth in the developed countries during the nineteenth century.

Railroads also have a long history in many developing countries, though in the nineteenth and early twentieth centuries their role often was limited to the transportation of agricultural and mineral products to seaports for export to Europe and North America. Countries purchasing these raw materials typically provided the financial resources to build the railroads and the other SOC associated with them. Under these circumstances, the linkage effects of the railroads with the rest of the economy were quite weak.

During the twentieth century, railroads in general have found it increasingly difficult to compete with road transport by truck, which provides greater flexibility and is directly accessible to a larger number of persons engaged in farming, commerce, and industry. While 52 percent of the World Bank's transport loans through 1956 were for railroad construction, the corresponding figure for 1967–1971 was a much lower 29 percent (IBRD, 1972: 152–153). Nevertheless, railroads still tend to be more efficient than road transport for moving large volumes of relatively low-value cargo over long distances.

---

3. By the *takeoff*, Rostow means a sudden acceleration in the rate of economic growth; the savings/investment rate rises significantly over a period of about two decades, and growth thus becomes self-sustaining. Rostow's theory of the takeoff stimulated a vast quantity of critical and supporting literature during the 1960s. Most historical evidence suggests that increases in the rate of growth occurred more gradually than Rostow's data suggested. The concept of a *leading sector* may also be questioned, since one can easily build a case for leading sectors other than the ones indentified by Rostow (e.g., ocean transport rather than cotton textiles in Great Britain, agriculture rather than railroads in the United States). The importance of a leading sector, in Rostow's view, is that it has powerful *backward and forward linkages*, to use Hirschman's (1958) terminology. In the case of the railroad, the backward linkages are to the coal, iron, and engineering industries, which provide inputs to railway construction, while the forward linkages are to those industries whose growth is stimulated by the availability of rail transport services.

Roads and Highways

While the importance of railroads in World Bank transport-sector lending was declining, the share of roads and highways rose dramatically from 24 percent during 1945–1956 to 60 percent during 1967–1971. This surge in road and highway construction is to a large extent a reaction to the neglect of roads—particularly in rural areas—during the colonial period. This does not mean that road construction is the "key" to late-twentieth-century economic growth and development. As we noted above, the expansion of economic activity in regions served by new transportation facilties also depends on complementary government action to encourage investment in agriculture, industry, and other economic activities.

A country's road transport network consists of *primary* roads (highways) connecting major urban centers; *secondary* roads tying smaller urban areas to the primary road network; and *farm-to-market* (access) roads giving farmers direct access to this mode of transportation. Depending on the circumstances, major emphasis in road construction might best be placed on access roads rather than an expansion of the primary or secondary road network. Determination of priorities requires a careful evaluation of the various alternatives, using the project evaluation techniques to be described later in this chapter.

The development of truck transport has provided good evidence that latent entrepreneurial skills do indeed exist in developing countries and will become manifest when opportunities to exercise them become available. Particularly in the poorer developing countries, trucking tends to be a highly competitive activity, with most operators owning just one or a few trucks. National railway systems, by contrast, tend to be monopolistic entities saddled with bureaucratic and political problems. In an interesting account of road-versus-rail transport in Nigeria, Hirschman (1967: 139–148) shows how problems of tribalism, corruption, and managerial inefficiency plagued the railroads much more than trucking, where individual entrepreneurs were more easily able to accommodate these characteristics of Nigerian society.

One of the major problems of road projects in developing countries has been poor maintenance. In some countries, roads have deteriorated rapidly either because contractors have not built according to specifications or because truckers have overloaded their vehicles and have the political power to prevent effective enforcement of weight regulations. Government officials often find it difficult to understand the economic value of proper road maintenance, and international agencies, despite strong efforts, have had only a mixed record in improving maintenance practices.

TELECOMMUNICATIONS[4]

The basic telecommunications facility is the public telephone network, though telegraph and postal services are also of major importance in South Asia and Africa. Relatively minor investment in additional equipment enables the telephone network to provide services such as telegraph and telex facilities and radio and television transmission.

There is strong demand for telecommunications services in most developing countries, as measured by the backlog of requests for telephone connections. New subscribers in some countries must sometimes wait several years to obtain service. The World Bank reports that the return on investment to expand the telecommunications network sometimes is close to 50 percent. It is nevertheless difficult to determine the contribution of telecommunications to economic growth. While the services provided clearly improve the operation of product and factor markets, by facilitating contacts between buyers and sellers, they often serve final consumption purposes rather than investment purposes. Determining the marginal productivity of investment in telecommunications, compared with other types of SOC, is thus difficult.

Investment in telecommunications typically accounts for a modest 3 percent of total public-sector investment. But there is great potential for growth. In 1970 there was only 1 telephone per 100 persons in developing countries, compared with 18 per 100 in Western Europe and 55 per 100 in North America. There is also room for considerable improvement in the quality of service in many developing countries. This will require replacement of obsolete equipment with new facilities and an upgrading of management capabilities. In some countries, telecommunications service has been so poor that governmental and industrial groups have established their own private systems. The unit cost of such systems is much higher than that of an efficiently operated public system.

ELECTRIC POWER[5]

Electric power accounts for perhaps 15 percent of public-sector investment in developing countries, and in the early 1970s investment in power facilities was reported to be increasing by 10 percent annually (IBRD, 1972: 221).

Shortages of electric power can be a bottleneck to a country's industrial development. Firms with prospects for high profit rates and access

4. Most of the information on telecommunications is drawn from IBRD (1972: 195–214).

5. Most of the information on electric power is drawn from IBRD (1972: 215–238).

to suppliers' credits can overcome this obstacle by importing their own generators; but the electricity so supplied (and hence the cost of their products, to the extent that they have market power) will be costlier than that which could be supplied by a large public power facility. Smaller firms may lack the credit to pursue this option, and the formation of new firms may be discouraged if an assured power supply from a public facility is not available.

Public-sector electric power projects can be quite costly. During 1967–1971, the average World Bank power loan was $20 million. This figure excludes additional contributions to the same projects by other international agencies as well as contributions by the host government. International financial assistance is usually necessary for power projects, not just because of their high cost and long payoff period but also because a high proportion of project inputs must be imported (about 50 percent of the value of hydroelectric plants, plus a high percentage of the cost of transmission and distribution equipment). Foreign lending agencies usually provide funds for the foreign exchange component of a project, while the recipient country is expected to provide most if not all of the resources for local currency expenses. Projects are sometimes delayed for several years because the recipient country finds it difficult to meet its financial commitments.

Another reason why construction of power facilities may be delayed is that governments of developing countries are reluctant to raise power consumption charges so that a project is self-financing—i.e., generates sufficient revenues of its own to repay the loan without recourse to general budget revenues. Even more than in the United States, raising utility rates in developing countries provokes a negative public reaction, and a government whose political power base is weak finds it politically risky to authorize rate increases. International lending agencies, on the other hand, want to be assured that a project is financially viable. This writer is aware of one loan which was delayed for four years because of a stalemate over rate increases.

Electric power facilities in developing countries are highly concentrated in urban areas, but electricity is increasingly being spread to the countryside. Still, most rural residents in developing countries do not have access to electric power. This not only deprives them of a consumer service that is an important component of welfare but also limits the scope for the development of agriculture and small rural industries. Measuring the benefits of electricity in rural areas is more difficult than in urban areas. To the extent that rural electrification permits the establishment of small-scale industrial enterprises and provides power for irrigation pumps, one should consider not only the direct benefits but also the secondary and indirect benefits (i.e., the multiplier effects of these investments). In addition, the significant social (and political) benefits of rural electrification should be taken into account. It has even been claimed (without much supporting evidence) that electrification lowers birth rates by providing alternative nighttime activities. One of the major problems with rural electrification has been that low-density loads make financial returns low, even when rates are comparable to those in the cities. But if the social rate of return is as high as some observers believe, subsidies to the operating entities can be justified.

DETERMINING INVESTMENT PRIORITIES

If some economists had their way, investment priorities would be determined simply by ranking projects according to their *benefit-cost ratios* or *internal rates of return* (explained below). SOC projects would be compared not only with each other but also with directly productive activity (DPA) projects in agriculture and industry. However, this approach is too simplistic, both for theoretical reasons and also because it ignores valid noneconomic criteria which public decision makers must take into account.

The Interdependence of DPA and SOC

On theoretical grounds, a simple ranking of SOC and DPA projects ignores the fact that these two types of investment are interdependent. SOC projects will not have favorable benefit-cost ratios or internal rates of return (or, in the language of chapter 2, low marginal capital-output ratios) unless complementary DPA projects are also undertaken. SOC which has a high rate of unused capacity is not productive capital. Obviously, if SOC is abundant, there will be incentives for DPA projects to be established. But we should remember that markets in developing countries are imperfect, and government action may be essential for stimulating investment in DPA projects. Such action could include the provision of medium- and long-term credit through public development banks; assistance in identifying domestic and overseas markets; and vocational, technical, and on-the-job training programs to provide skilled labor to industry and agriculture.[6] In some cases, governments may wish to make their own DPA investments.

Because SOC and DPA projects are interdependent, it is impossible

---

6. A case can also be made, under certain circumstances, for a development strategy based on deliberate SOC *shortages*. See Hirschman (1958: Ch. 5) for an excellent discussion of this strategy and of the relationship between SOC and DPA generally.

to determine the productivity of one type of investment unless assumptions are made about the availability of the other.[7] This is very difficult to do when all new investment possibilities are considered simultaneously —something that is rarely if ever done because of the manpower and financial burdens this would impose. In practice, investment projects tend to be considered individually, based on rough calculations that they are likely to be economically feasible or politically desirable. To the extent that only "pure economic" criteria are involved, the decision to go ahead with the project or not is based on whether the expected internal rate of return (IRR) or benefit-cost ratio (B/C) is favorable.

Benefit-Cost Ratios

Since social overhead capital projects benefit society as a whole, their economic evaluation differs from project evaluation in a private enterprise, where managers are interested in the expected *financial* rates of return to a proposed new investment. A profit-maximizing firm has little if any interest in external costs and benefits; and noncash costs and benefits, while sometimes important to a firm, frequently are ignored.[8] Social benefit-cost analysis, however, must take these matters into account. Needless to say, this is no easy matter.

Benefit-cost (B/C) analysis involves a comparison between the discounted present value of the future expected project benefits and the discounted present value of costs during the project's lifetime.[9] In symbolic terms, B and C, are defined as follows:

$$B = \frac{b_1}{(1+r)} + \frac{b_2}{(1+r)^2} + \cdots + \frac{b_n}{(1+r)^n}$$

$$C = \frac{c_1}{(1+r)} + \frac{c_2}{(1+r)^2} + \cdots + \frac{c_n}{(1+r)^n}$$

7. One of the arguments for a big push investment strategy (see chapter 2) is that the simultaneous promotion of SOC and DPA activities will ensure that there is a high rate of utilization of new SOC capacity.

8. A frequently used illustration of external costs is the case of a profit-maximizing firm dumping its waste materials into a river. This type of waste disposal is chosen simply because it is the least expensive method. The additional costs of water purification are borne by downstream users. An example of an external benefit would be an increase in land values if a particularly desirable firm moves into a community. Noncash costs or benefits can arise if a change in the work environment affects worker productivity.

9. Alternatively, B/C ratios may be computed by comparing the present value of net benefits with the present value of capital costs plus operation and maintenance costs.

where B = present value of gross benefits
C = present value of gross costs
b = gross benefits in years $1, 2, \ldots, n$
c = gross costs in years $1, 2, \ldots, n$
r = social rate of discount (e.g., .10)

If $B/C > 1.00$, a project is considered to be economically justified, though it might not be undertaken if alternative projects have higher ratios. If $B/C < 1.00$, the investment is not fully recovered, and it can be justified only if noneconomic factors are taken into account (see below).

Benefit-cost ratios are very sensitive to the discount rate used in the analysis. A private firm would want to use the cost of borrowing money,[10] but in social benefit-cost analysis it is more appropriate to use an estimate of (1) the society's "social rate of discount" or (2) the opportunity cost of capital. The social rate of discount is a measure of the society's preference for present goods over future goods. The stronger is the preference for present goods, the greater is the social rate of discount—i.e., the "reward" consumers would have to be offered to forego consumption and save instead. In developing countries, interest paid on savings accounts is not necessarily a good indication of the social rate of discount, since interest rates are often subject to government regulation and capital markets are imperfect in other ways. Moreover, we would know little about the time preferences of the great majority of the population who have no institutional savings. The opportunity cost of capital—a measure of alternative production foregone—is likewise difficult to measure. In developing countries, it is usually assumed to be between 8 and 15 percent (Gittinger, 1972: 61).

The choice of discount rate is extremely important in determining the economic viability of SOC projects. The lower the discount rate, the higher the present value of future benefits. This is particularly relevant for multiple-purpose river development projects, where most of the benefits are delayed for a number of years from the time construction begins. The U.S. Army Corps of Engineers has been criticized for using interest rates that are below the opportunity cost of capital in order to justify projects which are of dubious economic merit. The same thing has sometimes occurred in developing countries.

Other games, too, can be played with B/C analysis. In developed countries, recreational benefits of multiple-purpose river development projects are often exaggerated because of a failure to subtract recreational losses to other areas as vacationers are diverted away from those areas

10. Actually, private firms rarely use B/C analysis; instead, they rely on IRR or other discounted cash flow measures. In most cases, B/C ratios are used in evaluating water resource projects (Gittinger, 1972: 60).

to the new project area. Only the net increase in recreational benefits should really be counted. Analysis of land settlement projects sometimes fails to consider possible declines in output in the areas from which the settlers have come. If a little imagination is used in choosing assumptions, many projects of dubious economic viability can be made to look good.

Internal Rates of Return

Internal rate of return (IRR) analysis is generally preferred to B/C analysis by the World Bank and other international financial institutions. The internal rate of return is simply the discount rate which makes the present value of a project's *cash flow* equal to zero. The cash flow in this sense differs from the definition used in financial analysis by including, for the life of the project, all true costs and benefits, whether or not a cash payment or receipt takes place and regardless of the method of financing. Unpaid labor, for example, is a true cost of production in public works projects, and some means has to be found to impute its value (see below). If the internal rate of return exceeds the opportunity cost of capital, the project is deemed worthy of financing; if not, it is rejected—at least on purely economic grounds.

In symbolic terms, the IRR is computed as follows:

$$NPV = 0 = \frac{B^*_1}{(1+r)} + \frac{B^*_2}{(1+r)^2} + \cdots + \frac{B^*_n}{(1+r)^n}$$

where NPV = net present value
B^* = net benefits
r = internal rate of return (e.g., .20)
$1, 2, \ldots n$ = years (n is the length in years of the project's life)

Net benefits (B^*), which typically are negative in the early (construction) years, are determined by subtracting project costs from project benefits in each year. If the project replaces an existing facility (or if we are comparing, say, agricultural production with and without an irrigation system), annual benefits and costs are both expressed on a net basis —i.e., benefits without the project are subtracted from benefits with the project, and the same is done with costs. Calculation of the IRR involves some trial and error work, but the availability of present value tables makes this a relatively easy task.

Shadow Prices

In financial analysis, benefits and costs are valued at market prices. Taxes are treated like any other cash flows. To economists, however, subsidies and taxes distort the allocation of resources. Economic analysis of projects —i.e., calculation of social IRRs or B/C ratios—thus considers subsidies and taxes as transfer payments. It also calls for adjustments when costs and benefits do not accurately reflect scarcity values. These adjustments involve the substitution of *shadow prices* for market prices.

Since most factor and product markets in developing countries are imperfect, it is tempting to use shadow prices for almost all cost and benefit items. This, however, is very risky, since it is not always clear what a competitive market price might be. One suggestion for dealing with this problem is to use world market prices as shadow prices (Little and Mirrlees, 1974). This procedure is easier to defend for industrial projects than for SOC projects. In the former case, the output at least is usually a product which could have been imported rather than produced domestically, and its economic value can be regarded as no higher than the import price of the commodity (excluding tariffs and other distortions). In the case of highways, dams, and most other SOC, however, we are dealing with products that do not enter into world trade. With regard to inputs, both SOC and DPA projects use relatively unskilled labor and other services that are always purchased locally rather than imported; in other words, there is no world market price.

Given these difficulties, it is advisable to be cautious in the use of shadow prices. For SOC projects, they are most appropriately used under the following circumstances:

1. Exchange rates in developing countries are frequently overvalued —e.g., the official exchange rate may be 40 pesos (P40) to the dollar, while in a free foreign exchange market the rate would likely be P50 = $1. An overvalued exchange rate artificially encourages imports; in our example, the importer has to give up only P40,000, instead of P50,000 for a $1,000 piece of equipment. If there is good reason to believe that the exchange rate is overvalued, a *shadow exchange rate*, reflecting what is believed to be the currency's free-market value, may be substituted for the official exchange rate.

2. The marginal productivity of unskilled labor may be less than the wage rate. This is particularly likely to be true for rural SOC projects utilizing unskilled labor which otherwise would be seasonally idle because of crop-cycle patterns. Under these circumstances, the opportunity cost of labor, if not zero, is at least very low, and a shadow wage rate lower than the actual wage can be justified.

Sensitivity Analysis

Both B/C and IRR calculations may be sensitive to assumptions that have been made about project costs and benefits. Accordingly, *sensitivity analysis* is advisable to determine how project viability might be affected by increased costs or lower project benefits. For SOC projects, time delays and cost overruns need to be considered, as well as the possibility that projected use of the facility (e.g., freight volume on highways or electricity consumption) has been overestimated. If project viability is found to be very sensitive to key assumptions about which considerable uncertainty exists, it may not be advisable to undertake the project unless these uncertainties can be reduced.

Noneconomic Considerations

There are several reasons why an SOC (or DPA) project with a B/C ratio of 1.50 might be preferred to one with a ratio of 2.00. In fact, some projects might be considered desirable even if they have B/C ratios of less than 1.00 or IRRs lower than the opportunity cost of capital. For example, a government might wish to assist a region which is particularly impoverished and geographically isolated by building a road connecting that region with major transportation arteries elsewhere in the country, and by constructing a series of local public works projects to provide jobs and income. The underlying motives may be either humanitarian or obviously political (e.g., blunting secessionist tendencies, courting votes), but in either case, we are dealing here with legitimate concerns of national governments, elected or otherwise. An economic advisor who argues strongly against this package of projects on the grounds that the B/C ratio is only 0.983 is likely to be looking for another job within two hours. On the other hand, an advisor who can clearly and tactfully show why a B/C ratio of 0.50 calls for a consideration of other alternatives is performing a valuable service. International agencies are well aware that noneconomic considerations are important elements of project analysis, and they do not rigidly adhere to a B/C ratio of 1.00 or an IRR higher than 8 to 15 percent. Projects which seem to have merit from a social development standpoint will be approved under these circumstances provided that the B/C or IRR figure is reasonably close to the standard criterion.

What is "reasonably close," of course, involves a qualitative judgment. There are, though, other ways of dealing with social development concerns. The World Bank, for example, has been experimenting with methods for incorporating income distribution criteria explicitly into B/C or IRR calculations.[11] In theory, this could be done in a number of ways; but basically, what is involved is a determination that a dollar's worth of benefits to low-income farmers or urban dwellers should be valued at some multiple (> 1) of a dollar's worth of benefits to their high-income

11. See, for example, V. C. Nwaneri, "Income Distribution Criteria for the Analysis of Development Projects," *Finance and Development,* 10 (March 1973), 16–19, 37.

counterparts.[12] This, too, involves a value judgment, but at least the importance of social development concerns is made explicit and an attempt is made to quantify social benefits. This same type of analysis can also be used to give differential weights to project benefits according to their geographical impact, their employment effects, or other social considerations.

Finally, it should be noted that B/C and IRR analysis, even when adjusted by shadow prices which accurately reflect free-market conditions, implicitly accept the existing distribution of income. In other words, actual or estimated free-market prices are determined by supply and demand *given the present distribution of income.* A redistribution of income would affect prices in both product and factor markets, thus changing their B/C ratios or IRRs and in some cases altering the relative ranking of proposed projects. If income redistribution is considered desirable, simulation exercises could be undertaken to determine how B/C ratios or IRRs might be affected. Admittedly, such exercises would have to rely on much guesswork, but some efforts along these lines would be useful.

SUMMARY

Factor and product markets in developing countries are far from perfect, and even if they were, the market mechanism would be unable to provide the desirable amounts of public goods and services. Accordingly, it is unrealistic to assume that market forces, by themselves, can efficiently allocate resources on an economywide basis. Even in predominantly market economies, governments can do much to improve resource allocation by investing in social overhead capital and market information services. In countries where the state chooses consciously to influence the speed, structure, and social impact of economic growth—i.e., where development, rather than growth, is the major concern—decisions regarding social overhead capital can have a major effect on policy objectives. In the next chapter, we consider public investment in education, health, and nutrition, some of the most important dimensions of almost everyone's concept of well-being.

---

12. This implies acceptance of the hypothesis that the marginal utility of income declines as income rises; or, plainly stated, that an extra dollar means more to a poor person than to a rich one. While this hypothesis has been used to support progressive income taxation, traditional economic theory has usually rejected it. Common sense, however, suggests that the hypothesis is valid. Support for this view from a higher authority is found in the biblical message of the widow's mite in Mark 12:41–44: After observing the poor widow's offering to the temple of two small coins, which seemed insignificant alongside the contributions of the wealthy, Jesus remarked that "this widow has given more than any of the others; for . . . she . . . has given all that she had to live on."

Suggested Readings

Gittinger, J. Price. *Economic Analysis of Agricultural Projects*. Baltimore: The Johns Hopkins University Press for the World Bank, 1972.
> Written in informal language for project evaluation practitioners, this World Bank manual is an excellent introduction to B/C and IRR analysis. It includes a step-by-step case study.

Hirschman, Albert O. *Development Projects Observed*. Washington, D.C.: The Brookings Institution, 1967.
> Drawing on personal observation of eleven projects in eleven countries, Hirschman advances some general conclusions about the factors determining project success and failure. While underlying economic costs and benefits are obviously of primary importance, Hirschman also makes it clear that politics, government leadership, management, and administration must also be taken into account. Especially valuable are the discussions of how policy makers respond to changing circumstances affecting the projects.

Hirschman, Albert O. *The Strategy of Economic Development*. New Haven: Yale University Press, 1958.
> This is one of the classics in the literature on economic development, noted particularly for its presentation and defense of the "unbalanced" side of the old balanced-versus-unbalanced-growth debates. Chapter 5 contains a provocative discussion of the relative importance of social overhead capital versus directly productive activities (i.e., agriculture and industry) in the process of economic growth and development.

International Bank for Reconstruction and Development. *World Bank Operations: Sectoral Programs and Policies*. Baltimore: The Johns Hopkins University Press for the World Bank, 1972.
> A nontechnical review of major issues and problems in the various sectors of the economy, and a summary of how the World Bank has responded. Individual chapters focus on agriculture, industry, transportation, telecommunications, electric power, water supply and sewerage, education, population, tourism, and urbanization.

Little, I. M. D., and J. A. Mirrlees. *Project Appraisal and Planning in Developing Countries*. New York: Basic Books, 1974.
> Little and Mirrlees are the authors of a proposal, originally made in the late 1960s, to use world market prices as shadow prices for project inputs and outputs. Though adopted by some international lending agencies, this procedure is still very controversial.

Rostow, W. W. *The Stages of Economic Growth: A Non-Communist Manifesto*. Cambridge, Eng.: Cambridge University Press, 1960.
> Rostow regards social overhead capital formation as an important precondition for what he calls the "takeoff into sustained growth."

Wilson, George W., et al. *The Impact of Highway Investment on Development*. Washington, D.C.: The Brookings Institution, 1966.

The authors examine highway projects in nine developing countries. Sensibly, they do not regard transport (or anything else) as the "key" to economic growth. In some of the cases studied, the authors conclude that development of the areas served by the highway would not otherwise have occurred, though factors other than the highway were also necessary. In other cases, highway construction simply was a response to development that was occurring anyway.

7

The Role of
Government
Education, Health, and Nutrition

Few persons would deny that education and health are important aspects of human welfare. Government can play an important role in improving the well-being of its citizens not only by devoting more resources to health and education but also by designing programs in such a way that the poorest groups in the society directly benefit from them. Without attention to the distribution of benefits, it is by no means certain that health and educational programs will reduce inequalities. We shall consider this issue in more detail in chapter 11.

Education and health are both public goods, though their degree of "publicness" varies greatly according to the type of health or education service. At one extreme are programs such as malaria eradication, which come quite close to being pure public goods. If an effective program exists, no one can be prevented from "consuming" the benefits of that service, and one person's consumption does not take away from that of others. Such a program has obvious positive effects not only on individual well-being but also on society as a whole by increasing the quality of available labor. (The quantity of labor is also increased, but this may be a mixed blessing.) At the other extreme are partially subsidized, noncredit courses offered by public institutions in such subjects as flower arranging and bird watching. While these courses may be of great satisfaction to the individual taking them, it is doubtful that one's ability to tell a sparrow from a bluejay has any effect whatsoever on the welfare of others. In other words, virtually all the benefits are private. Between these two extremes is a variety of health and education programs in which both private and public benefits are important. To the extent that public benefits are present, consumers' true preferences will be understated in the marketplace, and at least partial public financing can be justified. Like the social overhead capital discussed in chapter 6, health and education projects are often costly, and in many cases the benefits are concentrated in the long run.

MEASURING EDUCATION AND HEALTH AS DIMENSIONS OF WELL-BEING

The importance of education and health as dimensions of well-being is highlighted in a "Physical Quality of Life Index" (PQLI) recently developed by Morris D. Morris.[1] The PQLI has three component measures: life expectancy at birth, infant mortality, and literacy. In comparison with some of the other comprehensive measures of development discussed in chapter 1, the PQLI has two major attractions: (1) its simplicity and (2) its focus on outputs (or direct measures of well-being) rather than inputs (indirect measures such as physicians per capita, intake of calories, or years of schooling). Accordingly, this index is receiving considerable attention as an alternative, or supplement, to per capita GNP figures for measuring development. Rankings of selected developing countries according to this index, and raw data for its component parts, are presented in Table 7.1. Note that countries with similar per capita GNP figures sometimes have very different PQLI ratings (e.g., India and Sri Lanka).

While this interest in an alternative welfare indicator is encouraging, the PQLI has a number of serious drawbacks, including the following:

1. It ignores other important dimensions of welfare, including employment, housing, income (which, other things being equal, provides freedom of choice of consumption items), and active participation in social and political affairs.

2. Despite its simplicity, the PQLI is ambiguous in concept. A physical quality of life index presumably measures improvements in physical well-being, and data on life expectancy and infant mortality clearly are appropriate. Morbidity statistics are also important indicators of physical well-being but are not included in the PQLI, presumably for lack of data. Literacy, on the other hand, is *not* an indicator of *physical* quality of life but rather is part of a less distinct dimension of well-being which includes availability of opportunity. Ambiguous indices can be badly misinterpreted.

3. Literacy statistics are notoriously deficient. Reported literacy rates do not refer to the same year, and data for some countries are ten

1. "A Physical Quality of Life Index," in *The United States and World Development: Agenda 1977*, ed. John W. Sewall (New York: Praeger Publishers for the Overseas Development Council, 1977), pp. 147–154.

TABLE 7.1
Per Capita GNP (1974), Health and Literacy Statistics, and Physical Quality
of Life Index, Selected Countries, Latest Available Data

	Per Capita GNP, 1974	Life Expectancy at Birth	Infant Mortality per 1,000 Live Births	Literacy Rate	PQLI[a]
Africa South of the Sahara					
Niger	120	39	200	5	14
Kenya	200	50	119	20–25	40
Ghana	430	44	156	25	31
Zambia	520	44	160	15–20	28
Angola	710	38	203	10–15	15
North Africa and Near East					
Yemen, People's Republic	220	45	152	10	27
Egypt	280	52	98	26	46
Morocco	430	53	130	21	40
Turkey	750	57	119	51	54
Saudi Arabia	2,870	45	152	15	29
South and East Asia					
Sri Lanka	130	68	45	81	83
India	140	50	139	34	41
China	300	62	55	25	59
Malaysia	680	59	75	41	59
Taiwan	810	69	26	85	88
Latin America—Caribbean					
Haiti	170	50	150	10	31
Bolivia	280	47	108	40	45
Cuba	640	70	29	78	86
Costa Rica	840	69	45	89	87
Venezuela	1,970	65	54	82	80
Developed Countries					
Sweden	7,240	75	9	99	100
United States	6,670	71	17	99	96
U.S.S.R.	2,600	70	28	100	94

Source: John W. Sewell et al., The United States and World Development: Agenda
1977 (New York: Praeger Publishers for Overseas Development Council, 1977),
Table A-3, pp. 160–171, based on data collected by various agencies identified in the
source.
[a] Based on a maximum rating of 100, held by Sweden.

to twenty years old. For many countries, experienced observers believe that
functional literacy—the ability to understand simple written instructions
and to make elementary arithmetical calculations—is only about half the
reported literacy rate. Functional literacy usually is attained only after

three to four years of schooling and even then is maintained only if used. To place so much reliance on an indicator that is seriously deficient can result in some very misleading relative country rankings. Moreover, literacy has only a quantitative dimension; yet two countries with a reported (or even actual) literacy rate of, say, 70 percent might have very different average years of schooling (or skill levels).

4. All three indicators are assigned equal weights. While any weighting system is of course subjective, the rationale for equal weights is difficult to understand, except as a tentative scheme subject to change after widespread consultation concerning the relative importance of each indicator. One hopes that interviews will be conducted not just with "experts" but also with a random sample of persons in both developed and developing countries whose welfare is being measured. The proponents of the PQLI argue that it avoids ethnocentric biases to a large degree, but it would be useful to have this assertion checked by research in a number of countries with widely different cultural characteristics and levels of per capita income. It would also be interesting to see if perception of welfare within a country varies according to such factors as income level, urban-versus-rural residence, and ethnic group.

5. Another aspect of the weighting problem concerns the use of two health indicators which on the surface appear to be interrelated. Preliminary indications are that they are not as closely correlated as one might imagine, but this should be confirmed by more sophisticated statistical tests.

6. The overall index ranks countries on a scale of 1 to 100, with the country having the highest rating for each separate indicator assigned a value of 100. This gives high-income countries—which have an average rating of 95—very little opportunity for improvement. On the other hand, one would expect that PQLIs will rise sharply in many developing countries over the next decade, resulting in a significant closing of the "PQLI gap" and thus leading to complacency about "progress" in the developing world. A more comprehensive welfare indicator, giving developed and developing countries equal opportunity for advancement, would likely tell a very different story.

7. Finally, the PQLI says little about the distribution of health and education benefits among the population. At the least, it would seem desirable to have an urban-rural breakdown of the index, to determine if the gap between urban and rural welfare is increasing or decreasing. Admittedly, even this simple disaggregation is not possible in all countries, but where the data do exist, disaggregation would be highly desirable.

These critical comments should not be taken as an outright rejection of the PQLI. It has promise, but considerable refinement is needed before it can be considered a comprehensive measure of development. Morris and his collaborators are well aware of its limitations and have prepared a revised version which should be published soon.

EDUCATION

The justifications for government financing of education may be grouped into two categories: economic and social. One of the economic rationales is that education is a public good, since the community at large benefits from the increased productivity associated with a better-educated and trained labor force. Business operators, for example, gain because the higher incomes permitted by increased productivity expand the markets for their products. Even the retired and the unemployed benefit to the extent that more resources are available to assist them.

Another economic argument for public education is that ignorance of the benefits of education would lead many individuals to undercon-sume it, in terms of their own self-interests, if it were provided only in the marketplace. Particularly in rural areas, parents may not demand education for their sons and daughters, believing that children, over their lifetimes, contribute more to the family income by staying at home than by going to school. Often this assessment is correct, but not always.

Studies of investment in education, in both developed and develop-ing countries, show that the rate of return is generally favorable—though they sometimes attribute to schooling[2] the formation of skills which some individuals would have developed by other means. At another level of analysis, research on economic growth in the United States has suggested that at least 40 percent can be attributed to education and to research and development. Frederick Harbison, a manpower economist who has done considerable research on the role of education in development, has gone so far as to write a book entitled *Human Resources as the Wealth of Nations*. In Harbison's view, the goals of development should be "the maximum possible utilization of human beings in productive activity and the fullest possible development of the skills, knowledge, and capacities of the labor force" (1973: Preface). If these goals are achieved, he argues, higher living standards and a more equal distribution of income are the likely results.

Government support for education, as Harbison implies, can also be justified as desirable social policy. If education and training are avail-

2. Passage through a certain number of years of school does not necessarily imply education in the sense of both acquiring knowledge *and* being able to utilize it for change. For a discussion of the difference between education and schooling, see Illich (1971).

able only in the marketplace, the poor will have little if any access to all but the informal education characteristic of a traditional society. Such education is unlikely to include literacy, nor will it investigate possible technological changes in agriculture. Under these circumstances, any economic growth that occurs is virtually certain to widen income inequalities.

In such an environment, there may nevertheless be opportunities for a few individuals from low-income families to obtain formal, institutional education. Subsidized education, for example, may be provided by religious or other private groups. In this connection, it is interesting to note that many leaders of independence movements in Africa began their education in missionary-supported schools. Another way that some of the poor might benefit is through on-the-job training in industrial and commercial establishments. In the absence of government-supported education and training, however, only a tiny percentage of low-income family members will have an opportunity to increase their earning power or otherwise improve their welfare.

So far, we have considered education simply as an investment good. It is, of course, also a consumption good and can be justified as an end in itself, since it enhances people's knowledge of their environment and presumably enriches their lives. On the other hand, some would argue that greater awareness of one's environment might only serve to increase psychological disorders. It has also been said that education which does not improve job opportunities simply confirms in an individual a feeling of inferiority.

Determining Investment Priorities

How much should governments spend on education, and how should the education budget be divided among primary, secondary, university, technical, and other types of education, e.g., adult literacy? The answers to these questions are not easy. First of all, they depend upon the relative importance of education as an investment good and as a consumption good. To the extent that consumption is emphasized, a decision will have to be made on how equally this form of consumption should be distributed. If education is regarded primarily as an investment good, as is generally the case, rational determination of spending priorities can in theory be made by several methods, including (1) the *rate of return* approach, which compares for the various levels of education the benefits of investment (mainly in the form of increased productivity and thus in lifetime incomes) with the costs (including income foregone because students are out of the labor force), and (2) the *manpower requirements* approach, in which the amount and type of education and training are made to conform to the manpower needs implied by the goals in the country's development plan.

Each of these two approaches has serious drawbacks. The rate of return approach, as we have already indicated, attributes higher earnings too much to formal schooling. It also assumes that earnings reflect marginal productivity, when in fact they are also influenced by custom and other institutional factors. Moreover, this approach is based on present labor market conditions, which might change significantly over the long run if there is a rapid expansion in the number of graduates at the primary, secondary, and postsecondary levels. For example, if the supply of skilled labor expands more rapidly than the demand, the relative wages of skilled workers will tend to fall. In other words, the marginal productivity of investment in education will be declining, and beyond a certain point, rates of return may be unfavorable. On the other hand, the rate of return approach completely ignores the value of education as a consumption good, and it is unconcerned with issues such as income distribution. The manpower requirements approach, which looks to the future, attempts to balance manpower supply and demand through planning. But it must be admitted that developing countries have had little success with economic planning (see chapter 8), and serious errors in forecasting manpower needs can easily be made.

Whichever of these two approaches is used, spending on education cannot be regarded in isolation, for both political and economic reasons. With regard to the latter, we pointed out in chapter 2 that investment in physical capital will be highly productive only if complementary factors of production are available. The same reasoning can be applied to investment in human capital. If graduates of universities, secondary schools, and technical schools cannot find jobs because of the lack of physical capital, natural resources, and other productive factors necessary for the tasks for which they were prepared, then there is in effect overspending on education and training relative to other types of investment. If there is a surplus of skilled workers, the result will be (1) unemployment, (2) "visible underemployment" (less than full-time work), (3) "invisible underemployment" (work in occupations requiring skill levels lower than those for which people have been trained), or (4) emigration to other countries where the skills in question are in short supply (the so-called "brain drain").[3] In each case, the government fails to receive the benefits of its investment in skill formation, and individuals (except for some of those who emigrate) find their personal objectives frustrated.

---

3. An extreme case of brain drain has occurred in Haiti, 80 percent of whose professionals were said to be working outside the country in the mid-1960s. Political conditions in Haiti and very low salaries contributed to this outflow.

Politics affects educational spending decisions in a number of ways. Given a government's revenues from taxes and other sources, and its perceived limitations on deficit spending, the total budget for a particular year is determined, and education must compete for funds with public works, military outlays, electric power, and a host of other activities. There are always more claims on the budget than there are funds available, so cuts have to be made in some (if not all) requests. These cuts are not made in accordance with comparative data on rates of return on the various competing projects—such data, in fact, are rarely available. The chief executive may still have a rough idea of the productivity of alternative investments, but he or she must also respond to short-term political realities. If votes are needed in an election year, small public works projects may be initiated in towns all over the country, and education (except for school construction) may be neglected. Some chief executives may feel that staying in power requires permanently generous allocations to the armed forces, or tax breaks and subsidies to the commercial and industrial elites.

Pressures for education, however, are also strong, particularly in urban areas, where many parents are willing to make great sacrifices to provide their children with as much education as possible.[4] Universal primary education has been espoused widely—perhaps universally—in the developing countries, and sometimes it is constitutionally obligatory. But the human and financial resources necessary for rapid achievement of this goal are lacking, and the promise has gone unfulfilled despite very rapid increases in educational budgets in many countries.[5] At prevailing (very low) teachers' salaries, it has been estimated that universal primary education in the Sahelian countries of Africa would require 10 to 15 percent of the GNP, well beyond these countries' capabilities.[6] Consider, too, the case of Nigeria, Africa's most populous country, which in the early 1970s decided to achieve universal primary education by 1976. Attainment of this goal would have required a quadrupling of the number of teachers from 150,000 to 600,000, an impossible task for a teacher-training system capable of graduating only 12,000 new teachers a year. Even with

---

4. In Ecuador in about 1970, I observed that the annual cost of nominally free public secondary education could easily amount to $50—several weeks' or a month's wages for many workers, who nevertheless tried desperately to secure for their children one of the limited number of openings at this level. The costs of secondary education included not only books, supplies, and uniforms but also almost-forced contributions to school fund-raising events and birthday gifts to teachers.

5. Harbison (1973: 55) reports that in the typical African country in the early 1970s, at least 20 percent of government spending (and often more than 33 percent) was on education.

6. Francis J. Lethem, "Innovation in Education in Western Africa," *Finance and Development,* 11 (December 1974), 26–28, 42.

its considerable revenues from petroleum exports, the Nigerian government will find that achievement of universal primary education is a long process unless it is willing (and able) to radically reorient budget priorities and mobilize human and financial resources, as China and Cuba have done with considerable success. Few governments, however, have the power to make such rapid changes.

Governments which are strongly responsive to pressures for increased primary education may end up with another kind of problem. So many resources are spent at the primary level that insufficient funds remain to satisfy the demands of primary school graduates for a place in secondary school. Those who are forced to enter the labor force at a lower level than they had hoped for, and with limited opportunities for advancement, are likely to be discontented with the existing social and political systems and may well be responsive to the call of political leaders challenging the existing government.

As we indicated above, there can also be too much emphasis on secondary and higher education, especially if governments believe it necessary to accede to the demands of middle- and upper-income groups or of provinces wanting their own universities. In this case, it will be skilled workers and professionals who will be discontented because of underemployment or even unemployment.

The Low Status of Technical Education

Another of the many educational problems facing developing countries is the lack of interest in technical education. Surveys of secondary students have shown that the overwhelming majority are in school to become "certified" (as opposed to educated) for white-collar jobs that convey (or preserve) middle-class status. Technical occupations—even if they pay more than some white-collar clerical jobs—have lower status. The middle-class aversion to working with one's hands can have some curious results. For example, this writer's wife has taught in a secondary school in Ecuador where the chemistry experiments were performed by the teacher's *assistant* and observed by his students, who were not expected to replicate them even though the school had the resources to make this possible.

Similar attitudes may be found at the university level. Students are attracted in large numbers to the prestigious fields of law, medicine, and architecture, or to education and the humanities, but not to fields like industrial or sanitary engineering, agronomy, and other applied sciences. Jokes about surplus lawyers abound in the international development fraternity, and in some countries there are also too many doctors. The latter may seem paradoxical in view of high death and morbidity rates; but effective demand for medical services in predominantly market economies is limited by low incomes, and doctors tend to concentrate in large urban centers where the professional, social, and cultural environment is more to their liking than that of rural areas (see below). Doctors may thus join the brain drain, while at the same time the countries from which they come will have to import the services of engineers, scientists, and business managers.

Technical skills can be acquired not only in the classroom but also on the job. Indeed, on-the-job training is often preferable to technical secondary education, which can be three to four times as expensive as general secondary education and in practice has often been of poor quality. Still, technical education can be economically justified, provided that it concentrates on basic technical skills that do not quickly become obsolete as technology changes and can easily be transferred from one industry to another. Highly specialized skills can be learned more effectively through on-the-job training by those with basic general and technical skills.

Other Educational Problems

We have only begun to discuss the problems plaguing education in developing countries. Others of importance include the following:

1. *Education as a preparation for more education.* In most developing countries, primary education is not regarded as a terminal program providing specific skills, but rather as a ticket to secondary school. This might be justifiable in a country where virtually all primary school graduates continue their schooling; but in developing countries, most of them generally cannot continue because there are too few places. The educational system treats them, in effect, as failures; they are not well equipped to do skilled or semiskilled work (though they do have the advantage of functional literacy), and in rural areas they may not know any more about modern methods of farming than their parents. Similarly, secondary schools are, in effect, channels for universities; terminal "tracks," or tracks leading to technical institutes, are rarely available. Again, those who do not go on to the next level are regarded as failures, rather than as persons with different aptitudes which might be further developed through formal education or training. Apart from the waste this implies in economic terms, this kind of educational system exacts a heavy psychological toll on those who are unable to realize their (unrealistic) hopes for moving up the educational ladder.

2. *High dropout rates.* In most developing countries, only a minority of those who enter first grade will finish primary school. For all of Latin America, a UNESCO study published in 1971 estimated the percentage who graduated to be less than 40 percent. In Brazil in the late 1960s, the figure was 27 percent. In Haiti, the poorest country in the

Western Hemisphere, 50 percent of those entering urban primary school finish the curriculum, but in rural areas the figure is an appalling 3 percent. Reasons for high dropout rates include parents' desires to use children as a source of labor, lack of facility in the language of instruction,[7] and poor nutrition and health. To the extent that children take up space but do not become functionally literate, the investment in their schooling yields little if any social return and probably few personal benefits. Since those who drop out tend to come from poor families, efforts to narrow inequalities by rapidly expanding education can often have just the opposite effect.

3. *Overcrowding, lack of books, and lack of equipment and supplies.* It is not unusual in developing countries for primary and secondary school classes to contain sixty to eighty students. It is also not unusual to find that students have no books and the teacher has no blackboard. Given the pressures for universal primary education, and the fact that teachers' salaries (as in the developed countries) account for most of the education budget, this preference for quantity rather than quality of education should not be surprising.

4. *Urban-rural imbalances.* Children in urban centers have a much better chance of going to school than those who live in rural areas, where political power is relatively weak. And those who manage to complete the primary cycle in rural areas often can continue their education only in the cities, where the curriculum may have no relevance to the problems of the countryside. Even in rural high schools, the curriculum may be oriented toward urban occupations. This inattention to rural problems, coupled with a lack of demand for skilled jobs in rural areas, means that these areas lose many of their most talented young people to the cities, thus exacerbating urban-rural differences in levels of living.

The list of educational problems is by no means exhaustive; many others could have been noted if space limitations had not intervened. But enough has been said to make it clear that educational programs in the developing countries are seriously deficient. At the same time, it is important to remember that political and bureaucratic considerations make change difficult to accomplish.

Reforming General Education

General education in the developing countries has come under considerable attack as not being relevant to the needs of these countries. What good is Latin, French literature, and philosophy, it is argued, when what is really needed are subjects like accounting and, in rural areas, agron-

---

7. In Haiti, for example, the language of instruction is French, yet 80 percent of the population speaks only Creole.

omy. This writer is quick to defend the value of a liberal arts education, but not as it is practiced in many developing countries, where there is too much emphasis on rote learning and not enough on problem solving. Formal education in rural areas, where most people in the developing countries live, too often emphasizes urban cultures and urban values. It would be more responsive to rural needs if curricula were redesigned to combine, for example, the teaching of mathematics with information on factor inputs, production costs, crop yields, and the economics of marketing and storage. Art and music appreciation could be based on local artistic and musical heritages, and indigenous verbal literacy heritages could be put into written form.

Consideration should also be given to expanding nonformal education—i.e., all types of education outside the highly structured, graded school system. This includes such diverse activities as on-the-job training, agricultural extension, adult literacy, mass education via television, and short courses imparting basic technical skills. Nonformal education is particularly valuable if it combines basic literacy and arithmetical skills with agricultural extension and training in handicrafts or repair skills. This approach, which is being tried in a number of African countries,[8] has the potential to improve rural welfare at less cost than formal primary education, and it provides the necessary basis for the formation of cooperatives and other community organizations.

Paulo Freire (1970) and Ivan Illich (1971) support nonformal education in combination with consciousness-raising among the oppressed.[9] The 1972 UNESCO-sponsored study *Learning to Be* stresses the concept of "lifetime education" and the greater role that noneducational institutions should play in guaranteeing this "universal right." China has combined formal education with work experience and apprenticeship programs, which begin at the secondary level even for the professions.[10] Recent worldwide experience in nonformal education is still too limited to attempt an overall evaluation of this promising strategy. It is important to remember, however, that any evaluation must go far beyond traditional B/C analysis to include the effects of nonformal education on income distribution and the quality of life.[11]

8. Lethem, op. cit.

9. The Freire method was introduced in northeast Brazil on a pilot scale in 1962, with financing from U.S. AID. However, AID soon got cold feet because of the program's revolutionary potential. When the Brazilian military assumed control of the government in 1964, the program was terminated and Freire himself was exiled. The Freire method has been very influential among social reformers and revolutionaries in Latin America and in developing countries generally.

10. R. P. Dore, "The Future of Formal Education in Developing Countries," *International Development Review*, 17, No. 2 (1972/2): 7–11.

11. For a review of the strengths and weaknesses of various types of nonformal education, see Harbison (1973: Ch. 4).

A Final Note on Priorities within the Budget for Education

Development economists generally agree that governments should pay greater attention to the formation of human capital; but there is disagreement as to whether primary, secondary, or postsecondary education should receive more attention. The answer probably depends on the individual country, but the weight of the evidence suggests that the emphasis should be on primary education and on the provision of more nonformal education and training at the postprimary level. Such a strategy, it would seem, should include both curriculum changes—with less emphasis on Western content and methods—and measures to give students a more realistic picture of job expectations. It should also ensure that sufficient semiskilled or skilled jobs are available for those who become functionally literate.

HEALTH

The World Health Organization (WHO), a United Nations agency, defines health as the "state of complete physical, mental, and social well-being" and not merely the absence of disease or infirmity. As with education, government investment in health can be justified on both economic and social grounds. The economic case rests mainly on the fact that health programs are to one degree or another public goods. This is particularly true of programs for eradicating or controlling major diseases. The rational individual's expressed demand for malaria control services, for example, would be much lower than his or her actual demand, since the risk of contracting the disease is low if a control program exists, and persons could not be excluded from "consuming" the benefits. For most health services, the entire community, not just the direct beneficiaries, stands to gain because a healthier labor force is a more productive one. Another economic argument for public investment in health services is that many persons, out of ignorance, would underconsume these services—in terms of their own self-interest—if provided only in the marketplace.

Investment in health programs can also be justified by social considerations. Some people, for example, believe that everyone, regardless of income, should have an equal opportunity to enjoy good health and access to preventive care, and to receive treatment when health status deteriorates. This is part of the rationale for the comprehensive national health service programs found in most developed countries (the United States is a notable exception) and in some developing countries. No country actually provides perfect equality of access to all types of health care, and in developing countries which do manage to provide health care services to a high proportion of the population (e.g., China and Cuba), it is not clear if the range of services offered is very wide.

Preventive versus Curative Medicine

An ounce of prevention may not be worth a pound of cure, but it is often worth several ounces. In other words, preventing a condition can be much more cost-effective for a society than treating it and suffering both economic and personal losses when people are disabled or die. The costs of health services are relatively easy to measure in comparison with the benefits. For example, even in developed countries, economic analysis of water supply projects rarely includes public health benefits because it is hard to separate the benefits of potable water from those of proper nutrition, housing conditions, medical services, etc. In developing countries, determining benefits—and therefore health investment priorities—is even more difficult because data on morbidity and mortality, which are poor enough in developed countries, are even more unreliable or incomplete.

Despite the difficulties of determining the viability of health projects and programs in strictly economic terms, there is good reason to believe that investment in many preventive health programs has a high payoff. These include potable water and sewerage systems, malaria eradication projects, and antituberculosis campaigns.

Water and Sewerage Projects[12]

All human beings must obtain water one way or another in order to survive. They must also dispose of their own and other types of wastes. Water supply and waste disposal systems are public goods because of their relationship with health status. Diseases associated with contaminated water and/or poor sanitation include gastroenteritis (inflammation of the stomach and intestines), a major cause of death in many developing countries; parasitic diseases; dysentery; and typhoid.

There are substantial economies of scale in the provision of both potable water and sanitary waste disposal systems. A central water supply or sewerage system can deliver water or carry away wastes more cheaply than trucks. Indoor or neighborhood water taps can save hours of time that otherwise would be spent transporting water from the nearest source if neighborhood truck service is not available. Because the benefits of potable water are more obvious and more private than those of sewerage

12. Much of the information in this section is drawn from IBRD (1972: 241–254). See the Suggested Readings in chapter 6 for the full reference.

systems, and because costs are usually lower, sewerage systems often have lower priority than water-supply systems. Investment in both, however, can usually be justified economically even without taking into account the public health benefits.

Although substantial investments in water and sewer systems were made in the 1960s, particularly in Latin America, only 25 percent of the urban population in developing countries received water from household or courtyard taps in the early 1970s. Another 26 percent had access to water from public standpipes, leaving 49 percent with no public water service. Even fewer urban residents had sewerage service. In Latin America, according to estimates made by the Inter-American Development Bank (IDB), only 38 percent of the urban population was served by sewerage facilities in the early 1970s; in Asia and Africa the figures were much lower. Public water and sewer systems are usually available only to a tiny fraction of the rural population.

Water and sewerage systems in urban areas have been plagued by two major problems. First, the rapid growth of urban populations (often 5 to 8 percent annually) has placed a great strain on capacity. If new customers are connected to a system faster than its intended capacity expands, the quality of service deteriorates for all customers. The World Bank reports that in one city in South Asia, 40 percent of the water entering an overloaded system was lost in distribution. Service was available only a few hours daily in each neighborhood, and customers were forced to invest in roof storage tanks and pumps. A second, and related, problem is that of poor management, a reflection both of the underdevelopment of entrepreneurial skills and of the difficulty of relating costs to benefits. One management shortcoming with clear negative implications for public health is inadequate attention to maintenance and repair. If water pressure drops, seepage from contaminated ground and nearby sewerage pipes increases. Service interruptions increase the risk of disease to the extent that unsafe water must be substituted for potable water.

The first problem noted above constitutes *prima facie* evidence that additional investments in water and sewerage systems would be productive. During the 1960s, most external finance for water and sewer systems came from private suppliers and bilateral aid programs. The principal source of multilateral assistance was the IDB. The World Bank's interest increased after 1970, and it now lends more for water and sewerage projects than the IDB. World Bank lending in this field amounted to $335 million in 1976. International agencies are also providing technical assistance to improve the management of water and sewerage systems.

As we have indicated, the public health benefits of potable water and sewerage systems are difficult to measure. There is little doubt, however, that they have made major contributions to lowering mortality and morbidity rates. Indeed, in the developed countries, there is good evidence that potable water and improved nutrition have done much more to improve health status than all types of medical care, including immunizations and antibiotics.[13] Since water and sewerage systems are concentrated in urban centers, however, they exacerbate urban-rural level-of-living differentials and contribute to migration from rural areas. To the extent that urban overcrowding has social costs, these should be subtracted from the benefits of improved sanitation. Still, the net social benefits are probably substantial.

Other Public Health Programs[14]

In the first two decades after World War II, one of the most significant and successful public health programs in the developing world was the eradication or control of malaria. This debilitating disease, spread by certain species of the *Anopheles* mosquito, can prevent an adult from working or at least lower his or her productivity. It can also be fatal, especially to children. In tropical Africa, it is estimated that one out of every four or five infants dies of malaria before the age of one.[15] Women with malaria often cannot breast-feed their children, and this has adverse effects on nutrition and susceptibility to disease (see below). Determining the economic impact of antimalaria programs is a difficult task, and the problem is complicated if we assume that a lower death rate, and therefore a higher population growth rate, would have offsetting costs in the form of a slower growth of per capita income (an issue we discussed in chapter 4). But when one considers humanitarian and other noneconomic arguments for eradication of major diseases, the case becomes a strong one.

Despite the successful eradication or control of malaria in some countries, the World Health Organization estimated that in 1965 this disease still affected at least 100 million persons, of whom 1 million died. Since then, the situation has worsened. In India, Sri Lanka, Haiti, Ecuador, and other countries where malaria had been effectively controlled, the incidence of the disease has been rising rapidly in the last ten to fifteen years. In India, for example, the number of reported cases increased from 100,000 on 1965 to 6 million in 1977.[16] The rising incidence of malaria

13. See Thomas McKeown, "Limits to Medicine," in *Conference on Future Directions in Health Care: The Dimensions of Medicine*, ed. Rick Carlson (Washington, D.C.: Blue Cross Association, 1975), pp. 24–38.
14. This section draws heavily on Kamarck (1976).
15. See "Malaria Strikes Back," an article by former WHO malariologist Gabriele Gramiccia, in the monthly U.N. publication *Development Forum*, 6 (May 1978), 1–2.
16. Ibid.

can be attributed to budgetary cutbacks in control programs, perhaps because of complacency resulting from earlier successes; failure to change control strategies, e.g., when mosquitos develop a resistance to DDT; a decline in the number of trained malariologists; and poorly maintained irrigation systems, which provide favorable environments for the mosquitos to breed.

Programs to halt the transmission of malaria in tropical Africa have been especially disappointing. Some species of the mosquito vector have developed a resistance to DDT and other insecticides (which themselves have undesirable effects). Researchers are now attempting to develop a vaccine, but in the meantime, antimalaria programs must continue to rely on such measures as spraying, draining of swamps, and clearing of bush.

Bilharzia, or schistosomiasis, affects even more people than malaria. Perhaps 200 million people suffer from this debilitating and sometimes fatal disease, which is transmitted by several species of a parasitic worm attacking the liver, spleen, and other organs. Bilharzia is found in virtually all of Africa and in various parts of Asia and Latin America. It became a particularly serious problem in Egypt following the construction of the Aswan High Dam, which converted running water to still and enabled the parasite to thrive—an example of how the public health consequences of development projects tend to get overlooked. One study, cited by Kamarck (1976: 63), found that one variety of bilharzia reduced the capability for work by 15 to 18 percent in mild cases and 72 to 80 percent in severe cases. However, Weisbrod et al. (1973), studying the impact of the disease in the Caribbean island of St. Lucia, where infection levels are intermediate, found that the impact on work capacity was less.[17]

The authors of the St. Lucia study were quick to point out the dangers of generalizing on the basis of one small country, and they called for additional studies of other countries where the disease is prevalent. But if their findings are confirmed, the B/C ratio or IRR of a campaign against bilharzia may well be unfavorable. This in itself would not be sufficient to recommend against a bilharzia control program, since the toll in human suffering should also be considered. But in countries where resources are scarce, funds might be better spent on other health or nutrition programs which yield greater returns. To date, no effective con-

17. The original study found that productive capacity of male plantation workers was reduced by perhaps 30 percent on a daily basis. Interestingly, though, those who were infected worked longer hours than noninfected workers, and there was no significant difference in average *weekly* earnings. A follow-up study, conducted in part to see if the longer-term effects of the disease might be more serious, found that labor productivity of infected workers was only 14 percent lower than that of noninfected workers. See Burton A. Weisbrod and Thomas W. Helminiak, "Parasitic Diseases and Agricultural Labor Productivity," *Economic Development and Cultural Change*, 25 (April 1977), 505–522.

trol for bilharzia has been found, and the cures have unpleasant side effects. The development of an effective control or cure, of course, could dramatically change the B/C picture.

Only brief mention will be made of several other diseases which affect residents of the developing countries, particularly those located in the tropics. River blindness, transmitted by a fly, affects some 20 million persons, particularly adult males in west and central Africa. The disease causes partial or total blindness, thus sharply lowering labor productivity. Efforts at eradication have had mixed success, and no cure has yet been found. Hookworm infects perhaps 500 million persons of all ages, causing anemia, apathy, and mental and physical retardation in children. Other parasitic worms cause filariasis, which affects an estimated 250 million persons. Tuberculosis affects several hundred million persons in the developing world. Data from India and Taiwan suggest that if 5 percent of those countries' health budgets were devoted to a tuberculosis control program, the returns on this investment would be a remarkable 21 to 1.[18]

Modern Medical Services

Given the poor health status of many residents of the developing world, one might think that there is a great shortage of medical personnel. But if one looks at effective demand, rather than at subjectively determined "needs," it can be argued that some developing countries actually produce a surplus of medical doctors. Medicine is a prestigious field of study at the university level, conveying (or preserving) status as well as the promise of a relatively high income. The great majority of medical school graduates have little interest in practicing their profession in rural areas, both because of the low effective demand at urban fee schedules and also because rural areas are lacking in professional networks and social amenities. Accordingly, there tends to be a great concentration of physicians in the large urban centers. It is not at all unusual for a capital city with less than 10 percent of the national population to have more than half of the country's physicians.

In some countries, urban-based physicians are underemployed. Some of them could easily find full-time employment serving small towns and rural hinterlands, provided that they were willing to accept an income significantly lower than what they could earn in urban areas if fully employed. Rural life, however, holds few attractions in comparison to another alternative—migration to a developed country. Many thousands of doctors from developing conutries now practice in the United States, Europe, and other developed parts of the world. This brain drain constitutes a loss of investment made by developing countries and can be considered as "reverse foreign aid." It is also an item that must be considered in calculating the costs of providing medical care in a developing country.

In theory, a variety of policies could be employed to deal with the curious case of the surplus physicians. If emigration could be prohibited, there would be downward pressure on salaries, thus reducing the number of entrants into medical schools; but few countries have the means to do this. Some persons probably enter medical school with no intention of practicing in their own country, but it would be almost impossible to identify them in advance and block their entry into medical school. Limiting the number of places in medical school is politically difficult. Physicians' salaries could be regulated to narrow urban-rural differentials, but few countries have the ability to do this effectively; even if effective, such a policy would encourage even more emigration. Some countries are experimenting with internship programs requiring one to two years' service in rural areas for new graduates, but enforcement is not easy. Medical services under social security programs could be expanded to raise effective demand in the wealthier developing countries, but this would tend to benefit only urban areas and might cause enrollments in medical schools to rise. Providing income supplements to doctors practicing in rural areas might be less expensive than losing through emigration the investment in training them, but when budgets are tight, such measures are restricted. In summary, there seems to be no easy answer to this peculiar supply-demand imbalance.

Hospitals, like physicians, are concentrated in urban areas. Because of ignorance, many people go to hospitals too late to receive effective treatment. In fact, hospitals are sometimes regarded as a place to die—a view sometimes reinforced by the sight of a cemetery adjacent to the hospital or nearby artisan workshops which specialize in children's coffins. How serious a problem this might be is not clear. However, to the extent that hospitals concentrate on the dying rather than those who can return in good health to the labor force, there is little if any return to the investment in hospital services. This is not to say that terminal patients should be terminated at the front door; rather, it calls for greater emphasis on early treatment—encouraged through educational and promotional activities, particularly among the poor—and on prevention.

Health service is a fertile field for greater use of intermediate technology (not just in developing countries but also in the United States). Most medical and other health services can be provided by nurses, nurse-practitioners, or other middle-level technicians trained to give routine examinations and treatment and to practice preventive medicine. Non-routine cases can be referred to full-fledged physicians. Middle-level technicians are less costly to train than physicians, and they are much less likely to emigrate. China is among the few developing countries whose health services are organized along these lines. In most other countries, there are at least two major obstacles to the use of intermediate technology in health services: (1) resistance by physicians and (2) the low status and salaries of health technicians, a situation which discourages interest in these occupations. Furthermore, if the U.S. experience is any guide, intermediate medical technicians would tend to distribute themselves geographically in much the same way as physicians. To ensure the desired coverage in rural areas, special attention would have to be given to incentives and/or controls.

Traditional Health Practices

Medical practitioners in developing countries do not always wear white coats and hang a diploma from Midwestern University Medical School on their office walls. Many of them are barefoot, wear paint on their faces, and operate out of grass huts. To regard these traditional practitioners as merely "witch doctors" relying on superstition would be a mistake. While it is true that some of their advice only aggravates medical problems and even leads to death, or tends to reinforce the social status quo, traditional medical practitioners have also discovered effective remedies for certain illnesses and injuries. They can also be very effective psychologists and psychiatrists, suggesting socially acceptable outlets for aggression and rage or providing comfort and reassurance to those with other troubles. These roles, incidentally, also occupy a good deal of the time of general practitioner M.D.s in the United States, whose patients' real problems are not always physiological. Even when the problems are physiological, maintenance of chronic patients (e.g., with arthritis) is heavily psychological.

Health programs in developing countries should consider using these traditional practitioners as allied health personnel, particularly in rural areas, instead of trying to displace them. The case for widespread use of middle-level medical personnel has already been presented. Traditional practitioners are good candidates for these positions because they already have some medical knowledge and their authority is respected. Their useful remedies can be accepted and employed, while those that are dangerous can be changed through training. For various reasons, incorporating traditional practitioners into modern health care programs may not always be feasible; but in most cases, this strategy deserves serious consideration.

Research

Research on major diseases in the developing world, particularly those peculiar to the tropics, has been limited. The leading members of the medical profession in developing countries usually have been trained in developed countries, where the major concern is with "Western" diseases, such as cancer and heart disease. While these are also present in developing countries, their incidence is usually relatively low (tuberculosis is the major exception), partially because of diet but largely because people die of other things first. However, effective demand for doctors' services in developing countries may be limited largely to a small elite, whose medical problems are more Western than indigenous. Even for those doctors specializing in indigenous diseases, there is often little local knowledge on which to draw because funds for research have been scarce. Few studies have been made of the rate of return to medical research or applied medical technology, but the experience of yellow fever and malaria eradication programs suggests that the payoffs may be quite high.

Since the budgets of individual developing countries are tight, and research tends to be regarded as a luxury activity, a few well-funded multinational research programs (e.g., for Latin America, Africa, Southeast Asia, etc.) might be able to contribute more than a large number of poorly funded programs at the country level. Such international programs would benefit from financial grants and technical assistance from developed countries.

NUTRITION

Nutrition, Intelligence, Health, and Development[19]

Overall health status is determined to a very large degree by nutrition. Particularly important is the nutrition received by the fetus during pregnancy, by infants, and by young children. There is good evidence that malnutrition during these periods has adverse effects on intelligence that are irreversible. A few recent studies have suggested that reversal is often possible, but more research is needed before we can be reasonably cer-

19. For summaries of the literature relating nutrition to intelligence and health, see Pedro Belli, "The Economic Implications of Malnutrition: The Dismal Science Revisited," *Economic Development and Cultural Change*, 20 (October 1971), 1–23; Marcelo Selowsky and Lance Taylor, "The Economics of Malnourished Children: An Example of Disinvestment in Human Capital," *Economic Development and Cultural Change*, 22 (October 1973), 17–30; and David Turnham, assisted by Ingelies Jaeger, *The Employment Problem in Less Developed Countries: A Review of Evidence*; Employment Series No. 1 (Paris: Organisation for Economic Co-operation and Development, 1971), pp. 80–92.

tain. Even if the effects of early malnutrition can be overcome, the cost would seem to be high in comparison with the cost of preventing the condition in the first place. If few funds are spent on prevention, a more costly cure is likely to receive even less attention.

Malnutrition affects not only mental faculties but also physical well-being and the capacity for work. Nutrition is clearly related to physical stature, which itself affects the capacity for certain types of work independently of how well fed a person might be as an adult. Caloric deficiency during the working years, of course, means that only limited energy is available for physical labor. Peasants disparagingly referred to as lazy are simply unable to work as much as a well-fed U.S. farmer. Deficiencies of calories, proteins, vitamins, and other nutrients directly cause diseases such as beriberi (thiamine deficiency), goiter (iodine deficiency), blindness (vitamin A deficiency), and anemia (iron or vitamin deficiency). They also increase the risks of infectious diseases by hindering the formation of antibodies. Diarrhea is a particularly serious problem after weaning, when unsanitary bottle feeding invites infection or a switch to less nutritious foods lowers resistance to disease.

In addition to affecting adversely the productivity of children who survive to adulthood, malnutrition is both a direct and an indirect cause of death during infancy (less than one year of age) and early childhood (ages one to four). A study by the Pan American Health Organization in various parts of the Americas found that 6 percent of all deaths in these age groups were attributable directly to malnutrition, while another 57 percent were associated with various types of malnourishment (cited in Eckholm and Record, 1976: 14). Measles and diarrhea, which rarely are fatal in the developed countries, are among the major causes of early childhood deaths in the developing countries. Apart from the human tragedies involved, these deaths represent a loss of human capital. Moreover, to the extent that food and other expenditures on children can be considered an investment in human capital, rather than consumption, the investment made prior to death will never be recovered.

Poverty and malnutrition can constitute a vicious circle. Because of limited family resources, children are malnourished and grow up deficient in both mental and physical abilities. Nutrition-related health problems cause higher absenteeism from school, and malnourished students are probably more likely to drop out of school than those whose nutrition is adequate. Disadvantaged in terms of mental faculties, these children will have low earning power as adults and thus will lack the resources required to provide adequate nutrition for their own children. Unless this circle is broken by special programs aimed at the nutritionally disadvantaged, economic growth is likely to widen both nutritional and income inequalities. Strategies for averting this outcome will be discussed at the end of this section.

Measuring Nutritional Deficiencies

There is disagreement among both economists and specialists on nutrition on how best to measure nutritional deficiencies. Reutlinger and Selowsky (1976: 8) note that "malnutrition should ideally be defined by its consequences, such as health status, rather than by nutrient intake." However, it is difficult to define health status, and, once defined, adequate data for measuring it are generally not available. Accordingly, nutritional levels are usually reported in terms of (1) average daily caloric intake, (2) daily protein consumption, and (3) measures such as the Gomez scale which are based on deviations from "normal" weights for each age.

Average daily consumption of calories is probably the most widely used single indicator of nutritional status. It is also a much-criticized measure because of its failure to consider other important elements of nutrition, such as protein and vitamin intake, and to discount for calories not absorbed by the body because of loss to gastrointestinal parasites. Moreover, caloric intake estimates are based on sample surveys. The results for a particular area may vary by 10 to 20 percent in accordance with seasonal differences in the availability of food. However, as we shall see below, protein consumption is also seriously deficient as an indicator of nutritional status. A study of 7,000 households in India suggests, in any event, that there is a close relationship between intake of calories and protein consumption. It was found that 95 percent of households meeting the caloric standards also received adequate protein, while 50 percent of those with substandard calorie intake also failed to receive sufficient proteins (Reutlinger and Selowsky, 1976: 9). If this emerges as a clear pattern in developing countries generally, a strong case could be made for continued reliance on the caloric intake measure.

Protein consumption data at the aggregate level fail to take into account the fact that alternative sources of protein have differing amounts of the various amino acids required by the human body. Animal proteins have amino acids not found in many vegetable proteins, and separate estimates of animal protein consumption are thus desirable. Such data are available for most developing countries, but apart from reliability problems there are also conceptual problems with the use of protein consumption data as indicators of nutrition. In particular, persons who receive less than the desired amount of calories will use proteins as a source of energy, and they are thus not available for such purposes as cell maintenance and cell formation. Under these circumstances, what may appear to be adequate consumption of proteins really is not.

Another problem with using protein data is that nutrition specialists disagree about what constitutes an adequate level of protein consumption. When the United Nations lowered its protein standards by about a third in the early 1970s, estimated deficiencies were drastically reduced and for some countries were eliminated. Recent research, however, suggests that the new standards are too low (Eckholm and Record, 1976: 9).

If the diet is low in both proteins and calories, malnutrition can take particularly severe forms. When the deficiency is greater for proteins, the result is *kwashiorkor*, a disease affecting the intestines, liver, and pancreas and causing the bloated bellies we often see in televised news reports from drought-stricken countries. If the deficiency is greater for calories, children—particularly infants—contract *marasmus*, which is characterized by very low weight and lethargy.

Data on other nutrients are less readily available at the national level than information on proteins and calories, though this information is often collected in studies of particular communities. Of the numerous minerals and vitamins needed by the human body, the most important are calcium, iron, vitamin A, thiamin (vitamin B_1) riboflavin (vitamin B_2), ascorbic acid (vitamin C), vitamin D, and niacin. In general, deficiencies of these nutrients are not as serious a concern as protein-calorie malnutrition. Still, the lack of specific nutrients can sometimes be a major problem in particular communities or among certain age groups.

Another frequently used measure of malnutrition is the *Gomez scale*, which is based on body weight. Children weighing 75 to 90 percent of standard weights by age are considered to be mildly malnourished, or to have what is called first-degree malnutrition; those whose weights are 60 to 75 percent of the standard are said to suffer from second-degree malnutrition; and those weighing less than 60 percent of the standard are classified as having severe (third-degree) malnutrition. Table 7.2 provides Gomez-scale data, together with protein and calorie indicators, for selected Latin American and Caribbean countries.

The Incidence of Malnutrition

Estimates of the extent of malnutrition in the developing world differ widely. Some observers maintain that roughly half the population is malnourished. A United Nations study in 1970 concluded that the percentage was more like one-sixth (460 million persons), but the nutritional standards employed were rather low (Eckholm and Record, 1976: 10). Whatever the true figure, the magnitude of the problem is clearly monumental.

Because of differences in climate, physiology, the age structure of the population, and other factors, standards of adequate nutrition cannot be regarded as uniform throughout the world. The Food and Agriculture Organization of the United Nations (FAO) has established regional standards for calorie consumption, and these, together with estimated actual consumption in 1965, are given in Table 7.3.

TABLE 7.2
Nutritional Indicators, Selected Latin American and Caribbean Countries,
Various Years, Late 1960s and Early 1970s

	Per Capita Calorie Consumption	Per Capita Protein Consumption	Percentage of Children under 5 Who Are Malnourished[a]	
			Grade II	Grade III
Argentina	3,036[b]	98.4[b]	n.a.	n.a.
Brazil	2,640	77.0	17.2	2.7
Colombia	1,812	46.1	19.3	1.7
Costa Rica	1,961	55.7	12.2	1.5
Cuba	2,688[b]	63.1[b]	n.a.	n.a.
Guatemala	2,048	51.0	26.5	5.9
Haiti	1,896[b]	46.5[b]	35.6	17.4
Jamaica	2,585	68.2	9.4	1.4
Mexico	2,077	67.1[b]	n.a.	n.a.
Paraguay	2,350	65.5	2.2	0.7
Peru	2,133	59.0	10.9	0.8
St. Lucia	1,684	51.4	9.0	1.9
Venezuela	1,320–2,175[c]	59.4–73.6[c]	12.2	1.4

Source: "Situación nutricional y alimentaria en los países de América Latina y el Caribe," Boletín de la Oficina Sanitaria Panamericana, 80 (June 1976), Tables 4 and 14, 503 and 511.
[a] Gomez scale.
[b] Calorie or protein availability.
[c] Based on local consumption surveys, 1966–1970.

TABLE 7.3
Recommended and Actual Calorie Consumption,
by Major World Region, 1965

Region	Average Daily Consumption of Calories	
	Standard	Actual
Latin America	2,390	2,472
Asia (excluding China)[a]	2,210	1,980
Middle East	2,450	2,315
Africa	2,350	2,154

Source: Reutlinger and Selowsky (1976: 3).
[a] In addition to China, these data also exclude North Korea and the former North Vietnam. In China, at least, average daily calorie consumption is believed to exceed the regional standard.

Only in Latin America was average calorie consumption above the recommended minimum. In Asia, the Middle East, and Africa, there were shortfalls ranging from 135 to 230 calories per day. To bring the averages for these regions up to the standards would require an additional 269 thousand million calories daily, or approximately 25 million metric tons of food grains annually (Reutlinger and Selowsky, 1976: 3).

These averages, of course, tell us nothing about the distribution of food consumption within regions or among different groups within each country. (Women and recently weaned children are particularly likely to be underfed.) If the estimated worldwide deficit is based on country averages rather than regional averages, the daily calorie deficiency rises to 314 thousand million. Finally, calorie consumption within countries is not evenly distributed among the population. In Brazil, for example, average consumption in the early 1960s was 2,556 calories, yet 44 percent of the population fell below the regional standards. If the population of all developing countries is divided into 8 income groups, and calorie consumption estimated for each group, the worldwide calorie deficit in 1965 rises to 350 to 488 thousand million calories daily, depending on the assumptions made about the elasticity of calorie consumption with respect to income. (Again, these estimates exclude China, where the incidence of malnutrition is thought to be relatively low.) On an annual basis, this deficit amounted to 4 to 5 percent of world food grain production at the time. For the lowest income group in Asia, average daily consumption was estimated to be only 1,671 calories (Reutlinger and Selowsky, 1976: 3, 28).

The regional distribution of the worldwide deficit in 1965 was as follows:

Latin America	9–15 percent
Asia	58–64 percent
Middle East	9 percent
Africa	17–18 percent

Asia accounted for well over half the total, but in relation to regional population, the deficit was greatest in Africa. Comparable data for more recent years are not available, but it is unlikely that the general patterns prevailing in 1965 have changed much since then.

Strategies for Alleviating Malnutrition

Nutritional levels and income are clearly related, but general economic growth cannot be expected to eliminate most of the nutritional deficit in the foreseeable future. If, from 1965 to 1990, it is assumed that (1) current rates of per capita income growth are maintained, (2) all income groups experience the same increase in per capita income, and (3) world food supply increases just enough to meet the increased demand, the total calorie deficit would be unchanged. More people would be suffering from malnutrition, but their proportion of the total population would be less and the average degree of malnutrition would likewise be lower (Reutlinger and Selowsky, 1976: 3–4). Without deliberate income redistribution policies, however, assumption (2) is not likely to hold up, and the incidence and average degree of malnutrition in 1990, other things being equal, would very likely be about the same as it was in 1965.

Income redistribution is only one of several strategies that might be considered for alleviating malnutrition in developing countries. Others include countrywide food price subsidies, food price subsidies oriented specifically to target populations suffering from malnutrition, and food stamp programs for the malnourished. Reutlinger and Selowsky (1976: 5–7) calculate that food programs for target groups are more cost-effective (i.e., they cost less per $1 of food made available) than either countrywide food price subsidies or income redistribution. For Chile, Selowsky and Taylor estimated that a program to provide milk to infants up to age two would yield a return of more than 20 percent.[20] Large-scale implementation of any of these strategies is difficult in most developing countries, not just because of limited government resources but also because of resistance from upper- and middle-income groups. China and Cuba are two countries which have been able to bring about a significant redistribution of food consumption, but only because their governments have a high degree of political power, commitment, and organization.

Programs aimed at target populations do exist in developing countries, largely on the basis of food donations from developed countries channeled through the United Nations World Food Program or through bilateral efforts such as the U.S. Food for Peace program. But these would have to be greatly expanded or supplemented by domestic programs if the incidence and degree of malnutrition are to be significantly lowered.

Developing country governments can deal with nutritional problems in several other ways. Eckholm and Record (1976: 50) suggest that a government agency be established to monitor the nutritional impact of major policies and programs. In Brazil, they point out, government policies led to a substitution of export-destined soybeans for the traditional beans grown for local consumption. While comparative advantage purists might argue that the foreign exchange earned from soybeans would permit Brazil to import even more food than it had to forego to produce soybeans, such an argument completely ignores the distribution of consump-

20. Selowsky and Taylor, "The Economics of Malnourished Children," p. 29.

tion before and after the crop substitution. It is doubtful that poor Brazilian farm families whose bean consumption declined received enough imported food to compensate them fully for their losses. Few developing countries have the ability to issue detailed "nutritional impact statements" for all major policies and programs, but it does not require too much sophistication to make qualitative judgments which identify potential problems such as the Brazilian case just described.

Studies relating nutrition and family size suggest that family planning programs can raise average nutritional levels. Nutrition tends to be poorer in large families and in families where children are closely spaced. Fewer children and greater spacing also improve the general health of the mother.

Another strategy for alleviating malnutrition is education, either as part of regular school curricula or through special programs aimed at target groups. Because of ignorance and superstition, many poor families (but by no means all) fail to allocate their limited resources rationally to maximize the amount of nutrition received per dollar spent. In some countries it is believed that pregnant women should not eat protein-rich foods such as eggs, chicken, milk, and fish. Experience in Haiti and elsewhere shows that nutritional levels can be raised by teaching mothers how to prepare nutritionally balanced meals from locally available, inexpensive foods. While the mothers are taking the course (which also includes health education) and assisting in food preparation, their children are fed an improved diet daily for three to four months. Most children show significent weight gains during the course, and a high percentage retain most of their gains after the course has terminated. Before an expansion of these programs is recommended, though, more needs to be known about B/C relationships. There is good reason to believe that they are unfavorable, but unless the B/C ratios are particularly low, such programs can still be justified on humanitarian grounds.

Educational and promotional programs might also be established to encourage breast feeding, the practice and duration of which are declining in the developing world, particularly in urban areas. This is attributable not just to increased female employment outside the home but also to emulation of middle- and upper-class social groups and promotion of bottle feeding by foreign-based firms marketing formula foods. Berg (1973: Ch. 7) shows that breast feeding is much less costly than alternative methods of providing the same nutrition.[21] A study in India found that 50 percent of a mother's income would have to be spent on food

21. An additional advantage of breast feeding is that it has contraceptive effects. Furthermore, social custom in some societies prohibits intercourse during breast feeding (Berg, 1973: 93).

providing nutrition equivalent to breast feeding. Findings like this might be considered as an argument for women to stay at home, but with urbanization and education, women will increasingly demand remunerative employment outside the home. It may also be difficult to overcome social pressures to abandon breast feeding. While the benefits of increased breast feeding seem clear, we need to know more about the costs of effective programs to encourage it. There is a good case for increased international financing of pilot projects to determine these costs. Experimental programs could include new types of mass communications techniques, which, despite their promise, have not been particularly effective in nutrition education (Berg, 1973: 81–88).

In theory, it should be possible to incorporate nutrition education into elementary and secondary school curricula at relatively little opportunity cost by foregoing the geography of Western Europe at the elementary level and the plays of Molière at the secondary level. A number of countries have experimented with elementary school garden plots, planted and cared for by the students, as a means of teaching about both nutrition and farm practices. These efforts have often been disastrous because of poor management and supervision. At the secondary level, resources that might be spent on nutrition education would in most developing countries reach only the small percentage of the population which already is relatively well fed and therefore stands to gain little.

Finally, there is what might be called the *technological approach* to combating malnutrition. In the larger, more urbanized, and relatively high-income developing countries, fortification of basic foodstuffs is a promising strategy (Berg, 1973: 108–118). Fortified food is indistinguishable in appearance and taste from nonfortified food, requires no special promotional costs, and can yield benefits quickly. With large-scale central processing, vitamin and mineral requirements in the average five-year-old's diet can be supplied at very low cost—a total of $0.28 annually in the late 1960s. Fortification of bread with soy flour can provide protein at one-tenth the cost of milk (Berg, 1973: 114). Benefits appear to be high in relation to costs under such circumstances, despite the fact that many consumers would have adequate nutrition even without fortification.

In the poorest developing countries, however, the scope for fortification is limited. Most people live on farms and consume their own food grains (rice, corn, wheat, etc.) and other basic foodstuffs. Even when processed food is purchased, processors may operate on too small a scale to make fortification possible without passing costs on to consumers. And when consumers can choose a lower-cost, unfortified product, most of them—especially those who most need the higher-priced alternative— will do so. Under these conditions, making fortification mandatory, and/or subsidizing fortified products, may be too expensive in relation to benefits. Still, some products, such as salt and cooking oil, are purchased by even the poorest rural families. Iodization and iron fortification of salt, and multiple fortification of cooking oil, probably have high internal rates of return in many very poor countries.

In the last few decades, several promising formulated foods have been developed. Most of these are vegetable-based substitutes for milk or meat, combining cereals deficient in certain amino acids with foods rich in them. Among the formulated foods with costs lower than milk or meat are Incaparina, a blend of corn and cottonseed flour; CSM (corn-soy meal); WSB (wheat-soy blend); and textured vegetable protein, usually made from soybeans and now available in a variety of forms in U.S. supermarkets. Despite their low cost relative to animal proteins (at least if the size of the market permits mass production), these new foods are still more expensive than wheat, corn, rice, and other lower-quality sources of protein. There is also an acceptability problem to be overcome. The contribution of formulated foods to alleviating nutritional deficiencies is likely to be minor in the short and medium run, but in the future they may constitute a major element of nutritional programs in many developing countries.

Another technological strategy is the construction of community fish ponds to provide a low-cost source of protein. Fish-pond culture has been successful in paddy-rice areas in Asia, but it requires a level of management which rural residents (and governments) in other developing countries cannot always supply.

SUMMARY

Education and health are important dimensions of welfare, and government investment in these areas can help reduce inequalities of living standards. By improving the productivity of the labor force, investment in health services, nutrition programs, and education can also have a positive impact on economic growth. Unfortunately, we still know too little about which specific investments are likely to be the most productive. In some countries, an expansion of primary education may be the most productive, while elsewhere the highest returns may come from increased education at the secondary level. Our models and our data are not yet good enough to give clear guidelines, which in any event would have to be supplemented by important social and political considerations. We are even less certain about B/C relationships for health programs and for nutrition programs, whose ultimate objective is improved health status.

We do know, however, that educational and health planning must pay close attention to the distribution of project benefits. It cannot be blithely assumed that programs in these areas will ultimately lead to a narrowing of income differentials. If greater income equality is desired in the long run, health and educational programs must focus explicitly on low-income groups in the population.

Suggested Readings

Berg, Alan, with Robert Muscat. *The Nutrition Factor: Its Role in National Development.* Washington, D.C.: The Brookings Institution, 1973.
An excellent, comprehensive analysis of the role of nutrition in development, with an emphasis on policy. The case studies and examples are especially valuable. This book is easily read by undergraduates.

Eckholm, Erik, and Frank Record. *The Two Faces of Malnutrition.* Worldwatch Paper No. 9. Washington, D.C.: Worldwatch Institute, December 1976.
The "two faces" are undernutrition in the developing countries and overnutrition in the developed countries. This is a good, short (63-page), nontechnical introduction to the subject.

Freire, Paolo. *Pedagogy of the Oppressed.* Trans. by Myra Bergman Ramos. New York: Herder and Herder, 1970.
Freire is a former education professor at the University of Recife (Brazil). His method of teaching adult literacy begins by identifying, for each community, a few dozen words of key social significance for that community. Literacy training is then combined with consciousness raising to encourage people to take action to solve their own problems. The Freire method has great—even revolutionary—potential for bringing about social change. Conservative governments in Latin America have sometimes resorted to armed force to prevent its use.

Harbison, Frederick H. *Human Resources as the Wealth of Nations.* New York: Oxford University Press, 1973.
A good, relatively nontechnical survey of the economics of education and manpower in developing countries. Attention is also given to employment problems. Harbison regards full employment of all individuals, and the maximum development of their capacities, as the ultimate goal of development. The title of the book reflects the author's view of the importance of education.

Illich, Ivan. *Deschooling Society.* New York: Harper & Row, 1971.
Austrian-born Ivan Illich, who has resided in Mexico since 1960, is a major advocate of the interests of developing countries. Illich emphasizes that schooling is largely a process of socialization to a modern industrial society characterized by a high degree of inequality. He stresses the importance of nonformal education, for both children and adults, which sensitizes them to their social environment and gives them the means to change it.

Kamarck, Andrew. *The Tropics and Economic Development: A Provocative Inquiry into the Poverty of Nations.* Baltimore: The Johns Hopkins University Press for the World Bank, 1976.

Chapters 7 and 8 discuss the major health problems in the tropics and evaluate the measures that have been taken to control them.

Reutlinger, Shlomo, and Marcelo Selowsky. *Malnutrition and Poverty: Magnitude and Policy Options.* World Bank Staff Occasional Paper No. 23. Baltimore: The Johns Hopkins University Press, 1976.

The authors argue that economic growth alone, with no attention to income distribution, will do little to alleviate malnutrition. Programs aimed specifically at poorly fed groups are necessary, they say, if the incidence of malnutrition it to be significantly reduced. Part of the analysis will be difficult for undergraduates to follow, but there are some valuable data on nutritional levels by income groups.

Weisbrod, Burton A., et al. *Disease and Economic Development: The Impact of Parasitic Diseases in St. Lucia.* Madison: The University of Wisconsin Press, 1973.

This study investigates the impact of schistosomiasis and several other parasitic diseases on (1) birth and death rates, (2) school performance, and (3) labor productivity. The authors find little if any effects of these diseases on (1) and (2), and the effect on (3) is less than might be expected.

8

The Role of Government
Economic Planning

Only fifteen years ago, the subject of government participation in the development process was hotly debated in the economics literature. Advocates of planning were vigorously attacked by those who thought resources would be allocated more efficiently, and growth would be faster, if reliance were placed on market forces. Proponents of government intervention replied that market forces in the developing countries were not doing their job, since economic growth rates then were still rather low.

Today, there is much less debate on this issue. Most economists now readily admit that market forces work even more imperfectly in today's developing countries than they did in eighteenth- and nineteenth-century Europe and North America. Rigid social structures and lack of educational opportunities restrict occupational mobility; poor transportation facilities inhibit geographic mobility; and weak or nonexistent capital markets make it difficult to attract savings and channel them into productive investments. Under these circumstances, governments relying on "free markets" are simply giving the rich continued freedom to exploit the poor.

By directly attacking market imperfections, governments can actually make it possible for market forces to work better. If new lands are opened by road construction, eradication of malaria, and provision of farm credit, workers will move—of their own accord—from densely populated areas to thinly settled areas where their marginal productivities and thus their incomes will be higher. Increased investment in education, especially if it is directed at providing skills that are in short supply, will improve occupational mobility. The establishment of public financial institutions, or the encouragement of private ones, can increase savings and investment.

Most developing countries, however, want to do more than simply improve factor mobility. They want significantly higher rates of economic

182

growth, and they see comprehensive macroeconomic planning as a means of bringing this about. Planning promises to avoid waste and duplication and to subordinate short-run private profits to long-run national development. It also provides a means for balancing competing private and intra-government interests. Finally, planning is viewed as a tool for promoting development by alleviating malnutrition and unemployment, reducing income inequalities, and otherwise meeting the basic human needs of a much greater share of the population.

Though most developing countries have adopted national development plans, there is little evidence that comprehensive planning per se has had a major impact on rates of economic growth. Likewise, it has had little effect on meeting development objectives. These are routinely listed in plan documents (e.g., lower unemployment rates, a more equal distribution of income) but are rarely incorporated into planning models, which focus on growth and on capital shortages as the major constraints to growth. On the other hand, there is little reason to believe that, on balance, comprehensive planning has had any serious negative effects. As one observer has commented, it has been "a disappointing irrelevance."[1] Meanwhile, the increasing complexity of economic activity in developing countries makes *micro*-level or sectoral planning ever more desirable. This has nothing to do with "socialism" but rather with the need to reduce risks. Those bastions of capitalism, the large, private corporations which dominate the U.S. economy, freely admit that internal planning is vital to their own operations.[2]

DEVELOPMENT PLANNING:
MEANING AND ORIGINS

Perhaps the first thing that should be said about planning is that it does not mean the same thing as socialism. The term *socialism*, before its meaning became obscured by politicians and the press, meant government ownership of the means of production. A socialist economy may rely

1. John Sheahan, "Comment" (p. 195), on Carlos F. Díaz Alejandro, "Planning the Foreign Sector in Latin America," *American Economic Review, Papers and Proceedings*, 60 (May 1970), 169–179. Though some observers would argue that the human and financial resources devoted to comprehensive planning are wasted, it is possible that there are enough indirect benefits to public sector decision making to match or exceed the costs. As Gerald Meier has put it: "The active process of planning may indeed be of more benefit than the actual plan, for it can demonstrate the need for the collection and use of more empirical information, promote the dissemination of knowledge, clarify objectives and choices, and indicate the political and administrative preconditions necessary for implementing policies" (*Leading Issues in Economic Development*, 3rd ed. [New York: Oxford University Press, 1976], p. 784).
2. For a good example of the importance of planning in private corporations, see John Kenneth Galbraith's description of the Ford Motor Company's introduction of the Mustang in the early 1960s (1967: 23–29).

heavily on comprehensive macroeconomic planning, but it can also make extensive use of the market mechanism to allocate resources, as in Yugoslavia. *Development planning* is simply the use by government of a coordinated set of policy instruments to achieve national or regional economic objectives. It is quite compatible with a capitalist economy which relies heavily on the market mechanism. For example, if a country's citizens have decided through the political process that a higher rate of economic growth is desirable, the government can employ tax credits, subsidies, and other policies to encourage a higher rate of investment by the private sector.

Development plans have been prepared by most developing countries, many of which have been influenced by the success of the five-year plans initiated in the Soviet Union in 1928. But it is not just the socialist nations among the developed countries which have engaged in planning; a number of basically capitalist countries, including France, the Netherlands, and Sweden, have also adopted it. As Galbraith (1967) has argued persuasively, planning has been increasingly employed by industry as well as government because of technological reasons, not ideological ones. The growing complexity of modern technology, the large sums of money required to take advantage of economies of scale, and the long time required from the conception of a project until its completion all demand careful consideration of the various aspects of a particular project. Since so much is at stake in large investment projects, private firms will be very concerned with minimizing risks. Thus they will generally defend the economic stabilization role of government budgets (a limited, informal type of planning), despite the impression one sometimes receives from the public pronouncements of business leaders.

In the United States, business leaders have had a curiously ambivalent attitude toward planning. The Marshall Plan for post–World War II European recovery received a great deal of support, and its success was widely praised; but during the 1950s "planning" became a code word for Soviet-style socialism. In essence, planning came to be viewed as an all-or-nothing approach to economic decision making; even when planning was far from comprehensive, it was denounced as "creeping socialism." In the late 1950s and early 1960s, however, the sluggishness of the U.S. economy, together with military and economic successes in the Soviet Union, led to a rethinking of U.S. attitudes toward planning. Commissions on "national economic goals" were established, and with the passage of the National Defense Education Act of 1958, the country took a significant step in the direction of manpower planning. When the United States joined in an "Alliance for Progress" with the Latin American nations, it made U.S. aid conditional upon the adoption of medium- or long-term development plans.

Other bilateral and multilateral foreign assistance agencies have also insisted on development planning. Individual projects, they are saying, cannot be considered in isolation, for they have far-reaching effects on the rest of the economy. Planning enables a country better to see these relationships. It also provides a framework within which projects can be ranked according to a hierarchy of priorities, as determined not only by their estimated internal rates of return but also by social and political considerations. Since there are always more project proposals than available human and financial resources can support, an orderly system of decision making is desirable for choosing those projects which maximize net benefits to a country.

COMPREHENSIVE MACROECONOMIC PLANNING

The Scope of Comprehensive Macroeconomic Planning

No country, not even the Soviet Union or China, attempts to plan the output of every single producing unit in the economy. But when a country, perhaps guided by an econometric model of the economy, attempts to influence both the major macroeconomic variables (GNP, the unemployment rate, the price level, and the balance of payments) *and* the (national) output of most major industries or sectors of the economy, we can say that it is engaged in *comprehensive macroeconomic planning*. It may do this by using various combinations of direct and indirect controls, examples of which will be given below. In the Soviet Union, most of the controls are direct, with national output targets for the major industries passed down through several layers of bureaucracy until each state-owned firm is assigned a specific output target. Countries like the Netherlands and France, where most enterprises are privately owned, rely more on indirect controls which seek to influence private decision making. In the developing countries, it is interesting to note that there is not always a close correlation between the scope of formal macroeconomic planning and the importance of the state as an owner of the means of production. India has had an elaborate formal macroeconomic planning mechanism since the early 1950s, but about 90 percent of manufacturing activity is in private hands. In Brazil and Mexico, on the other hand, the government owns a greater share of the means of production, but formal macroeconomic planning is less important.

The careful reader will have noticed that the word *formal* was quietly inserted in the last three sentences. This was done to introduce a distinction between what might be called form and substance. Many elaborate (or not so elaborate) plans in developing countries do little more than collect dust; the form is there, but there is no substance. Conversely, Japan, whose government says relatively little about comprehensive macroeconomic planning, actually engages in it to an important extent through close interrelationships among government, industry, and banking; the substance is there, behind the scenes, though the form is not.

Objectives, Goals, Target Variables, and Instrument Variables

Planning is always done for some purpose; it is not an end in itself. Objectives are usually stated very broadly, e.g., a higher standard of living, full employment, and greater equality in the distribution of income. Specific goals are then quantified for key economic variables which measure progress toward the broad objectives. These are the *target variables* of the plan. For comprehensive macroeconomic plans, the target variables for a particular year might be a GNP growth rate of 6 percent, an increase in employment of 4 percent, a rate of inflation of no more than 12 percent, and a balance-of-payments deficit that does not exceed $150 million. Targets may also be established for particular sectors of the economy: e.g., a 4 percent growth rate for agriculture, 9 percent for manufacturing, and 8 percent for construction.

The plan shows how the goals are to be achieved through the manipulation of *instrument variables*—the policy tools which the government has at its command. Instrument variables affect the target variables either directly or indirectly. *Direct controls* are those which interfere with market forces. To meet the inflation target, for example, a government may impose wage and price controls, and to minimize the balance-of-payments deficit it may restrict imports by rationing import licenses. Health goals may be met by requiring that all children in public schools be inoculated against certain diseases. A government also exercises direct controls to the extent that it is an owner of the means of production. A shift in sector priorities, for example, will be accompanied by a reallocation of the government's own investment funds, e.g., from manufacturing to agriculture. *Indirect controls* rely on the market mechanism to guide individual decision making in the directions outlined in the plan. Total economic activity can be increased by expansionary monetary and fiscal policies; but lower interest rates, or a higher tax credit for a new investment, will do little to affect the composition of output.[3] If a reallocation

3. Actually, these policies are not as neutral in their effects on resource allocation as might appear at first glance. For example, some industries—e.g., construction—are more heavily dependent on borrowed funds than others; thus they are more sensitive to changes in interest rates than industries dominated by a few large firms which rely mainly on internal sources of financing. An investment tax credit benefits capital-intensive industries more than labor-intensive industries, and in developing countries it encourages an often unwise substitution of capital for labor.

of resources is desired, indirect controls will have to be more specific, affecting some industries more than others. For example, tax rebates can be offered to firms producing for export markets but not to those producing for domestic consumption. Subsidized interest rates could be offered to farmers but not to manufacturing industries. Tariffs can be lowered to force domestic firms to be more competitive, and they can be increased to encourage more domestic production. In all of these cases, private firms still make the ultimate decisions; the government simply alters the figures which firms must use in making their investment decisions.[4]

The Planning Organization

Authority for planning typically is vested in a National Planning Board (NPB), whose head usually (but not always) reports directly to the chief executive. The NPB is staffed with economists, statisticians, and technical experts in various fields who use historical data to construct a model showing the interrelationships among the key variables in the economy. The model can be used to test for consistency among a particular set of targets. Referring back to our hypothetical example, the NPB is supposed to make sure that a 6 percent growth rate of GNP will be sufficient to achieve a 4 percent increase in employment without compromising the inflation and balance-of-payments objectives. It may turn out that 6 percent is insufficient, in which case the employment target will have to be lowered or the GNP target raised; the later course risks possible conflicts with other objectives.

This, at least, is an example of how a model *should* be used. Actual experience suggests that macroeconomic models in many countries have had little influence on the final design of the plan. Usually developed to a large extent by foreign advisors, these models may be understood only by a handful of NPB technicians. The NPB leadership may lack a clear understanding of what the technicians are telling them about the realism and compatibility of plan targets. As a result, plan targets may be determined more by political considerations than by economic feasibility.

In establishing national economic targets, the NPB cannot act on its own. If the plan is to have widespread support, there must be close coordination with other government agencies and consultation with representatives of the private sector. Since the interests of various government agencies will often be in conflict (not to mention conflicts between

4. In developing countries, only a small number of firms actually make formal IRR or similar calculations. Most business proprietors simply do some rough figuring on the back of an envelope or in their heads. They often make mistakes, as do proprietors in developed countries; but they certainly are able to distinguish between incentives and disincentives.

the private and public sectors), there must be room for compromise. If the NPB takes too rigid a stand, political support for the plan will be weak.

The most important support for the plan is that of the chief executive. If he or she does not stand behind the NPB's compromise goals, planning is not likely to be very effective, and policy and program decisions will continue to be made by traditional, often *ad hoc* methods. In many developing countries, this is precisely what happens. The NPB's authority and access to the chief executive are nominal only, and planning is little more than a formality.

Time Frames

Comprehensive macroeconomic plans can be placed into three categories on the basis of their time frames. *Long-term* or *perspective* plans usually cover a period of fifteen to twenty years. Since uncertainty increases with the passage of time, goals are highly aggregative, and these plans do not go into great detail on an industry-by-industry basis. The Soviet Union's perspective plan for 1960–1980 assumed that economic growth would average 7 to 8 percent annually. By the end of the plan, it was anticipated, socialism would be replaced by communism, with income distributed according to need, not productivity (Tinbergen, 1967: 52). These goals and objectives will not be met, but the plan has nevertheless been useful as a framework for shorter-term planning.

Perspective plans are particularly useful in planning for social overhead capital projects which have a long gestation period and are best built in stages. For example, it takes several years just to conduct a prefeasibility study and then a feasibility study for a hydroelectric power project. Construction may take four to five years. Since it is often easier to add a new stage to an existing facility than to build an entirely new one, the project design must allow for expansion. This means that the prefeasibility study requires an estimate of the demand for electricity twenty to thirty years or so into the future. A perspective plan provides such an estimate. Perspective plans are also useful for determining educational policy. If the projected age structure of the population ten years later shows a decline in the percentage of school-age children, building schools to relieve a present shortage of classrooms may not be advisable, since there would be vacant classrooms not far into the future. Some other solution to the current shortage can then be suggested.

The type of plan which most attracts the attention of the public is the *medium-term plan*, which commonly covers a period of five years. A good medium-term plan is very detailed, specifying year-by-year target variables and describing how instrument variables will be used to achieve the targets. Even over a five-year period, of course, unforeseen events— a prolonged drought, a sharp rise in imported energy prices, an increase in the world market price of the country's main export—can radically alter the economic scene. This calls for a revision of targets, and a good medium-term plan will allow for continual revision as economic conditions change.

Finally, there is the *annual operational plan,* based on the goals of the medium-term plan but providing, at least for the public sector, the same kind of detail as found in the government budget. In a rapidly changing economic environment, countries would be well advised to place more emphasis on annual planning than on tinkering with the medium-term plan, or to adopt "rolling plans" which each year extend the medium-term horizon by an additional year but concentrate on the current year.

A Simple Model

Macroeconomic models of developed economies can be extremely complicated, consisting of hundreds of variables and equations. In developing countries, however, these models are much simpler, for at least three reasons: (1) lack of financial resources necessary for designing and utilizing a complex model; (2) lack of the necessary technical skills; and (3) lack of reliable data. A simple model, it is true, has the drawback of not taking into account all factors that might have an important influence on a particular variable. For example, students who go beyond Principles of Economics 001 soon find that reliable consumption functions are more complicated than $C = a + bY$. Moreover, consumption functions for different categories of goods have different properties. On the other hand, a simple model has the advantage of being more easily understood by policy makers, whose recommendations are supposed to be based to a large degree on the model. In addition, if some key variables (e.g., consumption, investment, domestic savings) are estimated only at the aggregate level, rather than built up from measured component parts, disaggregating them generally means that the estimated component parts are less reliable than the aggregate.

Figure 8.1 illustrates a simple model of an economy divided into four sectors: a household sector, a financial sector, a production sector, and a foreign sector.[5] Each sector can be described by an equation (or, in the case of the foreign sector, by three equations) showing that the

---

5. This model is taken from *Manpower in Social and Economic Development,* Proceedings of the Fourth International Manpower Seminar, 1964 (Washington, D.C.: U.S. Agency for International Development [1964]). It is based on a presentation by Prof. Gustav Ranis.

Figure 8.1
A Simple Macroeconomic Planning Model

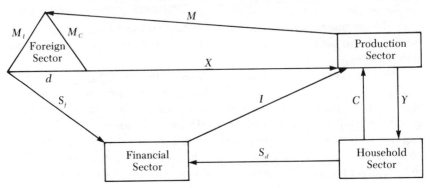

inflows into a sector are balanced by the outflows. These *tautological,* or definitional, equations are as follows:

$$Y = C + S_d \qquad \text{(Household sector)}$$

$$I = S_f + S_d \qquad \text{(Financial sector)}$$

$$C + I + X = Y + M \qquad \text{(Production sector)}$$

$$M = M_I + M_C$$

$$M_C = X + d \qquad \text{(Foreign sector)}$$

$$M_I + d = S_f$$

where Y = aggregate output (income)
C = consumption
I = investment
X = exports
M = imports
M_C = imports of consumption goods
M_I = imports of investment goods
S_d = domestic savings
S_f = foreign savings
d = deficit (difference between imports of consumption goods and exports)

If five of the six sectors are in balance, then the sixth must also be. In other words, there are only five *independent* equations. But since there ten variables, we need a total of ten independent equations to form a simultantous equations system in which we can solve for all the variables.

One of the early planning models for Pakistan chose the following additional equations, which describe *behavioristic* relationships:

$$Y = Y_0$$
$$C = f(Y)$$
$$I = k(Y)$$
$$X = X_0$$
$$M_C = f(Y)$$

The first of these equations simply says that output is determined exogenously—i.e., it is the target level of output established by the NPB. Exports are also determined exogenously, while consumption, imports of consumption goods, and investment are functionally related to income (and only income). The nature of each functional relationship is determined by historical data covering a reasonably long period of time.

Given a particular target level of income, the model tells us how this income will be divided between consumption and investment. It will also determine how much investment will be financed by foreign savings, including foreign aid. If the amount of foreign aid the country can expect to receive is less than the amount called for by the model, planners will have to consider lowering the target rate of economic growth or setting a higher export target and suggest policies for achieving it.

The Experience of Planning: Some Major Problems

The macroeconomic plans adopted by developing countries vary in complexity and technical soundness, but with few exceptions they have one common characteristic: their ineffectiveness. The acceleration in economic growth rates since 1960 has had little to do with the preparation of planning documents which prescribe the speed and direction of growth and identify the policy instruments that are to be used to achieve national economic objectives and goals. Indeed, economic growth has often proceeded in directions not foreseen by the plan, or if in accordance with the plan would have occurred even in its absence. If one is to look for explanations for more rapid economic growth in the developing countries, the reasons probably include more rapid growth in the developed countries, increased transfers of capital and technical assistance, better public administration, and improvements in the quality of human resources.

The principal shortcomings of macroeconomic planning in developing countries have been the following:

1. *Poor technical design.* This can occur simply because the government is not seriously interested in planning, undertaking it only as a *pro forma* exercise to satisfy international agencies or some domestic con-

stituency. But even when the commitment to planning is there, the soundness of the plan will be limited by deficiencies in both human and financial resources that can be overcome only partially with foreign assistance. Even if objectives and goals are clearly stated, they may be unrealistic or inconsistent because of balance-of-payments or manpower constraints. Specific actions necessary to achieve plan targets frequently are not identified. If they are, the costs of undertaking each action may not be calculated, and the plan may promise more than available resources can deliver. With time, these deficiencies become less serious as planners, economists, statisticians, engineers, and other technical personnel become aware of obstacles and interrelationships that initially escaped their attention. But in the early stages of planning, major errors are likely to be made.

2. *Poor data.* Macroeconomic data in developing countries usually are not very reliable. Savings and investment estimates may be particularly poor, and this means that the capital-output ratios used in the plan may be seriously in error. The estimated marginal propensity to import may ignore trends in contraband imports (which may increase significantly if legal imports are restricted). Poor data can lead a government to expand the economy too rapidly, thus inviting rapid inflation and a balance-of-payments crisis.

3. *Poor implementation.* Even a well-prepared plan will be ineffective unless careful attention is paid to *implementation*. A good plan clearly identifies investment priorities, and adherence to these priorities requires the cooperation of the various cabinet ministries and other implementing agencies. If these agencies are not adequately consulted during the preparation of the plan, securing their cooperation during the implementation phase will be difficult.[6] Even if there is consultation, an implementing agency must have a bureaucratic structure which links its programs directly with plan targets. This means that the agency needs to have a planning/programing unit of its own which works closely with the NPB. One of the most experienced observers of planning in developing countries has argued that "the absence of ineffectiveness of [sectoral] programing units is the most important flaw in the planning apparatus of even the more experienced less developed countries" (Waterston, 1965: 376).

4. *Public sector fragmentation.* In many developing countries, the central government has far from complete control over public sector revenues and expenditures, and its ability to reallocate public resources to meet plan objectives is thus limited. In Ecuador, for example, hundreds of autonomous and semi-autonomous government entities accounted for

---

6. On the other hand, if there is too much consultation, as in India, the planning process can become bogged down in endless discussion.

48 percent of all public sector revenues and 54 percent of public expenditures during 1969–1970—more than the central government proper. Together, these agencies usually have had a substantial budget surplus, but the central government has been able to tap only a part of it by pressuring the decentralized agencies into purchasing government bonds. Cash surpluses appear in part because these agencies receive some of their revenues through legislated tax earmarking, which automatically assigns an agency a fixed percentage of a particular tax without regard to the agency's year-to-year programing.

Policy control of decentralized agencies by central governments is less than complete, since many of them have powerful political constituencies which the central government must be wary of challenging. In the case of Ecuador, several of the most important decentralized agencies are regionally based, reflecting historic rivalries between the coast and the highlands. For example, there is a highway commission for Guayas Province which charges tolls and builds its own roads. National planners might conclude that the rate of return on additional road construction in Guayas would be 6 percent, compared with 20 percent in some of the highland provinces; but neither they nor the central government generally (which historically has been weak) have much power to reallocate resources away from Guayas toward other provinces.

Another reason for the existence of autonomous or semi-autonomous entities is that foreign assistance agencies often prefer to deal with specialized administrative units removed as much as possible from domestic politics. The establishment of such agencies has sometimes been a precondition for foreign assistance.

5. *Lack of support by the chief executive.* As we have already indicated, support from the head of government is crucial for the success of the plan (though it will not guarantee success). If this support is not forthcoming, priorities identified by the planners will be ignored, and agency heads will bargain for funds directly with the chief executive, circumventing the planning agency. In Ecuador, for example, planners had little influence under populist President José María Velasco Ibarra, who during his last administration (1968–1972) frequently attacked the NPB publicly and refused to adopt its plan for 1970–1973. In Velasco's view the "true needs of the people" were not those identified by the planners but rather schools, roads, potable water, and other infrastructure projects (whose location was often determined by domestic political considerations). Planning, in other words, was virtually a meaningless exercise.[7] A close observer of planning in Africa maintains that there is "no

7. See Clarence Zuvekas, Jr., "Economic Planning in Ecuador: An Evaluation," *Inter-American Economic Affairs*, 25 (Spring 1972), 45–73.

African state which is currently engaged in a serious planning effort, in the sense of using its plan as a guide to day-to-day policy decisions and the preparation of its budgets" (Killick, 1976: 163).

6. *Lack of private sector support.* Most developing countries have mixed economies, and planners thus must be concerned with private sector activity. The guidelines established in a comprehensive macroeconomic plan are usually mandatory for the public sector (at least by law, though not usually in fact), but they can only serve as guidelines for the private sector. Planning can be advantageous to the private sector by reducing the risks of new private investment. This requires mutual cooperation between the public and private sectors, so that each is aware of the other's broad intentions. The private sector wants to know about monetary and fiscal policy, tariff policy, and wage policy, all of which influence investment decisions. The public sector, on the other hand, has an interest in knowing what the private sector intends to do so that it can provide the stimulus or restraint deemed desirable to keep the economy moving toward the plan targets.

In many countries, there is a great deal of distrust between the private and public sectors. Planners may consider the private sector to be interested in personal gain rather than the national interest, while the business community fears that the planners will want to impose higher taxes to provide the resources needed to achieve public sector targets. Frequently, there is little consultation with the private sector during the preparation of the plan, a situation which only invites trouble during the implementation phase.

In a recent review of planning in developing countries, Tony Killick argues forcefully that its lack of success is due not simply to the factors noted above but fundamentally to "the naïvety of the implicit model of governmental decision-making incorporated in the planning literature" (1976: 161). Economists and planners, he says, implicitly assume that governments try to act in the national interest, as if it were possible to define clearly what this is and what kind of tradeoffs are necessary to maximize the country's "social welfare function." Also implied is a clear set of policy objectives, a high degree of centralization of government authority, and unity of purpose.

In most developing countries, however, society is pluralistic, with sharp differences existing not only among socioeconomic classes (or power groups) but also within them. Many unscheduled changes of government, for example, are due to deep divisions with the military. Under these circumstances, political power is fragmented, and no group can impose its own policies, unaltered, on others. Moreover, the weakness of political institutions makes it difficult for power groups to judge accurately the relative strengths and the policy positions of their competitors.

Given this situation, and the major economic uncertainties which government decision makers must face in preparing a medium-term plan, there is a natural tendency for governments to want to keep objectives and goals broad and priorities fuzzy. There is little scope, in other words, for the detailed, comprehensive, "rational" planning described in most of the literature on this subject.

Killick does not go on to conclude that all planning should be abolished, though he is skeptical about the advisability of continued attention to *medium*-term plans. Planning is still useful, he points out, for anticipating problems, reducing uncertainties, bringing order to the budgeting process, providing feedback, and in general introducing more rationality to decision making. Annual plans, Killick suggests, make more sense than five-year plans. A decade earlier, Waterston (1965) argued that countries whose governments lacked the authority and technical expertise necessary for comprehensive macroeconomic planning might best concentrate their efforts on project planning or sector planning (see below).

Planning from Abroad?

A case can be made that comprehensive macroeconomic planning for developing countries is being carried out not only by their own NPBs but also by one or more of the major development assistance agencies. The World Bank has developed its own macroeconomic models for some countries and, like U.S. AID and the Inter-American Development Bank, has made explicit its own ideas about development priorities in particular countries. Sometimes, an informal, even unspoken, consensus seems to develop among these agencies. Since the development assistance agencies together contribute more than half of the public investment funds for a number of developing countries, and since they have some influence over which projects will be financed, it is not at all farfetched to suggest that this constitutes planning from abroad.

MANPOWER PLANNING

During the 1960s, developing countries became interested in manpower planning as a means of solving some of the human resource bottlenecks that appeared to hinder achievement of development objectives. A comprehensive manpower plan acts as a bridge between the national development plan and the educational system, identifying the skilled human resources needed to fulfill plan objectives and showing how the educational system will provide the additional skills not imported from abroad. Thus conceived, comprehensive manpower planning implies acceptance of what in the previous chapter was called the manpower requirements approach to determining investment priorities in education. As we shall see, this demands that planning have a long-term perspective. (It is possible to conceive of manpower planning based on the rate-of-return approach to determining educational priorities, though this would be a more limited form of planning which could be used to rank alternative educational investments without reference to a national plan.)

A comprehensive manpower plan must adopt a long-term perspective because decisions made about educational priorities at the beginning of a medium-term plan will have an important bearing on manpower supply not only during the five years or so of this plan but also ten to fifteen years in the future. If the long-term macroeconomic plan calls for a doubling of chemical and petrochemical production in the next ten years, action will have to be taken right away to ensure that the required number of chemical engineers will be available. Unless a country wants to rely on foreign manpower to fill the gaps—which few if any countries want to do on a permanent basis—steps must first be taken to train more teachers of chemical engineers, build more classrooms and other facilities, and purchase needed equipment. Just to set up a program like this and to secure financing for it can take two or more years. Several additional years are then needed for the facilities to be built and for the new teachers to receive graduate-level training abroad in their specialties. Enrollments can then increase, but it will be another four to five years before the larger entering classes graduate.

Manpower plans must pay attention not only to highly trained specialists such as engineers, scientists, physicians, and managers, but also to nurses, engineering technicians, primary and secondary school teachers, skilled mechanics, repair specialists, and other middle-level manpower. Both formal and nonformal education must be considered.

If comprehensive macroeconomic planning is taken seriously and implemented reasonably well, the case for manpower planning is a compelling one. Potential shortages can be identified and monetary incentives used to guide people into shortage occupations. At the same time, disincentives or enrollment limitations can be used to reduce projected manpower surpluses. So long as performance under the macroeconomic plan is more or less on target, implementation of the manpower plan is likely to look rather good.

In practice, however, manpower planning has been just as disappointing as comprehensive macroeconomic planning. If plan goals and objectives are ignored by the chief executive, the economy will grow in different directions from those projected in the macroeconomic plan, and manpower needs will thus differ from those identified in the manpower plan. Unforeseen events can also blow the economy off course and thus change manpower needs. Finally, many developing countries find it difficult to use incentives and disincentives effectively to steer students away from high-prestige surplus occupations to low-prestige shortage occupation. It is easy to say that enrollments in law can be limited; but the unpopularity of such a measure might make it politically difficult to implement.

The fate of Ecuador's manpower plan is a good example of how ineffective this type of planning has been.[8] In 1965, foreign assistance was obtained to prepare a manpower plan based on the goals established in the comprehensive macroeconomic plan for 1964–1973. Field work began in January 1966, but publication of the results did not occur until August 1970 (though some data were available in late 1969). This delay meant that some opportunities were missed to implement medium- and long-term measures necessary to correct manpower imbalances projected for 1973 (and for 1980, the terminal date of the manpower plan). The long delay in the preparation of the manpower plan was caused primarily by lack of support for planning by the government administrations succeeding the one under which the plan was begun. Budget allocations to the NPB were cut, and few persons received the necessary technical training to assist in the preparation of the manpower plan. When the plan finally did appear, unforeseen events had made parts of it obsolete.

In recent years, there seems to have been declining interest in the kind of comprehensive manpower planning we have just described. At the same time, more attention is being given to the manpower implications of sector and project plans. In addition, there has been growing concern about finding jobs—or more productive jobs—for unskilled workers, whom comprehensive manpower plans tend to ignore on the grounds that their supply will continue to exceed the demand.

REGIONAL PLANNING

National economic plans sometimes establish goals for each of a country's regions, which may be defined by either political or natural boundaries. In the Soviet Union, for example, each of the fifteen republics has its own plan, and within the republics targets are established at the provincial and even the district level. Between 1957 and 1965, day-to-day administration of industrial enterprises was the responsibility of regional entities called *sovnarkhozy*, of which there were originally more than 100. Regional planning is also important in other Eastern European countries.

In the developing world, however, regional development planning is not even attempted by some countries with national plans, and where it exists it is usually ineffective. In Ecuador, for example, regional planning

8. Ibid., 66–68.

was incorporated into the ten-year plan for 1964–1973; but the NPB had few resources to devote to this task, and no meaningful planning at this level occurred. In the late 1960s, the NPB again stressed the need for regional planning as a means of (1) reducing regional inequalities, (2) providing for base-level participation in project planning and implementation, and (3) improving the allocation of national resources. Five regional groupings were proposed, and in three cases the new regions were to include one or more provinces in each of the country's three major geographic divisions: the coast, the highlands, and the eastern lowlands. It was argued—rather naïvely—that such groupings would help reduce historic interregional rivalries, particularly those between the coast and the highlands. Such considerations seem to have outweighed the economic factors, for some of the NPB's proposed regions were of dubious viability economically.

A more serious problem for the national planners in Ecuador was the prior existence of eight regional or provincial development organizations whose *raison-d'être* was implicitly questioned by the NPB. During the 1970s, the regional planning picture in Ecuador became highly confused when several regional development organizations were abolished by the central government but several new ones were established either by local initiative or by pressure placed on the central government by provincial interests. These regional organizations lacked a uniform structure, purpose, and relationship to the central government. Their territories sometimes overlapped, and some of them sought to usurp the functions of national ministries or specialized government agencies such as those dealing with irrigation and electric power. Their priorities did not always coincide with those in the national plan, which in any event was largely nonoperative.

The Ecuadorean case is not unique. Regional "planning" bodies in many other countries often are little more than lobbying groups organized by private economic interests or by local politicians looking for bacon to bring home to their constituents. In other cases, the main motivation may be genuinely humanitarian—e.g., to improve health and education for the masses in a particular region. In all these cases, though, regional development problems are not viewed with a national perspective. What may be considered a high-priority project by a particular region may be given low priority by national planners. Where the central government is relatively weak, compromises with local and provincial authorities will have to be made which may be inconsistent with the goals established in the national plan. National planning is thus ineffective, and regional "planners" often do not even bother to prepare a regional plan. Even in countries where regional planning nominally is integrated closely with national planning (e.g., India and Pakistan), administrative shortcomings have limited its effectiveness.

This not to say that regional planning in developing countries is always a failure. Waterston (1965: 548–549) reports that it has been successful in Malaysia and was making promising headway in one of Nigeria's four former regions (prior to the attempted secession of that region in 1966). In other cases, regional planning organizations have capably implemented a limited form of planning based on a few large regional infrastructure projects. In Ecuador, the regional organization for Manabí province has successfully planned and administered irrigation and water supply projects within its boundaries. On the whole, however, regional planning has been just as disappointing as national economic planning.

SECTOR PLANNING

During the past ten years, many developing countries—at the urging of the major international assistance agencies—have devoted a great deal of effort to sector planning. Where this type of planning is practiced, planning units have been established in the relevant government ministries or other agencies to coordinate or collaborate with the NPB in the preparation of medium-term and annual plans. For some sectors of the economy (e.g., electric power and transportation), long-term planning documents must also be prepared. A sector plan cannot be drawn up in isolation, since some assumptions must be made about macroeconomic trends in the economy. For example, all sector plans are dependent in part upon tax revenues, which in turn will depend on the overall level of economic activity (as well as planned changes in tax rates and tax administration). In the case of electric power, demand for electricity must be projected far into the future. This requires not only some assumption about the overall rate of economic growth but also about the sectoral composition of growth, since manufacturing is a particularly heavy user of electricity. Still, sector planning does not require the economywide detail necessary for comprehensive planning. Since its focus is limited, it is both technically and politically easier than comprehensive planning.

Like regional planning, sector planning can be an outgrowth of the NPB's comprehensive macroeconomic plan. However, in some countries the locus of planning now lies not in the NPB but in the planning units in the implementing agencies—at least for certain sectors of the economy. In Haiti, for example, the Ministry of Agriculture's planning unit has assumed major responsibility for agricultural sector planning, and its targets are not always consistent with those of the NPB. To the extent that one can speak of planning in Haiti, it is the Ministry of Agriculture's targets that are operative.

The growth of sector planning in developing countries should not be surprising, since it is a rational response to the disillusionment with comprehensive macroeconomic planning. In general, it is less technically demanding,[9] requires fewer political compromises, and gives the relevant agencies more of a vested interest in implementation by making them—rather than the NPB—primarily responsible for planning. International agencies are likely to continue encouraging sector planning, which—despite sometimes unrealistic goals—promises to be more effective than comprehensive planning has been.

PROJECT PLANNING

Even those who are opposed to comprehensive macroeconomic planning on philosophical grounds would find it difficult to make a good case against project planning. Economists strongly disposed toward free markets can readily accept the value of ranking projects according to their IRRs or B/C ratios and choosing those projects with the highest rankings. Those who believe that social considerations should also enter into the decision-making process have an interest in seeing that income redistribution goals, for example, are achieved at the least possible sacrifice of other goals.

Governments can play an important role in planning not only for social overhead projects but also for projects in manufacturing or other sectors of the economy in which private interests are expected to make most if not all of the investment. Since many potential private investors have very limited knowledge of production technology, export marketing, possibilities for joint ventures with foreign companies, taxes and tariffs, and other key information, government assistance in filling these knowledge gaps can constitute an important stimulus to private investment. In some countries, governments have established industrial promotion agencies to provide technical assistance to private enterprises and to conduct preinvestment or prefeasibility studies to separate promising projects from those whose prospects do not appear to be good. A preinvestment study will provide an estimate of project costs by major category; evaluate alternative project sites by analyzing soil conditions and considering the availability of water, power, and transportation; and assess the market for the industry's product. Given this head start, private firms find it much less of a burden to obtain the more detailed information that will be needed before a decision whether to invest can be made. Preinvestment studies can be included as part of a comprehensive macroeconomic plan,

9. In some countries, however, complex linear programing models have been prepared in the hopes that they will serve as a basis for agricultural sector planning. Preliminary indications are that they are not being used as much as their sponsors (the international developing agencies) had hoped, largely because the technical (and financial) demands have been too great. In addition, the usefulness of these models is sometimes limited by poor underlying data.

but they can also be conducted in the absence of such a plan. Even in the latter case, however, some assumptions about future economic growth have to be made.

Preinvestment studies are also important for social overhead capital projects proposed for government financing. As we noted in chapter 6, determination of IRRs for such projects is particularly difficult because of the importance of externalities on both the cost and benefit sides. Failure to consider all relevant benefits and costs can result in serious investment errors, both of commission and of omission.

SUMMARY

There is widespread agreement that comprehensive macroeconomic planning in the developing countries, with few exceptions, has failed significantly to increase economic growth rates or to affect other target variables. Still, it is not entirely fair to be so critical of planning per se, for in many countries what is called "planning" was never intended to be anything of the sort. Even in countries where serious planning has been attempted but has borne little fruit, poor performance is not due entirely to an unfavorable environment; the mistakes of inexperience and naïveté also have played a role. As experience is gained, it is quite likely that plan performance will improve in those countries that are seriously committed to it.

Notwithstanding the poor record of planning in developing countries, there is no noticeable trend away from it. Comprehensive medium-term plans continue to be prepared, with the blessing and sometimes the active support of the major economic assistance agencies. Interest also continues in manpower planning, though in the future this activity may be less comprehensive than some of the ambitious efforts in past years. Sector planning is becoming more important in many countries, but effective regional planning is still confined to a relatively few countries. Virtually everyone accepts the need for project planning, which in most developing countries will continue to require the assistance of foreign specialists for many years to come.

Suggested Readings

Bauer, Peter T. *Dissent on Development.* London: Weidenfeld and Nicolson, 1971.

> Included in this book is a good exposition of the philosophical case against planning (pp. 69–75), based on the argument that planning increases the power of government at the expense of individuals.

Galbraith, John Kenneth. *The New Industrial State*. Boston: Houghton Mifflin Company, 1967.

Galbraith argues that increasing technological complexity forces both business firms and governments to engage in progressively more detailed planning. He believes that this "technological determinism" will narrow the differences among various economic systems.

Griffin, Keith B., and John L. Enos. *Planning Development*. Reading, Mass.: Addison-Wesley Publishing Company, 1970.

A detailed description and evaluation of the techniques and practice of comprehensive macroeconomic planning; sector planning in agriculture, industry, and education; and population planning. Included are brief case studies of Latin America, Turkey, Ghana, Pakistan, and India.

Grossman, Gregory. *Economic Systems*. 2nd ed. Englewood Cliffs, N.J.: Prentice-Hall, Inc., 1974.

This short introduction to the subject of comparative economic systems includes a brief description of planning and how it is practiced in the Soviet Union, Eastern Europe, China, Cuba, France, Sweden, and the Netherlands.

Killick, Tony. "The Possibilities of Development Planning," *Oxford Economic Papers*, 28 (July 1976), 161–184.

This provocative review of planning experiences in developing countries argues that comprehensive macroeconomic planning has little chance for success in the pluralistic political environments which characterize almost all developing countries. Not opposed to planning on philosophical grounds, Killick argues that more limited types of planning would have greater effectiveness.

Lewis, W. Arthur. *Development Planning: The Essentials of Economic Policy*. London: George Allen and Unwin, 1966.

A detailed introduction to planning, written for "the intelligent layman." Basic techniques are explained, but the emphasis is on policy. Successful planning, Lewis argues, is based on "sensible politics and good public administration."

Tinbergen, Jan. *Development Planning*. Trans. by N. D. Smith. New York: McGraw-Hill Book Company, 1967.

A general introduction to development planning by a Nobel-prizewinning economist who has had many years of experience with planning in the Netherlands.

Waterston, Albert. *Development Planning: Lessons of Experience*. Baltimore: The Johns Hopkins University Press for the International Bank for Reconstruction and Development, 1965.

This is still the most comprehensive evaluation of development planning available. Drawing on his own experience as a World Bank advisor, as well as that of others, Waterston explains, using many examples, why planning has been a disappointment to its advocates.

9

Agriculture and Rural Development

Most people in developing countries earn their living directly from agricultural sector activities, defined broadly to include crop farming, livestock production, hunting, fishing, and forestry. A high percentage of the labor force in agriculture (70 to 95 percent in the poorest countries) means that productivity per worker is low. With little capital or land to work with, the average farmer produces scarcely more than enough to keep his or her own family—and that rather poorly. Only a small surplus is left to support workers in nonagricultural activities.[1] By contrast, only 4 percent of the U.S. labor force is engaged in farming, and yet the United States not only feeds its own population (often to excess) but also exports more than $20 billion worth of agricultural products each year, well above the value of its agricultural imports.

Per capita food production in the developing countries not only is low but has been stagnant since the early 1960s, as we shall see below. A country can experience economic growth with a stagnant agricultural sector, but it is likely to be growth without development. If living standards are to rise for the masses of people in rural areas, the productivity of agricultural labor will have to increase. There is no standard formula, however, for achieving productivity growth. As Hayami and Ruttan (1971) emphasize, each country must follow a unique process of technical change based on its original factor endowments and the pattern of its

---

1. This does not mean that most farmers in the least developed countries are pure subsistence farmers, producing food only for themselves and their families. In fact, they engage in considerable trade in agricultural products with each other, and many produce crops and livestock products for urban and export markets. In Haiti, the poorest country in the Western Hemisphere, nearly all farm families are market-oriented to a significant degree, with about half growing coffee as a cash crop. Production per farm, though, is very low.

resource accumulation over time. Technical change tends to be most effective, they argue, when it is based on research which seeks to economize on the relatively scarce factors of production. In the United States, for example, significant productivity gains were initially made largely through labor-saving mechanization. In Japan, on the other hand, increased productivity resulted mainly from biological research which improved seed varieties and made them more responsive to fertilizer, thus economizing on land.

In Hayami and Ruttan's view, successful agricultural growth and rural development require that a country's economic, political, and cultural institutions adapt creatively to technical changes that make growth possible (but not automatic). Their "induced development model" seeks to explain how "technical and institutional changes are induced through the responses of farmers, agribusiness entrepreneurs, scientists, and public administrators to resource endowments and to changes in the supply and demand of factors and products" (p. 4). They emphasize the importance of efficiently working *linkages* among the various markets and actors involved in agricultural development. In other words, Hayami and Ruttan are saying that there is no magic key to agricultural growth and rural development. Research alone, for example, is insufficient. Research results must be transmitted to farmers, and attention must also be given to credit, marketing, price policy, and other aspects of agricultural development. This calls for a carefully planned, multifaceted strategy, the need for which is the major theme of this chapter.

THE ROLE OF AGRICULTURE IN ECONOMIC GROWTH AND DEVELOPMENT

Agriculture plays many roles in the processes of economic growth and development, but most of them can be summarized under four headings: (1) providing more food and raw materials, (2) serving as a market for the products of the industrial sector, (3) supplying savings to other sectors of the economy, and (4) providing productive employment. Let us take a close look at each of these.

The first role of agriculture may seem obvious, but on close examination we can see that its importance goes beyond the need to keep a growing population alive. If the food supply is increasing more slowly than the population, nutritional standards either will be lowered or will be maintained by increasing food imports. Spending scarce foreign exchange on food means that less is available to import capital, technology, skilled labor, and management—the factors of production that tend to be in short supply in developing countries. Poor agricultural performance, in other words, hinders the growth of the rest of the economy and limits the resources available to promote development.

In most developing countries, the agricultural sector not only produces food for domestic consumption but also supplies a major share—if not virtually all—of the foreign exchange earnings from commodity exports. While it is true that reliance on primary products for export has its dangers, recent research suggests that the instability of primary product prices has been less damaging to most developing countries than is commonly supposed (see chapters 5 and 15). Still, reliance on just one or two major agricultural exports can be quite harmful to some countries, which would be well advised to diversify their export bases. In the last ten years, developing countries have come to recognize that export opportunities have been greater than they previously realized, and this, together with disappointing experiences with import-substitution development strategies (see chapter 10), has led many of them to return to export-based strategies of development. The more agricultural products a country can export, the more foreign exchange it has available for those items needed for the industrialization process—as well as for food products which can be produced more cheaply overseas than at home.

Another important aspect of food production is its contribution to the formation of human capital. Until quite recently, economists tended to regard food strictly as a consumption good. We now recognize that part of food utilization really should be considered an investment which improves the quality of the labor force. Malnutrition causes both mental and physical retardation, and poor diets also affect general health. As a result, worker absenteeism is higher and on-the-job productivity lower than would be the case with a well-nourished labor force. Food consumption in developing countries, as we saw in chapter 7, is deficient not just in calories but also in proteins. Particularly lacking, in many cases, are some of the amino acids abundant in animal proteins but not in other sources of protein.

A slowly growing agricultural sector can also result in inflationary pressures. Aggregate demand for farm products in the developing countries has been growing not only because of population growth (2.5 percent annually) but also because of rising per capita incomes (and average annual increase of 3.4 percent since 1960) and a relatively high income elasticity of demand (YED) for food (the percentage change in food demand divided by the percentage change in income). It has been estimated that the YED for food is approximately 0.5 to 0.6 in most developing countries compared with only 0.2 to 0.3 in the better-fed developed countries. The increase in food demand is given by the following formula:

$$\dot{D} = \dot{P} + (YED)\,\dot{Y}$$

where $\dot{D}$ = the rate of growth of food demand
 $\dot{P}$ = the rate of growth of population
 $\dot{Y}$ = the rate of growth of per capita income

Substituting the above figures into this equation, we obtain $\dot{D} = 2.5 +$ 0.5(3.4), or 4.2 percent, as an approximation of the situation in the "typical" developing country. If domestic food production is not growing this rapidly—and particularly if food imports are limited by foreign exchange constraints—both the absolute and the relative price of food will tend to rise. These inflationary effects will be particularly burdensome for the very poor, who spend 50 percent or more of their income on food.

The second major role of the agricultural sector in the process of development is to provide a market for the products of the industrial sector. The speed of the industrialization process itself will depend on how rapidly agricultural incomes are rising. If economic growth is confined to urban areas, the domestic market for manufactured goods will be very restricted and import substitution possibilities thus will be limited. In the early periods of economic growth, rising incomes in the agricultural sector can expand the market not only for light consumer goods (radios, bicycles, kitchen utensils, etc.) but also for agricultural implements and, in the larger countries, tractors and other agricultural machinery.

Third, the agricultural sector is important as a source of savings. In a very poor country not blessed with petroleum, copper, other minerals, or tourist attractions, more than half the national income is likely to be derived from agriculture and closely related activities. If that is where the income is, that is where the savings potential will be. Tapping that potential may not be easy (see chapter 13), even if the agricultural sector is growing rapidly. The task is even more difficult if agricultural output is increasing only enough to keep up with population growth.

Thus far, we have seen that a stagnant agricultural sector limits the possibilities for growth elsewhere in the economy by restricting the supply of foreign exchange, the quality of the labor force, the demand for manufactured goods, and the supply of savings. In the last few decades, poor agricultural performance has had another serious consequence for developing countries: rising levels of unemployment and underemployment. Accordingly, we should add a fourth major role of agriculture in the process of development: providing jobs. Early development theorists paid little attention to this role, because historical experience suggested that agriculture best aided the process of development by *releasing* labor to other sectors of the economy. Indeed, some models assumed (incorrectly, most agricultural economists now believe) that the marginal productivity of agricultural labor in developing countries was zero. But in a world where population is growing rapidly and urban-based economic sectors seem unable to create enough jobs (other than those of a menial and low-paying kind) to satisfy both the natural population increase and the migrants from rural areas, increasing attention is being paid to the possibilities for increasing employment in agriculture. This is a subject to which we will return in chapter 12.

TRENDS IN WORLD FOOD PRODUCTION

The performance of the agricultural sector in most developing countries has been disappointing. Table 9.1 shows that *total* food production in the developing countries has been rising just as fast as in the developed countries; but *per capita* output rose by only 0.6 percent annually from 1954 to 1964 and for the next ten years did not rise at all. In the developed countries, on the other hand, per capita food production in these two decades rose at annual rates of 1.7 percent and 1.8 percent, respectively. There was some improvement in 1975 and 1976, when per capita food production in the developing countries rose by a total of 5 percent, but it is too early to tell whether a long-term upward trend has been re-established.

Table 9.2 presents data on per capita food production and per capita total agricultural production for major developing regions and selected countries. Africa has the poorest record, with per capita production during 1974–1976 some 7 percent below what it was in the early 1960s. Latin America and the Far East show only slight gains during this period. The best records—and they are by no means spectacular—are in the Near East and in the centrally planned Asian economies, though in the latter case the figures are based on considerable guesswork and thus are the subject of controversy.

Within each region, country performance varies considerably—even

TABLE 9.1
Growth of World Food Production, 1954–1974
(average annual percentage rates of change)

	1954–1964			1964–1974		
		Food Production			*Food Production*	
	Population	*Total*	*Per Capita*	*Population*[a]	*Total*	*Per Capita*
Developed Countries	1.3	3.0	1.7	1.0	2.7	1.8
Developing Countries	2.4	3.1	0.6	2.6	2.6	0.0
Total	1.9	3.0	1.0	1.9	2.7	0.8

Source: Clifton B. Luttrell, "Food and Population: A Long View," *Federal Reserve Bank of St. Louis Review,* 58 (May 1976), 2–10.
[a] 1964–1973.

TABLE 9.2

Indices of Per Capita Food Production and Total Agricultural Production,
Major Developing Regions and Selected Countries, 1974–1976 Average
(1961–1965 = 100)

	Per Capita Food Production	Per Capita Total Agricultural Production
All Developing Market Economies	103	101
Africa	93	93
Algeria	80	81
Ghana	87	88
Ivory Coast	135	128
Nigeria	85	85
Tanzania	116	107
Tunisia	135	134
Latin America	105	100
Bolivia	122	127
Brazil	122	110
Chile	97	95
Costa Rica	138	131
Mexico	103	95
Paraguay	98	103
Near East	108	107
Afghanistan	95	95
Egypt	104	99
Iraq	85	85
Sudan	118	116
Turkey	115	117
Far East	103	102
Burma	91	91
India	99	98
Philippines	107	106
South Korea	116	120
Centrally Planned Asian Economies	111	113
China	113	115
North Korea	107	106

Source: Food and Agriculture Organization of the United Nations, *Production Year-book*, 30 (1976), Tables 6 and 7.

more than indicated by the data in Table 9.2. Per capita food production since the early 1960s has risen relatively rapidly in such diverse countries as Bolivia, Brazil, China, Costa Rica, Ivory Coast, South Korea, Sudan, Tanzania, Turkey and Tunisia. Notable declines in per capita food production have occurred in Algeria, Burma, Ghana, Iraq, and Nigeria, among others.

To generalize from diverse country experiences in agricultural development is hazardous, since a great many factors affect what happens in a particular country. In many cases, though, rapid population growth is a major reason for poor agricultural performance, especially where little unused arable land remains or where bringing it into production is quite costly. Population pressures have forced farmers to adopt practices that deplete the fertility of the soil, thus lowering its productivity (see chapter 16). In these cases, production increases depend mainly on the adoption of new technology. This, in turn, depends both on domestic research and extension efforts and on the availability of foreign exchange for the importation of fertilizers, irrigation pumps, agricultural machinery, and other inputs. With the supply of foreign exchange limited in most developing countries, it is not surprising that technological change often proceeds at a snail's pace.

It should not be assumed, however, that rapid population growth and foreign exchange bottlenecks explain away the entire problem. In the next section, we will discuss the numerous other obstacles to increasing food output per capita, most of which can be overcome by enlightened government policy.

Most governments in developing countries have given a relatively low priority to agriculture. In some cases, political leaders have virtually equated development with industrialization and have encouraged import-intensive, high-cost projects which impose heavy foreign debt burdens on their countries. Ghana, under its former president Kwame Nkrumah, provides a classic example of this development strategy. The agricultural sector often is severely squeezed to provide the savings necessary to finance industrial products. In Argentina, for example, the Perón government established a state trading agency in the late 1940s to purchase farm products at low prices and sell them in world markets at prevailing prices, which then were quite high. While this agency's profits helped industry grow rapidly in the short run, agricultural production declined, reducing the country's ability to meet industry's import requirements and thus eventually slowing industrial growth. Another example is the collectivization of agriculture in the Soviet Union in the early 1930s, which also had adverse effects on farm output.

It is not hard to understand why agricultural development tends to be neglected in developing countries. Confusing the *symbols* of development with the *process* of development is an easy mistake to make. It is difficult to see that the symbols of development (e.g., automobiles and steel mills) are there in large part because of prior growth in agriculture. Furthermore, there are great pressures on political leaders to produce short-run results. A steel mill, an international convention center, a highway, or an automobile assembly plant can be pointed to as visible evidence of "development." It is much more difficult to score political points with an agricultural experiment station or an enlarged and better trained extension service, which lack the glamour of industrial projects and whose benefits are less visible and are long-run rather than short-run.

OVERCOMING OBSTACLES TO AGRICULTURAL DEVELOPMENT

Just as there is no single "key" to economic growth or development, there is no single solution to the poor performance of the agricultural sector in most developing countries. Increasing agricultural growth rates requires a multifaceted attack on a number of interrelated problems, ranging from land tenure arrangements to government price policies. To begin with, let us see why the "problem" of primitive technology has a "solution" that is much more complex than the simplistic one of "increasing the use of machinery and equipment." After thus illustrating the interrelationships among the various components of an agricultural development strategy, we will then focus on the individual components separately.

Technological Change

In chapter 3, we discussed in some detail how difficult it is to convince farmers to change, especially if they are illiterate and unacquainted with high-yielding methods of production. We also pointed out that poor farmers in developing countries, though suspicious of change, are not "happy peasants" who actually like being poor. It is hard to believe that people enjoy seeing half their children die before adulthood, being denied an opportunity to acquire their own land, not being able to send their children to school, or living most of their lives with intestinal parasites. The problem is not one of basic unwillingness to change; rather, it is one of reluctance to change *if the risks of change are not adequately covered.*

If farmers are to adopt new technology, they will either have to borrow more money to purchase modern inputs or have to commit more of their own resources to their farm operations. In either case, they stand to lose more in the event of crop failure than under traditional methods of production. Since they will be ill-at-ease with the new technology for a few crop cycles, they must have some assurance that success with the new technology will provide them significantly higher incomes than they would receive under traditional methods of farming. If the potential gains are perceived to be relatively small, it is unlikely that the new method will be adopted, and this decision is perfectly rational in view of the risks involved.

Inducing farmers to change requires, among other things, agricultural research and a skilled extension service to transmit research results directly to farmers. Academic training for extensionists is not enough.

Even an illiterate farmer can spot an "asphalt agronomist" who has no feel for rural life. Farmers are not likely to place much trust in a technician who has little on-farm experience; neglects to consider regional and location-specific differences in soils, rainfall, or pest problems; and shows little respect for local traditions and values.

Farmers are also unlikely to adopt new methods of production— even if they can perceive clear potential benefits—if they have no *means* to make the change. Basically, this means credit. The so-called Green Revolution in rice and wheat production (Brown, 1970) is not based only on "miracle seeds"; indeed, use of the new seeds without changing other practices will increase yields very little. The key to sharply higher yields is use of the new seeds in combination with a package of new practices, including land leveling, irrigation, timely fertilizer application, and proper weeding. This requires a great deal of credit and managerial expertise— both of which are in very short supply. Accordingly, the Green Revolution has tended to benefit medium-size and large landowners more than small farmers (owners and nonowners alike), who have little access to credit and limited managerial experience. Furthermore, the Green Revolution has sometimes had undesirable employment consequences, as wealthy farmers with large plots often have found it profitable to substitute machinery for labor.

In summary, what appears to be a technology problem is not quite as simple as that. The adoption of new technology is intimately tied up with the supply of credit, the land tenure structure, the availability of foreign exchange, and other factors. Modern technology alone, then is not the key to successful agricultural development.

Agricultural Research

The growth of agricultural productivity in the developed countries can be traced largely to basic and adaptive research. Numerous studies have shown that investment in agricultural research can have high internal rates of return, and there is widespread agreement among agricultural economists and other specialists that developing countries can profit from increased investment in research.[2]

2. For a brief review of studies attempting to measure the productivity of research, see Thomas M. Arndt and Vernon W. Ruttan, "Resource Allocation and Productivity in National and International Agricultural Research," Seminar Report, Agricultural Development Council, Research and Training Network, New York, September 1975. While the methodologies of some of these studies were criticized by many of the fifty-four participants in the conference on which this report is based, most of these agricultural economists and research specialists felt confident that rates of return to investment in research were generally high. (This is not to say, of course, that all agricultural research is productive.) This section on agricultural research draws heavily on the Arndt-Ruttan summary of the conference papers.

The results of agricultural research are to varying degrees public goods. One person's consumption of new knowledge leaves others no worse off, and once this knowledge is available, it is difficult to exclude others from consuming it. This is particularly true of information on crop rotations, fertilizers and irrigation practices, optimum planting times, plowing techniques, and similar crop and livestock practices. But where the product of research is an improved input (e.g., hybrid seeds) the consumption of which can be effectively restricted, private firms as well as public agencies will engage in agricultural experimentation. Only rarely, however, does one find research conducted by individual farmers. Such efforts are restricted by high capital and recurrent costs, long payoff periods, and the inability of farmers to obtain compensation for the benefits received by others.

The great bulk of agricultural research continues to be in the developed countries, despite substantially increased outlays in the developing countries during the past two decades. In 1959 global spending on agricultural research totaled $1.3 billion, of which $141 million, or 11 percent, was in the developing countries. By 1974 these figures had risen to $3.8 billion and $957 million, respectively. Even though developing countries now account for 25 percent of the total, research on tropical crops is much less advanced or extensive than research on temperate zone crops.

Within the developing countries, some of the most important research is being conducted by nine major international research institutes and two other international programs, whose combined 1974 budgets amounted to $34 million. The importance of these organizations goes far beyond their 3.6 percent share of developing-country agricultural research in 1974. The two oldest and best known—the International Center for the Improvement of Maize and Wheat (CIMMYT) in Mexico and the International Rice Research Institute (IRRI) in the Philippines—developed the "miracle" wheat and rice seeds associated with the Green Revolution, whose principal impact has been in Asia. One analyst has estimated that these seeds added $1 billion to Asian grain production during the 1972–1973 crop year. The international institutes also play important roles in training indigenous researchers and in transmitting information to national organizations in the developing countries.

These national organizations play a vital role in the transfer of technology. Indeed, a major study of agricultural research concludes that "the successful absorption of foreign-generated technology depends on domestic research capabilities."[3] Domestic research is necessary to adapt new seeds and other imported technical innovations to local environ-

---

3. Robert Evenson and Yoav Kislev, *Agricultural Research and Productivity* (New Haven: Yale University Press, 1975), p. 160.

mental conditions. In many developing countries, these efforts are primitive and unproductive, with poorly trained technicians conducting simple, textbook experiments that often duplicate work done elsewhere. Even if researchers are well trained, their efforts may be concentrated on sophisticated technologies which only a handful of farmers are financially capable of employing. Intercropping systems employed by small farmers are often ignored because of the widespread but erroneous belief that total productivity is always highest with pure stands, not when several crops are grown simultaneously on the same plot. The international professional rewards system even leads some researchers to continue studying Michigan or Ohio soils after completing their degrees in the United states and returning to their own countries. Another common shortcoming of research efforts is a focus on maximizing yields rather than profits per hectare.

An effective national research program requires a corps of well-trained technicians whose salaries are high enough to keep them from emigrating. Contacts with international research institutes must be established, and researchers must have access to journals, abstracts, and other publications. All this costs money, and as a low-visibility effort with a long payoff period, research is often given a low priority by politicians, whose outlook tends to be short-run.

Extension Services

The results of agricultural research are unlikely to reach many farmers unless extension personnel take these results to the field. The county extension agent has been an important change agent in the United States, where extension, research, and education have been closely integrated in a decentralized system based on cooperative efforts between the U.S. Department of Agriculture and the land-grant universities. In the developing world, extension has played a particularly important role in Taiwan's notably successful agricultural development.

Extension programs, however, are not always successful, as demonstrated by E. B. Rice's (1974) detailed evaluation of the U.S. government's efforts to develop extension services in Latin America. These programs, begun in 1942, sought to demonstrate how knowledge about modern techniques could be transferred to farmers (particularly small farmers), and to create independent institutions capable of carrying on this work once U.S. advisors had completed their tasks. In Rice's judgment, this effort failed for at least two major reasons. First, the attempt to establish a permanent extension institution was a mistake given administrative, bureaucratic, and political conditions in the region. Second, the U.S. extension model brought to Latin America was faulty, being too concerned with the process of education and paying insufficient attention to the creation of favorable conditions (e.g., credit, supplies, markets, and prices) necessary to induce farmers to adopt the technologies they were being shown.

The framework out of which a viable extension institution was to emerge was the so-called *servicio*, a largely autonomous entity staffed by U.S. and host-country personnel who jointly occupied the key administrative and technical positions. This temporary structure, however, was too isolated from the indigenous bureaucratic environment, and it collapsed when a policy decision in Washington led to an abrupt termination of the *servicio* arrangements in the early 1960s. As extension personnel were absorbed by Ministries of Agriculture, salaries tended to decline, working conditions deteriorated, and political influences on program operations increased. The only real alternative to the *servicio*, in Rice's view, would have been to place the extension service *within* the Ministry of Agriculture and to arrange for close coordination between extension and other ministry activities. However, this strategy might well have been just as unproductive, since the institutional environment in most of the assisted countries did not permit the degree of coordination necessary to make extension efforts effective.

The weight of the evidence leads Rice to conclude that extension played only a minor role in increasing productivity in the twelve countries studied. Even when extension personnel functioned effectively in coordinating extension work with other development activities, the marginal contribution of extension appears to have been small. Moreover, in Rice's view, whatever contribution extension does make, it is the extension *function* that counts. The existence of an independent extension service is neither a necessary nor a sufficient condition for the profitable introduction of new technology, since the extension function can be performed by development banks, agrarian reform agencies, commercial supply houses, or other such institutions. Indeed, Rice maintains that the proper place for extension advisors is on the staff of one of these development organizations, where their role would be not only to transmit knowledge but to promote the adoption of new technologies. Extension, in other words, must be integrated with other development activities. Successful development projects, Rice finds, tend to involve "strong institutional organization and direction of the production-distribution system," and "extension services typically have not been involved in these institutional arrangements" (p. 328).

In addition to demonstrating once again the importance of coordination among policy instruments, Rice's study provides another valuable lesson: the danger of transferring developed-country institutions to developing countries without paying adequate attention to the environment in which those institutions are expected to function.

Agricultural Education

Educational systems in developing countries typically neglect agriculture at all levels. Primary-school curricula are urban-oriented, even in rural areas. School gardens, designed to give students experience with simple farm technology, are often so poorly managed that they reinforce negative attitudes toward agriculture as a low-status occupation. This writer is aware of one instance in which working in the school garden has been used as a form of punishment. Since many students (especially those who do not go beyond the primary level) will end up working in agriculture, the failure to acquaint them with better techniques of farming represents a lost opportunity to make a productive investment in human capital. Much of the investment actually made will have a low payoff.

Secondary schools, as we noted in chapter 7, tend to be viewed as conduits for higher education. There is little technical training to develop middle-level skills in extension, agricultural engineering, or research. Universities may graduate enough agronomists to meet the *effective* demand by government and the private sector, but training often emphasizes classroom exercises at the expense of field work, thus limiting the effectiveness of these graduates in research and extension activities.

Also neglected is continuing education to upgrade skills, introduce extension agents to new technology, or acquaint them with crops whose importance in the economy is increasing. In the Eastern Caribbean island of Antigua, older extension agents have received no training for fifteen years, and their expertise is largely limited to sugar cane and cotton, the production of which has virtually ceased. Even the few new extension agents have little training in livestock operations or fruit and vegetable production.

Perhaps the major obstacle to more effective agricultural education is attitudinal. In much of the English-speaking Caribbean, negative attitudes reflect both an understandable reaction against the legacy of plantation agriculture based on slavery and the attractiveness of jobs in industry and tourism. In one island, the head of government publicly expressed his desire to see the day when none of his constituents would have to cut cane. In another island, a "critical strategic objective" of the national development plan is "to lessen drudgery in agriculture." Meanwhile, agricultural production stagnates or is declining, and the food import bill is rising rapidly, thus reducing the amount of foreign exchange available for the expansion of industry and other economic activities. Unemployment rates have risen sharply since 1960, particularly among young people who prefer joblessness in the cities to farming. It will take exceptional leadership to overcome these negative attitudes and reorient educational curricula.

Irrigation

Many developing countries have made substantial investments in facilities to provide irrigation water from surface or underground sources. World Bank loans for irrigation totaled $564 million (8.5 percent of all IBRD/ IDA lending) in fiscal year 1976, and additional facilities were to be constructed under other loans for comprehensive area development projects.

Irrigation can contribute to increased agricultural production in several ways. First, it can bring into cultivation areas where soils are suitable for farming but lack of rainwater makes non-irrigated cultivation impossible. Israel has brought such land under cultivation with considerable success. Second, irrigation can increase crop yields by regulating the flow of water in accordance with requirements during various phases of the crop cycle. Irrigation is particularly important for maximizing the benefits of the new rice and wheat varieties. Third, irrigation can permit two or more crops per year to be grown on land that will support only one crop under rain-fed conditions. Finally, irrigation systems can be designed to control flooding and thus reduce crop damage from this source.

Having made irrigation sound like the long-lost key to solving the world's food problem, we should hasten to dash some cold water on this optimistic viewpoint. An experienced irrigation specialist with AID has warned that irrigation projects in the drought-plagued Sahelian region could well become "enduring monuments to failure." He and his coauthor cite two major problems that have plagued irrigation projects in other developing countries: (1) high construction and operating costs and (2) management problems. Flood irrigation systems usually cost $2,000 to $5,000 per hectare, and sprinkler or drip systems may cost up to $10,000. Only high-value crops can be grown profitably when costs are in the upper part of this range, and greater amounts of credit are needed.[4]

Administrative and managerial problems can easily result in unfavorable B/C ratios. Poor technical management can cause salinity or sedimentation of canals. Government mediation of water-rights disputes may be time-consuming and costly. Fee structures can result in inefficient use of water (underconsumption if fees are too high; overconsumption and waste if they are set too low). Fee collection costs may be high if fees are paid in kind. Farmers often have difficulty understanding complex systems and cannot see the social value of running a system beyond their own headgates. In these cases, government operation of the system is necessary, thus adding to overhead costs. In India and Pakistan, canal systems and management practices were designed to avert famine, and

4. Gary Nelson and Fred M. Tileston, "Why Irrigation Projects May Become 'Enduring Monuments to Failure'," *Focus: Technical Cooperation*, Supplement to *International Development Review*, 19, 3 (1977/3), 22–24. (Tileston is the irrigation specialist; Nelson is an agricultural economist.)

thus water is spread thinly according to rigid guidelines which fail to consider efficient use. Farmers have no control over the amount or timing of water that will be made available and thus cannot count on planting at the optimum time for maximizing yields (Johnston and Kilby, 1975: 415–416). Nevertheless, they generally know when water will be available to them, and despite less-than-optimum conditions, irrigation has played a major role in the encouraging expansion of grain production in South Asia in the last decade.

The very mixed results of irrigation projects in developing countries provide a warning that these investments must be carefully planned and potential problems clearly identified. In addition to the problems noted above, attention should be given to (1) farmers' willingness to adopt radically new technology, (2) the effects of agricultural chemicals on ground and surface water, (3) possible increases in the incidence of malaria and bilharzia, and (4) the distribution of benefits among large, medium-size, and small farmers.

Mechanization

All too many agricultural specialists have assumed that the success of mechanization in raising production in the United States can be duplicated in the developing countries. Advice to this effect ignores economic, agronomic, and institutional factors in these countries that may make mechanization too costly, too environmentally harmful, and—for small farmers—too impractical in comparison with labor-intensive methods of production. Moreover, it can have serious adverse effects on rural employment. This is not to say that mechanization is never desirable in developing countries, only that it has been unwisely promoted in many instances.

A good example of unwise mechanization was the establishment of a machinery pool in Bolivia's eastern lowlands in the mid-1950s, following the completion of a road connecting this very promising agricultural area with the major population centers (and thus markets) in the highlands. Under a U.S. government program, machinery was leased to local farmers, at highly subsidized rental rates, for land clearing and cultivation. Another artificial stimulus to mechanization was a provision in the 1953 agrarian reform law permitting large landowners to retain large tracts of land if they demonstrated through the use of machinery that they were operating efficient "agricultural enterprises." After the rental subsidy was terminated, large farmers quickly shifted back to labor-intensive methods of clearing and cultivation, which were perceived to be less costly when machinery was priced realistically. Meanwhile, land clearing by unspecialized bulldozers resulted in the loss of loamy topsoil and exposed the sandy subsoils to leaching from heavy rains and wind erosion.

To be fair to those who advocate greater mechanization, it should be noted that the use of machinery is often costly simply because farmers are not well trained in its use and no provision is made for maintenance and repairs. If proper attention is paid to these problems, the case for mechanization becomes stronger. Furthermore, mechanized cultivation and land preparation is quicker than hand methods, thus permitting more favorable adaptation of the crop cycle to climatic conditions and making possible higher yields in some cases. In addition, it may permit double-cropping of land that otherwise would have to be single-cropped. Land leveling can help raise rice yields.

In practice, production and marketing problems, as well as poor managerial skills, keep these potential gains from being realized. Although mechanization can sometimes increase both production and employment, the effect is often simply to replace labor with capital while increasing production negligibly, if at all. Machinery may appear attractive only because an overvalued exchange rate, subsidized credit, or tax policy makes its price to the purchaser (or renter) lower than its scarcity value.

Mechanization tends to benefit medium- and large-scale farmers more than small farmers, because the latter usually do not have access to medium-term credit for machinery purchases—or short-term credit for rental—from banks or from farm equipment dealers. To the extent that mechanization is successful in raising productivity and income, it will thus make the distribution of rural income more unequal. Mechanization can also affect income distribution if it results in a net displacement of labor. While this sometimes occurs, widely differing estimates of the labor-displacing effect of machinery in various countries indicate that we still know too little about the importance of this effect.

If employment and income distribution objectives are considered important, a sensible set of mechanization policy guidelines, suggested by William Cline,[5] is the following: (1) Governments and international agencies should support mechanization only when it clearly increases output; (2) machinery should be made available on a rental basis to all farmers; (3) encouragement should be given to intermediate technologies such as improvement of implements, as opposed to the use of tractors and combines; and (4) machinery prices should reflect their scarcity values.

Land Tenure Reform

In most Latin American countries and in a number of others throughout the world, the land tenure structure is a major obstacle to agricultural development. There are two important dimensions of this problem: (1)

5. William R. Cline, "Interrelationships between Agricultural Strategy and Rural Income Distribution," *Food Research Institute Studies*, 12 (1973), 151.

land tenure arrangements per se (i.e., the form in which agricultural land is held—freehold, leasehold, etc.) and (2) the distribution of agricultural land.

Let us deal first with the issue of land distribution. A major study of seven Latin America countries, based on census data during the years 1950–1961, found that the distribution of agricultural land was particularly unequal in Colombia, Ecuador, Guatemala, and Peru. In those countries, 64 to 88 percent of the land was held by only 2 to 6 percent of the farm operators. At the other extreme, 64 to 90 percent of the farms, occupying only 5 to 7 percent of the land, were in "subfamily" units averaging about 2 hectares (1 hectare = 2.47 acres). A subfamily unit was defined as one too small "to provide employment for . . . two people with the typical incomes, markets and levels of technology and capital . . . prevailing in each region" (Barraclough and Domike, 1966: 395). Households in this category had to supplement their farm income with earnings from other economic activity (part-time or seasonal work on other farms, production of handicrafts, domestic service, etc.). The situation has changed little since 1960, except in Peru, where a significant amount of land redistribution has occurred since 1968.

If small farmers had access to more productive technology, many of them could appreciably increase their income, as has been demonstrated on farms of only a few hectares in Japan and Taiwan (created, incidentally, by agrarian reform programs supported—and in the case of Japan imposed—by the U.S. government after World War II). But in Latin America, even though most small farmers own their own land,[6] few have access to credit or to supporting services, such as extension and research, which are necessary for significant productivity gains to be achieved. The reasons are both economic (e.g., administrative costs on small loans cannot usually be covered by normal interest-rate charges) and political (larger farmers use their political power to claim most of these services).

If small farmers cannot obtain credit or other needed services, a logical alternative means of increasing their incomes, in the opinion of some reformers, is to give them more of another factor of production: land. Thus the confiscation of large landholdings, and their distribution in "economic-size" units to small farmers, is sometimes advocated. (Alternatively, land could be transferred to cooperatives or operated as state farms providing employment and other services to rural residents.) Since the politically powerful are just as unlikely to give up their lands as they are to ensure that small farmers have good access to bank credit, it is unrealistic to think that a significant redistribution of land can be

---

6. In the seven-country study cited above (which included Argentina, Brazil, and Chile, in addition to the four countries already mentioned), the percentage of subfamily units owned ranged from 52 to 81 percent.

quickly achieved in a nonrevolutionary atmosphere. Even in revolutionary settings—e.g., Mexico under the Cárdenas administration (1934–1940), Bolivia in 1952–1953, and Peru for a few years after 1968—land redistribution was less extensive than its proponents had hoped for and slowed markedly after the initial impetus. In other cases, much of the land distributed to small farmers (e.g., in Venezuela during 1945–1948 and Chile during 1970–1973) was given back to the original owners following a change in government. Where an evolutionary approach to land redistribution has been adopted, change has usually been very slow; some programs are little more than tokens. Among Latin American countries, only in Cuba, where large private holdings were converted to state farms, has there been a truly radical change affecting most of the country.

Let us now turn to the issue of land tenure per se. Farmers who lease their land from private landowners, paying rents in cash or surrendering a share of their production, usually do so under terms that give them little security. Rental agreements are likely to be verbal rather than written, and of short-term duration. The lack of tenure security discourages long-term investment, and there is not even much of an incentive to increase the use of current inputs, since most production gains are likely to be appropriated by landowners in the form of higher cash rents or crop shares.

Large landowners, too, sometimes have little incentive to increase productivity. If land is concentrated in a few hands, food production is destined only for an (isolated) regional market, the incomes of the masses are kept around the subsistence level by the social-political structure, and the supply of capital and labor is relatively fixed, increased output will lead to falling prices.[7] This could be prevented if productivity gains were shared widely, thus increasing the effective demand for food, since the poor have a higher income elasticity of demand for food than the rich. However, those who hold power usually are unwilling to let it be eroded voluntarily. Even if there are potential gains to large landowners from increased productivity, this class does not appear to be motivated only by profit. Status may be determined more by acreage owned and farm workers controlled than by size of bank accounts. Under these circumstances, new farm techniques will be adopted only if they do not upset the social structure (Feder, 1971).

In some countries, large landowners have another reason not to make investments on their land—the increased incidence of land invasions and other manifestations of rural unrest and, correspondingly, the greater likelihood of land redistribution, either by force (as in Bolivia in the early

---

7. Anthony Bottomley, "Monopolistic Rent Determination in Underdeveloped Rural Areas," *Kyklos*, 19 (1966), 106–118.

1950s) or by planned government action. Some parts of Latin America (particularly the Andean highlands, where production is almost entirely for the domestic market) are caught in a serious bind. Neither has there been effective agrarian reform—which has the potential to increase farm output significantly—nor do large landowners have the assurance that there will *not* be agrarian reform sometime in the near future. Thus relatively few farmers of any size have both the incentive and the means to make long-term investments to increase productivity.

A decade or two ago, it was frequently argued that redistributing land from large to small farmers would result in lower yields. This view is not supported by recent research, which has shown that production usually expands, farmers' incomes rise, and employment increases.[8] The value of production per hectare of agricultural land is frequently much higher on small farms than on large farms (Barraclough and Domike, 1966), though there is some evidence that this is due in part to a higher average quality of land.

Despite this favorable postredistribution record, it should not be assumed that land distribution is both a necessary and a sufficient condition for progress in agriculture. Indeed, land redistribution alone sometimes leaves the small farmer no better off than before the reform. If farm incomes are to rise steadily, agrarian reform must be comprehensive, including provisions for credit and for technical assistance in production and marketing. Even in these cases, farm production and incomes may not rise if other government policies fail to provide the right kind of incentives.

A good example of ineffective government policies is the situation in some of the Eastern Caribbean islands, where the decline of sugar and cotton production has resulted in government purchase of private estate lands. Some of these lands are being made available to small- and medium-size farmers under long-term leasehold arrangements. Farmers generally pay low rents, and a high percentage of them have access to one or more government services (credit, extension, marketing, subsidized tractor services, animal health services, etc.). One might think that this type of land tenure reform would significantly increase production. However, this has not occurred, partly because government policies, particularly in marketing, have not provided the right kind of incentives (see below). It is also possible that the long-term lease arrangements (20 years or more in some cases) are not providing the degree of security that the governments expected.

8. Dale W. Adams, "The Economics of Land Reform in Latin America and the Role of Aid Agencies," AID Discussion Paper No. 21 (Washington, D.C.: U.S. AID, 1969).

In most countries where landholdings are highly concentrated, land redistribution has been a slow process, affecting a relatively small percentage of farmers. Overcoming social and political obstacles requires a strong and determined government sympathetic to the plight of the masses and able to stand up to resistance by large landowners. Even if a government can overcome these obstacles, it still has a financial obstacle to surmount, since an effective, comprehensive reform requires the diversion of considerable resources away from other economic activities.

Colonization

Particularly in Latin America, where (as in Africa) there are still large expanses of uncultivated arable land, colonization programs have been viewed as a means of relieving population pressures in areas where the average landholding, small to begin with, is becoming even smaller. In some countries, colonization programs have been undertaken as a deliberate alternative to the redistribution of private land that is already being farmed. Since it is government land that is being colonized, and since financing on favorable terms can be obtained from foreign assistance agencies, the landowning elite has not strongly resisted this use of public-sector funds.

Most programs for bringing new agricultural land into production may be broadly placed into two categories. If the government builds roads into an area, takes steps to eradicate malaria or other diseases, but offers little if any direct assistance to settlers, the process of settlement is referred to as *spontaneous colonization*. In other words, once the land is opened up, settlers decide on their own—with no "market interference" —that their economic situation is likely to improve by moving. Even if no homesteading legislation has been passed and their tenure status is insecure, they still find migration attractive if arable land is abundant in the area of settlement. Most of the land available for colonization is in tropical or subtropical areas where settlers can practice "slash-and-burn" farming: clearing a few hectares by hand, farming the land until the soil has been depleted, then moving on to another location and letting their initial farm site return to its natural vegetation. This is a primitive farming technique, but if a farmer has no access to credit he has little choice —except to move back to his original home, where conditions may be even worse.

The other type of settlement is usually referred to as *directed colonization*. Under these programs, the government builds access roads leading away from the major penetration road; divides the land into parcels; enacts homesteading legislation; builds schools and clinics; provides agricultural extension services; and makes credit available to settlers. Not all directed programs provide this full gamut of services, though some of them have attempted to do so.

Spontaneous colonization is far more important than directed colonization,[9] and it may surprise many readers to learn that it has generally been much more successful from a benefit-cost standpoint than directed colonization programs (Nelson, 1973). Indeed, some of the latter can rightly be termed financial disasters, costing thousands of dollars per family settled but providing benefits whose present value is much lower than their costs.[10] Directed colonization programs have been plagued by mismanagement and paternalism, and land has sometimes been distributed not to bona fide poor farmers but rather to military officers and NCOs, lawyers, and other middle-income urban dwellers. Promised services have not been provided, either because costs were underestimated or because other programs have had a higher-priority claim on scarce government resources. Crop recommendations by extension agents have often been disastrous because of lack of knowledge of tropical soils or the high cost of marketing cash crops. Farmers who have borrowed for these crops may be left heavily in debt. And if credit is not available, soils on what are supposed to be permanent farm sites will deteriorate because of the lack of ability to purchase fertilizer.

Small farmers, functionally illiterate though most of them may be, often prove to be better decision makers than government advisors. If spontaneous colonists are relatively far from markets, or the price of cash crops is low, they will concentrate on subsistence crops. When access to market improves (e.g., with the construction of an all-weather road) or the price of an annual cash crop rises, they will shift to crops destined for the market. The great majority make such changes without access to bank credit, relying on their own savings (often held in the form of livestock) or borrowing from private moneylenders in what is called the *informal* or *noninstitutional* credit market.

Not all spontaneous colonization, of course, is successful. Poor soils, diseases and pests, flooding, drought, and other problems will cause some settlers to abandon their farms. Furthermore, some readers may be concerned about the lack of attention to education and health services implied by spontaneous as opposed to directed colonization. Actually, this is not as much of a disadvantage as it may seem. In the first place, many of the promised health services often are never provided in directed projects,

9. For example, in Bolivia's colonization zones, 86 percent of the settlers as of January 1975 were living in areas that had been brought into production through spontaneous settlement.

10. In fourteen such programs reviewed by Nelson (1973: 190–191), the average commitment of public funds per family settled, through 1968, was $4,500.

and schools may not provide enough education for functional literacy to be achieved. Secondly, as the economic situation of settlers improves, pressures can be exerted on the government to provide schools and clinics. Finally, it must be remembered that most colonists had little if any access to health services or education in their regions of origin, so by migrating they are unlikely to be worse off in terms of these dimensions of welfare.

In summary, many economists who ten years ago were skeptical of colonization are giving it a second look—at least in its spontaneous form. Agrarian reform has been slow in most countries, and for political reasons prospects for land redistribution in the near future are limited. Continued population pressure on the land makes spontaneous colonization an increasingly attractive response to the lack of action on the redistribution front. Recent research shows that the B/C ratio for such investment can be favorable.

Group Farming and Other Forms of Cooperation

The economic case for group farming, or for other forms of cooperation among small farmers, is based on two major arguments: (1) economies of scale are present under existing production technologies and marketing arrangements, and (2) a larger scale of operations permits more productive technologies to be employed. With regard to the first point, there is little doubt that groups of small farmers have more power to bargain for lower input prices and higher prices for their output. If a group's land is farmed as a single unit, less labor time is needed, other things being equal, than for farming the land in small, individually operated parcels. Even if a group wishes to retain individual-plot farming, economies of scale can be achieved through common hiring of mechanized plowing services or sharing of other traditional inputs. It is often easier for small farmers to obtain credit as a group than as individuals, and the pooling of their resources can make it possible for them to purchase small tractors, irrigation pumps, and other machinery and equipment, thus enabling them to employ more productive technologies. This does not necessarily mean that labor inputs will decrease. Indeed, more intensive agriculture and the ability to grow more than one crop a year can increase the demand for labor.[11]

Cooperative efforts may take a variety of forms. In some cases, farmers retain ownership of their individual plots and farm them as separate holdings. Elsewhere, land may be owned in common or by the state

11. The employment implications of technological change in agriculture will be discussed in more detail in chapter 12.

and farmed by a group of persons as a single unit. Among the various types of cooperative efforts are the following.[12]

1. *Producers' associations.* These are often large-farmer organizations, concerned only with one crop or type of livestock, which operate primarily in the political arena—e.g., to lobby for tariff reductions on imported inputs, lower export taxes, more credit, etc. However, they may also engage in a variety of other activities. For example, the Windward Islands Banana Growers' Association (WINBAN), which serves small as well as large farmers, conducts research, buys fertilizer and sells it to members on favorable credit terms, and markets its members' production.

2. *Marketing cooperatives.* Marketing cooperatives are similar to producer associations like WINBAN, though they tend to be smaller and confined to a particular community, whereas producers' associations are usually national or regional organizations. Their activities are limited largely to cooperative purchase of inputs and marketing of their members' principal crop (or crops).

3. *Production cooperatives.* Production cooperatives take many forms. Sometimes they are organized initially to purchase land for their members, and title to the land may be held by the cooperative rather than by individuals. Land may be farmed as a single unit or as individual plots. Members of production cooperatives often apply for credit as a group and jointly purchase a tractor or construct irrigation works. Production cooperatives often engage in marketing as well.

4. *Communes.* In a true commune, property is held in common, decision making is shared by all participants, distribution is egalitarian, and children are carefully socialized to the group's norms. The Hutterite colonies and the Israeli *kibbutzim* are among the few groups which come close to being pure communes. China's so-called communes are less pure.

5. *Collective farms.* The Chinese "commune" as well as the Russian *kolkhoz* (nominally a type of producers' cooperative but actually controlled largely by the state) fall into this category. In both systems, group members are permitted to have small plots of their own, and in both countries farmers seem to work harder on these plots than on the collective farm proper, which is operated as a single unit. Distribution is not egalitarian, as work incentives are offered.

6. *State farms.* A state farm operates very much like an industrial

12. For a discussion of several other typologies of group farming and cooperative schemes, see Peter Dorner and Don Kanel, "Group Farming Issues and Prospects: A Summary of International Experience," Seminar Report, Agricultural Development Council, Research and Training Network, New York, November 1975. The papers on which this conference report is based are published in *Cooperative and Commune: Group Farming in the Economic Development of Agriculture*, ed. Peter Dorner (Madison: The University of Wisconsin Press, 1977).

factory, with employees having clearly identified roles as managers or hired workers.

Given what seem to be significant economic advantages of cooperation among small farmers, it is reasonable to ask why small-farm agriculture in developing countries is not always dominated by communes, marketing cooperatives, producers' associations, and similar groups. One might also ask why cooperative efforts have often failed or have had only a mediocre record in increasing agricultural production and rural levels of living. The answers are complex, and certainly vary from country to country (as does the degree of cooperation); but some common problems may be identified, including the following.

1. Distrust of individuals outside the close circle of family and relatives. Many farmers fear—often with good reason—that some members of a proposed group would seek to dominate it to further their own selfish interests.

2. A strong desire on the part of individuals—apparently to satisfy some deep-seated psychological need—to have land they can call their own. Even in the Soviet Union and China, political leaders have found it to their advantage to permit farmers on collective farms to have small, privately controlled plots.

3. Managerial and administrative problems. Cooperative efforts have often failed because management (elected as well as imposed) has been too authoritarian. But failure can also be caused by management that is too democratic, permitting all voices to be heard but delaying important decisions or adopting consensus decisions that minimize individual risk but fail to maximize group welfare.

4. Resentment of outside control. Where cooperatives or other groups have been established or sponsored by the government (or even by nongovernment organizations), outside leadership has sometimes been imposed upon a community. Especially if outsiders are unresponsive to a local group's priorities, resentment against them can sabotage cooperative efforts. This occurred in Bolivia during the 1950s, and the word "cooperative" now has strong negative connotations in that country.

5. Use of cooperatives to further political objectives, to the neglect of their economic functions. This problem, related to that described immediately above, was another reason for the failure of the Bolivian government's cooperative program in the 1950s.

6. Lack of production incentives. Where group solidarity is strong (e.g., among the Hutterites or in the Israeli *kibbutzim*), individuals will be highly motivated to work for the welfare of the group. Motivation is also likely to be high in cooperative efforts where individual rewards are determined primarily by individual efforts. But where group cohesion is weak, land is farmed as a single unit, and the political authorities have

decided upon a relatively egalitarian distribution of benefits, it has been difficult to motivate farmers to become more productive. Creation of group solidarity on the basis of a new set of norms is no easy task (China has been relatively successful, but efforts in Cuba and Tanzania have been disappointing), and throughout the world people seem to be less responsive to nonmonetary incentives than to monetary rewards.

Production Credit

Government neglect of the agricultural sector is usually reflected in the distribution of credit granted by public financial institutions, which tend to focus on modern industrial activities. Private banks typically concentrate on short-term commercial operations, and their loans to agriculture go primarily to large landowners or to finance traditional exports. Fertilizer dealers and other input suppliers will sell on credit, but usually only to large or medium-sized landowners.

Small farmers generally have no access to bank credit unless they are landowners. Even then, most will be bypassed, not just because the risk of lending to them is perceived (usually incorrectly) to be relatively great,[13] but also because the administrative costs of processing loan applications are high in relation to the small amounts requested by farmers with only 1 or 2 hectares of land. Small loans are simply unprofitable for commercial banks, and even government development banks must keep administrative costs down if they are to become financially self-reliant, covering all costs from the margin between their borrowing and lending rates and leaving some resources for expansion.

Farmers who have no access to bank credit may obtain resources in the noninstitutional credit market, where lenders include relatives, friends, merchants, and those private lenders sometimes referred to as "loan sharks." In India it was estimated that 60 percent of all agricultural credit in 1971–1972 was provided through noninstitutional channels, while elsewhere in Asia the figure was perhaps as high as 80 percent. In Latin America and Taiwan, on the other hand, the noninstitutional market at this time was providing only 10 to 30 percent of all agricultural credit.[14] Annual interest rates in the noninstitutional market often reach 20 to 40 percent, and rates as high as 10 percent a month have been reported. Private moneylending has been defended on the grounds that it is better

13. There is growing evidence that default rates are higher for larger farmers than for smaller farmers (Lipton 1976: 546, 548).

14. Hayami and Ruttan (1971: 271) and Lipton (1976: 544, 548). For a recent review of research on the noninstitutional credit market, see U Tun Wai, "A Revisit to Interest Rates Outside the Organized Money Markets of Underdeveloped Countries," *Banca Nazionale del Lavoro Quarterly Review*, No. 122 (September 1977), 291–312.

than no credit at all and that transactions are voluntary—i.e., farmers have the option of declining to borrow. High interest rates often can be justified by the risks involved, and in any event recent research suggests that *average* noninstitutional interest rates are lower than commonly believed (Lipton, 1976). Moreover, many small farmers prefer noninstitutional credit because repayment schedules are more flexible than for lower-interest public credit.

While it is true that noninstitutional credit may be better than none at all given existing social, political, and economic structures, these structures are sometimes (though by no means always) used to exploit the small farmer. For example, in areas with only one or a few potential sources of credit, a competitive money market does not exist and lenders can make monopoly profits. And where the marketing system is likewise primitive and uncompetitive, farmers may have little choice but to pledge their crops to those with monopsony power.

Governments have attempted to provide an alternative to the noninstitutional market by establishing their own credit institutions, but since public resources are limited the amount of credit made available usually is relatively small. Moreover, even government credit institutions typically require collateral in the form of a land title, thus shutting their doors to cash tenants or sharecroppers.

The record of public agricultural credit agencies in developing countries is mixed at best. Michael Lipton (1976: 548), in reviewing recent research on this subject, is less charitable; in his view, "most institutional lending to farmers in most LDCs is in a mess." Administration is often weak or simply corrupt, and loans may benefit primarily those who have alternative sources of credit but who prefer the public institution because of subsidized interest rates and longer repayment periods. Low interest rates prevent a credit institution from growing through internal accumulation of resources and make it dependent on government subsidies. This limits the growth of public credit (while at the same time private bank credit may be restricted by interest rate ceilings).[15] Lipton (1976: 548) notes that in some South Asian languages the word used for "loan from the government" means "assistance" or "grant," which is indeed how many farmers view public credit programs, even where language does not facilitate this interpretation. Such an attitude results in high default rates and encourages overinvestment in fertilizers, chemicals, machinery, and equipment at the expense of labor, draft animals, and the use of crop rotations, including green manures.

---

15. The conclusion that interest rate regulations restrict the supply of credit is based on a review of agricultural credit programs in Latin America by Dale W. Adams (cited in Hayami and Ruttan, 1971: 271).

Although increased credit would appear to be crucial for more rapid agricultural development, recent research (summarized in Lipton, 1976) has suggested that lack of institutional credit is not as serious a constraint to agricultural development as most observers have assumed. Farmers seek credit not only for production purposes but also to finance basic consumption needs and to repay debts. When market conditions encourage increased agricultural production, farmers will reallocate resources borrowed in the noninstitutional market and spend more on production inputs. Moreover, there is a growing body of evidence that many small farmers, even in very poor countries, have savings (often held in the form of livestock or land) which can be utilized to take advantage of attractive market situations. One should be cautious, however, in accepting the "new consensus" regarding the importance of credit, for it seems applicable mainly to situations where farmers have an opportunity to increase their incomes by switching crops or by making relatively modest technological changes. Where radical new technologies are required (e.g., with the use of high-yielding grain varieties), credit is needed even by relatively affluent farmers.

Since some crop and livestock development programs are dependent on credit, governments have good reason to be concerned about improving efficiency in the use of credit. Two of the major policy implications of the "new consensus" are that (1) government credit agencies should take a tougher stance on defaults and (2) higher interest rates should be charged, both to promote more appropriate factor proportions in agriculture (more labor, less capital) and to permit credit agencies to add to their lending capacity over time. Higher interest rates can be borne by farmers (who already sometimes pay 20 to 40 percent to private moneylenders) provided that they have access to technical assistance and to markets. Governments are reluctant to permit higher interest rates, though, because politically this would arouse strong opposition.

Some governments have attempted to improve the efficiency of their small farmer credit programs by encouraging the formation of cooperatives and credit unions. Loans made to these institutions, rather than to individual farmers, can lower administrative costs per dollar lent, and they appear to give all member farmers an incentive to help each other by making the group jointly responsible for its members' debts. The U.S. government has provided considerable technical and financial assistance to such organizations, and other bilateral and multilateral assistance programs have also made significant contributions. Organizing small farmers, however, is a difficult task, since a high degree of mutual trust is necessary among the participants and strong cooperative traditions do not exist in many countries. Cooperatives, as we noted above, have had a mixed record in developing countries. Even successful efforts like the Comilla project in Bangladesh have improved farmers' welfare only at a high cost, and they have not been easily replicated in other areas.

If cooperatives and credit unions have often been disappointing as vehicles for channeling credit to small farmers, alternative program possibilities need to be explored if governments are concerned about the distribution of credit. The problem of distribution, however, is not just an administrative one; it is also a problem of power. Unless this aspect of the problem is effectively tackled, even an efficiently administered credit program is likely to result in a very uneven distribution of benefits.

Transportation

We have already seen, in chapter 6, that lack of good transport facilities limits the scope for agricultural development. Crops whose production costs are competitive with those in other countries often cannot enter world markets because internal and external transportation costs are too high. High transportation costs also can discourage the use of modern inputs. In Bolivia, for example, farmers purchasing fertilizer in the capital city of La Paz had to pay $0.35 to $0.48 per kilogram of urea in 1969, compared with $0.20 in the United States and $0.20 to $0.25 in Mexico, Peru, and Venezuela. In remote rural areas, the price of fertilizer was several times as high as in La Paz, making its use unprofitable for most farmers.

Investment in roads and other transport facilities can lower the cost of producing food and delivering it to domestic markets. It can also enable producers to enter export markets. If the economic system is one in which production units (individuals, cooperatives, etc.) have an incentive to react to input/output price changes, then the market signals generated by transport investment—unless contradicted by other government intervention—will lead farmers to expand production. However, markets work imperfectly in developing countries, and other government programs are necessary to ensure that farmers' responses to transport investment will be quick and large enough to justify the investment. Highway or rail projects with high expected internal rates of return may turn out to have low *ex post* IRRs because of inattention to complementary investments. Projected beef exports, for example, may not materialize because of the government's failure to institute a program to control hoof-and-mouth disease—a public good which private producers will not rationally purchase as individuals. Grains destined for the export market may rot because the government fails to provide sufficient credit for private trucking fleets and storage facilities or delays its own investments in these areas. Lack of production credit may also limit increases in agricultural output.

In countries where farm input/output prices are controlled by the government, transport investment will not automatically stimulate production. If we assume that both production and distribution activities are government owned, though, then the effect of transport investment—holding input and output prices constant—is to increase the surplus (savings) obtained from the agricultural sector. This surplus could be used to increase the supply of agricultural inputs or to lower retail agricultural prices; but it might also be diverted to finance investments in other sectors of the economy.

Marketing and Storage

If marketing and storage problems are neglected in commodity production programs, farmers (rationally) may not respond to market incentives for increasing production; and if output does increase, the pressures on the distribution network may result in higher spoilage rates. Hayami and Ruttan (1971: 216) point out, for example, that inadequate storage facilities in the early years of the Green Revolution prevented some farmers in the Philippines from growing two rice crops a year. In northern India, wheat production increased in response to the availability of new seed varieties, but because storage facilities were in short supply, wheat had to be stored in schools or in the open air, where it was subject to considerable damage by rodents and moisture. In the northern Altiplano of Bolivia, it is estimated that up to 20 percent of the principal staple—potatoes—is lost in storage.

The lack of storage facilities not only results in crop damage but also contributes to extreme seasonal price fluctuations, as commodities glut the market after harvest time but are in short supply several months later. For crops which can be stored for long periods of time, the lack of storage facilities also aggravates annual price fluctuations. Price uncertainties can discourage production, though the importance of this disincentive is sometimes exaggerated.

Packaging and handling methods are often poor in developing countries, and this can result in considerable damage during shipment, particularly for perishables moving by truck over rough roads. This is a major reason why 25 to 40 percent of a country's banana crop often does not meet export standards.

The lack of uniform grades and standards—another common characteristic of markets in developing countries—can discourage efforts to improve product quality and can also contribute to waste. If there is little difference in price among the various cuts of beef, either because of price controls or because local tastes are "unsophisticated" (from the producer's viewpoint), ranchers will have little incentive to fatten cattle to obtain higher-quality cuts or to slaughter carefully.[16] Inadequate sanitary standards in slaughterhouses may prevent a country from taking advantage of export opportunities. If grain millers do not control for broken kernels, moisture, foreign material, mold, and insect and pest damage, export possibilities are likewise limited and producers cannot receive the higher prices which some local customers would be willing to pay for a higher quality product.

Production increases and quality improvements can also be discouraged by oligopsonistic conditions in the markets where farmers sell their crops and livestock products. Such conditions have been documented in many countries, but the extent to which producers are "exploited" by intermediaries is often exaggerated—just as it is in the United States. Detailed studies of marketing in Haiti and Bolivia, for example, show that marketing for most crops is highly competitive at the assembly, wholesale, and retail levels. If marketing margins sometimes seem relatively high, this is usually because of spoilage risks or the very low volumes handled by most intermediaries, whose net incomes are quite low.

The lack of a nationwide market price information system can lead farmers to make incorrect decisions regarding which crops to plant, when to sell, and the desirability of on-farm or community-level storage facilities. To the extent that price information stimulates the construction of storage facilities, seasonal price fluctuations would be narrowed.

Most of our comments thus far have assumed that marketing and storage are predominantly or exclusively private-sector activities. In many developing countries, however, the government plays the dominant role, even though production may be in private hands. This is particularly true of former British colonies, many of which have set up marketing boards to purchase, store, and sell major commodities. Marketing boards have functioned successfully in countries like Australia and Canada, where they have sometimes caused price fluctuations to narrow significantly, thus stabilizing farm incomes as well as providing an assured market. But in developing countries, their record is not so good. Apart from a lack of technical knowledge (e.g., appropriate storage conditions, off-season opportunities in developed countries), marketing boards often suffer from a lack of general managerial expertise, and they may require heavy government subsidies. In the Eastern Caribbean island of Antigua, the marketing board buys a wide range of products, paying prices that seem to be based on (poorly) estimated costs of production plus a standard percentage margin, without regard to quality or to demand factors. One of the results of its policies is an annual cucumber glut and the con-

16. Someone once remarked—not entirely in jest—that the ratio of the price of sirloin to the price of bone was a good indicator of a country's level of development.

sequent dumping of large quantities of this vegetable. The rational response to this situation would seem to be a lowering of the price paid for cucumbers and an increase in prices paid for products for which expanded marketing opportunities exist. That this has not been done is due partly to a political commitment to support small farmers' incomes; but this same objective could be met much more efficiently if the marketing board's technical and managerial expertise were upgraded.

Despite the numerous problems mentioned above, marketing systems in developing countries operate more efficiently than is sometimes assumed. Hayami and Ruttan, for example, cite studies in Asian and African countries which show that for commodities for which demand and productivity are growing slowly (mainly grains), "the product market is relatively efficient in transmitting price information and incentives between consumers and producers, and any arbitrary power to modify price behavior is of short-run or local significance" (1971: 267). Intermediaries often play an important role as a source of credit for small farmers. Where competitive conditions prevail, interest rates are relatively low, and by providing credit, intermediaries can often build up regular sources of supply. In Haiti, spoilage is relatively low because goods move to market in small volumes on foot power and exchange hands quickly. Also, marketing is an important source of employment and income for a high percentage of both rural and urban families. In Bolivia, the technology exists to reduce banana spoilage in storage, but given the low volumes handled by most wholesalers, the investment they would have to make cannot be justified on benefit-cost grounds. Credit could be made available to promote consolidation of wholesaling activities and thus achieve economies of scale, but this would have serious negative employment consequences.

Price Policy

Governments in developing countries can influence the prices of farm outputs and inputs in a variety of ways. In response to consumer pressures, maximum prices are often established at the producer, wholesale, and/or retail levels for basic foodstuffs. Such a policy is politically attractive in the short run, but the long-run effect may be to raise prices by discouraging domestic production and forcing the country to increase its reliance on imported food. Maximum prices may also be established for other purposes. In the late 1940s, as we noted earlier in this chapter, Argentina created a state trading company which squeezed savings out of the agricultural sector to finance an ambitious industrialization program. The low prices paid to farmers, however, had a negative effect on production, and this aggravated a balance-of-payments situation which was deteriorating for other reasons. In response, the government raised relative agricultural prices in the early 1950s, but this did little to stimulate increased output because farmers were not confident that the more favorable prices would be permanent.

Administrative controls in developing countries are not always effective in keeping prices low to consumers. Often they are only a minor nuisance to farmers rather than a disincentive to production. If enforcement is weak because the government does not directly purchase farm commodities and lacks the manpower and administrative expertise to police private-sector transactions, products will sell openly above the official maximum prices. In other cases, black markets will develop.

Governments in developing countries (as in developed countries) must be responsive not only to consumer pressures for lower prices but also to demands by producers for higher prices. This sometimes results in the establishment of price support schemes for selected products. These can be effective in stimulating production (often at the cost of a subsidy) if the government is the sole purchaser or if it can buy (and store) enough of a product to affect its market price. But if the government relies only on private-sector compliance with minimum support prices, such schemes are likely to be ineffective.

Government can also influence the price of agricultural *inputs*.[17] Minimum wage legislation, for example, can raise production costs and reduce a country's competitiveness in export markets, as has occurred in the English-speaking Caribbean. Tariff policy will affect the use of machinery, fertilizer, and other imported inputs. So will policies affecting the availability and cost of credit. Exchange-rate policy will affect both the competitiveness of exports and the factor proportions used in agriculture. An overvalued exchange rate—common in developing countries —discourages exports and artificially stimulates the substitution of capital for labor.

Changes in price policy, by themselves, will not stimulate agricultural development; markets in developing countries just do not work that well. But if governments are trying to encourage production of particular commodities through research, extension, credit, and other programs, they should be aware that all their efforts can be negated by inappropriate price policies. Often they are very much aware but feel compelled by political considerations to follow policies which in the economic sphere are contradictory. If the true economic costs of contradictory policies were known, this would be less of a problem.

---

17. The beneficiaries of input policy changes may be primarily large farmers or small farmers, depending on the policy instruments used.

Agricultural Sector Planning

It should be clear by now that there is a strong case for agricultural sector planning and programing in developing countries. Among the arguments that can be used to build this case are the following.

1. The record of agricultural development in developing countries has been worsening, and there are growing pressures for governments to reverse this trend in order to relieve nutritional, employment, income-distribution, and balance-of-payments problems.
2. The obstacles to more rapid agricultural development are numerous and interrelated, and a unified set of policies is needed to identify and eliminate bottlenecks.
3. Some key elements of agricultural development, including research, extension, and irrigation, are to a large extent public goods.
4. Government actions (e.g., market price information systems, crop insurance programs, road construction, land tenure reform) can make product and factor markets function more efficiently.

There is danger, however, in trying to make agricultural planning too comprehensive. If human and financial resources are limited, spreading them thinly over all crops, regions, and points of market intervention can be unproductive. There is much to be said for concentrating resources on a small number of programs focusing on a particular crop and/or a particular region. Planners should seek to identify all important elements involved in crop or area-development programs and to develop administrative mechanisms through which these various elements can be coordinated. The present writer was involved in the development of a rice production program in Ecuador's Guayas River Basin, the components of which included land tenure reform, cooperative formation, irrigation, marketing reforms, credit, and extension. This program required the cooperation of a number of government agencies, and a special unit was created to administer field operations. Two years after the program went into effect, significant social and economic changes had occurred.[18] Similar programs have been undertaken in many other countries, though not all of them have been successful.

The history of planning in developing countries suggests that primary responsibility for agricultural planning should be given not to the National Planning Board (NPB) but rather to a planning/programing unit within the Ministry of Agriculture. Being intimately involved at the planning

18. Clarence Zuvekas, Jr., "Agrarian Reform in Ecuador's Guayas River Basin," *Land Economics,* 52 (August 1976), 314–329.

stage, the ministry will have more of a vested interest in implementation than if primary responsibility for planning rested elsewhere. (Coordination with the NPB, of course, is still desirable.) Many Latin American and Caribbean countries have adopted this approach to planning, but it is too early to tell what the long-term results will be.

The Chinese Experience[19]

The remarkable transformation of Chinese agriculture since 1949, accomplished with much less human suffering than that of the Soviet Union in the 1930s, has attracted the attention of many economists and political leaders in developing countries who have been seeking models for transforming their own agricultural sectors. Prior to 1949, ownership of rural land in China was concentrated in the hands of a politically powerful elite. A large proportion of farmers had no land of their own but rented their plots from these large landowners, whose local monopsony power enabled them to charge high rents. Immediately upon attaining power in 1949, the revolutionary government under Mao Tse-Tung and his followers decreed that rental payments would be drastically reduced and began to take steps to expropriate large landholdings and distribute the land to former tenants. This task was accomplished by 1952 and was accompanied by the establishment of mutual aid teams among small land holders. These teams were then transformed into larger cooperatives, still larger collective farms, and finally, beginning in 1958, into communes with a membership of several thousand families and a land area varying from 3,000 to 12,000 hectares.

Each commune is divided into brigades, which in turn are divided into several teams of twenty-five to forty families. Each team is responsible for carrying out day-to-day farming activities on part of the commune's lands, which may be devoted to the production of a number of different crops as well as to livestock and forestry activities. The net income of the commune is divided among its members in accordance with "work points" earned for performing various tasks. Commune members also have small private plots which provide much of the pork and vegetables in their diet. Construction and maintenance of roads, irrigation canals, and other infrastructure is usually the responsibility of the brigade. Brigades also may own industrial production facilities, though

---

19. This section draws heavily on Sartaj Aziz, "The Chinese Approach to Rural Development," *International Development Review,* 15 (1974/4), 2–7, and John Wong, "Some Aspects of China's Agricultural Development Experience: Implications for Developing Countries in Asia," *World Development,* 4 (June 1976), 2–7. Aziz's assessment is perhaps too favorable, but it is useful for describing briefly what might be considered the "ideal" structure of the commune.

for economies-of-scale reasons much of the manufacturing activity in rural areas is carried out at the commune level or higher. The communes are responsible for building health and education facilities, which are staffed by medical and educational personnel provided by a unit of government roughly equivalent to the U.S. county.

One of the most interesting aspects of the commune system in China is the deliberate rural location of manufacturing activities, particularly those which provide backward and forward linkages with agriculture. Communes produce such products as refined sugar, powdered milk, paper, edible oils, and agricultural machinery and equipment. By providing these rural employment opportunities, and by tightly restricting the internal mobility of labor, China has prevented the rapid migration to the cities that has occurred in many developing countries; the urban population increased from 13 percent of the total in 1953 to just 16 percent in 1973. Restrictions on labor mobility, however, have had some negative consequences for agriculture, since labor is prevented from moving from areas where its marginal productivity is low to areas where it is high.

The government extracts a surplus from agriculture (i.e., forcibly mobilizes rural savings) through a tax in kind on agricultural production and through compulsory as well as voluntary sales by the communes, beyond their quotas, to the government. The agricultural tax was an estimated 13 percent of gross value of output in the early 1950s but currently is only 5 to 6 percent. Squeezing the peasants through post-quota sales at fixed prices appears to be much less severe than in the Soviet Union.

Evaluating the performance of Chinese agriculture is difficult because of the reluctance of the Chinese government to release detailed statistics and sometimes because of the deliberate falsification of data. Moreover, most "Western" visitors to China spend little time there and admit that what they are shown may not be representative. Nevertheless, there is widespread agreement among visitors of various political persuasions that the performance of Chinese agriculture has been impressive. The proportion of land under irrigation reportedly rose from 20 percent in 1952 to 78 percent in 1971, thus permitting more double- and triple-cropping. As we noted in chapter 7, there seems to be relatively little malnutrition. Farmers' living standards appear to be higher than in most Asian countries, and the gap between the highest and lowest rural incomes is reported by some observers to be only 2 to 1. Labor is close to being fully employed, though the marginal productivity of some activities (e.g., reclaiming the land by hand-carrying baskets of earth) is less than the consumption requirements of those performing these tasks. (The Chinese counter this neoclassical criticism by pointing out that some increase in production is better than the absence of any increase if labor is idle.) The soil erosion problem, neglected in the early years of the revolution, now receives considerable attention. Whereas the original strategy for increasing production was based on institutional reorganization, the emphasis is now on technological change.

Notwithstanding the numerous positive features of the Chinese experience with rural development, it is inappropriate to consider it a "model" that can be transferred to other developing countries. Indeed, the Chinese government itself has emphasized that an attempt to implement such a system elsewhere would be dangerous, since each country has a unique social, political, and institutional framework to which development strategies and program must be adapted.[20] Moreover, the present Chinese system is not one that has been adhered to rigidly, but one which has developed by evolution and probably will continue to do so. It is very unlikely that institutions similar to the present-day communes could be organized in other developing countries in just a few years. Complex structures like this take time to develop, and an evolutionary approach is more likely to succeed than one which challenges a great number of traditions, institutions, and power contenders simultaneously.

Still, the Chinese experience has a number of valuable lessons for developing countries. First, it illustrates the importance of establishing a strong institutional framework, whatever that framework might be. Second, it shows how a rejection of urban-biased strategies and the adoption of a balanced strategy with some proagrarian aspects can result in both growth *and* development. Third, it demonstrates the value of an integrated approach linking production, distribution, capital formation, industrialization, and numerous nonagricultural activities. For other countries to profit from these lessons, careful attention will have to be paid to management and administration. But above all, what is needed is political will.

SUMMARY

We have emphasized in this chapter that there is no single key to accelerating the growth of agricultural output. What is required is a comprehensive "package" of policies based on a clear understanding of interrelationships, complementarities, and conflicts among different policy actions. This package will vary according to the economic, agronomic, and institutional conditions prevailing in each country or region. For societies that are highly organized, the Chinese model of agricultural development may provide some valuable lessons. But in less centralized

---

20. Wong (op. cit., p. 494) points out that the countries whose agricultural structures are most similar to China's—Japan, South Korea, and Taiwan—have had successful agricultural development experiences on the basis of very different systems.

societies in which planning and administrative capacities are limited, it is perhaps best for policy makers to concentrate on a small number of commodities or geographic areas, and on incentive systems. Even these efforts may have little effect unless the government assigns a high priority to agriculture and commits both the economic and political resources necessary for policies to be carried out effectively.

Suggested Readings

Barraclough, Solon, and Arthur Domike, "Agrarian Structure in Seven Latin American Countries." *Land Economics*, 42 (November 1966), 391–424.

This article summarizes the findings of comprehensive studies of land tenure arrangements in Argentina, Brazil, Colombia, Chile, Ecuador, Guatemala, and Peru, conducted during the 1960s by the Interamerican Committee on Agricultural Development, a group supported by five U.N. and Western Hemisphere organizations.

Beckford, George L. *Persistent Poverty: Underdevelopment in Plantation Economies of the Third World*. New York: Oxford University Press, 1972.

The author, an experienced agricultural economist at the University of the West Indies, argues that the plantation system engenders "persistent poverty" which not even political independence has done much to change. The only escape, in Beckford's view, is the replacement of the plantation system by one that is based on indigenous institutions and geared more toward production for the local market and for a regional market integrating the economies of the small nations now trapped in persistent poverty. Beckford's detailed prescriptions are not too clear, but his analysis of plantation agriculture is well researched and insightful.

Brown, Lester R. *Seeds of Change: The Green Revolution and Development in the 1970's*. Foreword by Eugene R. Black. New York: Praeger Publishers, 1970.

This nontechnical book, written by a former U.S. Department of Agriculture official intimately involved in Green Revolution activities, is a good summary of the development of the "miracle" grain seeds and early experiences with them. Though more optimistic about the Green Revolution in 1970 than he is today, Brown was well aware when this book was written of the problems the new seeds might create.

Feder, Ernest. *The Rape of the Peasantry: Latin America's Landholding System*. Garden City, N.Y.: Doubleday and Company, Inc., Anchor Books, 1971.

This insightful study of the land tenure situation in Latin America is based on the author's field experience in Latin America, including work on the CIDA project, whose results are summarized in the Barraclough and Domike reference above. Using vivid examples from a number of countries, Feder argues that the *latifundio* system can be regarded as one of "unemployment agriculture" in which large landowners deliberately seek to keep small farmers' real incomes from rising.

Hayami, Yujiro, and Vernon W. Ruttan. *Agricultural Development: An International Perspective*. Baltimore: The Johns Hopkins University Press, 1971.

This book is a major contribution to the literature on agricultural development. The authors' theory of induced innovation argues that the growth of agricultural productivity depends on a country's capacity to develop technology that is appropriate to its factor proportions and consistent with its institutions. Most of the book compares agricultural development in the United States and Japan, but attention is also given to South Korea, Taiwan, and other developing countries. In addition to the theoretical material (somewhat difficult but by no means impossible for undergraduates to follow), the authors provide valuable descriptions of institutional change in U.S. and Japanese agriculture, and they summarize the results of scores of studies in both developed and developing countries.

Johnston, Bruce F., and Peter Kilby. *Agriculture and Structural Transformation: Economic Strategies in Late-Developing Countries*. New York: Oxford University Press, 1975.

This collaborative effort between an agricultural economist and an industrial economist emphasizes the interrelationships between agriculture and the rest of the economy. The authors contend that "a choice and sequence of innovations that is compatible with the progressive modernization of a large and increasing fraction of a country's small farmers has important economic as well as social advantages."

Lele, Uma. *The Design of Rural Development: Lessons from Africa*. Baltimore: The Johns Hopkins University Press for the World Bank, 1975.

Based on a detailed study of seventeen rural development programs in sub-Saharan Africa, this book argues that successful rural development requires an overall policy framework as well as an institutional framework conducive to the achievement of policy objectives. Differences between expected and actual project performance, the author argues, are often due to assumptions that are not consistent with the facts relevant to each unique situation.

Lipton, Michael. "Agricultural Finance and Rural Credit in Poor Countries." *World Development*, 4 (July 1976), 543–553.

In reviewing the recent literature, the author finds an "emerging consensus . . . that interest rates are much less 'extortionate', and farm activities much less often constrained by lack of credit, than was once thought."

Nelson, Michael. *The Development of Tropical Lands*. Baltimore: The Johns Hopkins University Press, 1973.

This study reviews the experience of twenty-four colonization projects in Latin America. Nelson finds that B/C relationships are more favorable for spontaneous colonization than for directed colonization projects.

Rice, Edward B. *Extension in the Andes: An Evaluation of Official U.S. Assistance to Agricultural Extension Services in Central and South America*. Cambridge, Mass.: The MIT Press, 1974.

Working imaginatively with poor data, this former AID "insider" seeks to explain why U.S. assistance efforts in agricultural extension had little impact on production and failed to leave behind permanent institutions once U.S. assistance was terminated. Rice argues that the extension model brought from the U.S. to Latin America was inappropriate, and that the bureaucratic environment in the region doomed the institution-building effort.

Schultz, Theodore W. *Transforming Traditional Agriculture.* New Haven: Yale University Press, 1964.

This short, easily read book argues, contrary to the views of many anthropologists at the time it was written, that farmers are rational economic beings. If they refuse to adopt new technologies, says Schultz, it is not because of stubborn resistance to change but rather because they lack incentives. Schultz's view is now widely accepted. However, because of ignorance of environmental factors and other externalities, farmers often make decisions which seem to be rational in the short run but which may have serious negative consequences in the long run.

10

Industrialization

Industrialization may be defined as the process of transforming raw materials, with the aid of human resources and capital goods, into (1) consumer goods, (2) new capital goods which permit more consumer goods (including food) to be produced with the same human resources, and (3) social overhead capital, which together with human resources provides new services to both individuals and businesses. If the new goods and services created by industrialization are not widely distributed among the population, it may be said that only economic growth is taking place. But if they are the types of goods and services that are used to satisfy the basic human needs of a large percentage of the population, then industrial growth is being accompanied by development.

Industrialization also contributes to the psychological dimension of welfare by giving a nation and its citizens a feeling of greater control over their economic lives. Industrialization is viewed both as a means of reducing dependence on imports (thus helping to overcome the foreign exchange constraint) and, at least in some countries, as a means of earning additional foreign exchange through an expansion and diversification of the export base. Foreign exchange earnings or savings can be used both to further expand industrial activity (and thus, it is hoped, to further reduce dependence on imports) and to increase imports of consumer goods and services which for various reasons cannot be produced locally.

Industrial activity, broadly conceived, includes manufacturing and the related sectors of mining and public utilities. Some writers would add construction to this list. In a very poor developing country, these activities together may account for only 10 to 12 percent of the national output and even less of total employment.

Most people in the manufacturing sectors of very poor countries will be engaged in artisan or handicraft activities, whose low productivity provides them little income.[1] When modern manufacturing activity begins, output per worker rises, permitting higher wages for those employed in the new firms. At the same time, however, artisans will find it difficult to compete with modern methods of production, and artisan employment may stop increasing or even decline. Thus, as manufacturing becomes steadily more capital intensive, employment in that sector grows more slowly than output. This tendency, combined with the small absolute size of the manufacturing sector in the initial years of development, means that even a rapidly growing industrial sector may provide only a small percentage of the increased jobs demanded by a growing labor force. We shall have more to say about the employment implications of industrial growth in chapter 12.

STAGES IN THE PROCESS OF INDUSTRIALIZATION

At the risk of overgeneralizing, industrialization may be described as proceeding through a series of stages, each dominated by the growth of particular types of manufacturing industries. In the first stage, the most important branches of the manufacturing sector tend to be food processing and the production of textiles and clothing. This should not be surprising, since the great bulk of consumers' budgets in low-income countries will have to be spent on necessities. Moreover, there tend to be few economies of scale in these activities, so that average production costs for small firms are not significantly different from those of large firms at prevailing levels of technology. Much of this early manufacturing activity does not truly represent increased output but simply a shift of production from the household, where it is unrecorded in the GNP statistics, to the factory, where it is. Examples would include flour milling, baking, brewing (beer is substituted for various "home brews" of roughly equivalent alcoholic content and social significance), and various items of clothing. A greater share of housing construction, too, is likely to be found in the marketplace. What this means, of course, is that the GNP statistics are likely to exaggerate the growth of industrial output. On the other hand, a shift from household to factory production also may result in an improvement in product quality (many people apparently think

---

1. In 1960 artisan employment accounted for 70 percent or more of total manufacturing employment in six Latin American and Caribbean countries: Bolivia, Ecuador, Haiti, Honduras, Nicaragua, and Paraguay (UN-ECLA 1966: 75). Many African and Asian countries are at even lower levels of development today than the above-mentioned countries were in 1960, and artisans probably account for more than 75 percent of manufacturing employment in some cases.

beer tastes better than home brew). This kind of welfare gain does not show up in the GNP statistics even in the highly industrialized countries.

As income per capita rises, the demand for light manufactured articles increases, and additional products for which economies of scale are not great will begin to be produced in the country. Many new industries may begin as assembly operations (transistor radios, bicycles, sewing machines, etc.), but over time an increasing percentage of the inputs will be produced at home. In other cases, products may be made directly from local raw materials (wooden kitchen utensils, leather goods, stoneware), or they may be fabricated locally from imported iron and steel or other intermediate products (tools, a variety of plastic products).

The growth rate of these industries depends not only on the rate of growth of GNP but also on several other factors. If the benefits of a rising GNP go only to a small segment of the population, demand for light manufactured products will rise more slowly than would be the case if the same GNP growth were shared by a larger number of people. Government policy is also critical. If these industries are given little tariff protection and have trouble getting credit, they will find it hard to compete with imports.

Returning now to our sequence of industrial stages, a further rise in per capita income will stimulate the formation of major consumer durable goods industries, such as those producing television sets, refrigerators, and automobiles. Furniture production will also be stimulated, though this is an industry in which production is likely to increase at an earlier stage because of the relatively simple technology and the availability of local raw materials. Significant economies of scale exist in some of these industries, and if governments try to stimulate output when domestic demand is still limited, production costs will be high and stiff tariffs will be required to protect local firms from lower-priced imports. More about this problem below.

In developing countries where significant increases have occurred in per capita incomes *and* where the absolute size of the domestic market is large (e.g., Brazil, Mexico, Iran), an economic case can be made for producing intermediate products (e.g., iron and steel, glass) or other products using advanced technology and having significant economies of scale (e.g., refined petroleum products). Fairly sophisticated machinery (including agricultural machinery) and other capital goods can also be produced fairly efficiently under these circumstances. Again, though, tariff protection is likely to be necessary initially.

In reality, the stages of industrial growth are not as orderly as we have just outlined. The above scheme is simply suggestive of the rough order in which industrial growth proceeds, based on what we know about consumer demand patterns, economies of scale, and technological considerations. It is not unusual, however, for industries to be established "out of sequence." There are at least four major reasons why this may occur.

1. In countries with significant mineral deposits or petroleum reserves, large-scale smelting or refining operations may be established at relatively low levels of development (though it is often more profitable for these operations to be carried out in the developed countries). This almost always involves foreign capital and foreign technical assistance, since a very poor developing country has neither the skilled labor and management nor the ability to mobilize the large amounts of domestic savings required by such industries.

2. The manufacture of some consumer durables—e.g., furniture— is labor intensive, based primarily on local raw materials, and does not have significant economies of scale. Production can thus easily begin in the early stages of development.

3. If a country adopts an export-oriented strategy of development, based either on the processing of local raw materials or on assembly operations, manufactured products can be produced before the local market is large enough to support such industries.

4. Finally, an import-substitution strategy of development can alter the sequence of industrialization by providing tariff protection and other incentives which permit industries with significant economies of scale to be established earlier than would be the case in an internationally competitive environment. This development strategy is examined in the following section.

IMPORT SUBSTITUTION

Import-substituting industrialization (ISI) is a development strategy based on the planned substitution of domestically produced goods for imports. It is a logical outgrowth of the declining terms-of-trade thesis generally accepted by most developing countries as a result of their experience with the Great Depression and its aftermath (see chapter 5). ISI appears to solve the terms-of-trade problem by diversifying developing countries' output and lessening their dependence on imported manufactured goods. There is also a gain in the important psychological dimension of welfare—which economists tend to underrate, if not ignore—as countries feel more in control of their own destinies.

Import substitution seems to promise very rapid growth, since an industry's growth rate is determined not just by the growth of domestic demand but also by the potential for replacing imports. This may be seen in Figure 10.1, whose horizontal axis measures time in years. The vertical axis measures the quantity of the product demanded, on a log (ratio)

Figure 10.1
Industry Growth Prospects via Import Substitution

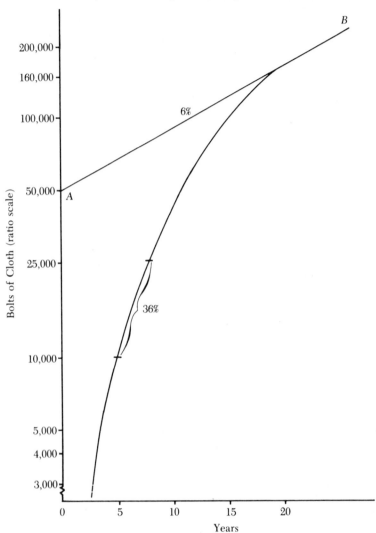

scale. This means that a constant rate of growth appears as an upward-sloping straight line. The faster the growth rate, the steeper is the slope. Let us assume that in Year 0 domestic demand for cotton textiles is 50,000 bolts of cloth, all of which is supplied by imports. Assume further that demand for cotton textiles can be expected to grow by 6 percent annually for the next 20 years, which would imply a demand of 160,000 bolts by Year 20. This is indicated by Line AB. Now assume that the government places a protective tariff on cotton textiles (or limits imports through a quota scheme), with the objective of completely eliminating imports by Year 20. If this strategy is successful, the cotton textile industry can grow during this period at a rate much higher than 6 percent. In Figure 10.1, for example, the line we have drawn indicates a growth rate of 36 percent between Years 5 and 8. The growth rate then declines gradually to 6 percent by Year 20, after which it cannot rise again unless domestic demand grows faster or export opportunities are available. But by this time, the country is likely to be ready for a new round of import substitution, based on consumer durables, so the industrial sector as a whole can still grow faster than the entire economy.

This promising scenario is in practice often thwarted by foreign exchange constraints. While it may appear that ISI reduces imports, this does not always happen, particularly in the short run. For one thing, there will be an initial large outlay for importing the machinery and building materials (structural steel, cement, etc.) necessary to establish the industry. Then, to the extent that they are not produced within the country, raw materials and intermediate goods will have to be imported. Even skilled labor and management services may have to be purchased abroad, not to mention patent and trademark fees and other costs associated with technology transfer.

The end result could well be a short-run *increase* in foreign exchange costs, particularly if a "crash program" of import substitution is pursued, as in Argentina in the late 1950s and early 1960s.[2] If foreign exchange earnings are not rising at the same time—as may well happen if agriculture is ignored in favor of industry—the process of ISI will have to be slowed.[3] Foreign exchange, of course, can be borrowed, but since it must eventually be repaid, this is only a short-run remedy. If export earnings continue to stagnate, debt repayment will take up an increasing proportion of these earnings, at the expense of imports needed by industry. And this will make foreign lenders hesitant to make additional loans until the country takes steps to increase exports. Private foreign investment is another potential source of foreign exchange, but many developing countries are reluctant to grant foreigners a major role in industrial development. This, too, is a short-run solution, since foreigners will want to remit future profits back to their home countries.

Thus, ISI does not so much eliminate imports as shift the composition of imports away from finished goods toward raw materials, inter-

2. See Clarence Zuvekas, Jr., "Argentine Economic Policy: The Frondizi Government's Development Plan," *Inter-American Economic Affairs*, 22 (Summer 1968), 45–73.

3. A major study of industrialization and trade policies in seven developing countries found that these policies overencouraged industry at the expense of agriculture. As a result, exports were discouraged, resources were allocated inefficiently, and the industrialization process itself was constrained. Moreover, industrialization policies were found to have negative effects on employment and to have widened income inequalities (Little, Scitovsky, and Scott, 1970).

mediate goods, and capital goods. In one sense, this makes the economy even more dependent on imports, since a foreign exchange crisis will force a halt to some construction activity and will cause workers to be laid off in industries not able to acquire all the inputs they need. When the finished product is imported, on the other hand, the immediate job layoffs occur only in the import houses, and the wastes of unused capacity are less.

Strategies of ISI usually involve significant protection to domestic industry in the form of high tariffs (or perhaps quotas) on the competing imported items. While such tariffs can be justified by the "dynamic comparative advantage" argument explained in chapter 5, some industries receiving protection have little chance of growing up in the foreseeable future because they lack the necessary economies of scale, technical expertise, or inexpensive inputs. They are established as political favors, and they can survive in the long run only with continued protection.

The automobile industry has been particularly wasteful of scarce economic resources. This is due in part to the fact that economies of scale are especially great in this industry. The United Nations Economic Commission for Latin America has estimated that unit costs of raw materials used by an automobile assembly plant producing 10,000 units annually are 25 percent higher than those for a totally integrated plant producing 300,000 units. For parts and pieces (40 percent of total production costs in the larger plant, compared with 15 percent for raw materials) unit costs are *80 percent* higher for the smaller plant.[4] Many automobile assembly plants in developing countries produce well below 10,000 units. In Argentina, for example, 19 of the 22 plants operating in 1960 had an average annual production of only about 3,000 units.[5] Most of these high-cost plants were unable to survive, even with high tariff protection. In Chile, the problem of low production volume per plant was complicated by a political decision to induce firms to locate automobile assembly operations in the northern city of Arica—1,000 miles away from the country's major markets for automobiles—by granting that city free port status. High internal transportation costs and numerous other problems resulted from this unfavorable location decision.[6]

Protective tariffs which remain high have several undesirable consequences. First, there is little incentive for firms to lower costs, since

4. United Nations, Economic Commission for Latin America, *Notas sobre la economía y el desarrollo de América Latina*, No. 143 (Nov. 16, 1973), p. 2.
5. *Review of the River Plate*, 126 (December 22, 1959), 24.
6. For a vivid description of the Chilean case, see Leland L. Johnson, "Problems of Import Substitution: The Chilean Automobile Industry," *Economic Development and Cultural Change*, 15 (January 1967), 202–216. The 20 automobile firms which located in Arica had a *total* annual production in 1963 and 1964 of only 8,000 units.

imports are restricted or shut off and the domestic market structure is likely to be one of oligopoly with collusive behavior. A rational policy under these circumstances would seem to be a planned reduction of tariffs in accordance with a published schedule, forcing the infant industries to grow up through external competition or to wither. Such a policy, however, is politically difficult (though not impossible) to implement, given the industrialists' influence in government. A second consequence of high protective tariffs is that potential export industries are penalized by being forced to buy either high-cost domestic inputs or imported inputs with a stiff tariff attached. This makes it difficult for a country to diversify its exports and provide additional foreign exchange for its development efforts.

On the basis of the above analysis, readers might be tempted to conclude that ISI is not a viable development strategy. That is not the impression we would like to leave. On the contrary, ISI can indeed be a successful strategy, provided that developing countries pay close attention to the foreign exchange costs of new industries. Some countries have encouraged capital-intensive methods of production but have not followed policies which encourage the full use of capital goods, most of which have to be imported. It is not uncommon to find 35 to 40 percent of capacity unused in developing countries, even during periods of rapid growth. This represents a considerable waste of foreign exchange. While technological imperatives often require the use of very capital-intensive methods of production (e.g., petroleum refining, steel, automobiles), other industries use capital-intensive methods only because government policy distorts relative factor prices, making capital cheaper and labor more expensive than would be the case without government intervention. In addition to these foreign exchange implications, capital-intensive methods of production also have serious employment consequences, a subject that will be discussed in chapter 12.

In essence, what we are saying is that an effective ISI policy, as Balassa and his associates (1971: xv) have emphasized, cannot be based on ad hoc responses to pressures by special interest groups. Rather it must pay close attention to balance-of-payments and other effects of ISI, and it must give *selective* encouragement to those industries which use a relatively high proportion of domestic inputs (including labor). As industrialization proceeds, more and more inputs will be produced domestically, making possible the gradual establishment of new industries without unusually high import requirements. Import substitution can be accelerated by widening the domestic market through income redistribution.[7]

7. For a recent defense of import substitution as a development strategy, see Alexander (1976).

What needs to be resisted is the temptation to succumb to the automobile-steel mill-refinery complex in the early years of the ISI process—particularly in the smaller countries, where the market is not large enough to take advantage of economies of scale. As we have said before, policy makers who become fascinated with these "sexy" industries are confusing the symbols of a developed economy with the processes of growth and development.

EXPORT-ORIENTED INDUSTRIALIZATION

Disappointment with ISI as a generator of rapid growth (and a provider of jobs) has led many developing countries to reconsider an export-oriented pattern of industrialization. Earlier, this strategy had often been rejected because it seemed to make developing countries too dependent on the developed countries. In addition, many of the latter were using tariffs, quotas, and other measures to restrict their imports of manufactured goods for which the developing countries seemed to have acquired a comparative advantage. The United States, for example, has used "voluntary quotas" to limit imports of textiles and footwear, and Latin American countries have charged (with some justification) that U.S. sanitary regulations covering canned fish and seafood are unduly restrictive, protecting U.S. producers rather than consumers. The European Economic Community (EEC) has been attacked just as vigorously by developing countries for its restrictive practices, especially for the products of developing countries not party to the Lomé Convention, which provides special treatment for former colonies of EEC members as well as some other African nations.

In the face of these very real obstacles to manufactured exports, many developing countries for a long time did little more than object that the international trade "system" was stacked against them. This was essentially true, but some countries nonetheless managed to increase their manufactured exports at very rapid rates. Examples include Singapore, Hong Kong, Taiwan, and South Korea in the Far East, and Mexico, Colombia, and Brazil in Latin America. For developing countries as a group, exports of labor-intensive manufactures increased at a healthy annual rate of 13 percent between 1953 and 1966.[8] Unpublished estimates by the World Bank show that the *real* value of manufactured exports by developing countries rose by 12.7 percent a year from 1965 to 1975. The growth rate was particularly rapid (14.6 percent annually) in the middle-income developing countries, which accounted for 90 percent

8. Gerald M. Meier, *Leading Issues in Economic Development,* 2nd ed. (New York: Oxford University Press, 1970), pp. 550–558.

of all developing-country export earnings from manufactures ($33 billion). In the poorest countries, on the other hand, the annual rate of increase was a modest 3.5 percent.

Approximately two-thirds of all manufactured exports from developing countries in 1974 were made by countries in South and East Asia, particularly Hong Kong, Taiwan, South Korea, India, Singapore, and Malaysia. Most of the remainder came from Latin America, with Africa and the Middle East each supplying only about 6 percent of the total.[9] Table 10.1 provides data for the principal exporting countries in the developing world in 1972 (when manufactured exports in current dollars were only about half their 1974 figures).

Two decades ago, the distingiushed economist W. Arthur Lewis remarked to his fellow West Indians that the fundamental problem regarding industrial exporting was not that the developing countries lacked a comparative advantage in manufactured goods; rather, it was "a lack of initiative, a lack of imagination, a lack of willingness to take the

TABLE 10.1
Principal Developing Countries Exporting
Manufactured Goods,[a] 1972

Country	Manufactured Exports (US$ million)
Hong Kong	2,635
Taiwan	2,489
South Korea	1,351
India	1,320
Singapore	893
Brazil	749
Mexico	647
Argentina	394
Pakistan	380
Malaysia	175
Colombia	172

Source: Deepak Nayyar, "Transnational Corporations and Manufactured Exports from Poor Countries," *Economic Journal,* 88 (March 1978), 62, and United Nations, *Yearbook of International Trade Statistics* (for Malaysia).

[a] SITC categories 5–8 minus 68.

9. Deepak Nayyar, "Transnational Corporations and Manufactured Exports from Poor Countries," *Economic Journal,* 88 (March 1978), 64. Taiwan, one of the two leading developing-country exporters of manufactured goods (see Table 10.1), is not included in the regional totals on this page.

risks of developing an export trade in manufacturers."[10] Success in exporting manufactured products requires an enlightened, comprehensive export development policy dealing with a variety of problems ranging from export credit shortages to government red tape. A striking, though admittedly extreme example of what an enlightened policy can accomplish is provided by the case of South Korea, where commodity exports increased from a mere $33 million in 1960 to $622 million in 1969 and $4.9 *billion* in 1975.[11] Even if one discounts for inflation, U.S. aid, and opportunities generated by U.S. intervention in Southeast Asia, this is a remarkable achievement.

RECENT TRENDS IN INDUSTRIAL OUTPUT

Although many countries have been disappointed with their ISI efforts, industrial output in the developing countries has nevertheless been growing faster than production in other economic sectors, and its share of the GNP has thus been rising. In 1970, 71 percent of all industrial output in developing market economies consisted of manufactured goods (see Table 10.2). Light manufacturing was slightly more important than heavy manufacturing in that year, but because of trends since 1970 their relative positions have been reversed. Mining accounted for 23 percent of industrial output in 1970, while the share of public utilities was 6 percent. Between 1970 and 1976, mining's share of industrial output declined, while those of manufacturing and public utilities increased.

Recent industrial growth has been much faster in the developing countries (a compound annual growth rate of 6.6 percent between 1970 and 1976) than in the developed market economies (3.4 percent), though not so fast as in the centrally planned economies (8.5 percent). The developed market economies were particularly hard hit by the world recession of 1974–1975, but even without these distorting effects, industrial growth in the developing countries would have been faster. Note in Table 10.2 that the rapid growth of industrial output in the developing countries is attributable mainly to the performance of manufacturing and not to the real growth of value added in pertoleum and other mining activities, which was relatively slow.

Data in Table 10.3 examine regional trends in manufacturing growth rates since 1960. These data make it clear that developing countries

10. W. Arthur Lewis, "Employment Policy in an Underdeveloped Area," *Social and Economic Studies*, 7 (September 1958), 48.

11. See Hyong Chun Kim, "Korea's Export Success, 1960–69," *Finance and Development*, 8 (March 1971), 14-21; and Amicus Most, *Expanding Exports: A Case Study of the Korean Experience* (Washington, D.C.: U.S. Agency for International Development, June 1969).

TABLE 10.2
Structure of Industrial Output in Developed and Developing Countries, 1970, and Growth of Industrial Output, 1970–1976[a]

	(1) Centrally Planned Economies[b]	(2) Developed Market Economies	(3) Market Developing Economies	(4) Latin American/ Caribbean	(5) Developing Countries in Asia	Indices of Industrial Output in 1976 (1970 = 100)				
						(1)	(2)	(3)	(4)	(5)
	(percentage composition)									
Total Industry	100.0	100.0	100.0	100.0	100.0	163	122	147	147	155
Manufacturing	89.2	88.0	71.1	82.3	64.7	166	122	152	152	154
Light[c]	29.3	29.0	37.1	39.1	36.6	141	119	141	136	146
Heavy[d]	59.9	59.0	34.0	43.2	28.1	177	123	165	166	164
Mining	7.9	4.9	23.0	11.5	29.9	138	104	125	104	150
Petroleum/ Natural Gas	2.8	1.8	16.8	6.3	25.5	148	114	129	94	155
Other	5.1	3.1	6.2	5.2	4.4	—	—	—	—	—
Electricity, Gas and Water	2.8	7.1	5.9	6.2	5.4	154	135	180	169	196

Source: United Nations, *Monthly Bulletin of Statistics*, November 1977, Table A.
[a] Based on indices of value added.
[b] Bulgaria, Czechoslovakia, East Germany, Hungary, Poland, Romania, and the Soviet Union.
[c] Food, beverages, tobacco, textiles, apparel, leather, wood, printing, publishing, rubber, plastics, and miscellaneous manufactures.
[d] Paper, paper products, chemicals, petroleum, nonmetallic minerals, basic metals, and metal products.

TABLE 10.3
Average Annual Growth in Manufacturing Output,
Developed and Developing Countries,
1961–1965, 1966–1972, and 1973 through 1976
(*percent*)

	1961–65	1966–72	1973	1974	1975	1976
Developed Countries	6.2	5.7	9.4	−0.6	−8.8	9.9
Developing Countries	8.7	8.7	11.0	7.2	1.7	n.a.
Africa South of the Sahara	9.3	8.8	4.9	7.7	3.6	n.a.
East Asia and Pacific[a]	9.1	14.5	18.9	7.8	7.6	n.a.
Latin America and the Caribbean	6.0	7.9	9.5	6.8	0.8	7.1
North Africa and Middle East	9.9	8.8	14.9	12.1	11.9	n.a.
South Asia	9.1	3.4	3.1	1.9	3.3	8.2
More Advanced Mediterranean Countries[b]	11.7	9.7	11.8	7.5	−1.2	4.9

Source: *World Bank Annual Report 1977*, Annex Table 1, pp. 104–105.
[a] Excludes mainland China and North Korea.
[b] Cyprus, Greece, Malta, Portugal, Spain, Turkey, and Yugoslavia.

were experiencing rapid industrial growth in the 1960s as well as in the 1970s. For developing countries as a group, the average annual growth of manufacturing output was 8.7 percent during 1961–1965 and again during 1966–1972. This was several percentage points higher than the comparable growth rates in developed countries during the same years. After accelerating to 11.0 percent in 1973 the manufacturing growth rate in developing countries fell to only 5.0 percent during 1974–1975, in response to the direct and indirect effects of the sharp increase in the price of petroleum, a key production input. Still, this was a much better record than that of the developed countries, where manufacturing output *fell* at an annual rate of 4.7 percent. The developed countries experienced a strong recovery during 1976, and partial data for the developing countries indicate that they did likewise.

Among the developing countries, the most heavily industrialized regions are Latin America and the Caribbean, where manufacturing's share of the GNP is about 25 percent, and the Mediterranean region, where it is about 27 percent. The least industrialized region is Africa South of the Sahara, where manufacturing averages no more than 10 percent of the GNP.

Looking at regional growth rates, we find that manufacturing growth has been most rapid in East Asia and the Pacific, where countries like Singapore, South Korea, and Taiwan have focused on export markets as well as import substitution, and in North Africa and the Middle East, where revenues from petroleum production have permitted manufacturing activity to expand rapidly from a relatively small base. The poorest performance, particularly since 1965, has been in South Asia, where political difficulties and natural disasters have taken a serious toll on India, Pakistan, and Bangladesh, three of the world's ten most populous countries.[12]

OVERCOMING THE OBSTACLES TO MORE RAPID INDUSTRIAL DEVELOPMENT

As with agriculture, there is no single key to the process of industrialization. A successful strategy, based either on export promotion or import substitution, must deal with a variety of problems. Let us take a brief look at some of these.

Lack of Financial Markets

Investment, or physical capital formation, must be matched by an equivalent amount of savings, either from within the economy or from abroad. Over the long run, the great bulk of savings must be provided by the developing country itself. As we shall see in chapter 13, securities markets in most developing countries are rudimentary and sometimes nonexistent, making it difficult for firms to raise money through stock or bond issues. Few people channel their savings into life insurance institutions. The lack of savings and loan associations or alternative sources of mortgage lending may hinder housing construction. Governments can help overcome these obstacles either by operating directly as financial intermediaries or by providing incentives for such entities to be formed in the private sector.

Shortages of Credit

A related problem is the shortage of industrial credit, particularly medium- and long-range credit for financing plant construction and the purchase of machinery and equipment. Commercial banks usually restrict their operations to short-term, working capital loans. Medium- and long-term credit may be available only from domestic or foreign suppliers of machinery and equipment, often at high interest rates and with short repayment periods. Some developing countries have remedied this problem by establishing specialized development banks (or *financieras*, as they are called in Latin America), either in the public sector or the

---

12. Political difficulties diverting resources away from economic growth and development included military confrontations between India and Pakistan, India and China, and East Pakistan and West Pakistan, As a result of the last confrontation, East Pakistan became the independent national of Bangladesh.

private sector. These institutions have been able to attract long-term loans, under favorable conditions, from the World Bank, the U.S. government, and other bilateral and multilateral lending institutions. Their record is mixed, but the more successful ones have played a major role in accelerating the pace of industrialization.

Shortages of Skilled Labor and Other Middle-level Manpower

While most developing countries have an abundance of unskilled labor, skilled laborers such as welders, machinists, tool and die makers, and repair specialists are often in very short supply. The same may be true of middle-level white collar workers, such as bookkeepers and engineering assistants. In some cases, these shortages may impose absolute limits on the output of a particular industry. Generally, however, industrial output can still increase, though more slowly and at higher costs per unit. Shortages will be filled by less trained workers; average labor productivity will decline, other things being equal; and labor costs per unit of output will rise. On-the-job training programs can provide the necessary skills, but at a cost to the employer. If skilled labor shortages persist for a long time, economic theory suggests that the wages of these workers will rise faster than wages and salaries generally. And that indeed is what we find in many developing countries. This can lead to the formation of a class of "privileged" workers whose objectives may have little in common with those of less fortunate workers and who may support different political parties or leaders.

As we pointed out in chapter 7, governments can help overcome manpower shortages by changing their educational policies to conform more closely with development objectives. They can also subsidize on-the-job training, which frequently is less costly than technical education in secondary and postsecondary institutions.

Lack of Entrepreneurial Skills

The important role of entrepreneurship in economic growth and development was discussed in chapter 3. One way for governments to overcome a shortage of entrepreneurial skills is to rely heavily on foreign entrepreneurship. Much of the recent rapid growth of Brazilian industry, for example, has occurred in foreign-owned firms.[13]

13. It has been estimated that multinational enterprises accounted for 43 percent of Brazil's exports of manufactured goods in 1969. Figures of 25 to 30 percent have been reported for Argentina, Colombia, and Mexico. For the Asian countries listed in Table 10.1, the importance of multinationals is less in all cases except Singapore, where the figure is nearly 70 percent (Nayyar, 1978: 62).

Not all developing countries, however, are willing to have their economies so dominated by outsiders., Alternatively, governments in these countries may deal with the entrepreneurial problem indirectly, through general policies increasing incentives to industry, or they may attack it directly in one of two ways. One is to provide supervised credit (i.e., credit and technical assistance) and special training programs, particularly for owner-operators of small and medium-size industrial firms. The other is for the government itself to assume an entrepreneurial role, either for those priority industries which the private sector neglects or for other industries for which state ownership is deemed to be in the public interest. One should not assume that public entrepreneurship is significant only under radical or "leftist" regimes. Conservative regimes, such as the present Brazilian government, have also supported a strong role for the state in the ownership and operation of industrial enterprises.

Electric Power Shortages

Shortages of electric power are sometimes exaggerated as obstacles to industrial development, but they should not be dismissed too lightly. A firm protected by high tariffs will find it profitable to install its own power units if it cannot purchase power from an existing system, provided that foreign exchange is readily available to import the necessary equipment. But even if there is no foreign exchange problem, use of a high-cost power source affects product prices and thus limits consumer demand. It also affects the prices of domestic inputs used by exporters, thus making it difficult for them to compete in overseas markets.

Large-scale hydroelectric power projects can bring about lower power costs, provided that domestic demand is sufficient to use the new facilities at close to full capacity. But these projects are costly and usually require substantial imports. Many developing countries have been able to obtain the necessary foreign exchange on favorable terms from the World Bank and other lending agencies.

Lack of Incentives for Exports of Manufacturers

Since manufacturers in developing countries often have little access to good information on overseas markets, and markets are imperfect in other ways, special incentives may be necessary and desirable to stimulate exports of manufactured goods. Apart from dealing with the general problems described above, governments can encourage manufactured exports in a variety of other ways. Among these are:

1. Special export credit facilities to provide working capital to exporters, to give them cash between the date of shipment and their

receipt of payment, and to enable them to extend credit to their customers.

2. Export credit insurance to cover both commercial and political risks.

3. Identification of market opportunities which individual firms have difficulty discovering on their own.

4. Participation in international trade fairs to publicize the country's products; to scout the competition; and to learn what potential buyers are demanding in terms of product standardization, delivery schedules, and other nonprice aspects of the demand side of the market.

5. Training for commercial attachés assigned to embassies in major importing countries.

6. Provision of export subsidies and other fiscal incentives.

7. Correction of overvalued exchange rates to make exports more attractive to importing countries.

8. Reduction of bureaucratic red tape in the application for export licenses and processing of export documentation. The process is sometimes so long and costly that it constitutes a major barrier for potential exporters.[14]

Considerable technical expertise is required in most of the above areas, and developing countries usually have few individuals with the necessary experience. A great deal of assistance is now available, however, from the United Nations Industrial Development Organisation (UNIDO), other U.N. agencies, and other foreign aid agencies. Not all of this assistance has been well utilized. In many developing countries, responsibility for export promotion—and for industrial development policy generally—may be fragmented among as many as a half dozen separate agencies, whose policies may not be well coordinated and can even be contradictory. As a result, the resources committed to industrial promotion may not have a high payoff.

Developing countries should be particularly careful about granting export subsidies and other fiscal incentives. Too often, the resulting foreign exchange and employment benefits are outweighed by the loss of fiscal revenue resulting from overly generous concessions granted to

---

14. An AID consultant examining the red tape problem in South Korea in 1964 prepared a case study showing how difficult it was for a local cotton goods producer to export his product. Starting with the first offer and continuing through the final shipment and receipt of the foreign exchange draft from the bank, the consultant found that "of the 37 steps [documented], 12 are involved in [the exporter's] own business negotiations and procedures. The other 25 steps require him to fill out 94 different types of forms with a total of 148 copies. Not including his own time required to gather the information necessary or to fill out the forms, it takes from 84 to 121 days to process the documents" (Most, op. cit., p. 99).

special interest groups. Used carefully, however, fiscal incentives can be a powerful tool for increasing foreign exchange earnings and stimulating cost-cutting measures by firms wishing to become competitive in export markets.

Overcoming Other Obstacles

Governments can assist the industrial sector in still other ways. Pre-feasibility studies can be carried out and circulated to potential investors, both domestic and foreign. Special technical assistance can be provided to artisans and other small businessmen. The construction industry—and its suppliers—can be stimulated by public housing programs. Fiscal incentives can be given for the establishment of new firms or the expansion of existing ones.

Regional economic integration—participation in common market schemes or free trade areas—can widen the market for some products (though other industries may be hurt by increased competition). But the experience of the Latin American countries (see chapter 15) suggests that the political will necessary to make such cooperation successful is generally lacking in the developing countries.

One other way in which industrial production might be encouraged is for governments to take steps to redistribute income from the wealthy to the poor, thus giving the latter a greater effective demand for a variety of light manufactured goods. Economic theory seems to indicate that demand for industrial products might thus increase significantly, since the poor consume a higher percentage of their income than the rich. Several recent studies, however, suggest that the effect of income redistribution on the growth of the industrial sector may be fairly small (see chapter 11).

INTERMEDIATE TECHNOLOGY

Developing countries have often followed industrial development policies which artificially encourage the substitution of capital, the scarce and therefore relatively expensive factor of production, for labor, the abundant and relatively cheap factor. Specific pro-capital policies will be discussed in chapter 12, where we examine their contribution to the serious unemployment problem in many developing countries. For the present, we shall simply assume that the employment consequences are in fact negative and consider briefly the possibilities of alleviating unemployment by increasing the use of "intermediate" or "appropriate" technologies which are much more productive than simple technologies, yet not so sophisticated as the very capital-intensive technologies designed for developed countries, where labor is relatively expensive.[15]

Sophisticated technologies economizing on labor, it should be pointed out, are sometimes "appropriate" for developing countries in the sense that they are so productive that unit production costs are potentially lower than those of alternative technologies, even though the cost of capital is relatively high. The *potential* advantages, however, will not necessarily be realized. Capital-intensive technologies tend to require a higher level of technical and managerial skills than those which are labor-intensive, and if these skills are in short supply, actual productivity may be considerably below potential. In addition, plant and equipment may lie idle for long periods of time because maintenance and repair problems are less easily solved. Under these circumstances, more labor-intensive technology requiring less sophisticated managerial and technical skills may prove to be in practice less costly per unit of output.

The late E. F. Schumacher (1973: 186), founder of the Intermediate Technology Development Group in the United Kingdom, admitted that intermediate technologies are not universally applicable, but pointed out that industries in which advanced technologies are clearly superior generally do not make products that help satisfy the basic needs of the poor majority. Products which do help satisfy these needs, on the other hand, are well suited to the use of intermediate technologies. These include building materials, clothing, simple household goods, agricultural equipment and implements,[16] and processed foods.

With specific reference to India, Schumacher called for a development strategy based on a regional or district approach, with districts apparently defined as being somewhat larger than the Chinese communes (see chapter 9). As in China, agriculture and industry would be closely related; production would be based mainly on local materials, and most would be for local use. This radical proposal—advocated earlier in India by Gandhi—implies a significant redistribution of income in favor of the poor. When combined with Schumacher's humanistic proposals for reforming economic and political structures, many persons find it a particularly attractive development strategy.

15. The late E. F. Schumacher (1973: 179–180) defined intermediate technology in terms of cost per job. Symbolically, he refers to it as a technology whose job creation costs are £100, compared with "£1,000" technology in developed countries and "£1" traditional technology in developing countries.

16. Simple, locally designed power tillers, motor pumps for irrigation, and small gasoline engines—produced at a cost within the reach of many small farmers—have been designed in some Asian countries. See Amir U. Khan, "Appropriate Technologies: Do We Transfer, Adapt, or Develop?" In *Employment in Developing Nations*, Report on a Ford Foundation Study, ed. Edgar O. Edwards (New York: Columbia University Press, 1974), 227–229.

However, there are at least two major reasons why such a strategy is not likely to be implemented successfully by many developing countries in the near future. First, significant income redistribution is politically very difficult to accomplish (see chapter 11). Second, notwithstanding the relatively simple technical and managerial skills required by any one intermediate-technology industry, a national development strategy based on district-level development requires a great deal of organizational ability—including the ability to organize into cooperative work arrangements individuals among whom a great deal of mutual mistrust may be present. In addition, a great deal of work would be needed to develop those intermediate technologies which do not yet exist.

Even if such a radical development strategy is not adopted, other steps could be taken to encourage greater use of intermediate technologies. In chapter 12 we list a number of factor-price distortions, artificially stimulating the use of capital, which could be reversed. Some industries might be encouraged to consider purchasing used equipment, which is less capital-intensive than equipment associated with new technologies. Though it may not always be possible to find sufficient numbers of older machines, or to obtain spare parts, some studies have concluded that utilization of used machinery is the optimal choice for certain industries.[17] A long-run approach for increasing the use of intermediate technologies calls for applied research by developing countries to develop technologies best suited to their factor proportions. Since many small developing countries would find it difficult to have their own research programs, the suggestion has often been made that groups of developing countries within a particular region, and at similar levels of development, jointly finance research on intermediate technologies. While some national and regional research has been initiated in recent years, it is still modest in scope.

INDUSTRIAL LOCATION POLICY

Unless specific attention is paid to the spatial aspects of industrial activity, industrialization in developing countries is likely to be geographically concentrated in one or a few urban centers. In Haiti there are few large manufacturing firms outside the Port-au-Prince area, and in Ecuador about 80 percent of manufacturing output is produced in Quito, the capital, and Guayaquil, the principal port. Although this concentration of industrial activity results from rational, profit-maximizing decisions

17. See, for example, Howard Pack, "The Optimality of Used Equipment: Calculations for the Cotton Textile Industry," *Economic Development and Cultural Change,* 26 (January 1978), 307–325.

by private firms, it has social costs in the form of widening regional income differentials and a variety of social problems in the large urban centers receiving heavy streams of migrants from rural areas and smaller cities. Thus there is a case for government intervention to channel new investment to locations outside the major urban centers.

Some developing countries have attempted to alleviate the problems of geographically concentrated industrialization by using a variety of incentive mechanisms to influence location decisions by private firms. These efforts have not been particularly effective in increasing the *share* of nonmetropolitan areas in industrial output. Even very generous tax, tariff, and credit incentives can fail to overcome the locational disadvantages of rural areas and small urban centers, particularly with respect to transportation costs (for both input delivery and delivery to markets) and supporting services.[18] Location in large urban areas enables firms to take advantage of *external economies* (see chapter 2) in obtaining credit, in drawing upon a trained pool of skilled manpower, and in the provision of electricity and other utilities. In addition, firms in larger urban areas have better access to government offices, both for obtaining information and technical assistance and for lobbying for legislation, regulations, and policies favorable to them. Finally, large urban centers offer a wide range of cultural amenities and a network of professional contacts that provincial capitals or rural areas cannot offer.

Tinkering with the market mechanism, then, is not likely to have a significant impact on industrial location decisions. Such an impact requires more radical action. In a country where the government wishes to leave industrial activity largely in private hands, one strategy that might be adopted is to stimulate the expansion of agricultural production, incomes, and employment. This would increase, in rural areas and small cities, the market for light consumer goods and agricultural implements that could be produced with the intermediate technologies discussed above. Moreover, greater farm production would create new opportunities for agricultural processing industries. This kind of strategy is not particularly easy to implement. Although governments in developing countries are generally more aware of the importance of agriculture than they were fifteen years ago, they will encounter stiff political resistance from urban interest groups in attempting to reallocate public resources in favor of infrastructure facilities and supporting services in rural areas. There would also be strong resistance to attempts to expand rural markets for consumer goods by redistributing rural income and wealth. A reformist

18. When incentives *are* generous enough to induce firms to locate away from major industrial centers, the result has often been an allocation of resources so inefficient as to more than offset the social and political advantages gained. Such was the case with the Chilean automobile industry, discussed earlier in this chapter.

government following such a strategy within a basically capitalist framework would have to be quite strong to make more than token changes in these directions.

If a government is itself an important producer of industrial goods, it is easier for decisions to be made to locate most new plants in smaller cities and rural areas. Even in these cases, however, governments must take into account the political opposition to such a strategy. Such opposition occurs not only in multiparty political systems but also in single-party or single-party-dominant systems where the balance of political power among the various interest groups supporting the party is such that social policy is relatively conservative (e.g., Mexico). Relatively few governments have the power to pursue the type of industrial location strategy followed by China—a strategy which the previous chapter showed to have a number of social and economic attractions.

SUMMARY

Manufacturing output in developing countries as a group has expanded at an annual rate of about 8.5 percent since 1960. Although this seems most impressive by historical standards, the pace of industrialization in many countries has not kept up with rapidly rising expectations. Moreover, industry has been most disappointing in the provision of new jobs, a subject which will be discussed in detail in chapter 12.

Government stimulation of industrial activity involves short-run costs, often significant ones. If additional credit is to be made available, more technical assistance provided, or subsidies increased, resources will have to be diverted from other items in the government budget, or the budget will have to be increased by taxing the private sector more. Even if money is simply printed, the result is likely to be inflationary pressures which "tax" some sectors of the economy and make industrial exports less competitive.

Whether industrialization is based on import substitution or on an export-oriented strategy, political factors will play a major role in determining the amount *and* the kind of government assistance to industry. While some governments have neglected their industrial sectors, there are also examples of government policies which have been too generous to industry in view of the benefits obtained. Short-run tax breaks, for example, do not always stimulate the extra production necessary to "pay back" the tax revenues foregone. High protective tariffs discourage competition and hurt export industries. Measures like these are adopted because industrialists have the political power necessary to obtain legislation favorable to them. What is good for Motores Generales, however, is not necessarily good for the country.

In concluding this chapter, it is useful to emphasize again that industrialization programs in developing countries can easily run into foreign exchange bottlenecks. Unless close attention is paid to this constraint —and to the potential of the agricultural sector for overcoming it through food import substitution and exports—industrial growth will be forced to slow down. Countries do not develop by industry alone.

Suggested Readings

Alexander, Robert J. *A New Development Strategy.* Maryknoll, N.Y.: Orbis Books, 1976.

The "new" strategy advocated in this easily read book is actually the familiar ISI strategy, which has disappointed policy makers in many developing countries. Alexander argues that the "post-import substitution crisis" can be avoided if policy makers attempt to expand the domestic market and are selective in the industries they seek to encourage. However, he tends to underestimate the balance-of-payments problems that an ISI strategy can generate.

Baer, Werner, and Larry Samuelson, eds. "Latin America in the Post-Import Substitution Era." Special Issue, *World Development,* 5 (January–February 1977).

The ten articles in this collection discuss the various industrialization policies adopted by Latin American countries in the last fifteen years in response to disillusionment with ISI strategies that characterized industrial growth from the late 1940s to the early 1960s. In general, the authors find that greater stress has been placed on export promotion. Continuing problems include the increased role of multinational corporations and the neglect of equity issues in some countries, and a focus on equity at the expense of growth in others (notably Chile under Allende and Peru after 1968).

Balassa, Bela, and Associates. *The Structure of Protection in Developing Countries.* Baltimore: The Johns Hopkins Press for the International Bank for Reconstruction and Development and the Inter-American Development Bank, 1971.

This study examines the effects of protection on resource allocation, exports, and economic growth in six developing countries (Brazil, Chile, Mexico, West Malaysia, Pakistan, and the Philippines) and, for comparison, one developed country (Norway). Balassa finds that ISI policy is rarely based on a consistent program; rather, it tends to be ad hoc in nature, responding to pressures by particular interest groups. Effects of protection on exchange rates, exports, prices, and other variables tend to be ignored. Conclusions are made which are said to be applicable to all countries, though it is recognized that policies must take into account each country's special circumstances. Suggestions are made for an "ideal" system of protection.

Eckaus, Richard F. *Appropriate Technologies for Developing Countries.* Washington, D.C.: National Academy of Sciences, 1977.

This compact report describes and evaluates alternative criteria for determining technological appropriateness. Particular attention is given to small-scale industry and to agriculture. Technological, institutional, and economic policies are recommended. Eckaus emphasizes the importance of social, political, and other noneconomic factors as determinants of technological choice.

Little, Ian, Tibor Scitovsky, and Maurice Scott. *Industry and Trade in Some Developing Countries: A Comparative Study.* New York: Oxford University Press for the Organisation for Economic Co-Operation and Development, 1970.

Based on detailed case studies of Argentina, Brazil, Mexico, India, Pakistan, the Philippines, and Taiwan, this book argues that industry in developing countries has been overencouraged relative to agriculture. The particular types of protectionist policies employed, the authors argue, have discouraged exports, contributed to inefficient resource allocation, widened income inequalities, and adversely affected employment in both agriculture and industry itself. The authors advocate a gradual transition to a more open economy, with lower tariffs and export taxes and active encouragement of exports.

Schumacher, E. F. *Small Is Beautiful: Economics as if People Mattered.* Introduction by Theodore Roszak. New York: Harper & Row, Publishers, 1973.

The late E. F. Schumacher was a leading spokesman for the "intermediate technology" movement. Schumacher's case for the use of relatively simple technologies for much (though not all) of manufacturing output in developing countries is based not only on their potential for providing employment but also on what he regards as the greater ability of small-scale organization to provide psychological rewards to individuals, Furthermore, he argues, village-based industrialization can provide substantial direct benefits to rural residents, thus slowing rural-urban migration. Schumacher recognizes that such an industrialization strategy requires a great deal of organization, but he underestimates the obstacles to achieving the necessary degree of organization.

United Nations. Economic Commission for Latin America. *The Process of Industrial Development in Latin America.* Document No. E/CN.12/716/Rev. 1. New York, 1966.

This study describes in considerable statistical detail the growth of industry in Latin America from the early twentieth century to the mid-1960s. Particular attention is given to industrial development policy, which is said to have had a number of serious shortcomings.

11

Income Distribution

Since developing countries began to assert themselves forcefully in the world political arena in the mid-1960s, the distribution of income and wealth among nations has been a widely discussed topic.[1] The very unequal division of the world's wealth was vigorously attacked by the developing countries at the first United Nations Conference on Trade and Development (UNCTAD) in 1964. Pressures on the developed countries continued at the three subsequent UNCTAD meetings and in other international forums, where various proposals for international income redistribution have been discussed and declarations calling for a "new international order" have been passed. The oil-producing countries demonstrated in the early 1970s that the developing countries themselves could seize the initiative, and the success of the OPEC cartel has led other developing countries to seek the formation of similar arrangements for other commodities (see chapter 15).

The recent achievement of political independence by dozens of nations, and the coming to power of more development-minded governments in other countries, have resulted in greater concern with income inequalities *within* developing countries. While most of them still seem to regard growth as their most important economic objective, greater equality in the distribution of income—an important dimension of development—is increasingly becoming an important secondary objective. Sometimes it has even rivaled growth in importance. China is one example; though in terms of explicit attention to income distribution, the best example is perhaps Tanzania.[2]

1. This chapter draws heavily on Zuvekas (1975), where more detailed documentation is provided.

2. See Paul Bomani (Tanzania's ambassador to the United States), interviewed by Douglas Ensminger, "Tanzania's Road to Development: Bringing Development to the People," *International Development Review*, 16, No. 2 (1974), 2–9.

THE DISTRIBUTION OF INCOME
AMONG NATIONS

Table 11.1 shows the heavy concentration of world output and income in the advanced industrial nations. Countries with per capita GNP of more than $3,000 had only 16 percent of the world's population in 1975, yet they accounted for 62 percent of world income. At the other extreme, countries with per capita GNP of $500 or less had 59 percent of the world's population but less than 10 percent of its income.

Actually, because of the way in which foreign currency data are converted to dollars, and the exclusion of much nonmarket activity from GNP estimates in developing countries (see chapter 1), Table 11.1 exaggerates the extent of international income inequality. Nevertheless, there is no doubt that in countries with three-fifths of the world's population, the average level of material well-being is far below that of the developed countries.

The data in Table 1.2 show that per capita GNP in the developing countries increased at an average annual rate of 3.5 percent between 1960 and 1971, compared with 3.8 percent in the developed countries. Accordingly, income distribution among nations become more unequal. Since 1971, however, this trend has been reversed. Per capita GNP in the developing countries rose at an average annual rate of 3.2 percent from 1971 to 1975, while in the developed countries the growth rate was only 1.8 percent. It is premature to conclude that a new long-term trend toward greater income equality among nations has been established, but there is at least a strong likelihood that this may be happening.

TABLE 11.1
The Distribution of World Income, 1975[a]

Per Capita Income (dollars)	Number of Countries	Population[b]		Aggregate GNP	
		Millions	Percent	Billion $	Percent
3,000+	26	643	16.0	3,746	62.0
2,001–3,000	15	430	10.7	1,141	18.9
1,001–2,000	17	331	8.2	412	6.8
501–1,000	25	237	5.9	168	2.6
201–500	33	1,227	30.6	403	6.7
0–200	30	1,150	28.6	169	2.8
Totals	146[c]	4,017	100.0	6,039	100.0

Source: Calculated from the *World Bank Atlas 1976.*

[a] Preliminary.

[b] The population total is higher than the estimates presented in Table 4.6.

[c] All World Bank member countries plus others with a population of at least 1 million in mid-1974.

INCOME INEQUALITY WITHIN NATIONS AND ITS RELATIONSHIP WITH ECONOMIC GROWTH

Historically, there has been a definite relationship between economic growth and trends in the distribution of income within countries. A quarter-century ago, Nobel prizewinner Simon Kuznets (1955) presented evidence showing that income inequalities widened in the early periods of growth of today's developed countries, a trend which was reversed after higher levels of per capita income were achieved. Recent studies have provided additional support for Kuznets' findings. There is also considerable evidence that most developing countries are likewise experiencing greater income inequality as economic growth occurs.[3]

A recent study by Irma Adelman and Cynthia Taft Morris (1977) examined the effects of economic growth on poverty in twenty-four nations during the first half of the nineteenth century.[4] Using quantitative and qualitative historical data, the authors sought to determine what changes occurred over time in the incidence of extreme material poverty. This was defined to include persons who were starving or destitute; whose consumption of staples was inadequate and consumption of meat, fish, dairy products, and pulses was infrequent; and who were in poor health as indicated by extreme overcrowding, very high mortality rates, and a high incidence of disease. Adelman and Morris found that rapid industrialization and commercialization (i.e., production for the market) systematically lowered the *absolute* standard of living of the poorest segments of the population. In Belgium and Great Britain, for example, rural handicraft workers suffered declining incomes because of increased competition from factory manufacturing. In all countries, the increased commercialization of agriculture led to higher rents among tenants and to dispossession of small landholders burdened by debt and lacking the resources to survive during periods of depressed market prices. In India, China, and parts of Belgium and Germany, population pressures led to subdivision of small landholdings, thus decreasing the average amount of land per family.

DOES INEQUALITY STIMULATE GROWTH?

Until quite recently, it was widely believed that a high degree of inequality in the distribution of income has a favorable effect on economic growth (if not economic development) because individuals in the upper-

3. See Zuvekas (1975: 10–18) for a discussion of some of the evidence.
4. In addition to examining some of today's developed countries, this study also looks at poverty in Argentina, Brazil, Burma, China, Egypt, India, and Turkey.

income brackets have higher average (and presumably marginal) propensities to save than those in middle and lower brackets. The higher the savings, according to this argument, the greater the amount of investment (capital formation) and, therefore, the more rapid the growth of output over time. Although the increase in income corresponding to the extra output may be distributed very unequally, enough benefits are alleged to "trickle down" to lower-income groups over the long run to "justify" their short-run sacrifices and make them tolerant of rising inequalities, which are perceived as temporary.

Kuznets adopted an agnostic position concerning the relationship between income inequality and rates of economic growth in the now-developed countries, and he was not at all convinced that extreme and widening inequalities in today's developing economies would have beneficial effects on economic growth:

> Because they may have proved favorable in the past, it is dangerous to argue that completely free markets, lack of penalties implicit in progressive taxation, and the like are indispensable for the growth of the now underdeveloped countries. Under present conditions the results may be quite the opposite—withdrawal of accumulated assets to relatively "safe" channels, either by flight abroad or into real estate; and the inability of governments to serve as basic agents in the kind of capital formation that is indispensable to economic growth. It is dangerous to argue that, because in the past foreign investment provided capital resources to spark satisfactory economic growth in some of the smaller European countries or in Europe's descendents across the seas, similar effects can be expected today if only underdeveloped countries can be convinced of the need of a "favorable climate" (Kuznets, 1955: 26).

There is no conclusive evidence for developing countries to support the traditional view that a more equal distribution of income would have significant negative effects on rates of productive investment or economic growth. Some economists, in fact, argue that the effects of income redistribution might even be positive. A more equal distribution of income, it has been hypothesized, will improve nutritional levels among the poor and increase both the quantity and quality of human capital. It has also been suggested that income redistribution might provide a positive stimulus to productive investment by increasing consumer demand, though several tests of this hypothesis have concluded that the effect would be small. Another theoretical argument for income redistribution, advanced by UN-ECLA (1970), is that a very skewed income distribution in the higher-income categories has a negative effect on domestic savings by causing upper-income groups to strive for an international rather than a national target standard of living. Those who doubt the validity of the demonstration-effect hypothesis will be skeptical of this argument.

An experiment to test the effects of income redistribution on economic growth was conducted by William Cline (1972) for Argentina, Brazil, Mexico, and Venezuela. Using simulation techniques, Cline found that greater income equality would result in slightly lower savings rates. However, greater spending on foodstuffs would tend to increase the demand for the relatively low-cost factors of production in agriculture— labor and land—thus lowering the capital-output ratio and partially offsetting the effects of a lower savings rate. Import demand would decline, but only by negligible amounts. The net result would probably be a reduction in growth rates, but only a slight one. Cline's pioneering study is a valuable one and indicative of one direction in which future research needs to proceed. But the data on which it is based are weak and limited, and one should not draw any definitive conclusions from it. Another problem is that the model does not trace the effect of demand changes on factor payments and then back to demand.

Another simulation exercise, based on a multisectoral model with 110 equations and 118 variables, was conducted by Alejandro Foxley (in Foxley, ed., 1975). The redistributive objective in this model was to provide all sectors of the population with a minimum level of basic consumption goods by the end of a given time period. The consumption data were generated from a household survey of 1,740 families in the greater Santiago (Chile) area. The model shows that a redistribution of consumption from upper- to lower-income groups would result in only a negligible decline in the growth of output, while the effect on employment would be positive and particularly favorable in agriculture, food processing, textiles, and clothing. One of the weaknesses of this model, however, is that the savings rate is assumed to be constant—i.e., unaffected by income redistribution.

The relationship between economic growth and income redistribution may also be linked to population growth. One study found that developing countries experiencing sharp reductions in birth rates in the 1960s had one common characteristic: they were countries in which a high percentage of the population shared the economic and social benefits of growth.[5] If it is true that rapid population growth has a negative effect on per capita economic growth, then this study suggests that income redistribution can favorably affect economic growth through its effects on the rate of population growth. However, not all economists believe that rapid population expansion is inimical to economic growth. Moreover,

---

5. William Rich, "Smaller Families through Jobs and Justice," *International Development Review*, 14, No. 3 (1972), 10.

fertility has recently declined in some countries where the benefits of growth do not seem to be widely shared, casting some doubt on the hypothesis linking fertility declines to income redistribution.

EXPLAINING WIDENING INCOME INEQUALITIES WITHIN DEVELOPING COUNTRIES

Kuznets pointed to rapid population growth and industrialization in societies with rigid economic and social structures as two major forces tending to widen income inequalities in developing countries. Industrialization under these circumstances, he pointed out, might "destroy the positions of some of the lower groups more rapidly than opportunities elsewhere in the economy may be created for them" (1955: 25). This would be particularly true if industrialization were based on capital-intensive techniques. Kuznets found—and this has been confirmed by subsequent studies—that incomes in developing countries were generally distributed more unequally in the nonagricultural sectors of the economy than in agriculture. Since economic growth tends to increase the size of the former relative to the latter, overall income distribution would become more unequal—at least temporarily.

Regressive tax and expenditure patterns have also been identified as factors contributing to widening income inequalities. However, given the limited availability of data on tax incidence and the distribution of the benefits of public spending, the degree to which these factors affect income distribution is very difficult to determine. In many developing countries, the tax structure appears on the surface to be regressive; but when tax incidence is considered, this picture might have to be modified. If all import taxes, for example, are passed on to ultimate consumers, they would be progressive since the average propensity to consume imports rises with income. Government expenditures may have little effect on the levels of living of the lowest deciles of income earners but may serve to narrow inequalities in the middle and upper deciles. But these are only speculations. Much additional research is needed to clarify the distributional impact of government budgets in developing countries.

A study by the United Nations Economic Commission for Latin America (UN-ECLA 1970) singles out two characteristics of Latin American countries which contribute to greater income inequalities in that region: (1) the different structure of production and greater productivity differentials among economic sectors compared with the developed countries and (2) the peculiar socioeconomic characteristics of the upper-income groups. With respect to the latter, it is argued that (a) the concentration of private property is greater, not only in agriculture but also in commerce, finance, and industry; (b) professional groups (physicians, architects, etc.) base their fees on international rather than national standards (and, it is implied, have the market power successfully to approach such standards); and (c) individual or family ownership of business organizations makes the accumulation of large incomes easier than under the corporate form of ownership prevalent in the developed countries. In Galbraithian fashion, it is argued that salaried managers in large, management-controlled corporations tend to receive lower incomes than independent business operators. Furthermore, since their income is mainly in the form of salaries, it is more easily taxed; and since managers' prestige depends on sales volume, they are relatively unconcerned with corporate profits taxes. These are interesting hypotheses, but ECLA offers little evidence to support a direct link between the above-mentioned factors and a relatively high degree of income inequality.

Numerous studies have argued that agricultural modernization without land tenure reform generally will accentuate rural income inequalities. Adelman and Morris, using an analysis of variance technique, found income inequality to be greater the better endowed a country was with land and natural resources and the greater the degree of technological dualism in the economy.[6] The latter relationship tends to support Kuznets' observation that economic growth itself is one of the major causes—if not the major cause—of income inequality.

Dependency theorists (see chapter 5) have argued that widening income inequalities in developing countries are related to the degree of foreign domination of the economy. Either through their ownership or control of the means of production, or through their relationships with local exporters and importers, it is maintained, foreigners (not necessarily intentionally) tend to strengthen the power of the upper-income groups, thus enabling them to gain more than proportionately from economic growth. Little quantitative evidence has been provided to support this hypothesis, but there is a strong likelihood that some such relationship exists.

MEASURING INCOME DISTRIBUTION WITHIN COUNTRIES: THE PROBLEM OF DEFINING INCOME

Even for developed countries, where income data are relatively good, there has been considerable controversy over both the degree of income

6. Adelman and Morris, "An Anatomy of Income Distribution Patterns in Developing Countries," *Development Digest*, 9, No. 4 (October 1971), 24–37. For a more extended discussion of this research, which measured 48 social, political, and economic characteristics for the countries studied, see Adelman and Morris (1973).

inequality and trends in income inequality over time. For the United States, estimates of trends in the last few decades have ranged from slightly greater inequality to slightly less inequality. Even when the underlying data are the same, the use of different methodologies or measures of income inequality can result in significantly different conclusions. In measuring income inequality in developing countries—and particularly in making international comparisons—it is important not only to be aware of these methodological issues but also to bear in mind that estimates of personal incomes generally are subject to a greater degree of measurement error than those in developed countries.

Conceptual and methodological problems, however, are probably the most important reasons why income distribution data should be regarded with a great deal of caution. Many of these problems can be summarized in the form of two questions: (1) what is income? and (2) how should a country's population be disaggregated into mutually exclusive income-earning categories? Additional problems arise because income is not identical with welfare, and it is the latter concept that is the true concern of those attempting to measure inequalities.

Let us consider first the question of how income is measured. There is a systematic bias toward exaggerating income inequalities because almost all estimates of personal income distribution either exclude noncash (imputed) income or limit its measurement to the value of food produced and consumed at home. Since the relative importance of nonmarket transactions tends to vary inversely with income, the amount of "true income" is underestimated more in percentage terms for the poor than for the rich. *True income*, as used here, can be defined as the actual or imputed market value of all goods and services consumed during a year, plus savings (or minus dissavings). This would include such imputed items as the rental value of owner-built housing, the value of personal services provided without charge within a household or community, and the value of clothing, implements, charcoal, and other items produced within a household from raw materials grown by or collected by household members.

It is difficult, of course, to measure the value of goods and services production not passing through the market. That is why, even in the United States, imputation of nonmarket income is restricted to the rental value of owned housing and the value of food directly consumed by the farm households producing it. In developing countries, the data on which income distribution estimates are based may exclude not only noncash income but also entire categories of workers. Estimates for some countries, for example, are based not on census or sample-survey questionnaires but rather on income tax returns or social security data which cover less than half the country's population. Other things being equal, such estimates tend to understate the degree of income inequality by excluding those too poor to pay income taxes or to have access to social security coverage. Furthermore, high-income earners in developing countries probably have a greater tendency to underreport income (particularly property income) than their counterparts in developed countries. It should also be noted that income distribution estimates in some countries are based on pretax incomes, while in other countries they are based on aftertax incomes.

In summary, the definition of *income* used to measure inequality varies considerably from country to country. Even for the same country, income inequality estimates for two different years may not be based on the same concept of income. This makes it difficult to determine changes in income inequality over time.

An additional complication, which only in the last few years has begun to receive much attention, is that demographic factors can significantly distort income inequality estimates. Most estimates of income distribution are based on family or household incomes, and while this is a more appropriate basis for determining inequalities than one based on individual income earners, we need to remember, as Kuznets has reminded us:

> that families or households differ substantially in size, as judged by the number of members, either in productive or younger and older ages; that, consequently, the conventional distributions of income among families or households by income per family or household make little sense, since they are affected by changing or different inequalities among families or households by size; that even after size distributions by income per family or household are converted into distributions of persons by family or household income per person, they still reflect differences in the age of the household head . . . , in the phases in the lifetime span of a family's income, which obscure our view of the differences in the longer, or lifetime, level of income.[7]

In examining demographic data for three developed countries (the United States, West Germany, and Israel) and two developing countries (the Philippines and Taiwan), Kuznets found that:[8]

1. Family or household income was positively correlated with family size in all five countries, but income per person (or per adult consumer-equivalent) was lower in the larger family or household units than in the smaller ones.

7. Simon Kuznets, "Demographic Aspects of the Size Distribution of Income: An Exploratory Essay," *Economic Development and Cultural Change*, 25 (October 1976), 1.

8. Ibid., 84–94. Kuznets reports a number of other findings in these pages.

2. There is a close relationship between family size and age of the family head. In the United States, for example, average family size rises from two at formation to a peak of nearly five in the 35–44 age bracket, then falls to about two and a half for heads who are 65 and older.

3. In the developed countries, income per family varies significantly according to age of the family head, roughly doubling from the under-25 group to the 45–54 age bracket, then falling to about half of this peak for the 65-and-older group. Given these wide swings in income by age of family head, *and* the fact that the proportion of both young and old heads of households is high in the developed countries, a substantial inequality component is built into conventional income distribution data based on income per family.

4. In the two developing countries, the proportion of young family heads is again relatively high, but that of older family heads is far lower than in the developed countries. Moreover, the fall in earnings for older age-of-head groups is much less pronounced than in the developed countries. Accordingly, the inequality component attributable to age-of-head differences is less than in the developed countries. This suggests that conventional income distribution data exaggerate income inequalities in developed countries relative to developing countries.

Defining income and adjusting family income data for family size and age of head are serious enough problems in attempting to measure the degree of income inequality in developing countries. To make matters worse, income is not equivalent to welfare—a point we emphasized in chapter 1. The purchasing power of income *within* a country, for example, will vary according to geographic location. The costs of housing and domestically produced food are lower in rural areas than in urban centers, and though the opposite may be true of the cost of manufactured goods, the overall purchasing power of a unit of currency still tends to be higher in the countryside than in the cities. Thus a rural family of five with a total income equivalent to US$ 800 would have a higher level of material well-being than an urban family of the same size, age distribution, and income. Another reason why income and welfare are not identical is that clothing and housing requirements for maintaining a given degree of physical comfort will vary according to temperature (both average and variability), rainfall, and other environmental factors. In the Andean countries of South America, for example, residents of the warm coastal lands need considerably less protection against the elements than do their compatriots in the cooler highlands.

The quality of life is also very much determined by the consumption of public goods and services not paid for in the marketplace. Schools, streets and roads, and public health facilities make important contributions to welfare, and they are generally more available to urban residents than to rural dwellers, thus offsetting the advantage the latter have in food and housing costs.

If we want to measure inequalities in level of living rather than income, we will probably have to wait many years before data are available to construct, for most countries, a multidimensional level-of-living indicator that can be disaggregated to yield an inequality measure. Meanwhile, we shall be forced to continue relying on income data which mean different things in different countries. This does not mean that the data are worthless for comparative purposes, but it does mean that a serious critical evaluation of income inequality in any particular country must be based on a clear understanding of what the data actually measure.

ALTERNATIVE MEASURES OF INCOME INEQUALITY

A number of different measures of income inequality have been devised. The discussion in this text will be limited to three of the most widely used ones. In addition to evaluating their conceptual strengths and weaknesses, we shall present data showing the rankings of a number of developed and developing countries according to each of these measures. Readers have already been warned not to accept these rankings at face value.

The "Functional" Distribution of Income

A rather crude measure of income inequality is the "functional" distribution of income between wages and salaries, on the one hand, and property income, on the other. Other things being equal, total income will be more equally distributed the higher is the wage-and-salary share of national income. This is so because wealth, from which property incomes are derived, has always been found to be distributed more unequally than current income. The greatest attraction of the functional-share measure is that it is available on an annual basis for many developing countries, thus permitting an evaluation of changes over time. But as we shall see below, it has some serious drawbacks.

Table 11.2 shows that the wage-and-salary share varied widely among Latin America countries during the 1960s, ranging from a low of 40 percent in Paraguay (1962) to a high of 63 percent in Nicaragua (1968). This compares with a figure of approximately 75 percent in the United States during the same period. The wage-and-salarly share tended to rise with per capita GNP, but the relationship was rather weak.[9]

9. A curvilinear line fitted to the data yields an R^2 of .06 for 1960 and .24 for 1968.

TABLE 11.2
Wage-and-Salary Share of National Income,
Latin American and Caribbean Countries,
1960 and 1968
(percent)

Country	1960[a]	1968[b]
Argentina	40.7	43.8
Barbados	60.9	60.9
Bolivia	42.6	43.8
Chile	51.6	50.8
Colombia	41.6	45.9
Costa Rica	61.9	52.5
Ecuador	52.9	53.7
Guatemala	46.8	50.1
Honduras	49.9	50.3
Jamaica	60.7	61.9
Nicaragua	61.4	62.9
Paraguay	40.2	43.6
Peru	46.2	47.8
Trinidad and Tobago	49.9	n.a.[c]
Uruguay	48.2	56.8
Venezuela	61.2	57.0

Source: Inter-American Development Bank, *Economic and Social Progress in Latin America,* Annual Report 1972 (Washington, D.C., 1973).

[a] 1962 for Paraguay and 1965 for Argentina.

[b] 1964 for Barbados, 1966 for Guatemala, 1967 for Ecuador, 1969 for Argentina, and 1970 for Colombia.

[c] n.a.: Not available.

Between 1960 and 1968 there was a slight tendency for the wage-and-salary share to rise, but part of this increase was perhaps due to a rise in per capita income levels and the associated shift of workers from self-employed to wage-and-salary status. The weakness of the relationships between per capita income and the wage-and-salary share is not surprising, since factors other than income significantly affect the functional distribution. These include the structure of economic output, factor endowments, government versus private ownership of wealth, and wage policies.

One of the major difficulties in making intercountry comparisons of functional shares is that these shares can fluctuate widely from year to year, particularly when governments take direct action to influence wage rates. In Argentina, for example, the prolabor policies of the Perón government pushed the wage-and-salary share from 45 percent in 1946 to 56 percent in 1949, a level that was maintained with relatively little fluctuation through 1954. But after the fall of Perón in 1955, subsequent governments followed policies which depressed real wages, bringing the wage-and-salary share down to 46 percent in 1959. Thus the choice of year can have a significant effect on a country's ranking according to the functional share measure. Another problem with this measure is that it does not sufficiently disaggregate types of income. Salaried corporation executives, for example, are lumped together with production and office workers, and thus considerable inequality can exist *within* the wage-and-salary category. There is a comparability problem, too, in comparing functional shares for developing and developed countries, since top executives in the former are less likely to be salaried and more likely to receive income that would be recorded as property income. In summary, the functional-share measure is of only limited usefulness as an analytical tool for measuring income inequalities.

The Lorenz Curve and the Gini Coefficient

Probably the best-known indicator of income inequality is the Gini coefficient, based on the familiar Lorenz curve, which relates income to the percentage of income recipients in different income brackets (the so-called *size distribution* of income). In Figure 11.1 the percentage of income recipients is indicated on the horizontal axis, the percentage of income on the vertical axis. If income were distributed equally among all income recipients, the Lorenz curve would be a 45° line running from the lower left-hand corner of the square defined by the two axes to the upper right-hand corner. But if incomes are unequally distributed, the Lorenz curve will fall below the 45° line, as shown by the solid line *ORSTUV*. Point *R* on this curve indicates that the poorest 20 percent of income recipients have less than 4 percent of the income. The next quintile receives about 6 percent of the income, giving the poorest 40 percent of the population 10 percent of total income; this is represented by point *S*. Points *T*, *U*, and *V* are obtained in similar fashion. The various points on this diagram may be joined by straight lines, but a curve drawn through them is a more accurate representation of reality since it takes into account the unequal distribution of incomes *within* quintiles.

The Gini coefficient is the quotient of the area between the 45° line and the Lorenz curve (A) and the total area under the 45° line ($A + B$). The more unequal the distribution of income, the larger is the fraction, $A/(A + B)$, and therefore the higher is the Gini coefficient.

Although the Gini coefficient is a better measure of income inequality than the functional-share measure, it has a number of drawbacks. First

Figure 11.1
The Lorenz Curve

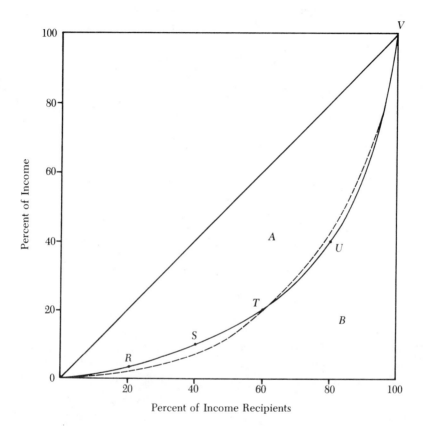

of all, a single coefficient—e.g., .50—does not indicate the degree to which various income groups are responsible for the overall index of inequality. For example, the second Lorenz curve in Figure 11.1 (the broken line) yields a Gini coefficient the same as that of the old curve *ORSTUV*. But in this second case, the poor have less of the total income, while income is distributed more equally among the upper- and middle-income groups.

Another problem with the Gini coefficient concerns the measurement of the area *A*. This is usually done by determining *B* and subtracting it from (*A* + *B*). One could obtain *B* by using integral calculus, but the first step—describing *ORSTUV* algebraically—is not an easy one. A common method of approximating the area under the curve is to connect the various points (*O, R, S, T, U,* and *V*, in the case of Figure 11.1) with straight lines, in which case B can be determined easily by adding the areas of a series of rectangles and triangles. It is clear, however, that this procedure gives an upward bias to B, thus *under*estimating the degree of income concentration. The fewer the number of income groups into which the population is divided, and hence the fewer the number of points that can be plotted, the greater the underestimate will tend to be.

Discussions of the mathematics of estimating the Gini coefficient can be much more complex than the paragraph above, but enough has been said to demonstrate that different methods of measuring the Gini coefficient can yield significantly different figures. Since not all researchers use the same methods, comparisons among countries can be misleading. When we combine this problem with those associated with defining and measuring income, discussed above, it becomes clear that the inequality ranking of any particular country should be viewed skeptically unless it can be confirmed by other evidence.

To illustrate how the definition of income and income recipients can affect the Gini coefficient, Albert Fishlow took income distribution data from Brazil's 1960 census and calculated four separate coefficients ranging from .50 to .59, depending on whether (1) the size distribution is based on family units rather than on the economically active population and (2) the data are corrected "to incorporate nonmonetary income excluded from the census inquiry [and] to reallocate income to family workers reported as economically active but without monetary remuneration."[10] Fishlow also notes that the income distribution tables he derived from the census differed from those of several other researchers.

Bearing in mind all these problems, let us examine some Gini coefficients for eight Latin American countries and five developed countries for the early 1960s (Table 11.3). Among the former, income concentration was greatest in Brazil and least in Argentina and Colombia. Other evidence tends to support the relative rankings of Brazil and Argentina, but there is reason to believe that inequality in Colombia is understated. At the same time, inequality in Costa Rica is very likely *over*estimated. In general, the data in Table 11.3 suggest that income inequality tends to diminish as the level of GNP increases. However, it is interesting to note that the differences in income concentration coefficients were greater among the developed countries than among the Latin America nations.

The UN-ECLA study (1970) from which these data are taken points out that there is less inequality among the lower half of income recipients in Latin America than in the developed countries. Thus "the greater

10. Albert Fishlow, "Brazilian Size Distribution of Income," *American Economic Review, Papers and Proceedings,* 62 (May 1972), 391.

TABLE 11.3
Gini Coefficients, Selected Countries,
Early 1960s

Country	Gini Coefficient
Latin America	
Brazil	0.575
El Salvador	0.54
Venezuela	0.54
Mexico	0.53
Costa Rica	0.52
Panama	0.49
Argentina	0.48
Colombia	0.48
Developed Countries	
France	0.52
Netherlands	0.44
United Kingdom	0.40
United States	0.40
Norway	0.36

Source: UN–ECLA (1970: 6).

[overall] inequality in the distribution of income in Latin America is due exclusively to the extreme inequality registered in the upper deciles" (p. 16). But the lower degree of inequality in the lower deciles is deceptive. In the developed countries, most of those in the two lowest deciles are "special cases"—retired persons, the frictionally unemployed (between jobs), very young workers, etc.—whose relatively low incomes reflect a temporary situation in their lives. (In Western Europe, almost half are not active members of the labor force.) In Latin America, the great majority of those in the lower deciles are employed persons with permanently low incomes.

The cross-section data in Table 11.3 lend some support to the Kuznets hypothesis regarding trends in income distribution over time (a widening of inequalities, then a narrowing once a certain level of development has been reached), but it would be useful to supplement them with data showing changes in income distribution over time. Data for seven countries (Argentina, Brazil, Ceylon, Colombia, India, Mexico, and Puerto Rico), indicating trends during the 1950s and 1960s, show that the Gini coefficient rose in all cases except for Ceylon where there was a slight decline. These data, as well as other quantitative evidence, support the widespread belief that income inequalities in developing countries have been widening, in contrast to the apparent narrowing that has occurred in developed countries (Tinbergen, 1975: Ch. 2). However, one should be cautious in making generalizations on the basis of rising Gini coefficients. In Mexico and Puerto Rico, for example, a rising coefficient did not mean that the income share of the wealthier groups had risen. In fact, it had fallen, with the middle-income groups gaining at the expense of both the lower 60 percent *and* the upper 5 percent. Moreover, alternative measures of income inequality actually suggest a reduction in overall income inequality in both these countries, as well as in Argentina.[11]

The "Target Group" Approach

The Gini coefficient is being widely replaced—or at least supplemented —by what might be called the *target group* approach to measuring income inequality. This approach focuses on the share of income received by the lowest-income groups and changes in that share over time. The World Bank focuses on the lowest 40 percent of the population (Chenery et al., 1974),[12] while Adelman and Morris (1973: 152) have in addition provided data on the lowest 20 percent and lowest 60 percent.

Data prepared at the World Bank are shown in Table 11.4. Apart from the usual problems of data reliability and compatibility, comparisons among countries are made difficult by the fact that the data do not refer to the same year, but rather to various years ranging from 1956 to 1971. Nevertheless, these data, and similar data prepared by Adelman and Morris, are the best available for comparing countries on a worldwide basis. The figures give broad support to the Kuznets hypothesis: the degree of inequality—as measured by the income share of the lowest 40 percent of the population—tends to be lowest in the very poorest countries and also in the wealthiest countries. In most countries where per capita income in 1971 was $200 or less, the lowest 40 percent of the population received 13 to 18 percent of total income, and in countries with a per capita income of $2,000 or more, the range was 14 to 20 percent. Meanwhile, the lowest 40 percent of income recipients had only 6 to 12 percent of the total income in most of the countries in the $200 to $700 per capita income range. The relationship between income inequality and income levels, however, is not a perfect one. A variety of institutional factors can cause countries to deviate from the historical trend described by Kuznets. Of particular note are the high shares of the low-

---

11. For sources, see Zuvekas (1975: 14–16).

12. A short article based on this report is Montek S. Ahluwalia, "Income Inequality: Some Dimensions of the Problem," *Finance and Development*, 11, No. 3 (September 1974), 2–8, 41.

est 40 percent of income recipients—up to 28 percent of total income—in the socialist economies of Eastern Europe, even those in which per capita income is well below the average for developed countries.

It should be noted that the data in Table 11.4 are based on pre-tax incomes. Information on after-tax income—very difficult to obtain for many countries—would show different relative rankings for some countries. If the overall tax structure is progressive, the share of the lowest 40 percent would tend to be higher and that of the upper 20 percent would be lower. But in some developing countries, after-tax income might well show an improvement in the relative position of the upper 20 percent at the expense of the middle 40 percent.

In comparing the World Bank data with the Gini coefficients in Table 11.3, we see that most countries have roughly the same relative rankings. There are significant differences, however, for Colombia and Norway, to which the measure of the lowest 40 percent share assigns greater relative inequality than the Gini measure. In the case of Norway, this is largely offset by a low share for the highest 20 percent of income recipients; there is no similar explanation for the difference in Colombia's ranking.

The data collected by Adelman and Morris for various years in the late 1950s and 1960s (1973: 152)[13]—not reproduced here—are broadly similar to those in Table 11.4, though for certain countries there are some significant discrepancies. These data, covering forty-three developing countries, show that the highest 20 percent of income recipients had an (unweighted) average of 56 percent of total income, compared with 57 percent for the fifty developing countries in Table 11.4.[14] For the lowest 40 percent of the population, the Adelman-Morris data show that the unweighted income share was 14 percent; the average among the developing countries in the World Bank study is 13 percent.

The Adelman-Morris data also focus specifically on the poorest 20 percent of income recipients. On the average, their share of total reported income was only 5.6 percent. The range (excluding a few peculiar cases at the extremes)[15] was from 1.9 percent in South Africa to 9 to 11 percent in such diverse countries as Burma, Greece, Surinam, and Tan-

13. See also Adelman and Morris, "An Anatomy of Income Distribution Patterns," p. 27.
14. In making this calculation, we include Bulgaria, Greece, Spain, Yugoslavia, and South Africa among the developing countries. The Adelman-Morris data include Israel and Japan, which sometimes were considered developing countries in the years to which the data apply but no longer can be placed in this category.
15. The 0.11 percent figure for Libya reflects that country's sudden emergence as a major petroleum exporter at a time when most of the population lived in extreme poverty. The 12 percent figures for Chad and Niger seem attributable to arithmetical errors.

TABLE 11.4
Cross-Classification of Countries by Income Level and Equality[a]

HIGH INEQUALITY
Share of lowest 40% less than 12%

Country (year)	Per capita GNP US$	Lowest 40%	Middle 40%	Top 20%
Kenya (1969)	136	10.0	22.0	68.0
Sierra Leone (1968)	159	9.6	22.4	68.0
Iraq (1956)	200	6.8	25.2	68.0
Philippines (1971)	239	11.6	34.6	53.8
Senegal (1960)	245	10.0	26.0	64.0
Ivory Coast (1970)	247	10.8	32.1	57.1
Rhodesia (1968)	252	8.2	22.8	69.0
Tunisia (1970)	255	11.4	33.6	55.0
Honduras (1968)	265	6.5	28.5	65.0
Ecuador (1970)	277	6.5	20.0	73.5
El Salvador (1969)	295	11.2	36.4	52.4
Turkey (1968)	282	9.3	29.9	60.8
Malaysia (1970)	330	11.6	32.4	56.0
Colombia (1970)	358	9.0	30.0	61.0
Brazil (1970)	390	10.0	28.4	61.5
Peru (1971)	480	6.5	33.5	60.0

MODERATE INEQUALITY
Share of lowest 40% between 12% and 17%

Country (year)	Per capita GNP US$	Lowest 40%	Middle 40%	Top 20%
Burma (1958)	82	16.5	38.7	44.8
Dahomey (1959)	87	15.5	34.5	50.0
Tanzania (1967)	89	13.0	26.0	61.0
India (1964)	99	16.0	32.0	52.0
Madagascar (1960)	120	13.5	25.5	61.0
Zambia (1959)	230	14.5	28.5	57.0
Dominican Republic (1969)	323	12.2	30.3	57.5
Iran (1968)	332	12.5	33.0	54.5
Guyana (1956)	550	14.0	40.3	45.7

LOW INEQUALITY
Share of lowest 40%, 17% and above

Country (year)	Per capita GNP US$	Lowest 40%	Middle 40%	Top 20%
Chad (1958)	78	18.0	39.0	43.0
Sri Lanka (1969)	95	17.0	37.0	46.0
Niger (1960)	97	18.0	40.0	42.0
Pakistan (1964)	100	17.5	37.5	45.0
Uganda (1970)	126	17.1	35.8	47.1
Thailand (1970)	180	17.0	37.5	45.5
Korea (1970)	235	18.0	37.0	45.0
Taiwan (1964)	241	20.4	39.5	40.1
Surinam (1962)	394	21.7	35.7	42.6
Greece (1957)	500	21.0	29.5	49.5
Yugoslavia (1968)	529	18.5	40.0	41.5
Bulgaria (1962)	530	26.8	40.0	33.2

284

Country (year)	Per capita GNP	1	2	3
Gabon (1968)	497	8.8	23.7	67.5
Jamaica (1958)	510	8.2	30.3	61.5
Lebanon (1960)	508	13.0	26.0	61.0
Uruguay (1968)	618	16.5	35.5	48.0
Chile (1968)	744	13.0	30.2	56.8
Spain (1965)	750	17.6	36.7	45.7
2				
Costa Rica (1971)	521	11.5	30.0	58.5
Mexico (1969)	645	10.5	25.5	64.0
South Africa (1965)	669	6.2	35.8	58.0
Panama (1969)	692	9.4	31.2	59.4
Venezuela (1970)	1004	7.9	27.1	65.0
Finland (1962)	1599	11.1	39.6	49.3
France (1962)	1913	9.5	36.8	53.7
Argentina (1970)	1079	16.5	36.1	47.4
Puerto Rico (1968)	1100	13.7	35.7	50.6
Netherlands (1967)	1990	13.6	37.9	48.5
Norway (1968)	2010	16.6	42.9	40.5
Germany, Fed. Rep. (1964)	2144	15.4	31.7	52.9
Denmark (1968)	2563	13.6	38.8	47.6
New Zealand (1969)	2859	15.5	42.5	42.0
Sweden (1963)	2949	14.0	42.0	44.0
Poland (1964)	850	23.4	40.6	36.0
Japan (1963)	950	20.7	39.3	40.0
United Kingdom (1968)	2015	18.8	42.2	39.0
Hungary (1969)	1140	24.0	42.5	33.5
Czechoslovakia (1964)	1150	27.6	41.4	31.0
Australia (1968)	2509	20.0	41.2	38.8
Canada (1965)	2920	20.0	39.8	40.2
United States (1970)	4850	19.7	41.5	38.8
3				

1 Income up to US$300 2 Income US$300–$750 3 Income above US$750

Note: The income shares of each percentile group were read off a free-hand Lorenz curve fitted to observed points in the cumulative distribution. The distributions are for pretax income. Per capita GNP figures are taken from the World Bank data files and refer to GNP at factor cost for the year indicated in constant 1971 U.S. dollars.

a The data used in the tables in this article are largely taken from Jain, S. and Tiemann, A. 1973, *Size Distribution of Income: A Compilation of Data,* Development Research Center Discussion Paper No. 4, World Bank, Washington, D.C.

Source: Montek S. Ahluwalia, "Income Inequality: Some Dimensions of the Problem," *Finance and Development,* 11 (September 1974), 4.

zania. These data also show that the average share of the poorest 60 percent of income recipients was 26 percent. The range for this group (again with a few necessary exclusions)[16] was from 15 to 17 percent in Colombia, Gabon, Iraq, Peru, and South Africa to 36 to 39 percent in Burma, India, Israel, and Surinam.

As with the Gini measure, it is useful to see if the target-group measure tells us anything about changes in income inequality over time. For the same seven countries for which Gini coefficients were available at two points in time (see above), estimates have also been made for the income share of the lowest 20 percent and lowest 60 percent of the population. Only in Brazil did the share of the lowest 20 percent of the population increase, but this finding can be disputed because of the method used to convert the Brazilian census data into quintiles. In the other countries, the share of the lowest 20 percent of the population declined. All seven countries showed declines in the share of income accruing to the lowest 60 percent of the population. Absolute declines in real family incomes occurred among the lowest 20 percent of the population in Ceylon, India, and Mexico. Other evidence (summarized in Zuvekas, 1975: 12–18) supports these findings that income inequalities, on the whole, were widening in developing countries during the 1950s and 1960s. Impressionistic evidence suggests that this trend may have been halted or even reversed in some countries during the 1970s, while in others it has increased. But insufficient data are available to make any firm conclusions.

Basic Needs Indicators

Dissatisfaction with income indicators as measures of well-being is leading many social scientists to regard favorably the "basic needs" strategy of development recommended by the International Labour Office (ILO). As defined by Francis Blanchard, the ILO's Director-General, basic needs are:[17]

> the minimum standard of living which a society should set for the poorest groups of its people. The satisfaction of basic needs means meeting the minimum requirements of a family for personal consumption: food, shelter, clothing; it implies access to essential services, such as safe drinking-water, sanitation, transport, health and education; it implies that each person available for and willing to work should have an adequately remunerated job. It should further

16. The figure for Libya this time is 1.78 percent. The 42.6 percent figure for Ecuador seems attributable to an arithmetical error.
17. International Labour Office, *Employment, Growth and Basic Needs: A One-World Problem*, intro. by James P. Grant (New York: Praeger Publishers, 1977), p. 7.

imply the satisfaction of needs of a more qualitative nature: a healthy, humane, and satisfactory environment, and popular participation in the making of decisions that affect the lives and livelihood of the people and individual freedoms.

Given the difficulties associated with the concept and measurement of income, measures of inequality based on the distribution of goods and services are an attractive alternative. Nevertheless, there are serious conceptual and data problems here, too. Moreover, the determination of basic needs involves a value judgment: who decides what is "basic"? Offsetting these difficulties, however, are several attractions. First, a basic needs strategy focuses on consumption, a more direct indication of well-being than income. Second, well-being or welfare is recognized to have a number of dimensions, each of which can be dealt with separately. Third, each country can determine its own basic needs indicators and focus its development strategies accordingly.

INCOME REDISTRIBUTION POLICIES

Before 1960, most development economists devoted little attention to income redistribution policies in developing countries. A major exception was Simon Kuznets, whose 1954 presidential address to the American Economic Association, cited above, highlighted this issue. Kuznets argued that the apparent widening of income inequalities in today's developing countries—given their very different institutional environments— might well lead to violent social upheaval and assumption of power by an authoritarian government which might draw upon the masses for support but prove to be more interested in economic growth than economic development.[18] Given the possibility of such an outcome, he maintained that revolutionary romanticism was just as dangerous for the welfare of the masses as laissez-faire romanticism. Kuznets believed that social change was both inevitable and desirable, and that pressures for such change were greater in today's developing countries than in the now-developed countries one or two centuries earlier. Accordingly, he challenged economists to find policies which would narrow income inequalities and thus avoid violent changes imposed by authoritarian governments. Appropriate policy prescriptions, he pointed out, required (1) an improved data base, (2) a better understanding of the institutional environment of the developing countries, and (3) greater knowledge of the causes of income inequality. Methodological approaches to the in-

---

18. It would appear that Kuznets had in mind the type of government exemplified by the Soviet Union under Stalin.

come distribution problem, he argued, must tackle all three problems, and this meant that economists must "venture into fields beyond those recognized in recent decades as the province of economics proper" (Kuznets, 1955: 28).

In the years immediately following the publication of Kuznets' presidential address, few economists responded to his challenge to identify appropriate policies for narrowing income inequalities. In the last fifteen years, however, considerable research on this issue has been conducted. Let us examine some of the results of these studies.

Fiscal Policy

Many economists have been skeptical about the efficacy of fiscal policy in redistributing income, but this prevailing view is being increasingly challenged, particularly as regards expenditure policy. Adelman and Morris, while finding that direct taxation is an ineffective tool for redistributing income, show that income inequalities are less the greater the share of net investment accounted for by the government.[19] This *might* mean that increased government expenditures will narrow income inequalities even if financed by an increase in taxes which does not change the overall progressivity of the tax structure. On the other hand, it might imply only that budgets at any given level should devote more resources to investment and fewer to current expenditures. Alternatively, what may really count is not the level of expenditures but the specific programs undertaken. Over the long run, a "basic needs" strategy may prove to be particularly effective in reducing the incidence of extreme poverty.

Education

In his influential 1961 article on human capital formation, Theodore Schultz noted that investment in human capital appeared to narrow income inequalities, though he cautioned that our knowledge of this relationship was very limited. Studies since then have tended to confirm such a relationship. Adelman and Morris (1973), for example, found that improvements in the quality of human resources—mainly through greater access to secondary and university education—constitute a particularly promising approach for reducing income inequalities. Most other studies, however, have found that redistributional effects are greatest if emphasis

19. Adelman and Morris, "An Anatomy of Income Distribution Patterns," pp. 36–37. A simulation model by Adelman and Robinson (1977) for South Korea also found that tax policy was relatively ineffective. For a summary of this study, and the two Adelman-Morris studies (1973, 1977), see Irma Adelman, Cynthia Taft Morris, and Sherman Robinson, "Policies for Equitable Growth," *World Development*, 4 (July 1976), 561–582.

is placed on primary education (see the references in Zuvekas, 1975: 20–21).

Agrarian Reform

As we noted in chapter 9, agrarian reform is widely believed to be a prerequisite for the success of traditional agricultural development programs aimed at lower-income groups. A review of nine countries experiencing major agrarian reforms (Japan, Taiwan, Egypt, Iran, Iraq, Kenya, Mexico, Cuba, and Chile) concluded that the effect on income distribution was positive, except perhaps in Iraq.[20] A study by William Cline concluded that land redistribution is the policy most likely to achieve both production increases and a narrowing of income inequalities.[21] The Adelman-Morris historical study (1977) found that the structure of land tenure was a particularly significant determinant of the extent of extreme poverty. The Adelman-Robinson simulation study of South Korea (1977) found that land reform was more effective in narrowing income inequalities than any other rural development strategy.

It is important to emphasize that agrarian reform generally must involve more than land distribution if incomes of the rural poor are to be significantly increased. Adelman, in explaining for another study the low statistical impact of agrarian reform in developing countries generally, argues that "the reason is probably that redistribution of land favors higher incomes for the poor only when supported by measures to maintain the productivity of the redistributional assets, supportive measures which are often not carried out."[22]

Agricultural Price Policy

The Adelman-Robinson simulation study (1977) found that the agricultural terms of the trade have a particularly significant effect on income distribution. An increase in relative prices received by farmers tends to narrow income inequalities, even though such price increases hurt the urban poor and benefit wealthy farmers more than proportionately. These movements toward greater inequality are more than offset by higher incomes for small farmers and, to a lesser extent, landless rural laborers. The authors of the study warn, however, that policy actions are needed to maintain a given relative price structure, since there is a natural ten-

20. Marvin Sternberg, "Agrarian Reform and Employment: Potential and Problems," *International Labour Review*, 103 (May 1971), 468–469.

21. William R. Cline, "Interrelationships between Agricultural Strategy and Rural Income Distribution," *Food Research Institute Studies*, 12 (1973), 139–157.

22. Irma Adelman, "Strategies for Equitable Growth," *Challenge* 17, No. 2 (May/June), 42–43.

dency for economic growth to be accompanied by declining agricultural terms of trade.

Industrial Development Policy

The distribution of income in urban centers generally is even more unequal than in rural areas. One important reason for this is that government policies—as well as the aid policies of foreign governments and international agencies—have tended to favor capital-intensive industrial development even though relative factor endowments may indicate that there is a greater scope for the use of labor-intensive techniques. Overvalued exchange rates, low interest rates, payroll taxes, tax advantages for the purchase of machinery, and the reluctance of aid agencies to make loans for local labor costs are some of the means by which capital-intensive development has been artificially stimulated. A reversal of these policies, by the same token, can stimulate urban employment and therefore narrow income inequalities.

The Adelman-Robinson model of the South Korean economy (1977) found that government policies favoring labor-intensive export industries resulted in a slightly more equal size distribution of income than would have occurred under a policy emphasizing import substitution. Interestingly, it was not the direct effects of this strategy that made the difference, but the indirect effects: an increase in the agricultural terms of trade and an acceleration of rural-urban migration.[23]

Population Policy

Over the long run, income inequalities might be reduced by policies designed to slow the population growth rate. Montek Ahluwalia (in Chenery et al., 1974: 17) finds that the income share of the lowest 40 percent of income recipients tends to be higher the slower is a country's population growth rate.

Direct Income Transfers and Subsidized Goods and Services

Direct payments to the poor, or the subsidization of food, housing, and other basic necessities, seem to be attractive policy options for narrowing

---

23. The terms of trade rise because the increased demand for food pushes food prices upward. Rural-urban migration narrowed income inequalities in Korea, but the authors note that too much migration can prevent this from happening.

inequalities because they can be focused exclusively on the poor without also directly benefiting middle- and upper-income groups. However, Adelman and Robinson (1977) note that such programs have several drawbacks. Over time, subsidy programs have a progressively smaller effect on income distribution since relative spending on necessities declines as income rises. More importantly, income-transfer or subsidy programs must be maintained year after year if their benefits are to last. This requires a heavy budgetary commitment and acceptance of a dualistic society.

Policy Packages

One of the most important conclusions of the Adelman-Robinson study is that policy packages can be more effective in narrowing income inequalities than any individual policy adopted in isolation. Thus an urban package combining public works and labor-intensive industry is the most effective urban strategy, though it is effective largely because rising agricultural terms of trade benefit the rural poor. Rural policy packages tend to be much more effective in narrowing income inequalities than urban ones.

Adelman and Robinson also experimented with combined rural-urban packages, simulating growth and distribution under a "market-socialism" strategy, a "reform-capitalist" strategy, and a strategy involving no reforms at all. After a decade, both the market-socialism and reform-capitalist strategies resulted in higher incomes for the seven lowest deciles than a strategy based on a continuation of existing policies. While incomes were highest under the reform-capitalist strategy, and the growth of output tended to accelerate, the initial narrowing of income inequalities was partially undone toward the end of the period. Under the market-socialism strategy, income inequalities continued to narrow, but growth tended to slacken toward the end of the period.

Concluding Comments

A sobering conclusion of all the studies conducted by Adelman and her collaborators is that reformist policies have at best only limited potential for narrowing income inequalities, especially if there is no fundamental change in development strategy. Even reformist measures require political decisions that will meet stiff resistance from those whose income shares stand to decline. Moreover, such measures, if implemented, tend to have only a temporary effect on inequalities. The effect is greater, and more permanent, if there is a shift in development strategy—e.g., to a broad-based rural development effort or to labor-intensive industrial exporting.

Still, a really significant and rapid narrowing of income inequalities is unlikely to occur in the absence of a true social and political revolution. Marxists would argue that such a revolution is bound to occur eventually in all countries. Even if they are right, the historical record—and traditional Marxist theory—suggests that most countries are in for a long wait. Some non-Marxists who deny the inevitability of revolution may be content to wait the gradual reduction in income inequalities that historically seems to occur after an initial period of widening inequalities. But others believe that reformist policies can and should be used to eliminate or cut short this initial period.

SUMMARY

The bulk of the evidence suggests that income inequalities have been widening in many if not most developing countries. There is also good reason to believe that the living standards of the very poorest members of society have declined in absolute as well as relative terms. These same trends appear to have characterized today's developed countries 100 to 200 years ago; but this is no reason to be complacent about income inequalities in developing countries today. As Kuznets warned a generation ago, social and institutional environments are different, and tolerance of inequalities is less in today's developing countries than during comparable periods in the history of the developed countries.

Measuring income inequality is no easy task, and frequently used indicators of inequality such as the Gini coefficient do not necessarily indicate what is happening to the living standards of the poorest members of society. The growing worldwide concern about the welfare of the very poor has prompted increased use of income distribution indicators which focus on the income share of the lowest 20, 40, or 60 percent of income recipients. More recently, economists have begun to shift from income data to "basic needs" indicators which more directly measure well-being.

Evidence from existing studies—which needs to be corroborated by additional research—suggests that policies for narrowing income distribution inequalities are likely to be ineffective when taken in isolation. Another important finding is that the indirect effects of policy measures are sometimes more important than the direct effects; this points to a need for systems approaches toward policy-oriented research. Rural-based strategies appear to offer greater scope for narrowing inequalities than urban-based strategies, but in the absence of a social and political revolution the reduction of inequalities is likely to be modest and gradual.

Suggested Readings

Adelman, Irma, and Cynthia Taft Morris. *Economic Growth and Social Equity in Developing Countries*. Stanford, Calif.: Stanford University Press, 1973.

This study provides comparative data on the income shares of the poorest 60 percent, middle 20 percent, and upper 5 percent of income recipients in forty-three developed countries for various years during the period 1957–1968. It also statistically analyzes the effects of thirty-five economic, social, and political variables on income distribution. The authors conclude that relatively few policy actions have a significant effect on income distribution, and that they benefit primarily the middle classes.

————, and ————. "A Typology of Poverty in 1850." In *Essays on Economic Development and Cultural Change in Honor of Bert F. Hoselitz*, ed. Manning Nash. Supplement to *Economic Development and Cultural Change*, 25 (1977), 313–343.

The authors examine qualitative and quantitative data on the incidence of extreme poverty in twenty-three countries in 1850. The countries— sixteen of which are now considered developed—are then classified into nine categories according to the extent of industrialization and commercialization. The authors conclude that structural change, by displacing society's poorest members, lowers their living standards. The faster the change, it appears, the more people will suffer.

————, and Sherman Robinson. *Income Distribution Policy in Developing Countries: A Case Study of Korea*. Stanford, Calif.: Stanford University Press, 1977.

Using an economy-wide planning model, the authors simulate the effects of various policy instruments (direct and indirect taxes, tariffs, interest rates, monetary variables, etc.) on income distribution. They also allow for different institutional arrangements regarding credit and factor markets. Fifteen categories of income recipients are identified. The study concludes that reformist measures generally have little impact on income distribution; significant redistribution requires structural change.

Cline, William R. *Potential Effects of Income Redistribution on Economic Growth*. New York: Praeger Publishers, 1972.

This study uses simulation techniques to examine the implications of income redistribution in Argentina, Brazil, Mexico, and Venezuela. Cline concludes that redistribution would probably reduce growth rates, but only slightly.

Foxley, Alejandro, ed. *Income Distribution in Latin America*. Cambridge, Eng.: Cambridge University Press, 1975.

Originally published in Spanish, this collection of articles examines a variety of topics concerning income distribution in Latin America. The studies deal with both theoretical issues and empirical research.

Kuznets, Simon. "Economic Growth and Income Inequality." *American Economic Review*, 45 (March 1955), 1–28.

Kuznets was one of the first economists to conduct detailed research on income distribution in both developed and developing countries. This essay stresses the importance of interdisciplinary research and the significant differences between the developed and developing countries. It also anticipates many of the policy issues of the 1960s and 1970s.

Tinbergen, Jan. *Income Distribution: Analysis and Policies*. Amsterdam: North-Holland Publishing Company, 1975.

This book summarizes and synthesizes the work of a number of social scientists on income distribution in *developed* countries. Tinbergen identifies three approaches to the problem of explaining income inequalities: the human capital school (supply-focused), the education planning school (demand-focused), and the demand-and-supply school, to which he belongs. Answers to the question "Can income inequality be reduced?" range from skeptical through not-so-skeptical to too-optimistic. Tinbergen's own research leads him to conclude that inequality can be reduced only if education expands faster than technological development. The policy recommendation that technological development be deliberately manipulated is relevant for developing as well as developed countries.

United Nations. Economic Commission for Latin America. *Income Distribution in Latin America*. New York, 1970.

This study is a detailed examination of income distribution data for eight Latin American countries, with particular emphasis on Argentina, Brazil, El Salvador, Mexico, and Venezuela. In addition to income concentration coefficients, the study also examines income distribution in terms of functional (factor-share), rural-urban, regional, and sectoral differentials. It also discusses the social, political, and economic causes and consequences of extreme inequality.

Zuvekas, Clarence, Jr. *Income Distribution in Latin America: A Survey of Recent Research*. Essay Series No. 6. Milwaukee: Center for Latin America, University of Wisconsin—Milwaukee, July 1975.

This essay surveys the post-1965 literature on income distribution in Latin America, summarizing major empirical findings and showing how——together with advances in economic theory—these have been altering economists' views concerning the relationship between income distribution and economic growth and development.

12

Employment

During the 1950s and 1960s, developing countries experiencing rapid economic growth generally found that growth alone did little to ease their unemployment and underemployment problems. Where growth was slower, these problems were usually aggravated. Thus employment, like the related issue of income distribution, has become a major policy concern of both national governments and international agencies during the 1970s. Some governments have taken direct action to reduce unemployment and underemployment because these conditions are regarded as morally unacceptable. Others, less sympathetic to the plight of the poor, have been concerned about the potential social and political problems created by the presence of large and growing numbers of people who are jobless, have only part-time jobs, or receive very little remuneration for their efforts.

Unfortunately, data on unemployment and underemployment in developing countries are poor—so much so, in fact, that it is often difficult to determine both magnitudes and trends. After looking at some of the statistical evidence, we shall show that reported unemployment and underemployment rates are so seriously deficient as indicators of well-being that many economists now advocate a very different approach to measuring the extent of the employment problem. The weaknesses of the traditional approach will be illustrated by a case study of efforts to measure rural underemployment in Haiti, where unrealistically high unemployment-equivalent rates, approaching 80 percent, have been reported.

Although the extent of underemployment is frequently exaggerated, it should be emphasized that employment problems in most developing countries are still very serious. In fact, open unemployment rates are probably *under*estimated. Much of the problem can be attributed directly or indirectly to rapid population growth, but government policies affecting choice of technology also play an important role.

THE STRUCTURE OF EMPLOYMENT IN DEVELOPING COUNTRIES

We noted in chapter 1 that a change in the structure of employment is one of the more notable features of the process of economic development. In the least developed countries, as much as 95 percent of the population may be engaged in agriculture, forestry, and fisheries, which together comprise what is called the *primary* sector of the economy. As productivity increases in agriculture, labor is released from primary production and moves into secondary and tertiary activities. The *secondary* sector, as defined here, includes manufacturing, mining, construction, and public utilities.[1] The *tertiary* sector includes transport, storage, and communications; finance, insurance, real estate, and other business services; personal services; and social and community services (private and governmental).

Table 12.1, which provides data on the structure of employment in twenty-four countries at various levels of development, shows that the economically active population tends to move out of agriculture into both secondary and tertiary employment as per capita income rises. Though we often associate high and rapidly growing service employment with a "postindustrial" economy, it should be noted that much of the increase in tertiary employment in developing countries does not represent white-collar employment but rather very-low-productivity jobs held by migrants from rural areas and city-born members of the urban population living in central city slums and squatter settlements. This kind of service employment—in jobs such as street vending, shoe shining, errand running, and other low-paying personal services—does not reflect widespread affluence but rather the failure of both agriculture and industry to provide sufficient numbers of jobs for new members of the economically active population.

---

1. Some economists place mining in the primary sector, since like agriculture it involves the direct extraction of a raw material. However, mining operations often include some transformation of the raw material and resemble manufacturing in other respects as well. Public utilities are sometimes considered as tertiary (service) activities.

TABLE 12.1
Sectoral Distribution of the Economically Active Population,[a]
Selected Countries, Latest Census or Survey Year
(*percentages*)

Country	Per Capita Income ($) 1974	Census or Survey Year	Sector of Employment		
			Primary	*Secondary*	*Tertiary*
Burma	100	1974–5	73	10	17
Nepal	100	1971	94	1	5
India	140	1971	72	12	16
Tanzania	160	1967	92	2	6
Egypt	280	1966	56	17	27
Mozambique	340	1970	74	13	13
South Korea	480	1975	46	24	30
Guatemala	580	1973	58	18	24
Dominican Republic	650	1970	56	14	30
Tunisia	650	1966	46	21	33
Cuba	710	1970	30	27	43
Algeria	730	1966	59	15	26
Peru	740	1972	44	20	36
Mexico	1,090[b]	1970	42	24	34
Iran	1,250	1966	47	28	25
Argentina	1,520	1970	16	32	52
Portugal	1,630	1970	33	33	34
USSR	2,380	1970	26	46	28
Italy	2,820	1976	16	43	41
Czechoslovakia	3,330	1970	17	48	35
Japan	4,070	1975	13	36	51
Australia	5,330	1973	7	36	57
Belgium	5,670	1975	4	39	57
United States	6,670	1975	4	32	64

Source: International Labour Office, *Yearbook of Labour Statistics 1976.*

[a] Excludes members of the economically active population classified only as unemployed, seeking work for the first time, or in the armed services, as well as workers whose sectoral employment is not clearly specified.

[b] Does not reflect the substantial devaluation of the Mexican peso in August 1976.

UNEMPLOYMENT AND UNDEREMPLOYMENT ESTIMATES

A comparison of urban unemployment rates in twenty-two countries during the 1960s (see Table 12.2) shows considerable variation in the percentage of those without jobs. Reported unemployment rates—some of which are very misleading—ranged from only 3 percent in India, Taiwan,

TABLE 12.2
Urban Unemployment Rates, Selected Countries, Various Years in the 1960s
(percent of the labor force 15 years of age and older)

Country	Total	Male	Female
Algeria	25	26	7
Argentina	4	3	7
Ceylon	15	13	26
Chile	6	n.a.[a]	n.a.
Colombia	14	10	18
Curaçao	19	n.a.	n.a.
Ghana	12	11	12
Guyana	21	18	28
India	3	3	3
Iran	5	5	4
Malaya	10	7	17
Panama	10	9	13
Philippines	12	11	13
Puerto Rico	10	11	8
Singapore	9	n.a.	n.a.
South Korea	9	9	8
Syria	6	6	6
Taiwan	3	2	7
Thailand	3	3	3
Trinidad and Tobago	14	14	16
Uruguay	12	n.a.	n.a.
Venezuela	8	n.a.	n.a.

Source: Turnham (1971).
[a] n.a.: Not available.

and Thailand to 21 percent in Guyana and 25 percent in Algeria.[2] A 1970 survey in Haiti reported a (very questionable) 49 percent unemployment rate in the capital. Unemployment rates for women are sometimes higher, sometimes lower, than for men. Rates for younger workers are almost always significantly higher than national averages, and young people, including first-time job seekers, often constitute the great majority of the unemployed. In Barbados, where the 1970 census reported a national unemployment rate of 7.7 percent, the unemployment rate for the 14–19 age group was 35.8 percent, compared with a very low 1.6 percent for those 25 years old or more. The 14–19 age group accounted for 66 percent of total unemployment, and the 20–24 group for an additional 20 percent.

A major worldwide survey of the employment problem in developing countries (Turnham, 1971) concluded that open unemployment rates

2. Economists who have studied development problems in India believe that open unemployment in urban areas was much higher during the 1960s than the reported rate of 3 percent.

in urban centers were usually higher than the published figures, but for developing countries generally they were probably not rising (or falling). However, since urban populations were growing quite rapidly, the numbers of unemployed urban workers were increasing at a disturbing pace even where unemployment rates were constant. Rural unemployment rates tended to be lower than urban rates—often considerably lower—but since population growth was faster in the cities than in the countryside, national unemployment rates were probably rising in many developing countries.

Scattered evidence from the 1970s suggests that the trend of the 1960s is continuing in a large number of countries. In some Latin American countries, however, lower urban unemployment rates have been reported, a reflection of the acceleration in economic growth in that region in recent years.

*Under*employment takes several forms and is more difficult to define than unemployment. One form of underemployment is represented by persons who are working fewer hours than they wish to be employed. It might appear that this could be measured easily by sample surveys, but it is not at all clear that we should regard as "underemployed" the relatively large number of people already working 40 to 50 hours a week but who would like additional work. In the Philippines, for example, a survey conducted in 1965 found that 62 percent of urban workers and 49 percent of rural workers seeking additional employment were working at least 40 hours a week at the time of the survey (Turnham, 1971: 60).

Another type of underemployment is that represented by persons working in jobs whose requirements are below the skill levels they have obtained through education and training. Ph.D.s driving taxicabs is a good recent example from the United States. Many economists also consider as underemployed persons who earn meager incomes as street vendors, bootblacks, porters, and other such occupations. But information on the extent of this type of underemployment—which is very difficult to measure—is hard to find.

Underemployment in agriculture is frequently measured by comparing number of days actually worked with the potential availability of labor for a "normal" year's work. Using this methodology, some writers have claimed that as much as 50 to 80 percent of potential labor time is unutilized in some countries. Such estimates, as we shall see below, are unrealistically high. However, the unemployment-equivalent rates of 14 to 32 percent calculated by the United Nations' International Labour Office for six Latin American countries are plausible.[3]

---

3. Regional Employment Programme for Latin America and the Caribbean (PREALC), *The Employment Problem in Latin America: Facts, Outlooks and Policies* (Santiago, Chile: International Labour Office, 1976), p. 38.

UNEMPLOYMENT AND UNDEREMPLOYMENT AS WELFARE INDICATORS

It is difficult to determine trends in unemployment and underemployment rates in developing countries because technical and financial resource limitations make accurate data collection difficult, especially on a regular basis. Disagreements on how to define the labor force, participation rates, and other key concepts limit the reliability of intercountry comparisons. Even for the same country, unemployment or underemployment estimates for different years may not be directly comparable because different methodologies were used.

Unemployment rates for some countries are calculated by dividing the number of unemployed workers by the *labor force* or the *economically active population*. The labor force is usually defined to include all employed persons and unemployed workers seeking work at the time of an employment survey or census. The economically active population, as defined by the International Labour Office, excludes students, women engaged solely in household work, retired persons, persons living entirely on their own means, and persons wholly dependent on others. Individual government statistics almost always exclude the same groups, but there is considerable variation among countries concerning the treatment of the armed forces, inmates of institutions, reservation residents, seasonal and part-time workers, and persons seeking work for the first time. This makes international comparisons difficult.

Particularly inconsistent are the differences among countries concerning the labor force status given to part-time and seasonal female workers. In most of Latin America, only 20 to 25 percent of the women are considered to be in the economically active population, even though a much higher percentage may be engaged in farm work, marketing, handicraft production, or other activities in addition to household management. In Bolivia, however, one set of government statistics shows that 60 percent of the women are economically active, and in Haiti the 1971 census reported that 70 percent of all women 15 years of age and older were in this category. Another definitional problem with unemployment rates concerns the status of younger workers. The usual practice is to exclude children below 14 to 16 years of age from the economically active population, but in some countries children only 5 years old may be included.

Problems in measuring open unemployment are serious enough, but in the case of underemployment the situation is far worse. Turnham (1971: 59) warns us that statements such as "30 percent of the labor force is underemployed" are very misleading unless we know something about the amount of additional work desired and the conditions under which it is wanted. Where attempts have been made to express this type of "visible underemployment" as a percentage equivalent of full-time employment, the result has often been an increase in unemployment rates of only 2 to 3 percentage points. Even such adjustments must be viewed with suspicion, since they may be based on questionable assumptions regarding such key issues as: What is a "normal" work week? How does one account for the apparent lack of correlation between average hours worked and desire for additional work? It is even more difficult to define and measure the "invisible underemployment" represented by people working full time but at less productive tasks than they are capable of performing.

Measures of rural underemployment are particularly troublesome, especially if it is implied that vast numbers of people could leave the countryside without affecting agricultural production. If technology is held constant, the physical removal of people might indeed cause production to decline, since all available hands may be needed for planting, harvesting, and certain other activities. True, these hands may appear to be idle much of the year, or the available work may be divided among all those present—leaving each one underemployed in the sense that slack-time tasks could be performed by fewer people. But it is not at all clear just how much underemployment exists under these circumstances. Many estimates of rural underemployment fail to take fully into account such activities as time spent on general farm management, small livestock operations, garden plots, marketing, acquisition of credit, community public works projects, food processing (both for market and for home consumption), maintenance and repairs, and production of clothing and other items which cannot be bought in the marketplace for lack of cash.

Another issue concerns the definition of a "normal" work year (in terms of days), particularly when only single cropping is possible—either for climatic reasons (as on the Bolivian Altiplano) or for technological reasons (e.g., the absence of irrigation water)—and no alternative employment opportunities are available. In the United States, we do not consider as "unemployed" the Minnesota farmers who spend three months of the year in Florida because there is little they can do on their farms during the winter. Instead, we say in effect that their normal vacation time is long. A comparable view might be taken in research on employment in developing countries, though this should not be seized upon as an excuse to brush rural unemployment problems under the carpet.

Available labor time is developing countries may also be overestimated by failing to take into account the fact that some rural residents considered as potential workers may not want to work on a full-time basis or may not even be in the labor force. In addition, malnutrition and illness probably limit significantly the ability of workers to do sustained work for long periods. Socioeconomic surveys in Bolivia suggest that in some areas 5 to 10 percent of potential labor time may be lost because of poor health.

Emphasis on unemployment and underemployment indicators fails to take into account the fact that many people counted as fully employed are working at such low-productivity tasks that they are no better off (in terms of nutrition, health, housing, etc.) than the openly unemployed or visibly underemployed. Indeed, they may be worse off. Bolivia before 1952 provides an excellent illustration of this point. Under a feudalistic system of agriculture known as the *colonato,* the rural poor had to spend as many as six days a week working for a large landowner, leaving them little time for their own plots. Not only was there no visible unemployment or underemployment, but one could even speak of "overemployment"! Some writers nevertheless have argued that "invisible underemployment" exists under these circumstances because of the very low productivity and/or income received. But this begs the question of what constitutes a "full employment" level of income and in effect shifts the focus of the problem from employment to productivity and income.

Because of productivity considerations, as well as measurement problems relating to unemployment and underemployment, Turnham (1971: 19, 59) advocates an income or "poverty" approach to the employment problem, with the emphasis on the *quality* (productivity) of employment rather than the quantity. Sample surveys, he suggests, could seek to determine what percentage of potential or actual full-time workers have incomes below some agreed upon poverty level. Changes in the employment situation would be measured by changes in the proportion of workers with incomes below this reference level. Turnham argues that the technical difficulties of such surveys are no greater than those of endeavors to measure unemployment and underemployment. What convinces him that such an approach is needed is his belief that a continuation of present economic growth trends will lead to an even more skewed distribution of income, thus increasing social and political tensions. Such tensions, of course, could have adverse effects on economic growth and development. At the same time, recent research, discussed in the previous chapter, shows that we can reject the notion that a more equal distribution of income would have significant negative effects on rates of productive investment or income growth.

Hollis Chenery and his collaborators at the World Bank and the University of Sussex share Turnham's view that the employment problem in developing countries is more appropriately viewed as an income problem: "The recognition that 80 percent or more of the low-end poverty group are employed in some fashion has shifted the focus of policy from increasing the quantity to improving the quality of employment."[4] L. S. Jarvis, in a Ford Foundation symposium on employment problems in developing countries (Edwards, 1974: 166), argues that

> employment, although an important subsidiary issue, is not the proper focus of policy concern is the less developed countries. . . . If . . . the primary issue is one of income distribution or, more broadly stated, equality of opportunity, it seems better to focus attention explicitly on this objective rather than on an issue which is only indirectly related, such as employment, and which may not result in the desired solution.

The importance of the income aspect of the employment problem is also emphasized by Yudelman, Butler, and Banerji (1971: 161), whose review of agricultural employment data leads them to question the fruitfulness of research for better measures of agricultural unemployment:

> Our consideration of employment has been of the factors limiting agricultural incomes and the provision of more opportunities for productive, remunerative employment in the agricultural sectors of developing countries. The question of how much involuntary unemployment there may be in traditional agriculture has been set aside, largely because when involuntary agricultural unemployment is properly defined (and defined in such a way as to be comparable with involuntary industrial unemployment) it becomes almost impossible to measure.

This statement is perhaps too negative, though the difficulties of measuring an improved concept of rural underemployment should not be underestimated.

MEASURING RURAL UNDEREMPLOYMENT: A CASE STUDY[5]

The lack of realism of many rural underemployment estimates can be vividly illustrated by examining some estimates from Haiti and showing how more realistic measures of available labor supply can drastically reduce estimates of the unemployment-equivalent rate (UER).

Rural underemployment in Haiti is widely reported to be a serious

4. Hollis B. Chenery et al., *Redistribution with Growth* (Oxford University Press for the World Bank and the Institute of Development Studies, University of Sussex, 1974), p. xvii.
5. This case study it taken from Clarence Zuvekas, Jr., *Land Tenure, Income, and Employment in Rural Haiti: A Survey*, Working Document No. 2 (Washington, D.C.: Rural Development Division, Bureau for Latin America, U.S. Agency for International Development, March 1978).

problem. One (unidentified) source cited in a report by the U.S. Agency for International Development (AID) has argued that the existing level of agricultural output could be produced by 30 percent of the agricultural labor force, working full time. But as the report noted, this estimate failed to take into account heavy seasonal labor requirements. In other words, removal of 70 percent of the economically active population in agriculture would cause a significant decline in agricultural output given the prevailing labor-intensive technology employed.

Even higher estimates of rural underemployment are made in the Ministry of Agriculture's 1976–1981 Plan, despite the fact that the ministry admits the existence of seasonal labor shortages. Initially, the ministry argues that the economically active population is 70 percent underemployed because the average number of days worked is "less than 120" per year. Later, the average number of days worked is placed at 100, including nonagricultural activities. Using the denominator apparently selected by the ministry, this translates into a UER of 73 percent. Finally, the ministry settles upon a UER of 78 percent, which, it is expected, will be lowered to 63 percent during the course of the plan.

There are a number of problems with the ministry's estimates. (1) No account is taken of the seasonality of labor requirements, and it is thus not possible to determine how many individuals could be considered surplus laborers in the sense that they could be transferred to other economic activities without affecting agricultural production. (2) All members of the economically active population 10 years of age and over are assumed to have the same capacity for work.[6] (3) Some persons reported to be in the economically active population in rural areas are not actively seeking work. (4) The UER refers to the entire economically active population in rural areas (including the 10.7 percent who work outside agriculture), so it is not clear what the UER in agriculture alone might be assumed to be. (5) No allowance is made for potential labor time not available because of poor health. (6) Even if the economically active population were in perfect health, a "normal" work year of 365 days is a rather extreme assumption. (7) Time spent in off-farm employment (including marketing) is almost certainly underestimated.[7] (8)

---

6. The full-time adult-male (15–54) equivalent work force is 81 percent of the total economically active population if we apply the following weights to various categories of rural workers:

Males, 15–54	1.00
Females, 15–54	0.80
All others	0.50

7. A study conducted for AID in the early 1960s estimated that the *average* woman in rural Haiti (not the professional intermediaries) spent 100 days a year in marketing activities. This estimate may be too high, but there is no doubt that marketing was (and still is) a very time-consuming activity.

Time spent in general farm management and household management is very likely underestimated.

Taking just points 2, 3, and 6 into account, the UER estimate can be reduced initially to 58 percent.[8] Further reductions, by considering points 5, 7, and 8, might also be substantial. (Taking point 1 into account in making this kind of adjustment is conceptually awkward, and it is not clear how point 4 would affect the UER in agriculture.)

Another estimate of the UER, in this case specifically for agriculture, may be made by determining labor requirements per hectare for each crop and then multiplying these figures (in work-days) by area under cultivation to yield total labor requirements. The results are then compared with labor supply figures. A comparison of the total labor requirement figure (362,700 work-years), as determined by one international agency, with agricultural employment in 1971 (1,433,202) yields a UER of 74.7 percent. (Actually, the calculated UER should be 72.4 percent. Because of an error in addition, labor requirements were underestimated by 33,300 work-years.) This procedure regards all of the economically active population as having the same work capacity; does not take into account nonagricultural work outside the household by 10 to 20 percent of the employed population; and ignores livestock, forestry, and fishing, which probably account for 10 to 15 percent of sector employment. Another problem is that the normal work-year assumed in making these calculations is 300 days, which this writer regards as too high. Finally, the estimate of land in crops is considerably greater (1,170,000 hectares) than the 1971 census figure for total land area in farms (863,520 hectares —which, admittedly, is too low). Adjustments by another international agency bring this UER estimate down to 48.8 percent, (or 46.5 percent, taking into account the error explained above), and a case can be made for reducing it further by lowering the number of days in the work-year and by taking a skeptical view of the reported land area in crops (and hence labor requirements).

This case study should warn us that estimates of rural underemployment should be regarded with great skepticism. Still, rural underemployment is usually a serious problem in developing countries, and with technological change, as we shall see below, it can increase. But if government policies focus too much on lowering UERs, there is a danger that productivity increases will be ignored; and such increases are necessary for sustained improvements in rural well-being.

8. The labor supply figure is first lowered by 19 percent to cover point 2; the resulting figure is then reduced by 2 percent to cover point 3. Finally, the second adjusted figure is multiplied by .658 to reduce the "normal" work year from 365 to 240 days, which may be considered an appropriate figure given the prevailing technology.

GROWTH AND EMPLOYMENT

One solution to the employment problem, in the opinion of some economists and policy makers, is to accelerate the rate of economic growth. This approach has worked in the developed countries, and at least until the 1970s economists could feel reasonably confident about their ability to determine fairly accurately the employment-inducing effects of economic growth. But while growth will almost always have a positive effect on employment, the magnitude of this effect in developing countries is very difficult to predict. Direct employment effects will be strongly influenced by relative price policies affecting choice of technology, while indirect employment generation will depend on what percentage of factor incomes goes to lower-income groups, who tend to spend a relatively high percentage of their incomes on labor-intensive goods. We shall discuss specific relative-price and income-distribution policies below. For now, however, let us briefly examine a few attempts to estimate how much growth is necessary for developing countries to reach what might be considered a full-employment situation.

In projecting unemployment trends in developing countries between 1965 and 1980, Turnham (1971: 115ff) assumes that the conversion of rural underemployment into open urban unemployment, a trend characteristic of the 1950–1965 period, will continue. Using two alternative assumptions about the historical relationship between output growth and employment growth during 1950–1965, he projects for 1980 increases in unemployment rates of 7 to 12 percentage points for developing countries as a group, assuming a continuation of past trends in the growth of output. A reduction of the unemployment rate from approximately 10 percent in 1965 to 5 percent by 1980 would require, according to Turnham's projections, a rate of growth of output averaging 6.4 percent a year —well above the 4.7 percent rate achieved between 1950–1952 and 1964–1966. For South America, the required growth rate would be 8.3 percent and for Middle America, 9.2 percent. These figures are somewhat higher than the 8 percent growth rate which the noted Argentine economist Raúl Prebisch estimated would have to be sustained for a decade to effectively eliminate unemployment and underemployment in Latin America.[9]

Turnham warns us, however, that an output or growth approach to solving the employment problem is extremely hazardous. An increase in the growth of GDP may simply be accompanied by an acceleration of the growth of labor productivity. If this happens, then a more direct

9. Raúl Prebisch, *Change and Development: Latin America's Great Task* (New York: Praeger Publishers, 1971).

attack on the employment problem is called for. On the other hand, Turnham suggests (p. 117) that "it is very likely that productivity growth will adapt to an important degree to the labour supply becoming available simply because most people will have to have some work." On the whole, "the fact of the matter is that we know very little about the employment/output relationship in less developed countries." Even if low-productivity employment grows rapidly in response to economic growth, the employment problem will not disappear; it will still be manifest as an income distribution problem. Specific policies and programs still would be needed to create higher-productivity jobs in both urban and rural areas.

THE EMPLOYMENT POTENTIAL
OF MANUFACTURING

As we saw in chapter 10, proponents of import-substituting industrialization (ISI) have counted on this development strategy to lower the incidence of unemployment and underemployment in both urban and rural areas. These hopes generally have not been met, both because ISI has proceeded more slowly than expected, and because it has been accompanied by policies which encourage relatively capital-intensive methods of production. Furthermore, the magnitude of the problem—in the face of rapid population growth—has been underestimated by most policymakers.

To illustrate this last point, let us assume that a hypothetical developing country has a total population of 4.8 million and a labor force of 1.6 million. The population is growing by 3 percent annually, and so is the labor force.[10] Employment in modern (nonartisan) manufacturing is 50,000, just 3 percent of the labor force—figures characteristic of a number of developing countries. Now assume that the country's modern manufacturing output is expanding by 12 percent annually, a very rapid rate of increase. Even if employment expands at the same rate (a very unrealistic assumption because of increases in labor productivity over time), the net increase in modern manufacturing jobs in the following year is only 6,000 (50,000 × .12), one-eighth of the total expansion of

---

10. Actually, the labor force is likely to be growing even faster, as falling infant and child mortality rates accelerate the rate at which new entrants into the labor force will appear some 15 years later. Also, greater life expectancy keeps people in the labor force for progressively longer periods of time. (To some extent, however, these trends may be offset by progressively higher secondary and postsecondary enrolment rates—i.e., delayed entry into the labor force.)

the labor force (1,600,000 × .03 = 48,000). Moreover, increased production in modern manufacturing is likely to displace several thousand workers in the artisan subsector.

Even with optimistic assumptions, then, industrial growth cannot be expected to make much of a *direct* contribution to employment in the early years of the development process. There may well be, however, notable indirect and income-induced increases in jobs in the services sector. An oft-cited study by Walter Galenson[11] found that growth of employment in manufacturing is associated with a substantial multiple of new service jobs, the creation of which was attributed to the rapid growth of manufacturing output, even if based on capital-intensive techniques. This implies that capital-intensive techniques may sometimes be preferable to labor-intensive techniques because the demand generated by higher output (and therefore income) will add to services employment more than capital goods take away from direct employment in manufacturing. One should not assume, however, that all of the growth in tertiary employment is attributable to income generation in manufacturing. Part of the growth might also be traced to increased agricultural production or higher government spending. Also, to the extent that capital goods have to be imported, the income- and employment-multiplier effects will take place abroad.

Much of the employment in the services sector, as we noted above, consists of low-paying jobs of a menial nature, providing just enough income on which to subsist. By contrast, capital-intensive firms rely heavily on skilled workers receiving relatively high wages. Thus rapid manufacturing growth based on capital-intensive techniques, while apparently helping to "solve" the unemployment problem, can lead to greater income inequality.

While capital-intensive techniques are unavoidable in some industries, in other cases there is some choice among alternative techniques, in which case profit maximization calls for use of the technique with which a given level of output can be produced at lowest cost. One might assume that developing countries would always choose the most labor-intensive techniques, since labor is the abundant and therefore relatively cheapest factor of production. Government policies, however, often bias business firms' decisions in favor of capital-intensive methods.[12] Some examples are as follows:

---

11. Walter Galenson, "Economic Development and the Sectoral Expansion of Employment," *International Labour Review*, 87 (June 1963), 510–519.
12. These policies are adopted in response to political pressures from business interests, who recognize that government policy can more easily lower the price of capital than the price of labor. In addition, as we note below, organized labor can also promote capital-intensive policies.

1. Tax legislation provides accelerated depreciation and investment credits for capital goods but no similar benefits for the hiring of more labor.
2. Overvalued exchange rates artificially cheapen the price of imported capital goods, which may be further stimulated by low or zero tariffs.
3. Nominal interest rates may be fixed by the government, and during periods of accelerating inflation *real* interest rates become low or even negative, thus stimulating borrowing by industrial firms for the purchase of capital goods.
4. Trade union pressures may lead to increases in wages and legislated fringe benefits in excess of productivity gains. In the absence of a competitive market, and hiding behind high tariff walls, business firms can pass these wage increases on to consumers. At the same time, they will find capital-intensive methods increasingly attractive. Rapid wage increases are of course welcomed very much by those who receive them (and who still are quite poor by developed-country standards), but the effect on *total* employment is negative. Furthermore, a class of privileged workers may be created whose interests may have more in common with the middle classes than with the urban masses.
5. Government policy may favor investment by foreign-based firms accustomed to capital-intensive techniques and unwilling to incur the expenses of developing alternative techniques that use more labor and less capital.

Apart from government policy, there are several other factors which tend to favor capital-intensive methods of production. Foreign loans—which often have a very high grant element (see chapter 14)—typically provide funds only for foreign exchange costs (i.e., imported capital goods) and not for local costs such as labor. Interest rates and loan terms on foreign suppliers' credits for capital goods may be much more favorable than those on short-term bank loans which might be available to hire more labor. Finally, some firms in developing countries (including government corporations) blindly imitate developed-country techniques and fail to search for less costly alternatives. With noncompetitive markets and tariff protection, the high costs of these techniques can readily be passed on to consumers.

A reversal of the government policies noted above could stimulate direct employment in industry without sacrificing output or the indirect employment gains in services. Governments could also encourage research on and development of intermediate technologies more suited to factor endowments in developing countries than highly capital-intensive techniques. International lending agencies could help by making more funds available for local costs.

POLICIES FOR INCREASING RURAL EMPLOYMENT

Disappointment with the limited ability of urban areas to provide reasonably well-paying jobs has led many economists to reconsider the employment potential of agriculture. The Chinese experience with rural development, reviewed in chapter 9, has demonstrated that agricultural modernization via labor-intensive techniques is a most promising way of directly creating jobs. In addition, a development strategy giving high priority to labor-intensive agriculture can contribute to growth and development in several other ways:

1. The foreign exchange costs of industrialization can be lowered if more food and agricultural raw materials are available for local processing.
2. Additional exports can be generated.
3. Agricultural growth would stimulate industrial activity (e.g., food processing, simple machinery and equipment production) in small cities and rural areas, thus easing urbanization problems in the larger cities.
4. Income is likely to be distributed more equally.

A successful employment generation program in rural areas will usually require a redistribution of land, coupled with credit, technical assistance, road construction, changes in marketing, and other programs designed specifically for low-income farmers and based explicitly on the use of labor-intensive techniques. Green Revolutions and other agricultural development programs not based on this approach have sometimes had a negative effect on rural employment. The same might be said of what can be called "indiscriminate mechanization," promoted by the same types of policies which encourage greater capital intensity in industry (ILO 1973).[13]

A labor-intensive strategy of agricultural development requires above all a political commitment to concentrate government resources on programs aimed directly and exclusively at the rural masses. Without this specific focus, the provision of credit, marketing services, improved seeds, roads, or other services is likely to benefit primarily medium- and large-scale farmers. The indirect ("trickle-down") benefits to small farmers will be few, and the employment effects could easily be negative if mechanization or livestock development is encouraged without regard to who the beneficiaries are likely to be.

---

13. This is not to say that all agricultural mechanization has negative effects. Where it permits farmers to plant two annual crops instead of one, mechanization can increase the demand for labor (see chapter 9).

Needless to say, a strong political commitment to small farmers is difficult to make, since governments in most developing countries are more responsive to—and often sympathetic with—the demands of the politically more powerful large farmers. Even in Mexico, where the principles of the 1910 revolution commit the government to serving the rural poor, and where agricultural growth has been more rapid than in most developing countries, underemployment has become a serious problem because the government's policies have in fact favored the larger farmers. Between 1950 and 1960, the number of landless rural laborers in Mexico increased from 2.3 to 3.3 million, while their average yearly days of work fell sharply from 194 to 100 and their real earnings declined from $68 to $56.[14]

Does this mean that a significant and rapid improvement in rural employment (and, more importantly, in the level of living of the rural masses) requires a social and political revolution? Perhaps it does. But the potential for true revolution exists only in a few countries, and where the rural employment picture does improve, it is more likely to do so slowly through reformist policies. This prediction may be discouraging or unpleasant, but to this writer that is what the historical record suggests.

Reformist policies may be adopted for several reasons. Conservative governments without the means for effectively suppressing rural unrest may conclude that this unrest can be defused only by making some concessions (colonization programs, roads, higher farm prices, credit, etc.) to the rural masses. Where political power becomes more widely shared among the various socioeconomic interest groups, moderate governments more sympathetic to the plight of the small farmer will come to power. Some international assistance agencies have committed themselves to focusing on the rural poor, and an increasing share of their budgets is being channeled in this direction. If, for any given country, a significant amount of money is made available, these agencies can exercise considerable leverage on a government's rural development policies.

The reformist approach cannot be expected to accomplish miracles in reducing the incidence of rural unemployment and underemployment. But modest improvements can be hoped for if appropriate measures are adopted. Among the more important steps that could be taken is a change in policies toward mechanization, along the lines suggested in chapter 9. As an alternative to mechanization, governments could give more attention to the adoption of what Yudelman, Butler, and Banerji (1971: 47–52) call "land-augmenting innovations"—i.e., innovations which increase output per unit of land. Evidence reviewed by these authors for

14. James P. Grant, "Accelerating Progress through Social Justice," *International Development Review*, 14 (1972/3), 2–9.

India and the Philippines (pp. 70–78) suggests that the introduction of high-yielding seed varieties, fertilizers, other chemical inputs, and irrigation increased labor use by perhaps 20 to 50 percent, other things being equal. A study by the Inter-American Development Bank reported that one community in Bolivia increased labor utilization by 30 percent simply by applying fertilizer to potato production. Land-augmenting innovations could be promoted directly through supervised credit programs, or indirectly encouraged by road construction and other activities that improve farmers' access to markets.

Government policy might also seek to expand rural employment opportunities in nonagricultural activities. Many countries have experimented with programs to increase artisan and handicraft production, but these efforts have generally had disappointing results. Export markets for these products are very competitive, and a significant breakthrough requires a degree of marketing organization that is difficult to achieve.

Little hope should likewise be held out for increasing rural employment opportunities through policies designed to promote a wide geographic dispersion of modern manufacturing activity. Even generous tax incentives often cannot overcome the locational disadvantages of rural areas or smaller urban centers, particularly from the point of view of transport costs and supporting services. At some point, of course, a subsidy will be high enough to stimulate geographic dispersion, but the cost might be difficult to justify even under liberal interpretations of social benefits. To be sure, there may be a few new opportunities for processing agricultural products in areas of high rural underemployment, but for many years manufacturing activities are likely to remain concentrated in the larger cities. Moreover, new agricultural processing activities in the smaller cities or in rural areas are likely to depend on the prior expansion of local agricultural output, income, and employment. Only where the government is willing to establish its own manufacturing enterprises outside the large cities is there much hope that this strategy will have a significant effect on rural employment within a reformist framework.

Finally, we may consider the employment-generation possibilities of rural public works projects, which many writers believe have great potential for absorbing seasonally idle labor—and increasing rural levels of living. Project possibilities include secondary and tertiary road construction, irrigation works, crop storage facilities, school construction, and tree planting and terracing to combat soil erosion. The labor for such projects will usually have to be remunerated in cash or in kind, but its opportunity cost can be regarded as very low or even zero for purposes of making social B/C calculations.

While there are good reasons to be optimistic about the potential of off-season employment opportunities of this kind, it should be noted that experiences with rural public works projects in developing countries have been mixed. Successful projects require not only money but also careful planning that takes into account what individual communities would most like to have. Care must also be taken to ensure that materials and other inputs not available in local areas can be obtained elsewhere on a timely basis. The amount of labor available, and precisely when it is available, must be accurately determined. Workers who are idle during periods of heavy rainfall cannot be used for projects which can be undertaken only when rainfall is scant. Above all, public works projects must be based on the kind of jobs that will create permanent, income-generating infrastructure.

Notwithstanding the many difficulties that rural public works projects might encounter, there is a good case for greater government attention to them. These projects are particularly attractive because they can be selected in such a way as to concentrate the direct and indirect benefits on particular target groups. Although much of the work thus provided would be of a one-time-only nature, some permanent maintenance jobs will have been created. Even more important are likely to be the income-induced jobs which would result from the higher farm incomes that rural infrastructure can make possible.

A major rural public works program would not be inexpensive. Heavy financial commitments, as well as commitments of scarce managerial resources, would be necessary. Even if a government's revenues are rising and foreign assistance is available, such a program would have to compete against other increasing claims on the budget. Individual projects would be economically justified only if their B/C ratio or internal rate of return exceeded those of alternative projects designed to increase rural employment and incomes.

SUMMARY

Even in developing countries where rapid economic growth has occurred, high rates of unemployment and underemployment have persisted. This lingering problem has become a serious policy concern of governments in these countries. A generation ago, developing countries were counting heavily on industry to make a major direct contribution to reducing unemployment and underemployment rates. But industrial growth, though it has accelerated, has been slower than developing countries had hoped, and wittingly or not, developing countries have pursued industrial development policies which have caused employment to grow much more slowly than output. With industry not fulfilling its promise, increasing attention is being paid to agriculture and rural development as additional sources of employment opportunities.

Though employment is undeniably important as a policy objective, there is danger in a policy which emphasizes only an improvement in employment statistics—i.e., the quantity of employment. This could result in the creation of a host of low-productivity, dead-end jobs in which individuals have little opportunity for advancement. Lower unemployment and underemployment statistics could thus be accompanied over time by greater income inequality, little change in the absolute income of the poor, and increased social and political tensions. Policies focusing on income and productivity are more appropriate for improving the level of living of the masses. Increases in the rate of economic growth can help alleviate the employment/income problem, but often the number of new jobs created by growth policies alone is not large. In these cases, a reduction of unemployment rates and/or a decline in the proportion of those living below the poverty line will require the adoption of programs directed specifically toward the urban and rural poor.

Narrowing income inequalities and alleviating the employment problem are difficult tasks. What is needed most of all is the political will radically to alter existing policies, and this will is lacking in most of the developing world. Political revolution may establish strong employment policies in a few countries; but in most, changes in employment and income distribution are likely to be slow. Nevertheless, greater concern about these issues is influencing the policies of both national governments and international assistance agencies, and it is possible that this will soon result in modest improvements in the employment picture in a number of countries.

Suggested Readings

Edwards, Edgar O., ed. *Employment in Developing Nations*. Report on a Ford Foundation Study. New York: Columbia University Press, 1974.

> The twenty papers in this volume were sponsored by the Ford Foundation in an effort to evaluate alternative strategies for increasing both urban and rural employment in developing countries. In addition to the papers focusing on specific policies or sectors of the economy, there are case studies of Indonesia, India, China, and Chile.

International Labour Office (ILO). *Employment, Growth, and Basic Needs: A One World Problem*. Foreword by James P. Grant. New York: Praeger Publishers for the Overseas Development Council and the ILO, 1977.

> This book discusses the ILO's "basic needs" strategy, prepared for the 1976 World Employment Conference and endorsed in principle by the conference. This strategy is based on the premise that all people are entitled to minimum levels of personal consumption and access to social services.

————. *Mechanization and Employment in Agriculture: Case Studies from Four Continents.* Geneva: ILO, 1973.

The authors of the seven papers in this volume (including case studies of East Africa, Latin America, the Philippines, Sri Lanka, Pakistan, and southern Italy) agree that "distorted factor prices, resulting from overvalued currencies, low or negative interest rates, subsidized international aid programmes, etc., have encouraged a premature and socially undesirable substitution of capital for labour, especially on large holdings."

Turnham, David, assisted by Ingelies Jaeger. *The Employment Problem in Less Developed Countries: A Review of Evidence.* Development Center Studies, Employment Series No. 1. Paris: Organisation for Economic Cooperation and Development, 1971.

This is an excellent summary and interpretation of evidence from all parts of the developing world on the nature and extent of the employment problem. Especially valuable are the discussions of the poor quality of the data, which lead Turnham to advocate an income approach to the employment problem. Other topics of interest include discussions of rural-urban wage differentials, the employment implications of the Green Revolution, and the relationship between nutrition and productivity.

Yudelman, Montague, Gavan Butler, and Ranadev Banerji. *Technological Change in Agriculture and Employment in Developing Countries.* Employment Series No. 4. Paris: Organisation for Economic Cooperation and Development, 1971.

The authors review the literature on employment and technological change in agriculture and stress the importance of additional job creation in agriculture in the face of rapid increases in the labor force and the limited employment potential of manufacturing. They show that yield-increasing innovations can increase labor utilization. Mechanization often reduces the demand for labor, but selective use of machinery can sometimes intensify land use and thus expand employment.

13

Financing Development
Mobilizing Domestic Savings

Investment in physical and human capital must be matched by savings, either from domestic sources or from abroad. If growth is to be sustained and self-generating, most of the savings will have to come from the domestic economy. Foreign savings can be useful as a source of financing for domestic investment, but in some countries it has been viewed merely as a substitute for local resources. This can result in an unhealthy dependence—political as well as economic—on foreign savings from both public and private sources. Lack of domestic savings effort may also threaten future receipts of foreign savings. Private investors will worry about repayment prospects, while multilateral and bilateral agencies generally require "counterpart" contributions by the country receiving project assistance.[1] If receipts of foreign savings thus become erratic, and additional domestic resources are not mobilized when foreign savings decline, economic growth will be affected adversely.

There are two basic ways in which governments can attempt to increase domestic savings rates. First, they can encourage greater savings by the private sector—i.e., households and businesses. For this approach to be successful, incentives must be provided to induce people to forego consumption, and financial institutions must be established to mobilize savings and channel them into productive investments.

---

1. This is not to say that foreign assistance will always be denied when domestic savings efforts are weak. First, the dominant motives for bilateral assistance continue to be political. Second, aid motivated by genuine humanitarian concerns is increasing in importance and is provided with little regard for domestic savings efforts. Still, other things being equal, there is no doubt that failure to provide sufficient counterpart funds (a) slows cash disbursements under projects already approved by public assistance agencies, (b) delays the approval of funds for new projects, and (3) reduces, over the long run, the flow of public resources from abroad.

The second approach to mobilizing savings is for the government directly to appropriate private-sector income. Taxation is the most obvious method, but it is not the only one. The Soviet Union "squeezed" savings out of the agricultural sector a half century ago by forcing farmers to give up private plots and to join collective farms. The output of these farms was then purchased by the government at low prices to provide inexpensive food for industrial workers and to sell abroad to earn foreign exchange for the purchase of machinery. Similarly, as we noted in chapter 9, Argentina squeezed savings from agriculture in the late 1940s by establishing a state trading corporation which purchased selected farm products at relatively low prices and sold them in world markets at the high prices prevailing at that time. The savings thus appropriated were used primarily to finance an industrialization program. Other countries have used different kinds of forced savings schemes, among which compulsory social security contributions are the most common.

No government, of course, relies exclusively on one or the other approach. All use a combination of the two, the mixture depending largely on the political stance of the government and the attitudes of the population toward the two approaches. In any event, it is important to remember that the role of government is decisive. Even if primary emphasis is given to the first approach, financial institutions must have a favorable policy environment to develop and flourish.

THE SAVINGS CAPACITY
OF DEVELOPING COUNTRIES

We have seen, in chapters 2 and 3, that savings rates in developing countries are low not just because of low incomes (the "vicious circle of poverty" theory) but to a very large degree because of social and political factors and a very uneven distribution of income. As Arthur Lewis (1955: 236) has put it:

> No nation is so poor that it could not save 12 per cent of its national income if it wanted to; poverty has never prevented nations from launching upon wars, or from wasting their substance in other ways. Least of all can those nations plead poverty as an excuse for not saving, in which 40 per cent or so of the national income is squandered by the top 10 per cent of income receivers, living luxuriously on rents.

This is not to say that a development-minded government can relatively easily capture potential savings. The Soviet Union, as noted above, had to resort to armed force, at a considerable cost in human lives and the size of livestock herds (which, ironically, constituted disinvestment in both cases). Other countries, such as Japan and China in the years immediately after their respective revolutions (1868 and 1949), relied heavily on the threat of physical force if not actual force.

From the point of view of the individual, there is often little incentive to increase savings, or to convert existing wealth from physical assets (i.e., land and livestock) to financial assets. Even if individuals have the financial capacity to save, they may lack the psychological capacity, particularly if they see little prospect for improvement in their lives and if existing financial institutions are not trusted. Increasing the psychological capacity to save—by creating economic opportunities, financial incentives, and financial institutions that will be trusted—is no easy task.

RECENT TRENDS IN DOMESTIC AND FOREIGN SAVINGS

Table 13.1 shows that the domestic savings rate for developing countries as a group rose from 12.8 percent of GDP during 1951–1960 to 17.0 percent during 1961–1970. Though many developing countries were disappointed that their savings rates did not rise more rapidly, this overall increase of 4.2 percentage points is quite impressive in comparison with the increases in savings rates estimated to have occurred in the now-developed countries during the nineteenth century.[2]

The rise in developing countries' domestic savings rates continued into the early 1970s, reaching an average of 19.3 percent during 1971–1973. Subsequently, however, a sharp increase in petroleum prices and the onset of world recession slowed GDP growth rates in the developing countries and resulted in a sharp drop in the average domestic savings rate to 15.8 percent in 1974 and probably an even lower figure in 1975.[3]

The decline in savings rates was particularly severe in the low-income developing countries. Moreover, it began earlier in many of these countries, as a series of poor harvests and rising food prices in the early 1970s diverted resources from savings to consumption. In the sample of ten low-income developing countries covered by the data in Table 13.1, domestic savings fell from a weighted average of 14.7 percent of GDP during 1961–1970 to 13.8 percent during 1971–1973 and 9.7 percent in 1974.

Domestic savings rates in the middle-income developing countries are higher than in the low-income countries, and they continued to rise during

2. See Simon Kuznets, "Quantitative Aspects of the Economic Growth of Nations—VI: Long-Term Trends in Capital Formation Proportions," *Economic Development and Cultural Change*, 9, No. 4, Part II (July 1961), 1–124. Kuznets focuses on investment rates, but it is clear from the data that domestic savings rates, too, generally rose slowly.

3. Table 13.1 does not provide data for 1975, but Bhatt and Meerman (1978: 46–47) report that data from a limited number of countries suggest that the savings rate for developing countries as a group continued to decline in 1975.

TABLE 13.1
Gross Investment and Its Financing in Developing Countries, 1951–1974
(*percent of GDP*)

	1951–60	1961–70	1971–73	1974
All Developing Countries				
Gross Investment	14.9	19.2	20.8	21.5
Domestic Savings	12.8	17.0[c]	19.3	15.8
Foreign Savings	2.1	2.2[c]	1.7	5.2
Selected Middle-Income Developing Countries[a]				
Gross Investment	—	20.0	21.6	23.2
Domestic Savings	—	18.8	19.9	17.7
Foreign Savings	—	1.3	1.8	5.6
Selected Low-Income Developing Countries[b]				
Gross Investment	—	17.0	15.6[d]	15.8[d]
Domestic Savings	—	14.7	13.8	9.7
Foreign Savings	—	2.3	1.8	6.2

Source: Bhatt and Meerman (1978: 47).

[a] Egypt, Syria, Tunisia, Greece, Turkey, and Yugoslavia in the Mediterranean; Cameroon, Ghana, Ivory Coast, Senegal, and Sierra Leone in West Africa; South Korea, the Philippines, Thailand, and Malaysia in East Asia; and Argentina, Brazil, Colombia, the Dominican Republic, Guatemala, Mexico, Peru, and Uruguay in Latin America.
[b] India, Bangladesh, Sri Lanka, and Pakistan in South Asia; Kenya, Tanzania, Uganda, Ethiopia, Mali, and Sudan in East Africa.
[c] The figures in Table 1 of the source actually are 18.4 and 1.4, respectively; but the discussion in the text indicates that they should be 17.0 and 2.2. The original table also seems to report several other figures inaccurately. The sum of domestic and foreign savings does not always add to gross investment, for reasons that are unexplained; and other figures in the text do not correspond with those in Table 1.
[d] Based on data reported on p. 63 of the source.

the early 1970s. For the twenty-three countries in this category for which data are presented in Table 13.1, the weighted average domestic savings rate reached 19.9 percent during 1971–1973 before falling to 17.7 percent in 1974. Table 13.2 shows the savings rates for these middle-income countries by region.

TABLE 13.2
Savings Rates by Major World Region,
1971–1973 and 1974

	1971–73	1974
Mediterranean	18.6	13.5
Latin America	19.7	18.2
East Asia	22.1	21.0
West Africa	16.9	19.0

Source: Bhatt and Meerman (1978: 62–63).

In general, the decline in domestic savings rates in 1974 was not as great in the middle-income countries as in the low-income countries, and savings rates in West Africa actually increased. In the Mediterranean region, however, domestic savings rates declined sharply, especially in Egypt, Greece, and Yugoslavia.

As might be expected, the OPEC countries have experienced sharp increases in domestic savings rates as a result of the petroleum price increases they imposed in 1973 and 1974. Data in the World Bank's *Annual Report* for 1977 show that gross national savings in the North Africa–Middle East region rose from an average of 26 percent of GNP during 1966–1972 to 41 percent during 1973–1975.

For developing countries as a group, the decline in the domestic savings rate in 1974 was more than offset by an increase in foreign savings—i.e., the deficit in the current account of the balance of payments—from 1.7 percent of the GDP during 1971–1973 to 5.2 percent in 1974.[4] The investment rate thus continued to rise, even in many of the low-income countries. However, the increase in foreign savings occurred to a large extent through short-term borrowing, use of regular and special borrowing facilities in the International Monetary Fund (see chapter 15), and the drawing down of foreign exchange reserves. Clearly, foreign savings of this magnitude cannot be relied on for more than a few years. Over the long run, present investment rates can be maintained only if additional domestic savings are mobilized.

THE STRUCTURE OF DOMESTIC SAVINGS

In the centrally planned developing countries, public savings tend to be more important than private savings, though the absence of good data often makes it difficult to determine the relative importance of each. Elsewhere in the developing world, most domestic savings are mobilized through the private sector, with public savings generally accounting for less than 25 percent of the total and only 2 to 3 percent of GDP. There are important exceptions, however, such as Brazil, South Korea, and Yugoslavia (Bhatt and Meerman, 1978: 48).

Private savings are mobilized from both corporate and noncorporate sources, with the latter including households as well as small businesses. Corporate savings tend to be relatively small, as in the developed coun-

4. The 1971–1974 foreign savings figures in Table 13.1 are of questionable reliability since foreign and domestic savings combined do not add to the reported total investment figures.

tries,[5] while noncorporate savings usually account for more than half of total domestic savings.

MOBILIZATION OF PRIVATE SAVINGS: THE "FINANCIAL LIBERALIZATION" APPROACH

In the view of some economists, notably Edward Shaw (1973) and Ronald McKinnon (1973), the most effective steps that governments can take to stimulate the mobilization of private savings constitute what frequently is called "financial liberalization"—i.e., the dismantling of government controls over financial markets. Shaw regards liberalization as the key to "financial deepening," the "accumulation of financial assets at a pace faster than the accumulation of nonfinancial wealth" (1973: vii). Money and relative prices, Shaw argues, do matter in the development process, and financial liberalization—if coupled with fiscal policy reforms and other measures—can contribute positively to economic growth and development.

In the following paragraphs, we shall discuss four aspects of financial liberalization—(1) the provision of positive real interest rates, (2) control of inflation, (3) market-determined exchange rates, and (4) fiscal policy reforms—and assess the importance of their contributions to the mobilization of private domestic savings.

Interest Rate Policies

Savings are often discouraged by regulations which limit the interest rates at which banks and other financial institutions can lend money. These "usury laws," as they are sometimes called, are justified as protection for the poor. However, even when they actually benefit the wealthy much more than the poor—as is common in developing countries— interest-rate regulations continue to enjoy widespread political support. By making money available at less than the opportunity cost of capital— thought to be at least 8 to 15 percent in most developing countries— usury laws restrict the supply of savings by limiting the interest rates financial institutions can afford to pay depositors. Furthermore, if interest rates are below those that would prevail in unregulated markets, credit will have to be rationed since the quantity demanded exceeds the quantity supplied. The problem here is that private credit in developing coun-

5. During 1960–1969, corporate savings in France, West Germany, Japan, and the United States averaged only 2.3 to 4.7 percent of the GDP (Bhatt and Meerman, 1978: 52).

tries often is rationed on the basis of social and political considerations rather than economic merit. This writer has worked in several countries where a high proportion of "agricultural production credit" actually finances luxury consumption by the rich on heavily subsidized terms. Reforming the structure of interest rates will not eliminate such problems, but it should reduce their incidence.

Another problem with low interest rates is that they artificially encourage the substitution of capital for labor by lowering the relative price of the former. This not only has unfavorable consequences for employment but also increases the real (social) resource cost of production.

This is not to say that there is no place for subsidized interest rates in the process of growth or development. Indeed, they can be useful for achieving specific objectives, such as increased exports and—under certain circumstances—higher incomes for small farmers.[6] But if interest rates *generally* are well below market rates, savings will be discouraged.

Several developing countries have attempted to encourage domestic savings by substantially raising interest rates. The most dramatic example is South Korea, whose 1965 reforms were strongly influenced by the recommendations of Shaw and other like-minded advisors. Though the recommendation to pay interest on demand deposits was resisted, interest rates on time deposits were sharply increased, along with bank lending rates.[7] Largely in response to these reforms, private savings, virtually zero in 1964, rose to 8 percent of the GNP in 1969. Financial deepening occurred as the real money stock (M_2, or currency and demand deposits, plus time deposits) increased sevenfold over this period, amounting to 33 percent of the GNP in 1969 (still well below the U.S. figure in the same year of 64 percent). Despite higher real bank lending rates, private investment rose rapidly, as "large scale financing from organized sources became available to many [South] Korean enterprises in industry and agriculture for the first time, and contributed to the extraordinary growth in [South] Korean real output" (McKinnon, in McKinnon, ed., 1976: 76).

The South Korean experience, while impressive, was not without its problems. These have occurred, say Shaw and McKinnon, because liberalization did not go far enough. Specifically, McKinnon traces the resurgence of inflation in 1972 to the subsidized interest rates which exporters continued to pay, even after the 1965 reforms. As commercial banks liberally discounted export paper with the Central Bank, control over the

6. As noted in chapter 9, a low-interest-rate policy can be counterproductive as a means of raising small farmer income.

7. The weighted average of nominal interest rates on time deposits was increased to 24 percent, about double the previous figure. The "standard" nominal bank lending rate was raised from 14 to 26 percent (McKinnon, in McKinnon, ed., 1976: 76).

monetary base was lost. Investment continued to be strong, but investors found foreign long-term financing to be increasingly more attractive than domestic financing at high nominal interest rates.[8]

Controlling Inflation

There is a good deal of controversy about the effects of inflation on economic growth and development. Some economists, focusing on the demand for long-term loanable funds, have argued that investment is stimulated when inflation is accelerating because the real costs of interest and principal repayments are lowered. If noimnal interest rates are controlled, real interest rates might even become negative. Brazil and other countries have managed to sustain relatively high rates of growth even with rapid inflation. The financial liberalization school, however, argues that inflation has a negative effect on economic growth. Focusing on the supply side of the market, these economists maintain that the "inflation tax" discourages savings by reducing the real value of time deposits— an argument supported by a recent study of Latin American countries (Vogel and Buser, in McKinnon, ed., 1976: 35–70).[9] Inflation, it is said, causes domestic finanical assets (demand as well as time deposits) to be converted to consumption goods, relatively unproductive investment goods such as housing, and foreign financial assets. If the exchange rate is fixed, as is common under what Shaw calls "shallow finance," the domestic currency will become overvalued if the domestic inflation rate exceeds the rise in international prices. This makes exports less competitive and imports more attractive, and leads the country toward a balance-of-payments crisis.

One way of trying to overcome the disincentive effects of inflation on savings is to introduce *indexing* of government bonds and other financial instruments. Indexing has been used most notably by Brazil and provides for periodic upward adjustment of the nominal value of financial assets (e.g., bonds and savings accounts) so that their real value is maintained in the face of inflation. Most observers, however, believe that the benefits of indexation—at least in Brazil—have been exaggerated.[10] Opponents of indexation argue that it tends to institutionalize inflation and does not attack its basic causes.

---

8. Foreign loans, with an exchange rate guarantee provided by the Korean government or banks at a relatively low cost, could be obtained in the late 1960s at interest rates of 8 to 10 percent.

9. However, there was no conclusive evidence that inflation affected capital formation.

10. See, for example, Jack D. Guenther, " 'Indexing' versus Discretionary Action— Brazil's Fight against Inflation," *Finance and Development*, 12 (September 1975), 24–29.

Exchange-rate Policies

All too often, Shaw (1973: 221) argues, "lagging economies have chosen the worst of foreign-exchange regimes, disequilibrium money with excess demand repressed ineffectively by interventions." Attempts to maintain fixed exchange rates in the face of rapid, internally generated inflation ultimately will fail, and countries will be forced into massive devaluations, preceded by capital flight and requiring the adoption of a stabilization program in order to obtain balance-of-payments assistance from the International Monetary Fund (IMF).[11] The devaluation itself will raise the domestic price of both imports and exportables, and as flight capital flows back into the country, it provides a base for further monetary expansion. The inflationary impact of devaluation can be minimized if a country takes steps to restrict demand for goods and services by limiting monetary expansion, curtailing bank credit, and adopting other restraints in accordance with its agreement with the IMF. This will cause the economy to go into recession, with the poorest segments of the population tending to suffer the most. Often the social and political impact of the devaluation is such that the restraints are soon loosed. Angry workers are placated with wage increases, which employers pass on to consumers as higher prices, and deficit spending by the government increases. As growth resumes, governments tend to turn more to foreign savings than domestic savings, and the foreign exchange brought into the country in this fashion contributes to even greater expansion of the nominal money supply. A balance-of-payments crisis will occur again as inflation discourages exports and encourages imports, and this will result in another devaluation.

This "stop-go" pattern of economic growth in a crisis context, Shaw argues, "is not congenial for financial deepening and acceleration of private savings, more effective fiscal effort, and reallocation of resources to market opportunities at the new exchange rate" (p. 221). Developing countries can avoid many of these problems and stimulate private savings, he maintains, if they abandon fixed exchange rates, let their currencies fluctuate freely in accordance with market forces, and eliminate restrictions on private capital movements. The freeing of exchange rates presumably should occur when the economy is healthy, for if it is done during a period of crisis the effects will be very much the same as those of a massive devaluation.

This is not the place for an extended debate on the relative merits of flexible versus fixed exchange rates. Suffice it to say that events since

---

11. Political leaders, with good reason, fear the political consequences of devaluation, which tends to be viewed as a sign of weakness.

1971 suggest that the dangers of destabilizing speculation and other risks of exchange-rate flexibility have been exaggerated. Flexible exchange rates alone, however, will be insufficient to encourage greater savings. Positive real interest rates and appropriate financial institutions are also needed. Shaw argues, in fact, that the optimal strategy is to institute the full gamut of liberalizations "almost at once" (p. 251). Going this far, however, is probably politically unacceptable to most governments. Exchange-rate flexibility will be resisted by importers and industrialists who benefit from overvalued exchange rates (and who may be politically powerful), and governments are well aware that currency devaluation or depreciation is politically risky because of the social unrest it generates. Weak governments will avoid bold, everything-at-once actions, though they may be willing to implement some liberalization measures. It is no accident that the countries Shaw cites as examples where financial liberalization is occurring—Mexico, Taiwan, South Korea, Indonesia, Yugoslavia, Brazil, Iran, Malaysia (p. 113)—all have been led by a single, strong political party or clique for at least fourteen consecutive years.[12]

Fiscal Policy Reforms

Shaw regards fiscal policy reforms as a major component of a financial liberalization program. Tax systems in developing countries, he notes, are often inelastic with respect to income, and inelasticity combined with political pressures for government spending causes budget deficits which are covered by inflationary financing. Inflation, in turn, reduces the real value of demand and savings deposits. The fiscal systems of most developing countries contain a variety of subsidies to industrialists and other interest groups, and many of these subsidies are of questionable merit in terms of benefits to society at large in comparison with revenue foregone. Still, this writer sees more scope for subsidies than does Shaw, who is too sanguine about the ability of product, factor, and financial markets in developing countries to function efficiently on their own.

Concluding Remarks

Financial liberalization can make a major contribution to the mobilization of domestic savings, but this writer would not endorse it as unreservedly

12. It may also be no accident that economic *growth* has been rapid in all these countries, with annual rates of growth of per capita GNP ranging from 2.4 to 8.1 percent during 1960–1975 (*World Bank Atlas 1977*). The income distribution record, though, is mixed. Relatively low degrees of income inequality in South Korea do not appear to have been affected adversely since liberalization; but income distribution in Mexico and Brazil, already very unequal before liberalization, seems to have become even more skewed since these measures were adopted.

or with the same messianic fervor that Shaw brings to the subject. First, there are serious social and political constraints to liberalization in many developing countries, and the objectives of liberalization can easily be thwarted by opponents of measures which suddenly free markets that have been tightly regulated. Second, while liberalization may have a positive effect on economic growth, measures to reduce inflationary pressures (e.g., wage controls and credit restrictions) tend to discriminate against the lower-income segments of the population, thus widening income inequalities. While Shaw would argue that this effect is only temporary, experience in Latin American countries suggests that higher degrees of inequality may persist. Third, liberalization may encourage the type of private investment that makes income distribution more unequal. Finally, the strong antigovernment bias evident in Shaw's writings implies a limited scope for using public investment to narrow income inequalities and to accomplish other social and economic objectives. While Shaw is correct in pointing out that governments in developing countries all too often use increased tax revenues for consumption purposes rather than investment, this is not a necessary consequence of public resource mobilization. Moreover, some individuals would regard certain types of government consumption to be socially more desirable than private investment in industries producing durable goods which only the upper and middle classes can afford to buy.

Despite these reservations, the case for some liberalization remains strong if discretion is used to minimize adverse short-term effects on income distribution. We have already argued, in chapter 9, that heavily subsidized interest rates in agriculture are counterproductive for increasing small farmers' incomes over the long run. Shaw himself points out that overvalued exchange rates and subsidized credit to industry artificially encourage capital-intensive technologies at the expense of employment and income-distribution objectives. Finally, there is ample evidence that individual savings will increase significantly if positive real rates of interest are offered to depositors.

MOBILIZING PRIVATE SAVINGS: OTHER GOVERNMENT ACTIONS

Since an important share of private savings generally is contributed by businesses, governments can attempt to increase business savings by policy actions favorable to private firms. Tax incentives—e.g., accelerated depreciation allowances, tax credits for the purchase of capital goods, or tariff reductions—are frequently used for this purpose. While this form of subsidy can be justified on the grounds that it offsets the disincentive effects of imperfect capital markets (which make the cost of borrowing high), indiscriminate use of tax incentives can have high social and economic costs. First, tax incentives may stimulate foreign savings and investment more than domestic savings and investment. Second, tax incentives tend to be provided for the purchase of machinery and equipment but not for the hiring of labor. Thus they artificially stimulate the use of the scarce factor of production. Since a high percentage of capital goods will be imported, tax incentives also have unfavorable balance-of-payments implications. Third, problems are created for the government budget, which would be faced with a decline in tax revenues. Carefully and selectively applied to specific industries, tax incentives can be an important tool for mobilizing savings. All too often, however, selectivity is based not on economic considerations but rather on responses to pressures from specific business interests.

A more promising form of government action is to encourage the formation or expansion of capital markets. The absence or small size of stock and bond exchanges makes it difficult for businesses to expand by offering debt or equity issues to the general public.[13] While governments may not wish to directly operate securities exchanges, they can facilitate their development by passing enabling legislation or decrees, subsidizing technical assistance, and floating their own securities on the exchanges to help attract attention to these markets.

Governments can also encourage the development of cooperatives, credit unions, savings and loan associations, and other private institutions to mobilize the savings of lower- and middle-income groups. Many developing countries have taken advantage of technical assistance provided by the U.S. Agency for International Development and other foreign donor agencies for the establishment of these institutions, and the results have often been encouraging. While savings and loan associations have directly benefited middle-income groups almost exclusively, a secondary effect has been the creation of a considerable number of jobs in housing construction, thus benefiting lower-income workers as well. Cooperatives, credit unions, and savings clubs provide direct benefits to lower-income groups and often constitute an important source of credit for both rural and urban residents.

Governments sometimes choose to play a more direct role in the mobilization of small savings. Postal savings schemes, for example, have made significant contributions to domestic savings in Japan and Taiwan, and they have also been successful in some African countries.

---

13. It should be pointed out that many businesses in developing countries are family owned, and the owners are often reluctant to expand ownership beyond a small circle of family and friends. Businesses willing to go public, however, are restricted by the lack of capital markets.

As we noted in chapters 2 and 3, a substantial savings capacity exists even in the poorest countries and among very low-income groups in middle-income developing countries. In Taiwan, a farm household survey found that the average propensity to save (APS) ranged from .19 to .31 for all households during the period 1960–1974. Farmers with only 0.5 hectares of land or less had an APS of −.03 in 1960, but in subsequent years their APS has ranged from .08 to .21. Farm household surveys in other developing countries have found the APS to be .11 to .33 in South Korea (during 1966–1974, after a low of .04 in 1965, the year of that country's financial liberalization measures); .06 in West Malaysia; .12 to .37 in the Punjab of India; more than .30 in parts of Zambia; and .11 to .14 in one rural area in Ethiopia. Similar savings potential exists in most other developing countries, but in the absence of financial institutions much of this potential will not be translated into productive investment. According to Dale Adams, a leading rural credit specialist with experience in many developing countries, "the key element in a savings mobilization program [through rural financial markets] is the attractiveness of the reward paid on savings. Convenience, liquidity, and security of the savings, however, strongly complement the return paid."[14]

Another major type of financial intermediary is the life insurance company, an institution virtually unknown in many developing countries and relatively unimportant in most others. While life insurance might understandably be considered a luxury by all but a tiny percentage of the population in most developing countries, there is considerable scope for expansion of this form of savings in the wealthier ones. In Latin America, credit unions and other types of cooperatives have successfully used life insurance to mobilize savings.[15] Some governments might wish to consider direct operation of life-insurance schemes.

Governments have experimented with a variety of other measures to encourage greater private savings. To stimulate markets for long-term finance, Brazil has allowed taxpayers to substitute purchase of securities for tax liabilities, and Pakistan engages in open-market operations to stabilize equity prices (Shaw, 1973: 142). To some extent, these and the other measures described above can mobilize private savings independently of financial liberalization. But liberalization probably enhances their effectiveness, particularly if it emphasizes interest rate reforms and is not undertaken in a crisis atmosphere which results in the adoption of measures that cause real income of lower- and middle-income groups to fall.

14. Dale W. Adams, "Mobilizing Household Savings through Rural Financial Markets," *Economic Development and Cultural Change*, 26 (April 1978), 559. The savings data cited above in this paragraph are taken from this article.
15. Ibid.

TAXATION

Although governments in most developing countries have assumed an active role in stimulating economic growth or development, their share of the GNP is not as great, on the average, as might be supposed. A survey of government finances in forty-seven developing countries found that the average ratio of tax collections to GNP during 1969–1971 was a modest 15 percent, compared with 26 percent for sixteen developed countries in Europe and North America. If social security contributions are included, the difference is even greater: 16 percent in the developing countries and 34 percent in the developed countries. For individual developing countries, the tax ratio ranged from a high of 31.3 percent in Zambia to only 4.4 percent in Nepal (see Table 13.3).[16]

Duties on imports and exports are the most important source of tax revenue in developing countries generally, and in fourteen of the forty-seven countries in the study noted above they accounted for more than 40 percent of total tax revenues (see Table 13.4). As a general rule, the less developed the country, the more it relies on foreign trade for tax revenues. This pattern is explained by the following factors. (1) Income is difficult to tax if a high proportion is received in nonmonetary form, and the sales tax potential is limited by the high incidence of subsistence farming and barter transactions characteristic of the poorer developing countries. (2) Effective income and sales tax systems require administrative skills that are in short supply in developing countries. (3) Significant taxes on property are politically almost impossible to collect in countries where major property holders have most of the reins of political power. (4) Most imports and exports pass through a small number of ports and border crossings, where their volume and value can be measured and taxed relatively easily by a modest administrative staff. To be sure, some exporters and importers will seek to evade taxes by engaging in contraband trade, or they will try to lower their taxes by providing "favors" to the tax authorities or by underinvoicing their goods (i.e., having a fictitiously low price placed on the import or export documentation). But these problems are not as great as those encountered in trying to collect sales or income taxes.

Taxes on foreign trade, however, have several disadvantages. First, they are affected by sharp fluctuations in the volume and prices of traded commodities. This means that tax revenues are very uncertain from year to year. If they fall unexpectedly, planned spending will have to be cut. Or, if this is politically difficult, the government will have to resort to deficit financing, which may have inflationary consequences. Second, if

---

16. The study cited in Table 13.3 is an updated version of an earlier article by Raja J. Chelliah, excerpts of which are reprinted in Bird and Oldman (1975: 105–127).

TABLE 13.3
Tax Ratios and Indices of Tax Effort in 47 Developing Countries,
1966–1968 and 1969–1971

Taxes as a Percent of GNP[a]			Index of Tax Effort		
Country	1969–71	1966–68	Country	1969–71	1966–68
Zambia	31.3	28.6	Brazil	1.81	1.80
Zaire	29.4	23.4	Tunisia	1.64	1.30
Guyana	23.4	20.6	Egypt	1.49	1.34
Brazil	22.9	20.8	Ivory Coast	1.47	1.43
Tunisia	21.7	20.7	Sudan	1.44	1.10
Iran	21.6	18.0	Sri Lanka	1.37	1.27
Venezuela	20.4	20.7	Senegal	1.34	1.27
Ivory Coast	19.8	19.7	Taiwan	1.30	1.12
Chile	19.6	19.2	Zaire	1.28	1.44
Jamaica	19.4	16.7	Morocco	1.22	1.16
Malaysia	19.3	17.1	Turkey	1.20	1.16
Egypt	19.2	17.5	Malaysia	1.19	1.02
Sudan	18.2	13.0	Korea	1.18	0.97
Senegal	18.1	16.8	Chile	1.16	1.18
Morocco	17.8	16.5	Ghana	1.15	1.02
Taiwan	17.8	13.1	Zambia	1.11	1.18
Sri Lanka	17.7	16.3	India	1.09	1.05
Trinidad and Tobago	17.7	15.2	Kenya	1.09	1.16
Ghana	15.8	13.4	Guyana	1.06	1.03
Turkey	15.6	14.1	Mali	1.06	1.36
Korea	15.4	12.6	Tanzania	1.03	1.06
Kenya	14.4	12.2	Ecuador	1.00	0.98
Peru	14.2	13.7	Jamaica	0.99	1.03
Tanzania	13.9	11.1	Argentina	0.97	1.10
Ecuador	13.4	12.9	Costa Rica	0.97	0.81
India	13.4	12.2	Venezuela	0.96	0.97
Argentina	13.4	13.3	Burundi	0.95	0.86
Singapore	13.2	11.8	Thailand	0.92	1.00
Mali	13.2	13.4	Iran	0.91	0.97
Costa Rica	13.1	12.4	Colombia	0.90	0.80
Colombia	12.5	10.6	Peru	0.87	0.92
Thailand	12.4	12.4	Paraguay	0.87	0.80
Burundi	11.4	10.4	Trinidad and Tobago	0.83	0.70
Honduras	11.3	10.5	Upper Volta	0.82	1.18
Togo	11.3	9.5	Honduras	0.80	0.75
Lebanon	11.2	10.9	Singapore	0.80	0.75
Paraguay	10.9	9.7	Lebanon	0.78	0.86
Upper Volta	10.3	11.4	Togo	0.74	0.71
Indonesia	10.0	6.9	Pakistan	0.73	0.75
Philippines	9.1	9.1	Ethiopia	0.70	0.78
Pakistan	8.8	8.3	Philippines	0.68	0.77
Ethiopia	8.6	8.6	Indonesia	0.66	0.62
Bolivia	8.2	8.7	Guatemala	0.62	0.65
Guatemala	7.9	7.9	Rwanda	0.60	0.70
Rwanda	7.9	8.3	Mexico	0.49	0.77
Mexico	7.1	6.8	Bolivia	0.46	0.54
Nepal	4.4	3.2	Nepal	0.37	0.30

Source: Raja J. Chelliah, Hessel J. Baas, and Margaret R. Kelly, "Developing Countries'
Tax Effort Continues to Rise, Study Shows, *IMF Survey*, June 3, 1974, pp. 162–164.
[a] Excludes local government revenues in some cases. GDP is used in the denominator
in some cases.

TABLE 13.4
Sources of Tax Revenue in 47 Developing Countries, 1969–1971
(percent of total)

Direct Taxes	33.58	
Income[a]		27.30
Property		4.85
Poll and personal		1.43
Indirect Taxes	63.95	
Imports		24.43
Exports and other trade		7.66
Production and internal transactions		31.86
Other Taxes	2.47	
Total	100.00	

Source: Chelliah, Baas, and Kelly (see Table 13.3).
[a] Includes royalties on minerals.

foreign trade is not growing faster than GNP, the *elasticity* of this source of tax revenue will not exceed 1.00—i.e., taxes cannot rise at a more rapid rate than the GNP—and this will limit the government's ability to increase spending on educational facilities, infrastructure, other capital goods, and social services.[17] Third, taxes on exports have adverse effects on products subject to competitive pressures, while import taxes raise the cost of imported components of export goods as well as the prices of inputs necessary for increasing agricultural production.

For these reasons, many policy makers in developing countries are anxious to shift to other sources of tax revenue as soon as this is politically and administratively feasible. A progressive income tax has the advantage of having an elasticity greater than 1.00, since a rising GNP will push taxpayers into higher tax brackets. Many nominally progressive tax systems, though, are at best only proportional in reality. Tax liabilities can be withheld from the paychecks of civil servants and other salaried workers, but landowners, professionals, business owners, and other high-income recipients find it relatively easy to avoid (legally) or evade (illegally) tax payments to the government. If tax evasion can be reduced by better enforcement and other administrative reforms, income tax collections in most developing countries (and some developed countries) could be raised significantly without any increase in tax rates. Table 13.4 shows that income taxes accounted for 27.3 percent of developing countries' tax revenues during 1969–1971, but this figure is inflated by the inclusion of petroleum and other mineral royalties. In nineteen of the forty-seven countries surveyed, less than 20 percent of tax revenues came from income taxes.

---

17. Elasticity will be particularly low if the country relies heavily on specific rather than *ad valorem* import duties during a period of rapid inflation.

Where effective income tax administration is politically difficult, greater reliance can be placed on sales taxes. While these have the reputation of being regressive, they are not necessarily so. Small shops patronized by low-income groups, for example, can be exempted. So can food purchases, which take a higher percentage of a family's budget the lower is its income. In addition, a differential sales tax system can be employed, with higher rates applied to luxury and semiluxury goods consumed by upper- and middle-income groups.

While the taxing capabilities of developing countries are determined in large part by political factors, economic factors play a role as well. This has given rise to several efforts to prepare indices of "tax effort" to compare a country's actual tax collections with its tax "potential." For the forty-seven countries in Table 13.3, tax potential is based on per capita nonexport income, the share of mining (including petroleum) in the GDP, and the ratio of nonmineral exports to GNP—factors which were found to be significantly related to actual tax ratios. A tax effort index greater than 1.00 indicates that a country's tax collections exceeded its tax potential. During 1969–1971, twenty-two countries fell into this category, and most countries' tax effort ratios showed an increase from 1966–1968. This helps account for the rise in the average tax/GNP ratio from 13.6 percent in 1966–1968 to 15.1 percent in 1969–1971. Countries with tax ratios above the average generally have tax effort indices above 1.00, though there are some exceptions. Venezuela and Iran, both major oil exporters, have tax ratios above 20 percent but tax effort indices below 1.00; India is one of four countries with tax effort indices above 1.00 but tax ratios that are below average. Given the importance of political factors in tax collections, tax effort indices are at best only an imperfect measure of tax potential. It should also be noted that these indices do not necessarily imply any normative judgment about the desirability of increasing taxes. They merely show what, on the average, countries with a given economic structure have actually collected. Nevertheless, the temptation to use them normatively has been difficult to resist.

CONSUMPTION AS INVESTMENT (SAVINGS)

One result of economists' increasing concern with economic development, as opposed to economic growth, has been a radical change in the theoretical distinction between consumption and investment (and therefore savings). Certain goods and services traditionally classified as consumption, it can be argued, should really be considered as investment items which increase the ability of individuals to contribute to future output. The traditional definition of investment is thus incomplete. Economists who have urged developing countries to undertake more investment in the narrow sense of physical capital have in effect asked these countries to forego "consumption" expenditures on education, health care, and basic foods. Increased spending on these items, however, might have higher payoffs (rates of return) in terms of future output and income than spending on some types of physical capital; moreover, such spending can reduce disparities in levels of living.

Given this major shortcoming in defining investment, it is no wonder that economists studying developed countries have had difficulty explaining changes in capital-output ratios over time or in accounting for all of the sources of economic growth. As our definition of investment changes, we will need to do some redefining of savings, too.

SUMMARY

The mobilization of domestic savings is one of the most important roles of government in the process of development. Increasing domestic savings, however, is often politically difficult. Taxes are never popular, and governments whose political base is weak will find it very difficult to raise tax rates, introduce new taxes, or even enforce existing tax laws. If the government instead chooses to encourage increased private savings, this may require higher interest rates and control of inflationary pressures, measures which again are bound to arouse political opposition.

A government which finds it politically difficult to mobilize greater domestic savings can try instead to increase foreign savings by seeking foreign aid and private foreign investment (see chapter 14). But this policy is also politically risky because it will be viewed by some as a sellout to imperialist interests. Still, these critics may offer the line of least resistance.

If the government is weak, mobilization of savings will be dependent upon market forces, whose operation in developing countries is most imperfect. Perhaps the best hope for higher savings rates in these countries is the discovery of a natural resource such as petroleum, the development of which can be heavily taxed, thus relieving pressures to increase other kinds of taxes.

Suggested Readings

Bhatt, V. V., and Jacob Meerman. "Resource Mobilization in Developing Countries: Financial Institutions and Policies," *World Development*, 6 (January 1978), 45–64.

> This article reviews trends in domestic savings and investment rates in developing countries since 1950. It also discusses the effect of government policies on both public and private savings rates. The authors believe that special efforts to mobilize domestic savings are needed to offset recent unfavorable developments in the world economy.

Bird, Richard M., and Oliver Oldman. *Readings in Taxation in Developing Countries.* 3rd ed. Baltimore: The Johns Hopkins University Press, 1975.

This excellent collection of readings has been the major sourcebook in its field since the first edition appeared in 1964. The forty-one selections in the current edition are grouped under eight headings: fiscal policy and economic development, taxation and the external sector, taxation of income and wealth, taxation of consumption, taxation and incentives, agricultural taxation, urban finance, and tax administration.

Lewis, W. Arthur. *The Theory of Economic Growth.* Homewood, Ill.: Richard D. Irwin, Inc., 1955.

The discussion of savings and investment in Lewis' classic text, now a generation old, is still well worth reading. Lewis combines theoretical (but nonmathematical) considerations with empirical evidence and perceptive insights into the noneconomic obstacles to savings and investment.

McKinnon, Ronald I. *Money and Capital in Economic Development.* Washington, D.C.: The Brookings Institution, 1973.

McKinnon argues that market-determined interest rates will result both in greater mobilization of domestic savings and in a more efficient allocation of financial resources among investment projects. Like Shaw (see below), McKinnon draws heavily on the South Korean financial reforms of 1965 in support of his case.

————, ed. *Money and Finance in Economic Growth and Development.* Essays in Honor of Edward S. Shaw. New York: Marcel Dekker, Inc., 1976.

Readers with mathematical skills will profit from reading essays on financial repression in Latin America and financial liberalization in South Korea. More easily read are three essays (in a section entitled "Alternatives to Domestic Financial Intermediation") which take issue with some of the views of honoree Edward Shaw, whose 1973 book is summarized below.

Shaw, Edward S. *Financial Deepening in Economic Development.* New York: Oxford University Press, 1973.

Financial deepening is defined as the "accumulation of financial assets at a pace faster than accumulation of nonfinancial wealth." Shaw argues that decentralization and liberalization of economic decision making will encourage domestic savings and thus make economic growth both faster and more stable. There is little reason to dispute this hypothesis. However, the importance of financial liberalization is perhaps exaggerated, and insufficient consideration is given to alternative means of mobilizing domestic savings. Moreover, Shaw pays little attention to the strong likelihood that liberalization will widen income inequalities, though he is correct in pointing out that "shallow finance" sometimes has the same effect.

Wai, U Tun. *Financial Intermediaries and National Savings in Developing Countries.* New York: Praeger Publishers, 1972.

The author reviews both the theoretical literature and empirical studies regarding savings behavior in developing countries. Econometric tests show positive correlations between the degree of financial intermediation and national savings rates.

14

Financing Development
Foreign Aid and Private
Foreign Investment

Developing countries can supplement domestic savings by obtaining financial resources abroad, either in the form of loans and grants from international agencies and individual developed-country governments, or by attracting investment in fixed plant and equipment by private firms (or state enterprises) based in other countries. These resource inflows permit a country to undertake more investment than would be possible by relying on domestic savings alone. Simultaneously, foreign resource inflows can help a developing country overcome balance-of-payments constraints to the importation of raw materials, intermediate goods, capital goods, and technical services necessary to meet its growth and development objectives.[1]

To the extent that foreign aid must be repaid, and overseas investors wish to remit profits back to their home countries, foreign resources are only temporary solutions to domestic-savings and balance-of-payments constraints. Thus over the long run, exports of goods and services will have to increase to provide the foreign exchange necessary to meet the obligations of debt repayment and profit remittances. If poor export performance forces debt renegotiation, or if there is outright default, a developing country's ability to continue obtaining foreign financing will be jeopardized. This is why defaults have been rare, despite widespread popular opinion to the contrary.

Reliance on foreign aid and foreign investment, from whatever

---

1. In the "two-gap" model used by some aid planners in the 1960s, the domestic savings-investment gap is equal to the foreign exchange gap. The equivalence of the two gaps, derived from a basic national accounts identity, will be illustrated below. See Hollis B. Chenery and Alan M. Strout, "Foreign Assistance and Economic Development," *American Economic Review*, 56 (September 1966), 679–733.

source, results in a dependency relationship between developed and developing countries with which the latter understandably are ill at ease. Still, only a few developing countries totally (or almost totally) reject foreign resources, since such a rejection would restrict their development options and, other things being equal, their rate of economic growth.[2] Most of the developing countries' objections to specific aspects of foreign aid and private foreign investment are reasonable, well-founded criticisms based on the terms under which foreign resources are made available, not on the principle of foreign resource transfers.

FOREIGN AID

Defining and Categorizing Foreign Aid

Foreign aid, like "democracy" and "socialism," is a term that means different things to different people. In the United States, there is considerable public misunderstanding about why, how, and how much aid is provided. Aid is frequently referred to as a "giveaway," and some people seem to think that large bundles of federal reserve notes simply are dumped into the laps of key decision makers in developing countries. Opinion surveys have shown that the U.S. public believes the foreign aid program to be much larger than it actually is. The negative balance-of-payments impact in the United States also tends to be overestimated, since the return of aid dollars to purchase U.S. goods and services is not fully taken into account.

From the viewpoint of the recipient country, some economists tend to equate aid inflows with foreign savings. The latter is equivalent to the deficit in the current account of the balance of payments, as shown in the following rearrangement of terms from the basic national income identity for an open economy:

$$Y = C + I + (X - M)$$

$$Y + M = C + I + X$$
(sources of resources)   (use of resources)

Since $Y = C + S$, then:

$$C + S + M = C + I + X$$

$$S + M = I + X$$
(leakages)   (injections)

2. Other things, however, are not necessarily equal. As we note later in this chapter, foreign aid may substitute for domestic savings, not supplement it, as the two-gap model assumes. Moreover, it can be argued that dependence on aid and private foreign investment also restricts development options by forcing countries into growth patterns determined by the developed countries.

$$M - X = I - S$$
(foreign exchange gap)   (domestic savings-investment gap)

$$I = S + (M - X)$$
(investment)   (domestic   (foreign
savings)   savings)

To refer to all resource transfers from developed to developing countries as "aid" is misleading. This term should be reserved for outright grants and for a percentage of the face value of loans made on more favorable terms than those prevailing in commercial markets. Specifically, if a $10 million loan is made at the concessional interest rate of 3 percent with twenty-five years for repayment, the amount of *aid* is not $10 million. Rather, it is the difference between the nominal principal and the discounted present value (see chapter 6) of the stream of repayments made on concessional terms. This figure may be referred to as the *grant content* of concessional lending.

Unfortunately, statistics on foreign aid generally lump together grants, concessional loans, and loans by such agencies as the U.S. Export-Import Bank, whose terms are close to those prevailing in commercial markets. A recalculation of aid statistics for the late 1960s, to include only the grant content of loans, lowers aid totals by perhaps 55 to 70 percent.[3] It also results in significant changes in the rank order of countries as aid donors relative to their GNPs. Adjusting the data for 1966, for example, transfers aid "leadership" among the Western bloc nations from Portugal to France. While a high proportion of French aid was in the form of grants, most of Portugal's "aid" consisted of the administrative costs of the colonial empire it was attempting—ultimately unsuccessfully—to maintain.[4]

Apart from the distinction between grants, concessional loans, and "hard" (commercial-type) loans, aid flows can be disaggregated in several other ways. For example, aid may be divided into military and economic categories. Ostensibly, military aid is provided to strengthen the national security of the recipient country (and donor country as well), while the purpose of economic aid is to promote development or at least growth. In practice, the distinction between these two types of aid is less clear. Military aid can free domestic resources for growth and development purposes, while economic aid likewise can permit more domestic resources to be allocated to military purposes.[5]

3. Jagdish Bhagwati, *Amount and Sharing of Aid*, ODC Monograph No. 2 (Washington, D.C.: Overseas Development Council, 1970), pp. 14–18.
4. Ibid., Table 9.
5. "Supporting assistance" provided by the U.S. government plays this latter role. In fiscal year 1977, supporting assistance ($1.7 billion) exceeded bilateral development assistance ($1.1 billion).

A similar distinction can be made between "aid aimed at the achievement of 'politically motivated' objectives" and "development assistance," or "aid . . . given exclusively in relation to the recipient's developmental needs." This distinction also is more apparent than real, since the notion of "pure development assistance" can be questioned both on theoretical grounds and on the basis of empirical observations. Indeed, the writer who neatly divided aid motivations into political and economic in the words quoted above admits that "all foreign assistance may be regarded as having its rationale in the foreign policy objectives of the donor; in this sense all aid is 'politically motivated'."[6]

Aid organizations sometimes separate their activities into "project aid" and "program aid." *Project aid,* as the name implies, is financial assistance in support of a specific project. *Program aid,* in theory, is aid in support of an entire development program; essentially, it is long-term balance-of-payments assistance, usually provided on concessional terms. (Balance-of-payments assistance available from the IMF and commercial banks, in contrast, is provided for short- and medium-term periods at market or near-market interest rates.) In practice, the distinction between project aid and program aid is fuzzy. Project aid is not given *in vacuo* but takes into account a country's macroeconomic situation and development objectives. Program aid typically is restricted to certain projects, or to certain types of imports.[7]

The Donor View: Motives for Foreign Aid

The motives for providing foreign aid are mixed. Most of them can be grouped into three categories: (1) humanitarian, (2) economic, and (3) political-national security. Humanitarian motives derive from feelings of individual or collective responsibility for alleviating poverty and promoting social justice, and may be based either on religious beliefs or on secular humanism. In most countries the "humanitarian constituency" for aid is small and fragmented into many groups which have experienced difficulty in joining forces to lobby for aid. Economic motives arise from individual or group self-interest. Businessmen often are strong supporters of aid if it is tied to purchases of goods and services in the donor country. Farmers may support aid if it promises to absorb surplus production, thus

---

6. Davison L. Budhoo, *The Integrated Theory of Development Assistance—An Initial Statement* (Mona, Jamaica: Institute of Social and Economic Research, University of the West Indies, 1973), pp. 3, 34, 5.

7. An intermediate category of aid is "sector aid," nominally an integrated package of assistance based upon interrelationships identified in a detailed analysis of economic sectors such as agriculture or health. In practice, sector aid often finances a loose collection of projects which may not be closely related but are lumped together for administrative convenience.

raising domestic farm prices. Some people have viewed aid as a means of improving the investment climate in developing countries. Political-national security motives are numerous. Aid has been used to secure military bases, influence voting in the United Nations, strengthen international alliances, promote the particular "ism" of the donor country, combat the "isms" of other countries, and keep countries politically neutral.

In the *bilateral aid* programs of major donor countries (i.e., country-to-country aid), political-national security motives generally predominate. The U.S. government has been quite frank in admitting this. Aid to Greece and Turkey after World War II was given specifically to counter threats of internal subversion by groups hostile to the United States (the "Truman Doctrine"). U.S. assistance to Western Europe, culminating in the Marshall Plan, was provided mainly because of the military threat posed by the Soviet Union. President Truman's "Point Four" program of technical assistance to developing countries was likewise rooted explicitly in political considerations. From 1951 to 1953, the U.S. aid program was directed by what was called the Mutual Security Agency. In the 1960s a pamphlet prepared for public distribution by the Agency for International Development (AID) began by stating openly that "the major objective of the U.S. foreign assistance program is to assist other countries that seek to maintain their independence and develop into self-supporting nations. The resulting community of free nations, cooperating on matters of mutual concern, offers the best long-run prospect for security and peace for the United States."[8]

This is not to say that other motives are absent. There is a humanitarian element in the U.S. foreign aid program, and it is not confined merely to disaster relief operations. The aid program has also been used to stimulate export sales by U.S. businesses and to support domestic farm incomes by creating a market for surplus agricultural commodities. But these motives are definitely secondary. U.S. aid has never been concentrated in the poorest or "most needy" developing countries (though there have been some recent moves in this direction) but rather in countries deemed most important from a national security standpoint.[9]

The situation is much the same for the Soviet Union. Cuba, a major recipient of Soviet aid, is one of the most developed countries in Latin

8. U.S. Agency for International Development, *Principles of Foreign Economic Assistance,* rev. ed. (Washington, D.C., September 1965), p. 1.
9. A high percentage of U.S. aid has gone to countries along the southern border of the Soviet Union: Turkey, Iran, Afghanistan, Pakistan, and India. Other major recipients of U.S. aid have included Taiwan, South Korea, the Philippines, and Panama, all countries where the United States has had a direct military presence. Pakistan and India, of course, contain a high percentage of the world's poor, and Afghanistan is one of the poorest countries in the world; but their poverty has not been the primary determinant of U.S. assistance. Equally poor nations in Africa received very little attention until the 1970s.

America. Targeted countries in Africa (including Egypt and Ghana, previously, and Ethiopia and Algeria currently) have been chosen for their political influence or strategic significance, not because of their level of development. The Chinese likewise have been politically selective in choosing aid recipients. Aid given by the European Economic Community is concentrated in former European colonies. But in some of the smaller European countries (e.g., Sweden), humanitarian motives play a strong role in determining aid priorities.

Multilateral aid—i.e., aid channeled through international agencies, such as the United Nations, the World Bank, and the regional development banks—may appear on the surface to be free of political motivations, but in fact these motivations are very much present. The World Bank was a creation of the Western nations, and its early efforts concentrated on the reconstruction of Western Europe after World War II. The United States, cool to Latin American proposals for a regional development bank for the Americas, quickly warmed to the idea after the Cuban revolution in 1959. It is no secret that the United States has used its voting power and political influence to curtail lending by multilateral institutions to countries whose governments were out of favor in Washington (e.g., the Allende government in Chile during 1970–1973). The multilateral lending institutions themselves are reluctant to make loan commitments in situations where the risk of default is high, since they wish to remain in good standing in world money markets, where they borrow a high proportion of their resources. Because they are structured as banks, they must look for bankable projects which directly or indirectly generate the funds needed for loan repayment, not for situations where aid is "needed" the most for humanitarian reasons.

Some critics of aid, notably Teresa Hayter (1971), have argued that World Bank aid, and the balance-of-payments assistance provided by the IMF (see chapter 15), are simply imperialist tools designed to promote or preserve the capitalist system. As such, it is argued, they differ little from the bilateral aid agencies of the United States and some other Western countries. Hayter is particularly critical of the efforts of the World Bank, the IMF, and AID to promote fiscal and monetary "stability," use of the market mechanism, and reliance on the private sector. Emphasizing such policies, she argues, these institutions tend to devote little attention to issues such as income distribution and social justice, or to the consideration of economic systems other than capitalism.

One does not have to be Marxist like Hayter to accept many of her criticisms as valid characterizations of aid policies in the past. On the other hand, it should be recognized that these policies have been (gradually) changing since Hayter's book was written (though not necessarily because of it), and both the World Bank and AID now give more explicit attention to social policy and development and no longer count on growth to take care of development objectives automatically. Moreover, there is good reason to believe that what appears to be "imperialist" behavior is in part a response by aid agencies to organizational constraints affecting their operations. Judith Tendler, a former AID official who is also well acquainted with the operations of other aid agencies, argues forcefully that "the more that donor organizations are able to impose order on the outside decision-making that affects their product, the better they can perform their task. In so doing, however, they bring dependency to those whose decision-making has been so ordered. Seen in this light, dependency is the result not necessarily of design but of an organization's attempts to do well" (1975: 109). While Tendler focuses on AID, she argues that similar organizational constraints affect the World Bank and other multilateral agencies.

Even if the "aid as imperialism" theory is not accepted, it still may be argued that the foreign assistance agencies' growing concern with development (as opposed to growth) is motivated ultimately by political considerations—i.e., the fear that growing inequalities will lead to social unrest and to political changes that may not be in the national-security interests of the United States and other Western donors.

The Recipient View: Attitudes toward Foreign Aid

Developing countries have mixed feelings regarding foreign aid. On the one hand, aid is a symbol of the dependency relationships from which most of them would like to become free. On the other hand, aid is viewed as a useful (though temporary) means of achieving economic independence more rapidly, and as such it is sought from both "anti-imperialist" and "reforming imperialist" developed countries. Representatives of developing countries have often argued that the developed countries have a moral obligation to provide aid so that international disparities in income and wealth will be reduced and the goal of eliminating poverty achieved more quickly. Aid has also been regarded as necessary to compensate for international trade patterns that have discriminated against the developing countries (see chapter 5). In addition, some countries have viewed aid as a form of reparations for what are regarded as the antidevelopment policies forced on the developing countries during the colonial period or during periods of military intervention. Vietnam's recent bid for U.S. assistance is a good example of the latter type of reparations requested.

Though foreign aid is generally accepted as helpful for achieving growth and development objectives, developing countries are very critical of the terms under which it is provided. We have already commented on aid donor insistence on monetary and fiscal "stabilization" as a precondition for some types of aid. Some bilateral aid programs are criticized for tying aid to the purchase of goods and services in the donor country, even though they may be secured elsewhere at considerably less cost.[10] Loan agreement documents are sometimes objected to—with justification —as challenges and insults to national sovereignty.

Other things being equal, most developing countries would probably prefer program aid to project aid, particularly if the valuable technical assistance now provided under project aid were still available for projects that the developing countries would be more free to choose. Donor agencies, however, are less willing to provide program aid than they were ten to fifteen years ago, apparently because they fear that the funds will not necessarily be used wisely to meet growth and development objectives. Developing countries are not pleased with the implication that they do not know what is best for them. Still, they value project aid, because it enables them to undertake high-priority projects at much lower cost (because of the favorable repayment terms and low interest rates) than would be possible without aid.

Because aid has been subject to more conditions than developing countries once hoped, and because its volume has been below expectations (see below), developing countries have become somewhat disillusioned with it. While they continue to lobby for more aid, on more favorable terms, their attention has increasingly turned in the last fifteen years to international trade reforms as an alternative source of foreign exchange.

The Volume of Foreign Aid

We have already pointed out that published figures on "aid" are misleadingly large. But recalculating them to arrive at grant-equivalent figures is a task beyond our resources. So we shall make do with what is available, having provided some indication of the degree of adjustment needed.

Table 14.1 shows the flow of aid and other financial resources from the seventeen member countries of the Development Assistance Committee (DAC) of the Organization for Economic Cooperation and Development (OECD), which includes most of the Western industrial nations. The data refer only to economic aid and thus exclude military assistance. Total financial flows more than doubled in real terms between 1960 and 1976, increasing at an annual rate of 6.1 percent. But a closer look at

10. Calculations by Mahbub ul Haq show that items procured by Pakistan under tied aid programs in 1965 were about 20 percent more expensive than they would have been without tying. Cited in Harry G. Johnson, *Economic Policies toward Less Developed Countries* (New York: Praeger Publishers, 1967), pp. 83–84.

TABLE 14.1
Net Flow of Financial Resources from DAC Countries to Developing Countries and Multilateral Institutions, 1960–1976
(millions of dollars)

	Current Dollars				Constant (1972) Dollars[a]			
Year	Total	Official Development Assistance	Other Official Flows	Private Flows	Total	Official Development Assistance	Other Official Flows	Private Flows
1960	8,115	4,703	262	3,150	11,817	6,849	382	4,587
1961	9,249	5,197	946	3,106	13,610	7,849	1,365	4,483
1962	8,437	5,438	546	2,453	11,959	7,708	774	3,477
1963	8,572	5,772	243	2,557	11,974	8,063	339	3,572
1964	9,645	5,952	−36	3,729	13,265	8,186	50	5,129
1965	10,320	5,895	304	4,121	13,886	7,932	409	5,545
1966	10,390	5,984	447	3,959	13,536	7,796	582	5,158
1967	11,435	6,536	518	4,381	14,471	8,271	656	5,544
1968	13,509	6,309	738	6,462	16,361	7,641	894	7,826
1969	13,778	6,621	571	6,586	15,888	7,635	658	7,595
1970	15,710	6,811	1,149	7,751	17,196	7,455	1,258	8,484
1971	17,245	7,759	1,271	8,215	17,960	8,061	1,324	8,556
1972	18,625	8,654	1,541	8,430	18,625	8,654	1,541	8,430
1973	24,628	9,351	2,463	12,814	23,278	8,838	2,328	12,112
1974	28,016	11,304	2,183	14,529	24,148	9,743	1,882	12,523
1975	40,378	13,585	3,024	23,605	31,749	10,682	2,378	18,560
1976	40,505	13,656	3,305	23,700	30,255	10,200	2,469	17,702

Source: Society for International Development, *Survey of International Development*, various issues, based on the annual reports of the Development Assistance Committee; and OECD (1977).

[a] Current dollars deflated by the U.S. implicit price deflator for GNP (1972 = 100).

Table 14.1 shows that most of the increase was accounted for by private loans and credits on commercial terms. *Official development assistance* (ODA)—government and international agency grants and loans with a grant content of at least 25 percent—increased at a real annual rate of only 2.5 percent. This means that real per capita ODA to the developing countries from the DAC countries was no higher in 1976 than in 1960, amounting to approximately $5 in 1976 dollars.[11]

For the DAC countries as a group, the total financial flows of $40.5 billion in 1976 amounted to 0.97 percent of their GNP. The United States was by far the largest contributor, with $12.3 billion. In relation to GNP, however, total financial flows from the United States were a modest 0.72 percent. Other major providers of financial resources, and of roughly equal importance during the 1970s, have been France, West Germany, and Japan (see Table 14.2).

TABLE 14.2

New Flow of Financial Resources to Developing Countries and Multilateral Institutions, by DAC Donor Country, 1976

	Millions of Dollars		Percent of GNP	
Country	Total Flows	Official Development Assistance	Total Flows	Official Development Assistance
Australia	527	385	0.57	0.42
Austria	372	39	0.92	0.10
Belgium	1,222	340	1.83	0.51
Canada	2,471	886	1.28	0.46
Denmark	485	214	1.27	0.56
Finland	66	51	0.24	0.18
France	5,318	2,146	1.53	0.62
West Germany	5,314	1,384	1.19	0.31
Italy	1,476	226	0.87	0.13
Japan	4,003	1,105	0.72	0.20
Netherlands	1,727	720	1.96	0.82
New Zealand	60	53	0.48	0.43
Norway	462	218	1.51	0.71
Sweden	1,134	608	1.53	0.82
Switzerland	1,350	112	2.28	0.19
United Kingdom[a]	2,176	835	0.99	0.38
United States	12,344	4,334	0.72	0.25
Total	40,505	13,656	0.97	0.33

Source: OECD (1977: 164–165).
[a] Estimate.

11. Aid from all sources amounts to about 2 percent of the combined GDP of the developing countries.

ODA resource flows in 1976 amounted to $13.7 billion, or 0.33 percent of the DAC ocuntries' GNP, well below the target of 0.7 percent recommended in a report prepared for the World Bank by the Pearson Commission (1969). Only three countries—the Netherlands, Norway, and Sweden—met or exceeded this target. The United States, the largest provider of ODA, ranked twelfth, with only 0.25 percent.

Estimates of economic aid provided by the Soviet Union, China, and other socialist countries are provided in Table 14.3. Though these figures are incomplete, notably because they exclude Soviet aid to Cuba, it is clear that aid flows from the socialist countries are considerably lower than those from the DAC countries. Also, a rather high percentage of the aid committed by socialist countries appears not to have been disbursed. Disbursements in 1976 totaled an estimated $950 million (excluding aid to Cuba), down from a peak of $1.1 billion in 1974. In real terms, they were 7 percent higher than in 1967. Much of Soviet and Eastern European aid is in the form of trade credits carrying higher interest rates and shorter repayment periods than is typical with ODA assistance. The smaller Chinese aid program, on the other hand, has a relatively high grant component: 87 percent in 1976, compared with 52 percent for the Soviet Union (OECD, 1977: 91).

In the last few years, the OPEC countries have become an important source of aid to developing countries. Total resource flows from those donors amounted to $1.7 billion in 1973 and nearly $8.0 billion in 1976 (see Table 14.4). These financial transfers averaged 3.6 percent of the OPEC countries' GNP during 1975–1976. The grant element in the OPEC countries' concessional commitments was an estimated 79 percent in 1976 (OECD, 1977: 86).

U.S. Foreign Aid

U.S. foreign aid is now much less than it was in the late 1940s and early 1950s, not just as a percentage of GNP but in real absolute terms as well. When the United States perceived a serious threat to its national security in the form of possible Soviet intervention in Western Europe, it responded in 1949 by committing 2.12 percent of its GNP to foreign economic assistance, most of it as grants under the Marshall Plan. The dollar figure that (fiscal) year was $5.5 billion, which in 1976 dollars would be equivalent to $14.0 billion. Commitments of economic aid in 1976, by contrast, amounted to only $3.9 billion in current prices, or just 0.23 percent of GNP.

These figures clearly demonstrate the weakness of the often-heard argument that the United States cannot "afford" to transfer more than $3 to $4 billion a year in economic assistance to the developing countries.

TABLE 14.3
Aid Commitments and Disbursements by Socialist Countries, 1954–1976[a,b]
(millions of current dollars)

Year	Total		USSR		Eastern Europe		China	
	Commit-ments	Disburse-ments	Commit-ments	Disburse-ments	Commit-ments	Disburse-ments	Commit-ments	Disburse-ments
1954–66	7,985	3,165	5,065	2,245	2,013	565	907	355
1967	473	525	291	310	132	115	50	100
1968	638	505	379	310	205	125	54	70
1969	933	525	494	355	426	100	13	70
1970	1,122	585	198	385	196	130	728	70
1971	2,171	795	1,125	440	484	165	562	190
1972	2,188	825	802	430	828	140	558	255
1973	1,573	895	661	490	484	175	428	230
1974	1,641	1,115	580	690	789	185	272	240
1975	1,994	825	1,299	485	422	200	273	140
1976	1,479	950	875	420	496	300	108	230

Source: U.S. Central Intelligence Agency, Communist Aid to the Less Developed Countries of the Free World, 1976, Publication No. ER 77-10296 (Washington, D.C., August 1977), p. 7.
a Economic aid only.
b Excludes aid to Cuba.

TABLE 14.4
Net Flow of Financial Resources from OPEC Nations to Developing Countries,
1973–1976
(millions of current dollars)

Country	1973	1974	1975	1976
Algeria	30	51	42	67[a]
Iran	5	739	936	795
Iraq[a]	11	440	251[a]	120[a]
Kuwait	550	1,250	1,711	1,875
Libya	404	263	363	373
Nigeria	6	135	348	177
Qatar	94	218	367	245
Saudi Arabia	335	1,622	2,467	2,826
United Arab Emirates	289	749	1,207	1,144
Venezuela	18	483	472	334
Total	1,740	5,952	8,164	7,955

Source: OECD (1977: 85).
[a] Estimated by the OECD.

At a time when its real GNP was much lower, the United States managed to give the equivalent of four times this amount. And, because of higher petroleum prices, it recently transferred to the OPEC countries additional financial resources equivalent to a large multiple of its current aid level, with fewer strains on the economy than had been predicted. The real reason for the presently low level of aid transfers is not lack of financial capability, but lack of political will. As explained above, the will to commit resources for aid is conditioned more by national security considerations than by humanitarian concerns. Apparently most people in the United States now see little threat to the country's national security from the developing countries. Or perhaps recent developments in Southeast Asia, Ethiopia, and elsewhere have led people to conclude that aid to developing countries will not be effective in strengthening U.S. security interests. Political support for aid is thus weak.

If the ability of aid to "buy" the goodwill of developing country governments is being questioned, there are good reasons for doing so. Frequently, this use of aid has helped maintain in power governments which have demonstrated little concern for employment, equity in the distribution of income, and other human and civil rights. Indeed, such aid may well prove to have been counterproductive to U.S. interests over the long run, as conservative regimes supported by the United States give way to governments with broader support but negative attitudes toward the United States acquired while their leaders were in the political opposition.

Marxists and other historical determinists would argue that the replacement of conservative governments by those with more widespread support is inevitable. Others seem convinced that elite-dominated ruling parties or institutions will mature and evolve into more democratic structures over time, as occurred in the United Kingdom and the United States. Adherents to the latter view tend to support aid policies which stress economic growth rather than economic development, the argument being that growth promotes stability, which in turn permits even more development over the long run. Those who believe in the probability, if not inevitability, of significant political change in the not-too-distant future, and who would like U.S. interests to continue being supported after the change, tend to argue for changes in U.S. aid programs. Specific changes that have been proposed include (1) greater concentration on projects and programs which *directly* benefit lower-income groups; (2) elimination of the requirement that most aid resources be used to purchase goods and services in the United States ("tied aid"); (3) a substantial increase in the amount of aid; (4) channeling a higher proportion of aid through international agencies; and (5) stricter adherence to the self-help principle (i.e., concentrating aid in countries which demonstrate a will to mobilize higher proportions of their own resources for the development effort).

Though such an approach would result in a redistribution of aid among recipient countries, it would be naïve to think that the humanitarian motive will prevail in the foreseeable future. The U.S. aid program (and that of most other donors) will continue to be motivated primarily by political considerations. Still, aid could do more to promote social change instead of giving the impression—rightly in some cases, wrongly in others—of delaying greater participation by the masses in the social, political, and economic lives of their countries. The U.S. aid program has in fact been moving in this direction, but conflicting policy directives and organizational constraints have made the pace of change slow. Among the organizational problems are that its administrative procedures favor large, capital-intensive, foreign-exchange-intensive projects. Small projects relying heavily on local labor are discouraged for being administratively cumbersome. Even recipient countries may find it attractive to support these biases (Tendler, 1975: Ch. 5).

The Role of International Agencies

International (multilateral) agencies are playing an increasingly important role as providers of both technical and financial assistance to developing countries. Table 14.5 shows that disbursements from these agencies amounted to $6.7 billion in 1976 (compared with official bilateral

TABLE 14.5
Financial Flows (Disbursements) from Multilateral
Institutions to Developing Countries, 1976
(*millions of dollars*)

Institutions	Total	Concessional
World Bank Group	3,243	1,326
United Nations	1,400	1,400
Regional Banks	936[a]	369[a]
EEC	559	501
OPEC and Arab Institutions	605	153[a]
Total	6,743	3,749

Source: OECD (1977: 65).
[a] Estimated by the OECD.

flows totaling $19.3 billion). Of multilateral flows, 56 percent are classified as concessional, though it should be pointed out that most of the remainder is provided on terms more favorable than those available from private sources.

The World Bank (IBRD),[12] established together with the International Monetary Fund (IMF) at the Bretton Woods Conference in 1944, is the most important source of multilateral finance. Most of its lending is for projects rather than programs. Disbursements by the IBRD and its affiliates amounted to $3.2 billion in 1976, close to half the multilateral-agency total. New loan commitments by the IBRD alone reached $5.8 billion in fiscal year 1977. Though supported by contributions from member governments, the IBRD raises most of its resources in international capital markets, where the backing of its member governments enables it to borrow funds and relend them at interest rates that may be several percentage points below those charged by private lenders. Moreover, the IBRD offers borrower governments a longer repayment period. One of its affiliates, the International Development Association (IDA), is funded by special contributions from member governments and lends for even longer periods of time (up to fifty years) at a zero interest rate. Its operations are concentrated in the poorest developing countries. The IDA's new commitments in fiscal year 1977 amounted to $1.3 billion. The other IBRD affiliate, the International Finance Corporation (IFC), helps stimulate private investment by taking equity positions in new or expanding firms (but rarely exercising its voting rights) and selling its shares once these firms are financially on their feet. The IFC's commitments in fiscal year 1977 totaled $207 million.

12. The organization's formal name is the International Bank for Reconstruction and Development.

In recent years the IBRD has strengthened its commitment to the poorest developing countries and the poorest segments of the population in developing countries generally.[13] It has also attracted an able group of economists and other specialists who have conducted innovative research on development problems. As a result, the World Bank has begun to shed its image as a builder of dams and roads. The proportion of its loans authorized for infrastructure projects, in fact, fell from 54 percent in 1967 to 30 percent in 1977. Still, some observers believe that the World Bank's rhetoric has outpaced its performance, and that it is still moving too cautiously in promoting development and social change directly instead of relying on growth to provide the resources necessary to meet development objectives—resources which may or may not be used for these purposes.

Other international lending agencies are the Inter-American Development Bank (IDB), established in 1960, and the newer and smaller Asian, African, and Caribbean development banks. The IDB's new commitments in 1977 totaled $1.8 billion, and the expansion of its membership in 1976 to include a number of European countries should increase its lending capacity. Political considerations often play an important role in the IDB's loan policies, particularly since the United States has an effective veto power on some loans. There has been growing concern in the IDB about the plight of lower-income groups, but the IDB's loan operations are still weighted heavily toward "safe" infrastructure projects or other projects which do not always focus directly on the poorest segments of the population. Still, the potable water and sewerage projects it has financed have made an important contribution to improving the health of the poor in both large and small urban areas.

In the field of technical assistance, the programs of the United Nations and its specialized agencies have rivaled the large bilateral effort mounted by the United States. A major criticism of U.N. programs has been that they lack centralized direction. The specialized agencies, such as the Food and Agriculture Organization (FAO), the World Health Organization (WHO), and the International Labor Organization (ILO), have had a great deal of freedom to "do their own thing." If the U.N. Resident Representative in a particular country *and* that country's planning/coordinating agency both lack power, duplication of effort and the undertaking of low-priority projects can easily occur.

Notwithstanding these and other problems that U.N. technical assist-

13. See Mahbub ul Haq, "The World Bank and the World's Poorest: I—Changing Emphasis of the Bank's Lending Policies," *Finance and Development,* 15 (June 1978), 11–14. The second article in the series, "The Bank and Urban Poverty," by Edward Jaycox, appears in the September 1978 issue (pp. 10–14) of this quarterly IMF-IBRD publication.

ance efforts have encountered, there have been some important accomplishments in some countries, and this writer would favor an expansion of U.N. activities relative to those of bilateral donors. This is not so much a reflection on the bilateral technical assistance programs of the United States and other countries—which often have been more innovative in dealing with low-income groups than U.N. programs—as it is a belief that bilateral aid in general has increasing political liabilities for donor countries. These liabilities can hinder the effectiveness of the ablest of technical advisors. On the other hand, bilateral aid—both technical and financial—sometimes has clear political advantages to donor countries, and it would be naïve to assume that the major donors would be willing to phase it out altogether.

Aid as a Substitute for Domestic Savings

In a controversial 1970 article that attracted considerable attention, K. B. Griffin and J. L. Enos argued on the basis of statistical evidence for thirty-two developing countries that foreign aid was being used as a *substitute* for domestic savings, not—as many economists had assumed— as a *supplement*. Specifically, their results showed that (1) domestic savings as a percentage of GNP were inversely related to the foreign savings rate and (2) roughly 75 percent of foreign aid inflows were devoted to consumption and only 25 percent to investment.[14]

The Griffin-Enos findings have been criticized on a number of grounds, including the following.[15] (1) Their data do not really measure "aid" but rather total (net) resource inflows, as defined by the current account deficit in the balance of payments. (2) The sample of countries chosen is nonrepresentative. (3) The time period used in the analysis (1962–1964) is too short. (4) Savings data in developing countries are notoriously poor. (5) The authors fail to demonstrate a causal (as opposed to statistical) relationship between foreign aid and domestic savings rates. One could just as well hypothesize that a decline in domestic savings rates (attributable, perhaps, to economic or political difficulties) causes foreign aid to increase.

Still, the critics tend to agree with Griffin and Enos' criticism of economic models which assume that $1 of foreign aid (or net foreign

---

14. K. B. Griffin and J. L. Enos, "Foreign Assistance: Objectives and Consequences," *Economic Development and Cultural Change*, 18 (April 1970), 321.

15. See the comments by Charles Issawi, Mitchell Kellman, and Simon Rottenberg, and the response by Enos and Griffin, in the October 1971 issue of the same journal. See also Gustav Papanek, "The Effect of Aid and Other Resource Transfers on Savings and Growth in Less Developed Countries," *Economic Journal*, 82 (September 1972), 934–950.

inflows) results in $1 in investment and imports. Some aid, it is admitted, is in fact devoted to consumption goods (though, depending on the type and distribution of consumption, this should not necessarily be criticized). Moreover, in some countries—Haiti is one recent example—the evidence is quite strong that foreign aid has indeed enabled developing country governments to lessen their efforts to mobilize domestic savings and even to reduce the real tax burden on middle- and upper-income groups. Under these circumstances, aid may be promoting economic growth, but it is doing little to lay a foundation for development.

The Issue of Absorptive Capacity

While it can be argued from a humanitarian or even a political viewpoint that the present volume of aid in general is too low, a case can be made that for specific countries it has sometimes been too high. In other words, the volume of aid may exceed a country's *absorptive capacity*, or its ability effectively to use financial resources and technical assistance supplied from abroad.

The absorptive capacity issue has at least three dimensions: the relationships between (1) the availability of host country financial resources and the counterpart requirements[16] of projects and programs assisted by foreign donors; (2) local manpower supply and manpower demand; and (3) local administrative/managerial capabilities and program requirements. None of these dimensions is easy to quantify. Indeed, trying to measure absorptive capacity is like trying to catch a will-o'-the-wisp. This writer, like others, once doubted that there really was such a thing; but recent experience in several developing countries has convinced him that the concept does in fact have analytical meaning.

It is important to recognize that absorptive capacity can be increased fairly rapidly in the short run or medium run if a government has the will (and the political power) to do so. With respect to the financial constraint, what is needed for the public sector as a whole is a transfer of resources from the private sector to the government, primarily through the tax mechanism (see chapter 13).[17] If the financial constraint is confined to a particular sector, such as agriculture or public health, it may be possible to overcome the constraint simply by reallocating the existing

---

16. Foreign donor agencies typically require that a percentage of the costs of projects or programs be financed by local resources. Generally, this percentage is lower the poorer is the country and the more serious are its budgetary and balance-of-payments problems.

17. This analysis implicitly assumes that foreign aid is channeled only through public-sector institutions. The great bulk of it in fact is; but even when aid is channeled through the private sector, similar absorptive capacity problems may be present.

level of public resources in favor of that sector. External donors can bypass the financial constraint by providing budget support to the developing country under one scheme or another.[18] However, this is only a stopgap measure, not a solution to the fundamental problem of mobilizing domestic savings in order to weaken dependency relationships with foreigners.

The manpower constraint can be relieved through classroom, internship, and on-the-job training programs emphasizing skills that are in short supply. Some high-level skills can be acquired only through graduate training abroad, leading to internationally marketable credentials. But shorter, nondegree courses or internships are sometimes quite adequate for providing the necessary skills, and they can do so in less time and with less risk that the trainee will be put into a position of being tempted by higher-paying jobs abroad. There is also considerable scope in most countries for expanding local training and education in secondary and postsecondary schools. Finally, greater use can be made of on-the-job training programs, particularly those that are built into projects financed by foreign donors.

Some observers believe that the most serious absorptive capacity problem is neither the financial constraint nor the manpower constraint, but rather the administrative/managerial constraint. Bureaucratic environments in many developing countries are not conducive to change and innovation. Decision making typically is highly centralized, and middle-level staff are given little initiative. Project implementation may be delayed for weeks because a cabinet minister or agency chief is out of the country and no one else can authorize even minor expenditures. In Bolivia the process of granting land titles to peasants proceeded slowly in the 1960s because the president insisted on personally signing each title—until an enterprising foreign advisor found a solution in the form of a signature machine. Other administrative/managerial problems include the lack of an effective reward/punishment system for encouraging productive work, arbitrary job assignments with little regard for specific skill capabilities, and assignments with little meaningful work content.

Still other administrative/managerial constraints are closely related to the financial constraints. Middle- and high-level government administrators, managers, and technicians often spend far less than eight hours a day on their jobs because their low salaries do not provide them the income to which they aspire. It is not uncommon for a government offi-

18. One common means of providing budget support is to make available to developing-country governments the local-currency proceeds from sales of U.S. agricultural commodities provided under P.L. 480. Some AID technicians privately refer to this as "funny money."

cial to be engaged simultaneously in private business or professional practice and perhaps also to teach at a local university or high school. Low salaries also have the effect of discouraging many of a country's most capable people from accepting government jobs. Inadequate budgets for supplies, equipment, and travel likewise restrict the effectiveness of government programs. Teachers whose students have no books, and extension agents who have no travel funds, are not as productive as their training would permit them to be.

If there is a rapid increase in the volume of aid to a particular country, or to a particular sector of its economy, severe strains are placed on the type of administrative/managerial structure described above. The relatively small number of capable and experienced administrators, managers, and technicians will be asked to assume greater responsibilities, particularly if there are no funds to hire additional staff in the numbers that would be desirable. As their burdens increase, the productivity of their efforts is likely to decline. Government agencies lacking the means to hire qualified managers from the outside will be forced to find project managers from among their technical specialists, who have little training or experience in management. These managers may be asked to serve simultaneously in a technical capacity in the projects under their direction.

Additional money obtained from local revenue sources can help ease administrative and managerial problems, but money can only go so far. Bureaucracies are slow to change, and the development of professionalism in management and administration may be hindered by the lack of a permanent civil service and by the frequent use of political criteria in decision making.

The managerial and administrative problems discussed above often make project implementation seriously deficient. This is not attributable so much to malevolent motives on the part of those in charge of implementation (though they are present, too, as they are in the developed countries) as to the nature of the system. Over time, as managerial and administrative experience is gained, project implementation will improve, though the process usually is slow. And if a government changes and the new leaders prove to be interested chiefly in personal gain or aggrandizement, improvements in implementation may suffer a setback.

Debt Relief

As developing countries have increased their borrowings from abroad, interest payments and amortization of their debts have required increasingly large outlays of foreign exchange. While some of the poorer developing countries have been able to obtain much of their recent aid in the form of grants or loans on highly concessional terms (0 to 3 percent interest, repayment periods of up to forty to fifty years, and grace periods of five to ten years), less-poor developing countries not eligible for such terms (and some that are) have relied heavily on private loans at high interest rates and with short repayment periods. Data from the World Bank's *Annual Report* for 1977 show that private loans accounted for 38 percent of the outstanding debt of the developing countries at the end of 1975, compared with 28 percent at the end of 1969.

If a country's foreign exchange earnings do not increase to meet debt-service obligations, imports will have to be restricted or the country must try to renegotiate its foreign debt. Twenty-two multilateral renegotiations, involving nine countries (Argentina, Brazil, Chile, Ghana, Indonesia, India, Pakistan, Peru, and Turkey) were approved between 1956 and 1973, and some of these same countries, as well as others, have been involved in debt renegotiations since then. A typical example is the rescheduling of $174 million of Argentina's debt principal, originally due in 1963–1964, for repayment over a six-year period (1965 to 1970). Because of the longer repayment period, and the relatively low (6 percent) interest rate on the new loan making this possible, this debt relief operation had a grant element of 13 percent. The grant element was even higher—from 48 to 61 percent—in debt renegotiations for Ghana (1970), Indonesia (1970), and India (1968).[19] While providing economic relief, debt renegotiations involve political costs to developing countries, since creditors require that debtor countries promise to take unpopular actions to "put their monetary and fiscal houses in order."

World Bank data for eighty-four developing countries show that their combined debt outstanding rose from $62.5 billion at the end of 1969 to $173.9 billion at the end of 1975.[20] The particularly sharp increase in 1974 ($30.9 billion, or 26 percent) resulted in large part from balance-of-payments difficulties caused by declining terms of trade and lowered demand for some developing-country exports. While the accompanying world inflation reduced the real value of existing debts, it increased both principal amounts and interest rates for new loans.

Of the eighty-four countries surveyed by the World Bank in 1975, sixteen had ratios of debt service to exports of commodities and nonfactor services of 15 percent or more, headed by Uruguay, where 46 percent of export earnings were needed to amortize debt principal and make interest payments. An additional eight countries had ratios in the 10 to 15 percent range. Falling export prices can quickly raise the debt-service/export

19. Thomas M. Klein, "Economic Aid through Debt Relief," *Finance and Development,* 10 (September 1973), 17–20, 34–35.

20. These figures exclude private debt not guaranteed by developing country governments. This amounted to an estimated $45.5 billion at the end of 1976 (*IMF Survey,* June 5, 1978, p. 172).

ratio, as happened in many countries in 1975. Petroleum-exporting countries have been more fortunate. In Iran, for example, the ratio fell from 19 percent to just 5 percent between 1972 and 1974. Among the major geographic regions, the highest debt-service/export ratios are in Latin America, where the capacity to repay foreign debt has been growing fairly rapidly, and in South Asia, where only since 1975 has there been much of an improvement in repayment capacity. Debt-service ratios are less than 10 percent for twenty-nine of thirty-four African countries south of the Sahara, and for seven of the eight countries in the East Asia-Pacific region.

The subject of debt relief has received considerable attention in recent Third World meetings, where it has been advocated as an effective and quick way of providing assistance to developing countries whose development prospects have received serious blows from world recession, world inflation, and sharply higher petroleum prices. Some developing-country leaders are advocating that *all* principal and interest obligations to nonprivate creditors be forgiven, at least for the very poorest developing countries. Until the overall economic situation improves in the developed world, significant steps in this direction will be politically difficult to take. But pressures for debt relief are bound to grow, and many observers believe that it is only a matter of time before most nonprivate debts are indeed forgiven for the poorest countries.[21]

PRIVATE FOREIGN INVESTMENT

Pros and Cons

The role of private foreign investment (PFI) is one of the most controversial topics in the field of development economics. At one extreme, there are those who argue that private investors take advantage of their business experience and monopoly power to drain resources from the developing countries, leaving them actually worse off than they were prior to the investment. Moreover, it is charged, they conspire with traditional elite groups to preserve the political and social status quo. At the other extreme, some private-enterprise zealots have claimed that only with substantial outside private investment and know-how can a country be pulled out of the quagmire of poverty and stagnation. For developing countries generally, the truth probably lies far from either extreme, though its exact location will vary from country to country.

21. In July 1978 the British government, though still opposed to generalized debt relief, introduced a bill in the House of Commons to cancel annual debt obligations of up to £60 million annually from 17 of the poorest developing countries (*IMF Survey*, August 14, 1978, pp. 255–256).

Both the extreme critics and the extreme supporters of PFI have frequently employed arguments of dubious analytical merit. For example, critics looking at balance-of-payments data sometimes find that more is being sent abroad in the form of profit remittances, royalties, and other transfers than is entering the country in the form of new investment, and cite this as proof of a net resource outflow or "exploitation." A more appropriate comparison, however, is between transfers abroad (plus retained earnings and local profit distributions) and accumulated investment—i.e., the rate of return on investment. Moreover, the counting of net external flows is incomplete, particularly because export earnings attributable to PFI are ignored. On the other hand, PFI supporters often go to the extreme of attributing *all* export earnings for a particular product, forever and ever, to the activities of the foreign investors who started the industry. While it may be true that the industry might not have existed without PFI, or might have been smaller, nationals of developing countries often can quickly learn the nuts and bolts of that industry's operations, so that continued foreign ownership cannot be justified on the grounds of technological expertise. A classic example is the Suez Canal, which contrary to widespread predictions was managed creditably by the Egyptians after they seized control of it in 1956. A more recent example is the petroleum industry, nationalized in whole or in part in many developing countries. Although the large private petroleum companies have not disappeared from the scene, the useful services they provide are now often contracted for under conditions determined largely by the developing countries, which have managed to obtain for themselves a higher share of the benefits of the original investment.

The attractiveness of PFI to developing countries is that it is a convenient way to help fill the gap between the domestic savings rate and the investment rate deemed necessary to achieve national economic goals. As we saw in the previous chapter, mobilization of additional domestic savings is difficult. This is particularly true if the government is trying to encourage the commitment of equity capital by local residents to projects that are large and relatively risky, and in which local entrepreneurs and potential entrepreneurs lack expertise. Unless the government itself is willing to assume the entrepreneurial role, foreign investment may be the only way for these priority industries to be established in the short run.

Foreign investors contribute more than just financial resources. They also provide managerial, administrative, engineering, and other technical skills that are in short supply, particularly in the poorest developing countries. Many of today's petroleum-exporting countries could not have developed their natural resource base without foreign assistance (though this could have been provided by public agencies as well as by private firms).

Offsetting the attractiveness of PFI have been a number of features to which developing countries understandably have objected. Many foreign firms have reserved all senior executive positions for their own nationals, at best training host-country nationals for middle-level positions with little management authority. Foreign firms may utilize capital-intensive technologies inappropriate to the host country's factor proportions.[22] They may do little to encourage local suppliers so that the import content of their operations can be reduced. The lavish spending patterns of some foreign nationals are bound to create social tensions and may have an undesirable demonstration effect on the aspirations of host-country citizens. Especially disturbing to some people is the interference of foreign firms in what are regarded as domestic political matters.

Not all foreign firms, of course, exhibit the kind of behavior described in the paragraph above. But the exploits of some, such as the United Fruit Company in Central America in the early twentieth century,[23] have tainted foreign firms generally, causing them to be viewed as threats to national sovereignty. Given the current strength of nationalism in developing countries, it is not surprising that the great majority of political leaders in the developing world frequently make sharp public attacks on PFI. Particularly singled out are the multinational corporations (MNCs),[24] which often (and sometimes with justification) are viewed as political agents of developed country governments.

Alternatives to Private Foreign Investment

As Vernon (1977: 161) has noted, perhaps only Burma and Cambodia can be said to have almost totally rejected private foreign investment. Other countries with widely differing political systems and ideologies have chosen to accommodate it to one extent or another. To the extent that a country chooses *not* to accommodate it, there are basically two alternatives: (1) greater encouragement of private domestic savings and investment and (2) state entrepreneurship.

The first strategy requires many of the financial measures described in the previous chapter. It also involves what Vernon (1977: 160) refers to as "unbundling" investment activities—i.e., not accepting the com-

---

22. As Vernon (1977: 161ff) points out, though, developing country governments themselves sometimes insist that the foreign investor use the newest available technology. Moreover, as we saw in chapter 12, their industrialization policies usually are biased in favor of capital intensity.

23. The United Fruit Company was sometimes more powerful than the governments in the Central American countries where it operated. Some country presidents were in effect puppets of the company.

24. Also referred to as multinational enterprises or transnational companies (enterprises).

plete "packages" offered by MNCs but encouraging and assisting local entrepreneurs to acquire the "components" separately by purchasing appropriate foreign technology through licensing and other arrangements, obtaining suppliers' credits and other forms of foreign financing, and developing their own marketing channels. Domestic financing can be provided through an expansion of commercial banking activity and the establishment of agricultural and industrial development banks *(financieras)*, which foreign aid agencies have been willing to support. In Vernon's view (1977: 160), the limited evidence available suggests that the net economic benefits of such a strategy, on the whole, would be similar to those of a strategy based on direct PFI. The model for successful implementation of an unbundling strategy is Japan.

Vernon warns that an unbundling strategy requires careful planning and a strong government commitment to supporting local enterprises. This commitment would involve such activities as making travel grants to private entrepreneurs wishing to investigate alternative technologies available in other countries; developing strong commercial sections in overseas embassies and consulates to gather intelligence on production processes and marketing activities; providing government guarantees for private loans secured abroad; making domestic credit available on favorable terms; providing education and training for skilled production workers and other manpower; and facilitating the development of backward and forward linkages in the domestic economy and abroad. The subsidy costs required for such a strategy could be offset by the benefits of more efficiently functioning markets. Many developing countries have scattered programs in most of the areas we have just mentioned; but these efforts are not carefully planned and coordinated, and the individual programs themselves are often too small to be effective. As Vernon puts it, most developing country efforts are "altogether inadequate for implementing a broad policy of unbundling" (1977: 173).

The alternative of state entrepreneurship—or what might be called direct unbundling by the public sector—is one whose appeal is not confined to "leftist" governments. Governments on the other side of the political spectrum, such as those in Argentina and Brazil, have also found state ownership attractive. This is probably explained by that imprecise term, "nationalism," which may be thought of as a desire by a country's people and government to exercise greater control over their economy at the expense of foreigners and the impersonal forces of the market which work to foreigners' advantage. Although governments in developing countries seem increasingly willing to undertake an entrepreneurial role, their ability to command the necessary financial resources is limited. To the extent that they are unable or unwilling to finance their planned investments by mobilizing domestic savings, state enterprises must seek funds abroad from international agencies such as the World Bank or from private or state-owned banks and suppliers. When the choice is restricted to the latter, the cost of borrowing may be unacceptably high, or the conditions may be politically unacceptable.

Most developing countries, as we have noted, have not tried to eliminate direct PFI altogether. Rather, they have sought to combine it, in varying proportions, with elements of the two alternatives described above. Often this involves the formation of *joint ventures*, or partnerships between one or more MNCs, on the one hand, and local private and/or public enterprises, on the other. This arrangement has the advantage of better access to financial resources, technology, expertise, and markets. Some critics will of course charge that governments engaging in joint ventures with MNCs, or encouraging MNCs to operate on their own, are merely "lackeys of capitalism." But when governments like those of China and Vietnam indicate a willingness to deal with MNCs, it seems clear that they perceive the advantages to outweigh the disadvantages.

The Issue of Profits

It is widely believed that MNCs make "exorbitant" profits on their operations in developing countries. This is not the picture one obtains from the published evidence, though there is widespread agreement that the published data are a poor measure of actual profits.

Table 14.6 presents data on rates of return on U.S. investments overseas during 1975 and 1976. Before commenting on these data, it is worth pointing out that most of this investment, contrary to widespread belief, is *not* in the developing countries. At the end of 1976, as may be seen in Table 14.6, 74 percent was in other developed countries; Canada alone accounted for 25 percent, more than all developing countries combined (21 percent). In the developing countries, manufacturing accounted for 39 percent of the total, petroleum for 10 percent, and all other activities for 51 percent. Of total investment in the developing world, 81 percent was in Latin America.

Reported rates of return on all U.S. investment abroad averaged just over 14 percent in 1975 and 1976. The figures were considerably higher for developing countries (25 to 29 percent) than for developed countries (11 to 12 percent), though if one disregards investment in the petroleum industry, which yielded unusually high profits in developing countries during 1975–1976, the figures are less far apart (16 to 17 and 12 to 13 percent, respectively). Excluding petroleum, the modest differential in profit rates between the two groups of countries is not surprising. Business operations are riskier in developing countries because of the higher probability of devaluation, currency inconvertibility, nationaliza-

TABLE 14.6

U.S. Direct Investment Position Abroad, 1976, and Adjusted Rate of Return on Investment, 1975 and 1976

	Direct Investment Position, End of Year, 1976[a] (millions of dollars)	Adjusted Rate of Return on Investment[b] (percent)	
		1975	*1976*
All Countries	137,244	14.2	14.4
Petroleum	29,713	20.1	18.1
Manufacturing	61,062	11.2	12.3
Other	46,470	14.6	14.9
Developed Countries	101,150	10.9	11.9
Petroleum	23,662	8.5	8.5
Manufacturing	49,699	10.6	12.5
Other	27,789	13.5	13.4
Developing Countries	29,050	29.1	25.2
Petroleum	2,882	288.5	109.9
Manufacturing	11,362	13.9	11.3
Other	14,806	18.7	19.7
International and Unallocated	7,044	5.6	6.8

Source: Obie G. Whichard, "U.S. Direct Investment Abroad in 1976," *Survey of Current Business,* 57 (August 1977), 33–39.

[a] Net book value of U.S. direct investors' equity in, and outstanding loans to, foreign affiliates.

[b] Ratio of adjusted earnings to the average of the direct investment positions at the beginning and end of the year. Adjusted earnings are the U.S. parents' shares of total earnings (net of foreign income taxes) of their foreign affiliates, plus net interest on intercompany accounts, minus withholding taxes.

tion, political unrest, and greater uncertainties in product and factor markets.[25] While the reported rates of return in developing countries might be considered comfortable, they could hardly be called exorbitant.

Reported profit figures, however, give a misleading picture of actual profits. Intrafirm pricing policies can significantly affect the distribution of profits between the parent company and its local affiliate. Other things being equal, MNCs will seek to maximize post-tax profits on their overall operations. Thus a parent firm experiencing an actual loss in its home-base operations can reduce the book value of its loss (and still have no tax liability) by using a variety of techniques to transfer home part of the

25. U.S. firms can obtain U.S. government insurance against the risks of currency inconvertibility, expropriation, and damage resulting from war, revolution, or insurrection. But even with this insurance (which is not available for all U.S. investments overseas) the risks of operating in another country are greater than those of domestic operations.

reported profits of an overseas affiliate (and thus reduce the affiliate's tax liability). For example, the parent firm can charge an artificially high price for the sale of intermediate products to its affiliate. It can also charge its affiliate management fees, royalty payments, and a high interest rate on intrafirm loans. In other words, the affiliate's costs are artificially increased, and its reported profits correspondingly reduced.

An important and influential study of intrafirm pricing practices in Colombia (Vaitsos, 1974) concluded that actual profit rates of MNC affiliates in that country averaged 40 to 135 percent, depending on the industry. Particularly important in explaining the discrepancy between these figures and the lower reported profit rates were transfer-pricing policies associated with the affiliates' purchase of intermediate goods and factor services from the parent. Vaitsos' findings have been criticized for relying too heavily on extrapolations from data obtained for the pharmaceutical industry, where profits were atypically high, and for failure to account for the free services (such as research results, patent rights, and trademark rights) supplied by parent firms to their affiliates (Vernon, 1977: 154–158). Nevertheless, there is widespread (though by no means universal) support for the broad validity of Vaitsos' findings, at least to the extent of concluding that actual profit rates are "significantly" higher than reported.

Regulating Private Foreign Investment

The desire to obtain a greater share of the benefits of private foreign investment has led some developing countries to adopt more restrictive regulations governing PFI. One of the best-known examples is Decision 24 of the Andean Common Market (ACM), which places limits on profit remittances; establishes timetables for conversion of some foreign firms to mixed firms (51 to 80 percent local ownership) or local firms (more than 80 percent); prohibits new foreign investment in public utilities, communications, news media, insurance, and banking; regulates royalty payments; and forbids specific restrictive practices commonly associated with technology transfer.[26] Decision 24 provoked a strong negative reaction by the Council of the Americas, which represents many large U.S.-based MNCs with business interests in Latin America. Some U.S. business executives commented, in effect, that the ACM could have sent the same message in just two words: "get out."

But the purpose of Decision 24 and similar regulations elsewhere in

---

26. For example, restrictions on production volume, exporting to third countries, use of competing technology, and requirements that all inventions or innovations made by the licensee or affiliate be turned over to the supplier of the technology.

the developing world is *not* to drive all foreign investors away. Indeed, these rules implicitly recognize, in the words of a U.N.-sponsored study on multinationals, that MNCs "have developed distinct advantages that can be put to the service of world development" (U.N. 1974: xii). The purpose of restrictive legislation is (1) to limit PFI to those cases in which it can make a clearly positive contribution to development by providing services more efficiently than any alternative source, and (2) to establish a framework for bargaining over the terms and conditions of PFI. Decision 24, it should be noted, contains many loopholes in the event that certain provisions prove to be more restrictive than deemed desirable. These loopholes have been liberally used by the ACM countries.

Many foreign business executives support foreign investment codes such as Decision 24 because they promise to provide greater stability in the "rules of the game." Arbitrary changes in these rules in the past, they point out, have often discouraged more investment than restrictive legislation per se.

The growing political power of the developing countries, and the recent publicity given to bribery, extortion, and other questionable practices associated with MNC activities, have placed the multinationals on the defensive. The United Nations "Declaration on the Establishment of a New International Economic Order," adopted in 1974, calls for regulation and supervision of MNCs within the framework of an international code of conduct, a draft of which has been in preparation for several years. In 1976 the OECD (Western industrial) countries adopted a set of voluntary guidelines to be recommended to MNCs operating in its member countries, and even some MNCs support the idea of "good conduct" codes. Vernon (1977: 214) points out, though, that the developing countries' public hostility toward MNCs is an obstacle to the adoption of an international code of conduct, since these countries would not simply be granted certain rights and privileges but also would have to accept certain obligations. Whether or not an international code is adopted in the near future, it is clear that the behavior of MNCs will be subject to ever-closer scrutiny by developing country officials, who are increasingly sophisticated enough to know what to look for.

SUMMARY

Countries having difficulty increasing their domestic savings rates can still experience rising rates of investment and economic growth by borrowing from abroad—preferably on concessional terms—or by attracting private foreign investment (PFI). These alternatives are particularly attractive if the country's growth or development objectives require the importation of capital goods and current production inputs. Such a net inflow of foreign exchange in the long-term capital account of the balance of payments, other things being equal, permits a country to run a current account deficit. The amount of the deficit is equivalent to what is termed "foreign savings," which added to domestic savings will equal total domestic investment.

There is no guarantee, however, that foreign aid and PFI will supplement domestic savings and permit a higher rate of investment. Several studies have argued that foreign aid tends to replace domestic savings, making little if any contribution to the investment rate. Although the results of these studies have been challenged, there is enough a priori evidence for some countries to be concerned pending a clarification of the issue by future research. If the replacement hypothesis is confirmed, the future of foreign aid will be cloudy indeed, at least to the extent that aid is given to foster development.

But what if, as we have argued, aid is not given primarily for this purpose but rather to attain political objectives? Should we not, then, judge the effectiveness of aid by how well these political objectives are met, regardless of the economic effects? And is this not rather difficult when there are multiple objectives which often come into conflict?

Developing countries have complained vociferously about the terms of foreign aid and PFI. And they have made it clear that they prefer to be helped instead by trade reform, a subject to be taken up in the next chapter. But the fact that both foreign aid and PFI continue to be sought by developing countries with various political orientations indicates that recipient countries still regard them as contributing positively to economic growth and/or development.

Suggested Readings

Hayter, Teresa. *Aid as Imperialism*. Middlesex, Eng.: Penguin Books, 1971.
On the basis of detailed observations of aid programs in Latin America, the author concludes that the efforts of the World Bank, the International Monetary Fund, and AID to influence economic policy-making represent attempts to promote or preserve Western-style capitalism in the developing countries. While this Marxist critique sometimes strays into polemicism and glosses over the complexities of aid-donor motivations, many specific criticisms of aid agency policies in the 1960s are well argued, well documented, and essentially valid.

Organisation for Economic Cooperation and Development (OECD). *Development Cooperation: Efforts and Policies of the Members of the Development Assistance Committee, 1977 Review*. Report by Maurice J. Williams. Paris, November 1977.

This annual publication provides detailed statistics on aid flows from seventeen Western developed countries to the developing countries. It also contains chapters on specific aspects of aid policies and programs.

Pearson, Lester B., et al. *Partners in Development.* Report of the Commission on International Development. New York: Praeger Publishers, 1969.

This report, commissioned by the World Bank, was widely discussed during the early 1970s. It called for developed countries to increase their aid commitments to 0.7 percent of the GNP and made specific recommendations in a wide range of fields, including trade policy and debt relief. The Commission members soberly noted that "no foreign help will suffice where there is no national will to make fundamental changes which are needed."

Tendler, Judith. *Inside Foreign Aid.* Baltimore: The Johns Hopkins University Press, 1975.

This insightful book by a former AID employee argues persuasively that the organizational environment in which an aid agency functions plays a major role in determining the projects that are selected for assistance and the design of these projects. This environment, which places pressures on agency employees to "move money," results in a bias in favor of large projects and projects with high foreign-exchange costs.

United Nations Department of Economic and Social Affairs. *Multinational Corporations in World Development.* New York: Praeger Publishers, 1974.

This study reviews the economic and political impact of MNCs in developing countries. It argues that MNCs have the potential to make a major contribution to development but maintains that their activities must be regulated at the national, regional, and international levels. Proposals for such regulation are presented.

Vaitsos, Constantine. *Intercountry Income Distribution and Transnational Enterprises.* London: Clarendon Press, 1974.

This study of affiliates of multinational corporations (MNCs) in Colombia found that actual profit rates were considerably higher than reported, largely because of the MNCs' transfer-pricing policies. Vaitsos' research results were well known in developing countries several years before publication in this book, and they have helped Colombia and other developing countries bargain successfully with MNCs to reduce disguised monopoly profits. Undergraduates will find parts of this book difficult, but the effort will be rewarding.

Vernon, Raymond. *Storm over the Multinationals: The Real Issues.* Cambridge, Mass.: Harvard University Press, 1977.

This is a short, easy-to-read, yet sophisticated work by one of the most knowledgeable students of multinational corporations (MNCs). Though Vernon is sometimes charged with being too partial to the MNCs' interests, his book is more balanced than most others written on this subject. Vernon's comments on data and research findings are valuable and insightful, even if one does not agree with all of his interpretations. Vernon sees a growing potential for conflict between the interests of MNCs and those of nation-states.

15

Reforms in the Structure of International Trade and Finance

For the past fifteen to twenty years, developing countries have lobbied aggressively in international organizations for actions to increase their export opportunities and to make their foreign exchange receipts less subject to changing economic conditions in the developed countries. They have also created forums of their own to assist and cooperate with each other, and to achieve greater bargaining power vis-à-vis the developed countries by adopting unified positions on key policy issues.

There are at least two major reasons why the developing countries have been seeking major reforms in international trade and finance. One, explained in chapter 10, is disappointment with import substitution and the concomitant acceptance—public statements to the contrary notwithstanding—of the economic interdependence of nations. The other, noted in chapter 14, is disillusionment with foreign aid as a means of transferring resources from the developed to the developing countries. Resource transfers via trade have fewer economic, political, and bureaucratic strings attached than those associated with aid.

The specific trade and financial reforms proposed by the developing countries have been many and varied. Among the most important have been those related to trade preferences, commodity agreements, compensatory financing during periods of falling export earnings, changes in the conditions attached to technology transfer, and a reduction in non-tariff barriers to trade in the developed countries. In addition to pressing for these changes, developing countries have actively promoted exports by taking domestic measures not requiring international agreement, and by attempting to integrate their economies more closely through regional organizations.

REGIONAL ECONOMIC INTEGRATION

After World War II, some developing countries were attracted to regional economic integration as a means of accelerating their economic growth. Widening the market for goods and services, it was believed, would lower production costs because greater economies of scale and external economies could be realized. Additional downward pressures on prices could be expected from greater competition among firms in the participating countries.

Economic theory and empirical studies suggest that if countries are at about the same level of development, and already conduct much of their trade with each other, there is a good chance that all will stand to gain from the greater specialization and division of labor resulting from integration of their economies. But where development levels are unequal, special provisions may be required to prevent the smaller and least developed countries from being hurt by increased competition from their partners.

Several levels or degrees of regional economic integration may be identified. A *free trade area* is the most limited. Member countries agree gradually to abolish tariffs and nontariff barriers to trade among themselves, but each retains its own restrictions against products from outside the region. Unification of tariff schedules applied to nonmembers results in a *customs union*. If, in addition, the factors of production are free to move among member countries, a *common market* is created. Higher degrees of economic integration may be achieved through harmonization of monetary and fiscal policies and the introduction of a common currency.

The European Economic Community (EEC) is the best-known example of successful economic integration among developed countries. A less obvious but also successful example is the United States, whose Constitution of 1787 abolished the trade restrictions imposed by the thirteen colonies on each other under the Articles of Confederation.

In the developing world, the most significant efforts at regional economic integration have been in Latin America. A Latin American customs union was proposed in 1948 by the U.N. Economic Commission for Latin America, and in 1951 the five Central American nations agreed to work toward integration of their small economies. After a decade of discussions, a treaty establishing the Central American Common Market (CACM) was signed in 1960. By the end of the 1960s, most trade barriers among the five member countries had been removed and a common external tariff nearly achieved. A regional bank had been created to finance projects that would promote economic integration. Intraregional trade expanded rapidly,[1] with industrial products accounting for 95 percent of intra-CACM trade by 1975. But factor mobility was considerably less than perfect, and most of the benefits of integration went to Guatemala and El Salvador—a situation that was untenable in the long run.[2] With the outbreak of the "Soccer War" between Honduras and El Salvador in 1969, the CACM suffered a setback from which it has not fully recovered. Once the process of integration lost its momentum, the individual governments began to reorient their trade strategies to emphasize the promotion of new export products to countries outside the CACM.

The Latin American Free Trade Association (LAFTA), also formed in 1960, comprises the ten Spanish- and Portuguese-speaking countries of South America plus Mexico. It has had even less success in meeting its objectives than the CACM. Although initial tariff cuts were achieved without too much difficulty, negotiations for further reductions became stalled because member countries were politically unwilling to see their less competitive industries decline or disappear as a result of competition from other LAFTA countries where comparative advantage lay. Some LAFTA members were particularly sensitive about prestige industries, such as automobiles and steel. The smaller countries balked at cutting tariffs on some products they did not yet produce (but wanted to), fearing that domestic production of these goods would become impossible if the larger countries secured a foothold. Almost no progress was made in reducing barriers to trade in agricultural products. The deadline for removing all remaining tariffs on intraregional trade in manufactures, originally set for 1973, was postponed to 1980, and even this date now seems

---

1. Intraregional trade (based on import data) rose from $32.7 million in 1960 to $299.1 million in 1970. This represents an annual rate of increase in current dollars of 25 percent. Since prices rose by only about 2 percent annually during this period, the real value of intra-CACM trade also increased very rapidly. See Inter-American Development Bank (IDB), *Economic and Social Progress in Latin America, 1976 Report* (Washington, D.C., 1977), p. 111.

2. Intra-CACM trade data for 1970, in millions of dollars, were as follows (IDB, op. cit., p. 112):

	Exports	*Imports*	*Balance*
Costa Rica	48.7	68.6	−19.9
El Salvador	75.0	60.6	14.4
Guatemala	106.4	65.0	41.4
Honduras	19.1	54.9	−35.8
Nicaragua	49.9	50.0	− 0.1

Data for 1975 show even greater disparities. Guatemala had a favorable balance of $80.1 million, while the four other countries had deficits ranging from $14.9 million to $23.4 million.

optimistic.[3] Still, intraregional trade has expanded, though not as rapidly as in the CACM.[4]

Some of the smaller and medium-sized LAFTA countries, fearing that the benefits of a fully functioning free trade area would go mainly to the larger countries (Argentina, Brazil, and Mexico), agreed in 1966 to form a common market among themselves, within the larger LAFTA framework. Three years later, the Andean Group was established by Bolivia, Chile, Colombia, Ecuador, and Peru; Venezuela joined in 1973. Free trade in industrial products was contemplated by 1980, though Bolivia and Ecuador, the least developed countries, were given longer periods of adjustment and other special benefits. At this stage, prospects for success of this integration scheme are fairly promising, despite a lengthening of some of the timetables, a relaxation of the rules of the common foreign investment code (see chapter 14), and the withdrawal of Chile in October 1976. But it is still too early to tell how strong the Andean Group ultimately will be. The same factors which slowed progress in LAFTA might limit progress of this more ambitious effort at regional economic integration.

Another integration effort in the Americas began in 1968 with the formation of the Caribbean Free Trade Association (CARIFTA), which united the economies of the English-speaking states in the Caribbean region. In 1973 CARIFTA was transformed into a common market (CARICOM), and a common external tariff was implemented in 1976. The Caribbean Development Bank (CDB), which borrows funds on favorable terms from major donor agencies, has quickly acquired a reputation as a solid financial institution.[5] An unusual feature of CARICOM is that more attention is being given to intraregional trade in agriculture than to trade in industrial products. Per capita food imports now exceed $80 annually in the region, and it is hoped that greater intraregional specialization and trade will help reduce this high and rapidly rising food

---

3. The disappointing progress of LAFTA has often been attributed largely to the fact that many of the tariff cuts were to be periodically negotiated, rather than made automatic. The problem, though, is not really an inappropriate mechanism but rather the lack of a strong commitment by the LAFTA countries to integration—a commitment that would have been necessary for reaching agreement on an automatic tariff-reduction mechanism.

4. Intra-LAFTA exports accounted for 11.6 percent of the regional total during 1974–1975, compared with 7.6 percent in 1962–1964. Excluding Venezuela, whose petroleum exports distort the data, the figures were 8.6 and 16.5 percent, respectively. Import data, however, show very little change. Intraregional imports rose only from 10.4 percent in 1962–1964 to 11.0 percent in 1974–1975 (11.7 and 11.8 percent, respectively, excluding Venezuela). See IDB, op. cit., pp. 101–102.

5. The CDB's first president was W. Arthur Lewis, a native of St. Lucia, whose classic 1955 text on economic development we have cited on several occasions.

import bill. Progress in agriculture has been disappointing, however, as the same nationalist forces that led in 1962 to the breakup of the West Indies Federation—a political union comprising most of the same states—have slowed or delayed the implementation of several regional programs.

In sub-Saharan Africa, five regional groupings which aim at least for customs-union status have been established: the Customs and Economic Union of Central Africa (four nations), dating from 1966; the East African Community (Kenya, Uganda, and Tanzania), formed in 1967; the Mano River Union (Liberia and Sierra Leone), created in 1973; the six-member Economic Community of West Africa, established in 1974; and the fifteen-member Economic Community of West African States, founded in 1975.[6] The East African Community is nearly lifeless because of political differences among the three member countries. The degree of integration within the other four groupings is still modest.

Regional organizations in other parts of the world have usually had less ambitious objectives, sometimes limited to consultation and cooperation in regional development projects and services. These groupings include the Maghreb Permanent Consultative Committee (Algeria, Morocco, and Tunisia), established in 1964 but moribund since 1970; the Association of South-East Asian Nations (Indonesia, Malaysia, the Philippines, Singapore, and Thailand), established in 1967 but plagued by political tensions between several pairs of member nations; and Regional Cooperation for Development (Iran, Pakistan, and Turkey), formed in 1964 but largely inactive until 1976, when agreement was reached to create a free-trade area over a ten-year period. Egypt, Iraq, Jordan, and Syria formed the Arab Common Market (ACM) in 1964, and the Sudan joined in 1977. Tariffs on intraregional trade were abolished in 1973, and a common external tariff is to be established by 1981. But the ACM still seems to be a weak organization.

In summary, regional economic integration, like ISI, has been a disappointing strategy of growth and development. Even when a number of developing economies have become integrated, their joint market is still relatively small, thus limiting the scope for economies of scale and for competition among firms. Moreover, imports of some goods are simply shifted from low-cost producers in the developed countries to high-cost regional producers protected by tariffs against the developed industrialized economies—a phenomenon known as *trade diversion* (as opposed to *trade creation*). Smaller and relatively poorer countries can actually suffer from economic integration if not compensated for disadvantages vis-à-vis their partners. But the major reasons for the disappointing results of economic

6. For a summary of the main provisions of these and other regional groupings, see Morton and Tulloch (1977: 305–308).

integration are political. Newly independent nations find it difficult to sacrifice recently won national sovereignty to a multinational authority. And in Latin America, whose nations have been independent for about 150 years, governments have found it difficult to resist pressures from powerful vested interests in agriculture, manufacturing, and trade.

UNCTAD

Along with attempts to increase trade with each other through regional economic integration, developing countries have been seeking ways to increase their exports to the developed countries. This objective has been pursued through two separate strategies: (1) domestic policy changes to improve incentives for exports, particularly of manufactured goods (see chapter 10) and (2) pressures on the developed countries to change the "rules of the game" applying to international trade, which we argued in chapter 5 historically have discriminated against the developing countries. At the United Nations Conference on Trade and Development (UNCTAD), held in Geneva in 1964, the developing countries presented a united front in asking the developed countries for trade preferences, commodity agreements, and other reforms in international trade and finance. In responding, the developed countries were far from united. Not only was there a split between Eastern and Western bloc countries, but the Western nations themselves were also divided. While the EEC was sympathetic to the demands of the developing countries, the U.S. position was intransigent. As a result, the conference produced few tangible results for the developing countries.

Nevertheless, the developing countries had demonstrated their ability to organize and unite behind a single platform, and the developed countries were placed on the defensive. Moreover, UNCTAD was able to become a permanent organization which established committees to give further study to major issues and began to make plans for a second conference. UNCTAD's first Secretary-General, interestingly, was the Argentine economist Raúl Prebisch, whose acceptance of this position represented a significant symbolic departure from the ISI policies he derived in the 1950s from his terms-of-trade thesis (see chapter 5).

Since 1964 there have been three additional UNCTAD conferences: at New Delhi in 1968, Santiago in 1972, and Nairobi in 1976. The developing countries have preserved their unity by meeting before each conference as the so-called "Group of 77" (actually now about 115) countries. Although the immediate results of the UNCTAD conferences have been disappointing to the developing countries, the pressures for change placed on the developed countries have resulted in some significant reforms in international trade and finance in the intervening years.

COMMODITY AGREEMENTS AND
PRODUCER CARTELS

One of the principal objectives of the Group of 77 has been the negotiation of a series of international commodity agreements for their major primary product exports. These agreements, ideally, would have two purposes: (1) to reduce price fluctuations and the resulting instability in major macroeconomic variables and (2) to raise the long-term trend of prices to compensate for what is perceived to have been past deterioration in the developing countries' terms of trade. More recently, some developing countries, notably Iran, have argued that the terms of trade should be stabilized by "indexing" primary product prices to the prices of manufactured goods.

By the mid-1960s, five international commodity agreements had been reached, independently of the pressures generated by UNCTAD. The most significant was that for coffee, one of the most important primary products in world trade. The others were for wheat, tin, olive oil, and sugar. These agreements, however, covered only a small percentage of total developing-country exports. The sugar agreement, moreover, ceased to function after the United States refused to import sugar from Cuba (though the United States had a special arrangement with some producing countries, as did the European countries for their former colonies).[7]

Before discussing subsequent efforts to obtain commodity agreements, it is useful to examine briefly some of the characteristics of these schemes and the conditions under which they are feasible or not feasible. Commodity agreements often involve the establishment of *buffer stocks* which are to be built up once prices fall below a certain level. The existence of these stocks would limit effective market supply and check the decline in prices. If prices rise above some agreed-upon maximum, the accumulated stocks would be sold in the open market, thus exerting a downward pressure on prices. Buffer stocks, of course, can be used only for nonperishable products. A major problem with these schemes is financing the purchase and storage of the commodities in question. Though some assistance has been available from the IMF since 1969, additional amounts are needed if buffer stocks are to be more widely used.

One way producing and consuming countries could deal with this problem is to establish a common fund to finance the accumulation of buffer stocks for a large number of commodities. This idea was proposed by the UNCTAD Secretariat and was adopted as a consensus resolu-

7. For a review of these agreements, see Tony Killick, "Commodity Agreements as International Aid," *Westminster Bank Review* (February 1967), 18–30, reprinted in Gerald M. Meier, *Leading Issues in Economic Development*, 2nd ed. (New York: Oxford University Press, 1970), pp. 772–778.

tion at UNCTAD IV in 1976, after the United States and some other developed countries backed down from the commodity-by-commodity approach they had favored. Even so, it was agreed simultaneously to seek agreements on individual commodities. The idea of a common fund is simply that of risk spreading. The total amount needed for financing would be less than the sum of the amounts required for agreements on individual commodities. A negotiating conference was to be convened before March 1977 to seek establishment of such a fund. Proposed contributors to the fund included exporting countries, OPEC members, developed importing countries, and multilaterial agencies. It was also suggested that part of the fund's resources be borrowed in private capital markets.

Given the scope of the proposal (eighteen commodities were mentioned in the UNCTAD resolution on commodity agreements, ten of which were to be included in the initial buffer-stock scheme)[8] and the size of the fund suggested by the Group of 77 ($6 billion), a high degree of international cooperation obviously would be required. The United States and some other developed countries committed themselves only to studying the idea, indicating that they would not necessarily contribute to a common fund even if a decision were made to adopt it. Negotiations between the developed and developing countries have thus far failed to resolve difference of opinion regarding the nature of the fund.

If a commodity agreement seeks not only to limit price fluctuations but also to raise average prices (or the long-term price trend line), an important consideration is the price-elasticity of demand (PED) for the product. If a 10 percent price increase causes quantity demanded to fall by more than 10 percent (PED > 1), export earnings will actually decline. This can occur for primary products for which there are close natural or synthetic substitutes. Commodity agreements for these products can hope to accomplish little more than price stabilization (Strategy A of Figure 15.1).

But if demand is price-inelastic (PED < 1), export earnings will rise if the average level of prices, or the long-term price trend line, can be raised (Strategy B). The recent case of petroleum provides a dramatic example of what can be done if producing countries can band together and raise prices without having to negotiate an agreement which also involves consuming nations. The quadrupling of oil prices transferred an

8. The ten commodities for which buffer-stock arrangements were proposed are coffee, cocoa, tea, sugar, cotton, rubber, jute, hard fibers, copper, and tin. Commodities for which other schemes were proposed are bananas, bauxite, iron ore, manganese, meat, phosphates, tropical timber, and vegetable oils. For a generally favorable reaction to the UNCTAD proposal, and a good review of the strengths and weaknesses of commodity agreements, see Isaiah Frank, "Toward a New Framework for International Commodity Policy," *Finance and Development*, 13 (June 1976), 17–20, 37–38. For a negative reaction to commodity agreement proposals, see Grubel (1977).

Figure 15.1
Commodity Price Stabilization: A Hypothetical Example

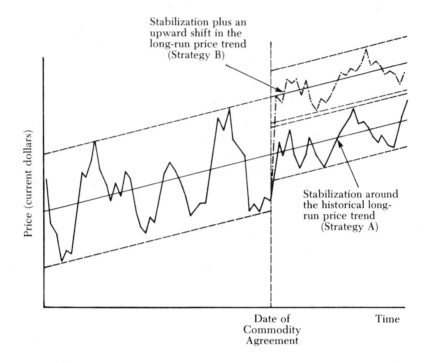

Stabilization plus an
upward shift in the
long-run price trend
(Strategy B)

Stabilization around
the historical long-
run price trend
(Strategy A)

Price (current dollars)

Date of
Commodity
Agreement

Time

additional $30 billion or more annually to the oil-producing countries, with no strings attached, far more than these countries (and developing nations as a group) had been receiving as aid subject to various conditions. The success of OPEC has understandably tempted other developing countries to seek the establishment of similar cartels for other inelastic-demand products.

However, there are limits to how far an OPEC-like strategy can be carried, since a significant short-run drain on the developed countries' international reserves would result in another world recession.[9] This, in turn, would lower the demand for primary products (i.e., shift demand schedules to the left) and place downward pressures on prices that would be difficult for developing countries to resist. It is instructive to note in this regard that *relative* petroleum prices (i.e., in comparison with the

9. While it is true that much of the additional foreign exchange transferred to the OPEC countries has returned to the developed countries to purchase goods and services, this return flow occurred with a lag, leaving many developed countries with serious balance-of-payments problems for several years.

prices of goods and services imported by the oil-exporting nations) have fallen since 1974. Maintenance of high *nominal* prices has been possible only because of production cutbacks, which some countries have resisted. Even with the cutbacks, quantity supplied exceeds quantity demanded at the current (mid-1978) nominal price, and some OPEC nations are unofficially selling petroleum at a discount.

Cooperation among countries participating in a commodity agreement is difficult to achieve, particularly if the agreement involves a large number of parties. Some countries may balk at a proposed quota based on their past market shares, arguing that their "natural" shares would be higher once new land or new mines come into production. A low-cost producer may argue for a relatively low price, hoping that this will force some of the competition out of the market. Inefficient producers, on the other hand, will argue for high prices. For many commodities, particularly those for which demand is price-elastic, the cooperation of consuming countries is essential for the agreement to work. Even if an agreement is established, countries with balance-of-payments problems may threaten it by shaving prices and increasing export volumes through illegal channels.

During the 1970s, attempts to reach new commodity agreements or to renew existing ones have met with mixed success. An agreement on cocoa was reached in 1972 but was only partially implemented while in force from 1973 to 1976. A second agreement, which like the first includes both buffer stocks and a quota scheme, covers the period 1976–1979. All major exporting countries are members, as are most importing countries with the major exception of the United States. It is difficult to tell how well the cocoa agreement will work in the long run. The stabilization scheme has never been used because market prices have exceeded the specified ceiling ever since the first agreement became effective. The International Coffee Agreement collapsed in 1972, and a new agreement was not negotiated until late 1975. Similarly, the International Sugar Agreement which expired in December 1973 was not replaced by a new agreement until October 1977. A banana agreement reached by a number of Latin American nations has not been effective because Ecuador, the largest exporter, and other major producing nations in Africa and Asia, have not participated. Even with full participation, the large number of producing countries and high perishability of bananas suggests that an effective agreement for this commodity is unlikely to be reached. International agreements for tin, wheat, and olive oil have been renewed, but the latter two contain no effective provisions for controlling prices and supplies.

To provide a better indication of how specific commodity agreements function, it is useful to review the major provisions of the new International Coffee Agreement, which became effective in 1976 and is scheduled to last for six years. The agreement, reached in late 1975, was the result of three years of discussions among forty-two producing countries and twenty consuming countries following the breakdown of the previous, relatively inflexible agreement during a time when prices were high and quotas were under attack because of the poor medium-term outlook for Brazil, the principal exporter. As in the previous agreement, the new agreement relies on export quotas, based on previous performance, to regulate supply. But quota controls are not to come into effect until prices fall below a specified minimum, and more specific provisions are made for suspending quotas during periods of prolonged price increases. To introduce additional flexibility into the quota system, both the global quota and individual-country quotas are divided into two parts: 70 percent is fixed, while the remaining 30 percent is to be allocated according to performance criteria, such as actual export volume and stocks. A proposed buffer stock scheme was deemed not feasible because of supply shortages. To protect consuming countries against supply interruptions and unusually high prices, the agreement provides for (1) prompt declarations of export shortfalls by producing countries and their redistribution to countries capable of supplying the necessary volumes and (2) measures to prevent deliberate shipments by any country of amounts less than its quota. Since prices have remained relatively high since the agreement came into effect, its strength has not really been tested.[10]

An important issue regarding commodity agreements or producer cartels—particularly if they are viewed as a substitute for aid—is the distribution of benefits among producing countries. In the case of petroleum, most of the benefits went to developing countries with relatively high per capita incomes. Though some relatively low-income countries also benefited (notably Indonesia and Nigeria), many non-oil-producing developing countries were faced with significantly higher import bills. For other commodities the distribution of benefits would vary, but there is no reason to believe that commodity agreements or cartels *generally* would contribute to a narrowing of income inequalities among the countries of the developing world. For commodities exported primarily by the higher-income developing countries, the effect would be just the opposite. Still, cartels and (some) commodity agreements would be effective in transferring resources from developed to developing countries. And to the extent that relatively affluent countries among the latter are willing to engage in aid programs of their own, as the OPEC countries have done, the benefits of higher commodity prices can be diffused more widely within the developing world.

The history of commodity agreements to date suggests that one

10. See *IMF Survey*, Dec. 15, 1975, pp. 368–369, and July 4, 1977, p. 223.

should be cautious about predicting significant transfers of resources from developed to developing countries via this mechanism. Nevertheless, even if the common fund scheme is not adopted, some new agreements for individual commodities are likely now that the United States—the major consuming country—is more favorably disposed to such agreements than it has been in the past.

TARIFF PREFERENCES

Developing countries have argued, with considerable justification, that the structure of tariffs in the developed countries (together with non-tariff barriers to trade) discriminates against them. Tariffs in the major developed countries generally average only 10 percent or less, but they are often much higher for the light manufactured goods in which the developing countries have a comparative advantage. One solution to this inequity, proposed at UNCTAD I by the Group of 77, was a "Generalized System of Preferences" (GSP) to be granted by the developed countries to manufactured and semimanufactured products exported by the developing countries. For all such commodities, it was argued, tariffs applied to the developing countries (but not other developed countries) should be reduced or even eliminated.

Progress toward adoption of a GSP was at first quite slow. The United States opposed it because the increased competition from developing countries would force many U.S. plants to close, leaving thousands of not-very-skilled workers without jobs—a situation which was politically unacceptable to many in both the executive and legislative branches of government. There was also opposition from some other developed countries. Some African countries seemed to prefer an extension of the regional trade preferences they enjoyed in the EEC, rather than a generalized scheme which would force them to compete with all other developing countries in European markets. Finally, in 1970, agreement was reached that each developed country (or group of developed countries, such as the EEC) would adopt its own GSP for a period of ten years.

Though most developed countries moved rather quickly to implement their GSP schemes, the United States was slow to muster the political will to act. Not until the Trade Act of 1974 (signed in January 1975) did Congress authorize the president to put the GSP into effect. As finally implemented in January 1976, the United States' GSP eliminated, for a period of ten years, all tariffs on more than 2,700 primary and manufactured products exported by ninety-eight independent developing countries and thirty-nine dependent territories. The political benefits of this action were offset not only by its tardiness but also by the legislated exclusion of certain countries because of "bad behavior" (e.g., membership in OPEC, failure to take action to prevent the export of illegal drugs, nationalization without compensation or negotiation). Furthermore, many important developing-country exports were declared ineligible, including certain types of textiles, iron and steel products, footwear, glass, electronic products, chemicals, ball bearings, and plywood.

These restrictions, and similar ones adopted by other developed countries, significantly limit the developing countries' potential gains from existing GSP schemes. For the developed countries as a whole, it has been estimated that only 39 percent of manufactured and semimanufactured imports from the developing countries are covered by the GSP. A similar situation exists for agricultural products. One attempt to measure the effects of GSP on developing country exports, based on 1971 trade data, concluded that annual exports would have increased by $1,387 million *in the absence of nontariff barriers to trade* (NTBs). But since NTBs are in fact significant impediments to trade in many manufactured products, the actual increase in developing country exports in 1971 attributable to the GSP was estimated to have been only $381 million. Of this amount, $233 million represented trade creation and $148 million was accounted for by trade diversion—i.e., a replacement of lower-cost exports from developed countries not benefiting from the GSP.[11]

As the GSP schemes come up for renewal in the next few years, developing countries will be seeking several major changes: (1) reduction or removal of NTBs (see below); (2) greater commodity coverage; (3) conversion of preferential tariffs to zero tariffs; and (4) fewer escape clauses which permit developed countries unilaterally to terminate GSP status for commodities whose importation causes "extreme hardship" to domestic producers. It is not clear how far the developed countries will go toward meeting these requests for liberalizing GSP schemes.

In evaluating the net benefits of GSP to the developing countries, one must ask a question raised in connection with commodity agreements: What is the distribution of benefits among the developing countries? Again, the answer is that the distribution of benefits has probably been quite unequal, with the relatively high-income developing countries benefiting much more than the poorest countries. The latter may have lower wages, but lack of complementary factors of production (particularly entrepreneurship) and misguided economic policies have prevented many of these countries from taking much advantage of GSP schemes. Since the market mechanism clearly has not brought forth much of a response

11. See Zubair Iqbal, "The Generalized System of Preferences Examined," *Finance and Development,* 12 (September 1975), 34–39. This article provides a summary table showing, for the Western countries with GSP schemes, the tariff rates and GSP status associated with major product categories. In addition to these Western countries, Bulgaria, Czechoslovakia, and Hungary have also implemented GSP schemes.

in these countries, there is a strong case for providing them assistance in export promotion. As we noted in chapter 10, the major source of assistance in this field has been the United Nations.

NONTARIFF BARRIERS TO TRADE

The significant reduction in average tariff levels in the developed countries over the last three decades has helped developing countries gain better access to overseas markets for their products. The GSP schemes, as we have just seen, have provided additional opportunities. But little progress has been made in lowering nontariff barriers to trade (NTBs). Many political leaders in developing countries view NTBs as evidence of hypocrisy, with developed-country leaders preaching to the developing countries out of one side of their mouths the advantages of free trade and competition, while promising their constituents out of the other side protection against free trade and "unfair" foreign competition. Some NTBs affect imports generally, but most are designed to protect specific products or services. Governments in developed countries considering the removal of NTBs must weigh carefully the political costs of withdrawing assistance to interest groups which may retaliate in large numbers at the polls and/or withdraw financial contributions to the party in power. In the United States, for example, the government is reluctant to remove quotas on the importation of textiles and clothing, industries which employ large numbers of poor, female, and minority workers with limited alternative skills. These industries, in which the United States is at a competitive disadvantage, are thus being phased out gradually—too gradually, in the view of the developing countries.

Other examples of NTBs about which developing countries have complained include subsidies to agricultural producers, especially in the EEC; shipping subsidies, particularly to the high-cost U.S. merchant marine; sanitary regulations which go beyond the protection of the consumer to also protect developed-country producers; and foreign aid tied to the purchase of high-cost goods in the donor country. For many products, these and other NTBs constitute more serious obstacles to trade than tariffs. Prospects for a significant reduction in NTBs are not bright. Developed countries have even found it difficult to reduce NTBs in their trade with each other.

REGULATIONS GOVERNING TECHNOLOGY TRANSFER

As we noted in chapter 14, multinational corporations establishing subsidiaries in developing countries, or granting licenses for the use of their technology, have sometimes taken advantage of their monopoly power to charge very high prices for the transfer of technology and to restrict its use. In some countries, subsidiary firms are limited to selling in the domestic market and are not free to compete with the parent company in overseas markets. They may also be forced to purchase machinery, raw materials, and intermediate goods from the parent company at artificially high prices. Royalty payments may be required even if patents have not been used. These practices have persisted because developing countries, until very recently, paid little attention to the conditions of technology transfer, concentrating instead on commodity pricing issues. Their lack of acquaintance with licensing arrangements, and with the availability of alternative sources of technology, placed them in a poor bargaining position with respect to the multinational corporations based in the developed countries.

In the last ten years or so, this situation has begun to change, largely through efforts of the developing countries themselves. Pioneering research by Latin American economists has helped clarify the issues surrounding technology transfer and has clearly identified specific forms of exploitation. Foreign investment legislation in the developing countries is now beginning to include detailed provisions governing technology transfer. The Andean Group's common foreign investment code, discussed in chapter 14, specifically prohibits the practices noted above, as well as many others. There is also more sharing of information among developing countries on technology availabilities, and there is growing interest in undertaking joint developing-country research on intermediate technologies appropriate to the factor proportions (labor-abundant, capital-scarce) typical of their economies. Developing countries would like to see technology transfer governed by an international code of conduct, but resistance to such a scheme by the developed countries is still strong.

ASSESSING THE EFFECTIVENESS
OF TRADE-ORIENTED GROWTH STRATEGIES

Developing countries began to shift their industrialization policies from import substitution to export promotion in the early and mid-1960s. Sufficient time has now elapsed to assess the effectiveness of this policy shift, and several evaluations have recently been undertaken. These suggest that trade-oriented strategies have been more promising than strategies emphasizing import substitution.

Studies in fifteen developing countries, sponsored by the Kiel Institute of World Economy in West Germany, found that exports of manufactured goods to markets in developed countries increased at an annual rate of 12.8 percent between 1962–1963 and 1972–1973.[12] Government export promotion policies were found to be strongly associated with improved export performance. While other possible explanations of better export performance were not systematically investigated, there is enough circumstantial evidence to support this conclusion. An appropriate exchange rate seemed to be a particularly important factor explaining increased exports, but the nature of the authors' model did not permit them to clearly identify the contribution of other specific policies.

Other studies, using widely differing methodologies, have concluded that the switch from import substitution to export promotion has resulted in more rapid rates of economic growth in countries making the switch.[13] These findings, when combined with recent (though mixed) evidence suggesting that export instability has been less harmful to developing countries than had once been assumed (see chapter 5), indicate that the export-oriented strategy has been a rewarding one.

One might ask, however, whether demand constraints might not make this strategy less attractive in the future, particularly for developing countries which have not yet gained much of a foothold in foreign markets and might be at a disadvantage in comparison with those that have. Specifically, it has been argued that if most developing countries try significantly to increase exports of manufactures, the result will be either to depress prices or to stimulate protectionist actions in the developed countries. An empirical investigation of the demand-limitation hypothesis has concluded that it is less of an obstacle than some observers have believed.[14] In the United States, for example, developing country imports accounted for less than 10 percent of the market for most product categories in 1971; and EEC data for 1973 show that developing country products accounted for only 8 percent of that market. Data for the United States and West Germany suggest that the income elasticity of demand for a number of manufactured imports averages about 3.00—i.e., a 3 percent increase in per capita income will increase the market for these imports by 9 percent. While there may be limitations to market penetration for some particular products, the danger of protectionist reactions—which resulted in increased NTBs during 1978—can be re-

12. Juergen B. Donges and James Riedel, "The Expansion of Manufactured Exports in Developing Countries: An Empirical Assessment of Supply and Demand Issues," *Weltwirtschaftliches Archiv*, 113 (1977), 58–87. The countries studied were Brazil, Colombia, Egypt, Hong Kong, India, Israel, Malaysia, Mexico, Pakistan, Singapore, South Korea, Spain, Taiwan, Turkey, and Yugoslavia.

13. Cited in Anne O. Krueger, "Alternative Trade Strategies and Employment in LDCs," *American Economic Review, Papers and Proceedings*, 68 (May 1978), 270–274.

14. Donges and Riedel, op. cit.

duced through product diversification. In addition, there is greater scope for increased trade in manufactures *among* developing countries; this trade now accounts for only about 30 percent of developing countries' manufactured exports.

Preliminary evidence from studies now being conducted by the National Bureau of Economic Research in twelve developing countries suggests that the employment impact of export-oriented strategies is favorable.[15] Little attention is being given, though, to the effect of export-oriented strategies on income distribution. It is interesting to note that the two countries cited as having the strongest export bias—Brazil and South Korea—have radically different income distributions. Brazil's is one of the most unequal in the world, while South Korea's is one of the most equal.

INCREASED BALANCE-OF-PAYMENTS ASSISTANCE FROM THE IMF

The Articles of Agreement of the International Monetary Fund, established in 1944, permitted member countries to obtain balance-of-payments assistance equal to 125 percent of their quotas. The first 25 percent, called the "gold tranche" because 25 percent of a member's quota had to be subscribed in gold, was available virtually automatically if requested by a country to help it overcome temporary balance-of-payments problems. Use of the four subsequent "credit tranches," each equivalent to 25 percent of quota, required that a country commit itself to progressively more stringent domestic policy measures designed to reduce its balance-of-payments deficits. The gold and credit tranches were to be repaid within three to five years. The domestic policy measures to which countries commit themselves in their "standby arrangements" with the IMF include credit ceilings, restrictions on monetary expansion, and budgetary constraints. In addition, standby arrangements often call for currency devaluation and elimination of multiple-exchange-rate systems.

During the 1950s and 1960s the IMF was frequently criticized, particularly in Latin America, for being excessively concerned with balanced budgets and price stability. While this writer is basically sympathetic to these criticisms, it should be pointed out that the IMF often was tolerant of violations of the terms of the standby arrangements. Moreover, it stressed—correctly, in our view—the importance of export promotion as a means of stimulating growth and development and helping to overcome

---

15. Krueger, op. cit. The countries being studied in this project are Brazil, Chile, Colombia, India, Indonesia, Ivory Coast, Kenya, Pakistan, South Korea, Thailand, Tunisia, and Uruguay.

balance-of-payments problems. Operating at this level, however, the IMF sometimes underestimated the political constraints on developing countries' policy actions, and it devoted little attention to the effects of its policy recommendations on lower-income groups.

Since the early 1960s, IMF assistance to developing countries has been liberalized in several important respects. In 1963 medium-term loans were made available to countries experiencing temporary declines in their export earnings because of falling export prices, adverse weather conditions, or other circumstances beyond their control. These loans do not affect countries' normal borrowing privileges under the gold tranche and the credit tranches. This *compensatory financing facility* was amended in 1966 to increase the benefits available. By the end of 1975, $1.4 billion had been provided to countries experiencing temporary export shortfalls. While this amounts to an average of little more than $100 million annually, and is in the form of loans, it was welcomed by many developing countries whose primary products are subject to sharp price fluctuations or the vagaries of weather.

In December 1975 the criteria for drawing on the compensatory financing facility were again liberalized, permitting countries to draw up to 75 percent of their quota (though only 50 percent during any twelve-month period). These revised criteria help account for sharply higher drawings under this facility in 1976: 2.3 billion Special Drawing Rights (SDR), or about $2.7 billion.[16] Two other factors, though, also were important: the world-wide recession in that year, and the closing of the IMF's temporary "oil facility" (see below) in May 1976. In 1977, as economic conditions improved, drawings declined to SDR 240 million ($281 million).

In addition to the compensatory financing facility, the IMF has developed other innovative schemes to provide greater assistance to both developed and developing countries with balance-of-payments difficulties.

1. A *buffer stock facility* was created in 1969 to help finance the accumulation and storage of selected commodities for which international agreements had been negotiated. Tin and cacao have been eligible for financing, but except for small amounts provided for tin, the buffer stock facility has not been used because prices of these commodities have been relatively high. Sugar was made an eligible commodity after a new sugar agreement was reached in October 1977.

2. In 1974 the IMF made arrangement to borrow SDR 6.9 billion

---

16. SDRs (Special Drawing Rights) are a form of international currency approved by the IMF in September 1967. SDRs equivalent to $9.3 billion were distributed to IMF members in proportion to their quotas during 1970–1972. Originally, an SDR was equivalent to one U.S. dollar, but it is now valued against a "basket" of sixteen major currencies. In mid-September 1978, one SDR was equivalent to US$1.27.

(about $8 billion) from oil-exporting countries and industrialized countries whose balance-of-payments situations were still relatively healthy after the petroleum price increases earlier that year. The resources in this so-called *oil facility* were lent to developed and developing countries experiencing unusually serious balance-of-payments problems because of the higher cost of imported petroleum. Repayment periods were as long as seven years, compared with three to five years under the IMF's normal operations. Table 15.1 shows that borrowings under the oil facility accounted for more than half the IMF's operations in fiscal years 1975 and 1976. The oil facility was terminated in May 1976.

3. An *extended facility* was established in September 1974 to provide assistance to countries whose balance-of-payments difficulties were expected to last several years or more. Borrowings may be spread over three years, with repaments to be made four to eight years after each purchase. Countries may borrow up to 140 percent of their quota in addition to borrowings under other facilities, so long as total borrowings do not exceed 265 percent. However, the policy commitments that must be made are just as restrictive as those under the normal credit tranches, and countries are especially reluctant to make such commitments for periods as long as three years. Use of the extended facility has thus been limited (see Table 15.1), with only Mexico, Kenya, and the Philippines having drawn on it through 1977.

Table 15.1
Borrowings under Various IMF Facilities,[a]
Fiscal Years 1973–1977[b]
(millions of SDRs)[c]

	1973	1974	1975	1976	1977
Gold tranche	641	607	981	1,324	161
Credit tranches	323	239	1,604	461	2,370
Buffer stock facility	5	—	—	5	—
Compensatory financing facility	206	212	18	828[d]	1,753
Extended facility	—	—	—	8	190
Oil facility	—	—	2,499	3,966	437
Total	1,175	1,058	5,102	6,591	4,910

Source: International Monetary Fund, *Annual Report 1977*, p. 51.

[a] Includes borrowings by developed countries under the gold tranche, credit tranche, and oil facility.

[b] May 1–April 30.

[c] One SDR (Special Drawing Right) was equivalent to US$1.15 in 1976 and US$1.17 in 1977.

[d] In addition, SDR 40 million of credit tranche purchases were later reclassified as having been made under the compensatory financing facility.

4. A *subsidy account* was established in 1975 to assist countries most seriously affected by the petroleum price increase. This account subsidizes interest payments on borrowings made under the oil facility. Through September 1977, eighteen beneficiary countries received SDR 41.3 million (about $48 million) in subsidy payments, lowering the effective interest rate on oil facility funds by about 5 percentage points to 2.7 percent.

5. In 1976 the IMF temporarily increased the size of the credit tranches from 100 percent of quota to 145 percent. This increase was in effect until April 1978, when higher quotas came into effect.

6. Also in 1976 the IMF created a special *Trust Fund*, to be financed by part of the profits from its sales of gold through periodic auctions, and from voluntary contributions or loans. Resources made available from the Trust Fund to low-income developing countries carry an interest rate of only 0.5 percent. The repayment period is ten years, including a five-year grace period. During its first two years, the Trust Fund made loans to forty-three developing countries for a total of SDR 841 million (approximately $1 billion).[17]

7. Finally, in 1977, the IMF approved a *supplementary facility* under which seven oil-producing nations and seven industrial countries subscribed SDR 8.7 billion (about $10 billion). This facility is designed to be used in conjunction with regular borrowings in the higher credit tranches or with the extended facility. Repayment may extend over seven years, including a three-and-one-half-year grace period. It remains to be seen whether developing countries will regard the supplementary facility as having the same drawbacks as the extended facility.[18]

Although the IMF's innovations may appear to be impressive, it should be emphasized that the grant element in its total operations is rather minor. Most of the IMF's resources should not be regarded as aid, and they were never meant to be.[19] Still, they are valued as balance-of-payments assistance, and newly independent nations are usually quick to seek IMF membership. It can be argued, though, that developing countries are almost blackmailed into joining the IMF. Membership in the Fund is required for countries wishing to join the World Bank, and

17. In addition, $363 million of the profits from gold sales were distributed to 104 developing countries in proportion to their quotas in the IMF. See *IMF Survey* (Sept. 4, 1978), pp. 266–268.

18. For a more detailed review of the various IMF facilities, see *IMF Survey* (Dec. 12, 1977), pp. 381–385.

19. Developing countries would like to see the IMF assume an aid role, specifically by giving them a disproportionately large share of new issues of SDRs. The original formula benefited the developed countries much more than the developing countries. Reluctance on the part of the developed countries to convert SDRs into an aid instrument is one reason (though by no means the only reason) why the creation of additional SDRs was not approved until September 1978.

being out of favor with the IMF makes private borrowings both more costly and more difficult to obtain. One does not have to believe in an international capitalist conspiracy to recognize that IMF policies, even though more liberal now than ten years ago, restrict the policy options of developing-country governments. Some would argue that "it's for their own good," but others are not convinced that this is so.

SUMMARY AND OUTLOOK

The recent reforms in the structure of international trade and finance have by no means resulted in a radical redistribution of wealth from developed to developing countries. Nevertheless, they are significant steps, and pressures for additional measures and quicker implementation seem likely to increase as developing countries acquire more political power in the international area. This power was greatly enhanced in the 1960s, not just because many developing countries became independent nations but also because they were able to put aside their many political differences to present a united front against the developed countries.

Future efforts by the developing countries to improve their gains from international trade and finance will not be limited to commodity agreements, trade preferences, technology transfer, nontariff barriers to trade, and balance-of-payments assistance. Other areas in which significant changes will be sought include shipping regulations, fishing rights, exploitation of the seabeds, and debt relief. In addition, developing countries will increasingly be adopting the kinds of measures outlined in chapter 10 to diversify and increase their exports.

It is likely that UNCTAD will continue as a major forum in which the developing countries present their viewpoints to the developed countries and seek concessions from them. Developing countries have also gained political strength within the IMF, though that organization's policies are still very much dominated by the developed countries. The Latin American nations are also using a regional forum to present their views and to negotiate with the United States and the EEC. These negotiations began with the formation of CECLA (Special Latin American Coordinating Commission), established in 1963, and are now likely to be sponsored by a new organization called SELA, the Latin American Economic System. This organization has been variously described as a replacement for the Organization of American States (minus the United States), a clearinghouse for ideas and technical assistance, a propaganda vehicle for the President of Venezuela, and a mystical idea with no solid base. Whatever it turns out to be, SELA is one more example of the many ways the developing countries are seeking to apply the principle that in unity there is strength.

Suggested Readings

Bhagwati, Jagdish N., ed. *The New International Economic Order: The North-South Debate*. MIT Bicentennial Studies Series, No. 2. Cambridge, Mass.: The MIT Press, 1977.

   This volume contains thirteen papers, of varying degrees of difficulty, on the subjects of resource transfers, trade relations, world food problems, and technology transfer. Also included is a panel discussion on the New International Economic Order.

Grubel, Herbert G. "The Case Against the New International Economic Order." *Weltwirtschaftliches Archiv*, 113 (1977), 284–307.

   The author argues that market forces would be more effective in relieving poverty in developing countries than planning and controls. He specifically criticizes current proposals for (1) negotiating new commodity agreements; (2) regulating the transfer of technology; and (3) linking aid to the creation of new SDRs by the IMF. As an alternative strategy for assisting developing countries, Grubel recommends that developed countries (1) remove tariffs and nontariff barriers to trade in manufactured articles; (2) continue to support the IMF, World Bank, and the General Agreement on Tariffs and Trade (GATT); and (3) increase official development assistance to at least 0.7 percent of GNP and remove all restrictions on the use of these funds.

Morton, Kathryn, and Peter Tulloch. *Trade and Developing Countries*. New York: Halsted Press, John Wiley & Sons, 1977.

   This is an easily read book describing in detail recent policy and institutional changes affecting developing countries and providing a great deal of valuable statistical information. It is essential, the authors argue, that developing countries regard international trade "neither as a panacea nor as an invention of 'foreign devils,' but as an instrument of development."

Tyler, William G., ed. *Issues and Prospects for the New International Economic Order*. Lexington, Mass.: D.C. Heath and Co., Lexington Books, 1977.

   The eleven papers in this volume discuss the economics and politics of commodity agreements, trade preferences, international monetary reform, foreign aid, private foreign investment, technology transfer, and debt relief.

16

The New Issues

*Limits to Growth, Energy,
the Environment, and the Changing
International Economic Order*

For a decade or so, many economists have been questioning the high priority given by most developing countries—and foreign assistance donors—to economic growth. If growth is the main policy objective, they argue, income distribution and other equity issues will be ignored; widespread improvements in human welfare—i.e., development—will thus occur slowly. Indeed, the experience of today's developed countries suggests that the living standards of the poorest segments of the population will deteriorate. Simultaneously, economic growth has been under attack from another quarter. Some environmental scientists fear that unchecked growth will make the earth unfit for human habitation not too many generations into the future. Predictions of widespread famine, increased deaths from pollution, and other such disasters are now commonplace. Finally, the "energy crisis" of the 1970s has caused many people to argue that economic growth should be slower in the future because it will be too expensive and not worth the price.

Are the no-growth proponents correct in their assessment of the future? Are we really getting close to the limits of growth? If we are, what does this imply for the developed countries, on the one hand, and the developing countries, on the other? If growth did have to come to a halt, would the developing countries accept a freeze in the existing distribution of income among countries? Or would they demand large resource transfers from the developed countries, backing up their demands with threats to use nuclear weapons or terrorism?

These questions cannot be brushed aside even by those who reject the argument that economic growth should come to a halt (for reasons to be explained below). For even if the world economy can continue to grow safely at recent long-term rates, pressures for greater equality in the distribution of world income will increase, and the developed countries will find that they cannot be resisted indefinitely. At the same time, to the extent that the environmentalists' arguments are valid—and many of them are—this should cause us to be more concerned with the quality of output. Similarly, if energy supplies fail to keep pace with the present growth of demand, pressures to conserve energy—or even to do without it for some purposes—will increase. The resulting changes in our pattern of demand, interestingly, could actually increase the prospects for *development*, both in the developed countries and in the developing countries.

THE LIMITS TO GROWTH

The most widely known study describing quantitatively the interrelationships among the various problems confronting humankind was published in 1972. Entitled *The Limits to Growth*, it was prepared by an international, interdisciplinary team headed by Dennis L. Meadows. The study was commissioned by the Club of Rome, an informal, nonpolitical association of some seventy-five eminent private citizens from twenty-five countries, established in 1968. Club of Rome members believe that traditional political, economic, and social institutions and policies are unable to cope with global problems such as food supply, population growth, environmental pollution, and natural resource depletion. Accordingly, they have sponsored a series of studies both to clarify the interrelationships among these problems and to identify promising new policies and institutions for helping to solve them.

The Limits to Growth, the first of these studies, employs a complex analytical tool called systems dynamics, developed by Jay W. Forrester of M.I.T.[1] The model used by Meadows and his colleagues describes the interrelationships and feedbacks among five key factors and shows how they affect the world's vulnerable ecological systems. The five factors, all measured in world totals, are population, agricultural production, industrialization, environmental pollution, and consumption of nonrenewable natural resources. Each of these factors affects the others and in turn is affected by them. Increased population, for example, requires more food

---

1. *Limits to Growth*, in fact, draws heavily on Forrester's 1971 study, *World Dynamics*. For a devastating critique of the Forrester model, see William D. Nordhaus, "World Dynamics: Measurement without Data," *Economic Journal*, 83 (December 1973), 1156–1183. Nordhaus argues that the model is seriously deficient because its assumptions are based on intuitive plausibility (to Forrester), not on actual data whose assumed relationships are verified by empirical study. Moreover, he notes, the model does not employ clearly defined concepts of consumption, output, or production functions; and there appears to be no means for allocating resources over time or between economic sectors. As we shall see below, some of these criticisms also apply to the *Limits to Growth* model.

production. This, in turn, depends on increased use of capital, which uses up scarce resources and produces pollution; and pollution has a negative effect on population.

The "standard run" of this model shows that the continued exponential growth of these variables would result in the collapse of the world's biological and social life-supporting systems in the second quarter of the twenty-first century. Population growth and industrialization are regarded as the ultimate culprits. A rapidly diminishing natural resource base will ultimately slow the growth of industrial output and then cause it to decline. Population growth and pollution will continue to grow for a while, but pollution (combined with decreased availability of natural resources and capital) will cause food output per capita to decline. This, in turn, will cause death rates to rise, a phenomenon exacerbated by a decreasing supply of medical services (which rely heavily on capital). Population begins to decline in about the year 2050.

Economists who have examined this model have been highly critical of it.[2] This is not to say that they reject the possibility of an impending ecological disaster. Indeed, they admit it may occur, but they fear that *Limits* will set people off in the wrong directions in seeking to avoid it. The methodological criticisms of the model center on its major assumptions. The "world model standard run" assumes a continuation of recent (1900–1970) trends in the five factors—until they start to conflict with each other. The authors claim that making the assumptions more realistic would postpone the crisis by only 20 to 30 years. A study conducted by the World Bank, however, suggests that using more reasonable assumptions provides an additional 100 to 200 years.[3] This might be sufficient time for the entire picture to change—e.g., through the harnessing of solar energy.

Let us take a closer look now at the major assumptions of the standard run.

1. *Population. Limits* assumes that population growth will be slowed only by increased industrialization. But many demographers believe that the major cause of declining birth rates (admittedly after a lag of one or more generations) is a fall in death rates rather than industrialization or higher incomes. Indeed, as we saw in chapter 4, there is evidence that birth rates are now falling in many developing countries, even in those where the level of industrialization is quite low.

2. *Technological change.* The model assumes a constant level of

2. See, for example, Everett E. Hagen, "Limits to Growth Reconsidered," *International Development Review*, 14, No. 2 (1972), 10–15; and Mahbub ul Haq, "The Limits to Growth: A Critique," *Finance and Development*, 9 (December 1972), 2–8.
3. Haq, op. cit., p. 4.

industrial and agricultural productivity, a curious assumption in view of historical developments in the past 200 years. While one should not place blind faith in technology, it is also unreasonable to have no faith whatsoever.

3. *Physical capital.* It is assumed that the amount of physical capital determines the amount of production. This ignores the results of recent research on growth in developed countries, which assigns to physical capital a relatively minor and probably decreasing role as a generator of growth.

4. *Land.* The supply of agricultural land available for food production is regarded as fixed. However, if synthetic fibers continue to replace natural textile materials (e.g., jute and cotton), additional land could be devoted to food production. Moreover, a great deal of arable land in the developing countries—particularly Africa and Latin America—is not now being used for growing crops. On the other hand, we should not be too optimistic about technical possibilities for bringing more land under production. As the authors of *Limits* correctly point out, the supply of fresh water will impose a limiting factor in many areas. There is also reason to be concerned about the declining productivity of much existing crop land because of inattention to soil conservation measures—an issue we shall discuss later in this chapter.

5. *Natural resources. Limits* assumes that the supply of natural resources is fixed. This ignores the fact that technological progress in the past 150 to 200 years has "invented" many new natural resources—e.g., petroleum, hydroelectric power, nuclear power, and aluminum. Moreover, estimates of existing mineral reserves may well be conservative.

6. *Pollution.* It is assumed that increased agricultural and industrial output is accompanied by a proportional increase in pollution. However, new capital is frequently less polluting than older capital. Furthermore, the technology already exists to eliminate most existing pollution at relatively low cost. The sharp reduction in automobile exhaust pollution since 1968 is a good example.

To avoid the catastrophe predicted by the "standard run," the authors of *Limits* say that the following would have had to occur between 1970 and 1975:

1. A fall in the world birth rate to bring it in line with the world death rate.
2. A reduction of 75 percent in natural resource inputs per unit of output.
3. A reduction of 75 percent in pollution per unit of output.

In addition, all growth in the capital stock would have to be halted by 1990.

As Hagen has pointed out,[4] apocalyptic models are likely to bring forth apocalyptic solutions, and that is what we have here. It is quite clear that, politically and socially, such goals could not be achieved in so short a time. Surely even the authors of *Limits* recognize this, though they have left us with an unrealistic solution, perhaps to frighten us into taking corrective action. Frightened people, however, need to know where to turn, and *Limits* provides too little guidance in this respect. The authors of *Limits* have protested that the qualifications of their model, and additional "runs" with less restrictive assumptions, have not been carefully studied, and in some cases they are right. But by focusing too much attention on the standard run, they have invited the sharp criticism to which they have been subjected.

A noted Pakistani economist, Mahbub ul Haq, has argued that "the basic weakness of the *Limits to Growth* is not so much that it is alarmist but that it is complacent . . . about the social and political problems which its own prescriptions would only exacerbate."[5] Although *Limits* recognizes that a freeze in the existing distribution of income in a stagnant world would lead to a confrontation between developed and developing countries, it glosses over the problem as if it were only of minor importance. But in fact it is a major issue which would have to be resolved. The possible solutions to the income distribution conflict—e.g., negative growth in the developed countries and positive growth in the developing countries, massive migration from developing to developed countries, or a world income tax—would not be easily agreed to by the developed countries, which now are reluctant even to transfer 1 percent of a rising GNP to the developing world. If agreement along these lines cannot be reached, some developing countries could well resort to terrorism or nuclear blackmail to obtain the resource transfers to which they would feel entitled.

THE SECOND CLUB OF ROME STUDY

The second report to the Club of Rome, *Mankind at the Turning Point (MTP)*, was presented in 1974 by Mihajlo Mesarovic of Case Western Reserve University and Eduard Pestel of Hannover University in West Germany. Like *Limits to Growth*, it is based on a complex computer model. Unlike *Limits*, though, *MTP* does not treat the world as a single unit but rather divides it into ten interdependent regions based on geography, culture, political systems, and levels of development. Each region is described mathematically as a separate "system" with its own peculiar

4. Hagen, op. cit., p. 14.
5. Haq, op. cit., p. 8.

set of economic, technological, and ecological relationships, as well as social and political ones. Thus each region faces its own particular set of limits, and regional catastrophes could occur before the entire world system collapses. In South Asia, for example, a food crisis is predicted even under very optimistic assumptions.

As *MTP* points out, the world has become increasingly interdependent, a fact that is easily seen in the rising importance of foreign trade in the GNP of most nations. Some developing countries are rich in energy resources and short of food, while in many developed countries the opposite is true. Better meeting the needs of both sets of countries would seem to require some form of international cooperation. Indeed, the basic message of the book is that *only* through international cooperation can a world catastrophe be avoided.

MTP develops a series of computer-projected "scenarios" over the next fifty years for such problems as food supply, population growth, and energy. For each problem, several alternative scenarios are devised to show the implications of various policies. In the case of population growth, for example, the *MTP* model shows that implementing an effective population policy in South Asia in 1995 instead of 1990 would result in the death of an additional 170 million children by 2025 (Mesarovic and Pestel, 1976: 81).

Another example concerns the narrowing of the per capita income gap between developed and developing countries. Nobel-prizewinning economist Jan Tinbergen has proposed that the gap be reduced to a 5:1 ratio for the poorest developing countries, and 3:1 for Latin America, by the year 2000 (the ratios in the early 1970s were 20:1 and 5:1, respectively). Mesarovic and Pestel (1976: ch. 5) argue that this would be economically and politically unfeasible. On the other hand, their model shows that continuation of historical trends would tend to widen the gap, a politically and socially dangerous development. Achievement of the Tinbergen target would be desirable, they say, but a more reasonable date would be 2025. The *MTP* model shows that achievement of this target would be much less burdensome to the developed countries over the long run if aid were significantly increased now rather than, say, in the year 2000, when such an increase might be politically unavoidable.[6]

In the area of energy, *MTP* (ch. 10) argues that reliance on nuclear energy amounts to the acceptance of a "Faustian bargain" with frightening implications—an argument with which many scientists would disagree. It is argued that primary reliance should instead be placed on

6. The resources transfer would not necessarily have to be in the form of aid. It could also occur through commodity agreements or other schemes to raise, over the long run, the relative price of developing country exports.

research into the development of solar energy. Once the technology has been mastered, it is suggested that solar farms be concentrated in the present oil-producing countries, which otherwise would face a severe economic crisis once their petroleum reserves are depleted. A decision to locate the solar farms there, if made now, would help secure the cooperation of the oil-producing countries in solar energy research. In the interim, it is argued, the developed countries should restrict their use of energy. This would not necessarily imply a slowdown in economic growth. It could be accomplished instead through a change in the composition of goods and services in favor of those which are less energy-intensive.

The message of *MTP* is appealing to those who wish to see violence and confrontation avoided, and who believe in what in the old days would have been called the brotherhood of man. Moreover, the authors are to be commended for making plausible policy suggestions for achieving international cooperation, such as the solar energy bargain described above. But one wonders if the message will be accepted by political leaders before a regional catastrophe develops. And even if they begin to cooperate then, will it be too late?

SOLVING THE FOOD AND POPULATION PROBLEMS: THREE QUESTIONABLE STRATEGIES

It is useful to consider the implications of three strategies that have been widely proposed for helping to solve the world's food and population problems. In brief, we may refer to them as the (1) stop-developed-country-growth, (2) no-food-aid, and (3) massive-food-aid strategies, each of which sees a close relationship between the food and population problems. The first and third are overtly humanitarian in calling for massive resource transfers to reduce international inequalities. The second, appearances to the contrary notwithstanding, is considered by some of its advocates to be humanitarian in that the ultimate survival of humankind is at stake. In this writer's opinion, all three strategies should be rejected—at least in their extreme forms—because their indirect effects may negatively affect the welfare of developed and developing countries alike. Let us see what these effects are likely to be.

1. *Zero or negative growth in the United States and other developed countries and massive transfers of resources to the developing countries. Sometimes included as a part of this strategy is the suggestion that food and other raw materials should be kept in the developing countries and not exported to the developed countries.*

To criticize this strategy may seem callous, but it is not inconsistent with the view that developed countries can and should transfer more resources to the developing countries. The question is how much more can be transferred in the short run without causing serious long-run problems for both developed and developing countries. A massive resource transfer to the developing countries, accompanied by zero or negative growth in the developed countries, would leave the latter less able to import raw materials and manufactured goods from the developing world. This would drive down raw material prices, which tend to fall faster than the prices of industrial goods. The resulting foreign exchange losses might more than offset the resource transfers from the developed countries. Thus the developing countries would be less able to import machinery, fertilizers, and other key inputs which they themselves do not produce. As we noted in chapter 15, only for a relatively few commodities is it likely that developing countries could form effective OPEC-like organizations to protect themselves against falling raw materials prices.[7] Moreover, few developing countries have the range of resources and size of market to imitate China's success with a policy of relative self-sufficiency.

Similar problems are encountered if developing countries stop exporting food to the developed countries. Increased food supplies in the former may not be consumed at home unless the effective demand for food is increased through a simultaneous transfer of income to those whose food consumption is deficient. This involves a politically difficult decision which must be made by the developing countries themselves. While increased food availability in the developing countries may cause prices to fall in the short run and permit more real consumption from a given income, the price declines will discourage increased output in the long run unless domestic demand for food is stimulated; this will result eventually in upward pressures on prices. Moreover, it may be difficult for incomes to rise if exports are restricted, since foreign exchange earnings will fall and industrialization efforts—as well as food imports—will be curtailed. In addition, imports of fertilizers and other key agricultural inputs may have to be reduced. This will further limit the ability of agricultural production to expand in the developing countries, where most of the expansion has to come from. This kind of scenario is not one in which conditions are propitious for a decline in birth rates.

Finally, consider from the developed countries' perspective the implications of zero growth in their economies for future agricultural production and population growth. Depressed economic conditions in the

---

7. A massive resource transfer did in fact occur after OPEC sharply raised petroleum prices beginning in late 1973. Since there was a lag before OPEC nations could act to reduce their huge balance-of-payments surpluses by importing more goods and services from the developed countries and by returning foreign exchange via the capital account, the developed countries were forced to contract their economies in an effort to reduce their balance-of-payments deficits. Non-oil-producing developing countries saw their growth rates decline during the resulting world recession of 1975–1976. OPEC strategists were well aware that additional massive resource transfers from the developed countries would have caused an even worse crisis, and that is why they have allowed the relative price of petroleum to fall.

developed countries will mean that fewer resources will be available to increase agricultural productivity in both developed and developing countries. Since about 80 percent of annual increases in food production now comes from productivity gains—given the limited amount of arable land not already under cultivation—this is an important consideration. It is important from an ecological standpoint, too. Productivity increases today are highly dependent on fertilizers and other chemical inputs which have negative environmental effects. If we are to lessen our dependence on chemical inputs without affecting crop yields, more research will be needed. The weaker are the developed economies, the fewer resources will be available to devote to this task. Moreover, fewer resources will be available for programs designed to reduce population growth in the developing countries.

Stressing the importance of growth is not to advocate growth for growth's sake. A growth strategy, for example, could be combined with measures drastically to cut developed-country consumption of energy and of animal proteins far in excess of nutritional requirements. This can be done with little sacrifice to growth by changing the composition of output and consumption in the direction of goods and services that are less energy-consuming and less damaging to the environment. Bringing about such a change is no easy matter. Moral suasion—exhortations to drive smaller cars, turn down thermostats, and substitute peanut butter for steak—is not very effective. The price mechanism can be a more effective tool, but consumer pressures make it difficult for politicians to raise taxes on energy consumption. Ultimately, though, it is difficult to see how drastic measures to reduce energy consumption can be avoided.

2. *Do nothing to combat starvation in the developing countries. Food aid will permit more people to survive (but at a miserable level of existence), thus aggravating the population problem.*

Apart from the ethical implications of this strategy, there are good economic and political reasons for not accepting it. Without food aid, widespread starvation would occur periodically in some developing countries, particularly in South Asia and the Sahel. The political implications of denying food aid are worth contemplating. Desperate situations will provoke desperate actions: destruction of property and lives, embargoes on exports to the developed countries, overthrow of governments, etc. The entire world political and social order may well be threatened. This danger was highlighted in a recent computer-simulated study by the Bariloche Foundation, a respected research institution in Argentina. This study concludes that destructive wars are a greater threat to the world than pollution or depletion of natural resources.[8] If such developments

---

8. See "Latin American Study Takes Grim View of Effect of World Food Shortages," *Christian Science Monitor,* June 11, 1974, p. 50.

take place, the economic capabilities of nations will be weakened, making it all the more difficult to solve the population problem by means other than the Malthusian checks of starvation or continued violence.

Alternative means for lowering population growth rates, as we saw in chapter 4, are strategies designed to have an impact on birth rates. These include family planning programs; public health programs to reduce death rates, and thus change attitudes toward family size; and continued industrialization/urbanization/modernization. If the developed countries refuse to provide food aid or to export food-production technology, it is difficult to see how developing countries will find the resources to pursue these alternative strategies.

It is also hard to see how incomes can be significantly redistributed in such an environment, unless by a violent revolution, which might damage the economy as much as help it, at least for a number of years. Income distribution is mentioned at this point because recent research has indicated that population growth rates have begun to decline significantly in countries where progress has been made in redistributing incomes from rich to poor. This redistribution has been accompanied by economic growth and indeed may have been politically possible only because of economic growth.

The discussion above suggests that an appropriate policy for aid to developing countries might be the following: direct food aid would be supplied in emergency situations, but not on a regular annual basis; a long-term strategy would focus instead on increasing agricultural production in the developing countries themselves and would require increased financial commitments by developing countries to their agricultural sectors. Limited food aid might be provided on the condition that developing countries take steps to distribute their incomes more equally. Dr. Norman Borlaug, the Nobel-prizewinning developer of the "miracle seeds," suggests that direct food aid be denied to countries refusing to take effective measures to control their populations. Since individual developed countries might find it politically difficult to tie their aid to such actions, direct food aid and agricultural technology transfer might best be provided through an international agency politically better able to make such requirements.

If the developed countries do not take steps along these lines, either bilaterally or multilaterally, then they are doing very little to affect population growth, apart from contributing to more starvation and violence— with possibly disastrous consequences for the world as a whole.

3. *To increase food consumption in the developing countries, the developed countries should concentrate on direct food aid, rather than seek to increase food production in the developing countries.*

A massive food aid strategy is just as dangerous as one which advocates no food aid at all. We should quickly get rid of the notion that the

United States and the other developed countries can provide enough food to bring everyone up to minimum nutritional standards; we cannot do it. We could, of course, close part of the gap by bringing marginal land under cultivation, but only at increasingly higher costs and with serious environmental risks (see below).

A much better strategy would be for the developed countries to concentrate on increasing food production in the developing countries, through programs which help these countries realize their potential comparative advantage. There are several reasons why this approach is preferable. (a) Large expanses of arable land are not being cultivated in some developing countries, particularly in Africa and Latin America.[9] (b) Significant yield increases are possible in the developing countries, at relatively low cost, *provided that governments in these countries follow appropriate policies with respect to prices, marketing, land tenure, and input distribution.* (c) Direct food aid tends to delay the implementation of programs by developing countries to increase their own food production. Too often, food aid has been seen as a substitute for domestic production, not as a supplement. (d) The balance-of-payments impact of massive food aid (which to some extent would substitute for commercial food sales abroad, thus lowering export earnings), and the resulting increase in food prices in the donor countries, would severely tax the developed countries' economies—assuming they could muster the political will to mount such a program in the first place. (e) Finally, direct food aid would tend to reinforce the dependency syndrome which developing countries are trying to escape. In this connection it is instructive to quote René Dumont, speaking at the U.N.-sponsored World Population Conference in 1974:[10]

> Today, the lack of caution about population and the lack of sufficient efforts in agricultural production are the accomplices of dependence. . . . I consider the population explosion to be the best ally of neocolonialism and dominating imperialism. In a few years, with the growing world scarcities, whoever wields the strategic arm of exportable wheat (therefore, North America) will wield an arm comparable to that of oil, and will be able to impose economic, and even political conditions on everyone else.

A long-term dependency relationship of this nature is politically and socially unhealthy for developing and developed countries alike.

9. In Africa, the presence of diseases is a major obstacle to settlement and cultivation of these lands (see chapter 2), while in Latin America the inequitable land tenure structure is probably the most important factor preventing cultivation.

10. René Dumont, "Population and Cannibals," *Development Forum* 2, No. 7 (September–October 1974), 2. Dumont urges greater sulf-sufficiency in food production and believes that greater food independence will result in slower population growth.

THE ENERGY CRISIS AND THE DEVELOPING COUNTRIES

The sharp rise in petroleum prices announced by the OPEC countries in late 1973 affected not only the oil-importing developed countries, but also caused serious balance-of-payments pressures in non-oil-developing countries (or NODs, as someone has dubbed them). Apart from having to pay higher prices for imported petroleum, many NODs suffered from falling prices for their exports as a result of the 1974–1975 world recession which the petroleum price increase helped bring about.

India, which in the early 1970s was importing 70 percent of its petroleum requirements, provides a good example of the impact of higher petroleum prices on the NODs: the price increase alone amounted to 40 percent of the value of its commodity exports in 1973.[11] Latin America, which unlike India had experienced an improvement in its balance-of-payments situation in the early 1970s, suffered a setback in 1974 as the foreign exchange costs for petroleum in the net importing countries rose to $4.9 billion, compared with only $1.1 billion in 1972. In Brazil alone, foreign exchange outlays for petroleum rose by $1.6 billion despite a fall of 24 percent in import volume.[12]

To help relieve the NODs' balance-of-payments problems, oil-exporting countries, as we saw in chapter 15, have established special funds to lend them money on favorable terms. But despite this rather substantial aid, many NODs are still having difficulty adjusting to higher petroleum prices. Unless additional aid can be obtained, some of them are likely to experience a number of years of slower growth. Meanwhile, they are (1) looking for ways to use energy more efficiently, (2) attempt-to mobilize domestic or foreign resources for petroleum and natural gas exploration within their own borders, and (3) seeking alternative forms of energy, including hydroelectric, geothermal, and nuclear power.

The petroleum crisis has had political as well as economic effects on the developing countries. As Raymond Vernon has pointed out (in Vernon, ed., 1976: 249–250), the initial effect of the OPEC actions was to increase developing-country solidarity in the international arena. Although the NODs were seriously affected by higher petroleum prices, these losses appeared to be more than offset by the prospects of substantial OPEC financial assistance as well as OPEC support for their efforts to exercise market power in negotiating international agreements for other primary products. How long this solidarity will last is difficult to say. It

11. P. D. Henderson, "India's Energy Problem," *Finance and Development,* 12 (December 1975), 21–24.
12. Inter-American Development Bank, *Economic and Social Progress in Latin America, Annual Report 1974,* pp. 49–50.

could be threatened by higher petroleum prices, slow progress in achieving other commodity agreements, sluggishness in OPEC aid disbursements (already of concern to some NODs), or even the development of a new dependency syndrome. But at present, there still seems to be a relatively high degree of unity among developing countries, despite considerable differences in political systems and development philosophies.

THE DESTRUCTION OF FOOD SUPPLY CAPABILITY

A recent study by Erik P. Eckholm (1976), jointly sponsored by the Worldwatch Institute and the United Nations Environment Program, has warned that the ability of many developing countries to produce more food is seriously threatened by damage to the physical environment caused ultimately by population growth in a socioeconomic setting which restricts farmers' options. Aptly entitled *Losing Ground,* this worldwide survey of environmental deterioration describes how much of the world's agricultural land is losing its fertility through erosion, desertification, salination, and other problems resulting from poor land use practices. These practices cannot be attributed simply to farmers' ignorance, though this often plays a role. More importantly, farmers have been forced to overwork once-fertile soil, and to farm steep slopes and other marginal lands, because they lack (1) access to modern agricultural inputs which can increase yields on good soils or (2) access to fertile but underutilized land on large private holdings or on government holdings in remote areas not opened up by transportation or the eradication of disease. In other words, environmental destruction occurs because short-term survival takes precedence over long-run productivity considerations.

Deforestation and the Cultivation of Steep Hillsides

For centuries, population growth throughout the world has been accompanied by the increased cutting of trees to obtain both fuel and new farm land. By 1950 perhaps one-third to one-half of the earth's original forest cover had been stripped. It is difficult to determine the rate at which the remaining forests are being cut down, but given the significant increase in world population growth since 1950, the process of deforestation has probably accelerated. If present trends continue, some observers believe that there will be virtually no forests left in some countries within a few decades.

Deforestation destroys an important ecological system sustaining agricultural production. Forests help hold the soil, preventing it from being washed away during rainstorms. The presence of trees makes it more likely that rainwater will soak into the ground, where it can seep into underground pools and springs. Forests also provide protection against wind erosion and play an important role in the recycling of oxygen, carbon, and nitrogen. If the cutting of trees is not accompanied by replanting and other soil conservation measures, erosion will begin to occur and eventually will become so serious that the land—especially on steep hillsides—can no longer be farmed. In Haiti it has been estimated that as much as a third of the original endowment of agricultural land has been removed from production through such processes, and the remaining hillside land is endangered. Nepal and Ethiopia are among the other mountainous countries where productive capacity has been seriously damaged by erosion.

Erosion affects not only hillsides but also adjacent lowlands. Rain falling on denuded hillsides runs off rapidly, causing floods which destroy crops in the plain below. The soil carried down from the hillsides is deposited as sediment in irrigation canals, drastically reducing the efficiency of irrigation systems and thus lowering crop yields. Siltation in riverbeds causes rivers to overflow their banks, sometimes damaging crops for miles in both directions and—as in India in 1978—claiming many thousands of lives. Siltation of reservoirs also contributes to flooding and in addition restricts the generation of hydroelectric power.

The cutting of trees without reforestation not only has serious implications for agriculture but also can create a fuel crisis. In most developing countries, wood is the principal source of fuel for 90 percent of the population. As demographic pressures increase and the supply of timber is reduced, both rural and urban residents find it more costly and more time-consuming to obtain wood and charcoal. The problem has been compounded since 1973 by the sharp rise in the price of kerosene, one of the principal alternative fuels. The fuel shortage is particularly acute in South Asia and the Sahel, the region immediately to the south of the Sahara Desert in Africa. It is also a serious problem in Haiti and in parts of Central America and the Andes. In India, farmers who do not have access to inexpensive firewood or charcoal burn dried dung, thus depriving the soil of nutrients equivalent to more than one-third of the country's consumption of chemical fertilizers (Eckholm, 1976: 105).

Reforestation campaigns seem to be one obvious way to reverse this environmental deterioration, especially on hillsides unsuited for farming under any circumstances but capable of supplying badly needed fuel on a regular basis if properly managed. Existing reforestation programs, however, have encountered a number of implementation problems. To begin with, countries find it difficult to mobilize the substantial financial and managerial resources needed just to offset the effects of population growth. Governments under pressure to produce growth or development results in the short run find it politically difficult to invest heavily in a program whose benefits are long run. Effectively administering a replanting campaign requires not only a high degree of organization at the national level but also organization at the community level to protect saplings against foraging by animals and to guard older trees against premature harvesting by both local residents and outsiders. Finally, farmers will be reluctant to invest in tree planting efforts unless their land tenure is secure. One of the few countries to have succeeded in reversing the deforestation process is China, but even in this highly organized society the task has not been easy and the cost has been high (Eckholm, 1976: 44–45).

Some hillside land can support sustained agricultural exploitation if terracing is employed to curtail erosion. But terracing will not be effective in all cases, since it sometimes results in landslides which expose too much infertile subsoil (Eckholm, 1976: 98). Moreover, terracing is a questionable investment on land that has already lost much of its original fertility, since the B/C ratio may be highly unfavorable. Finally, it should be pointed out that effective erosion control through terracing requires the cooperation and participation of all farmers on a hillside. If some farmers fail to participate in the construction or maintenance of terraces, the erosion control system will lose much of its effectiveness. Farmers can be enticed into building erosion-control structures through food-for-work programs sponsored by foreign donor agencies, but if they lack land tenure security the structures are unlikely to be maintained.

Desertification

Ecologically unsound farming practices have also caused desertification —loss of arable land in areas with low and often unreliable rainfall. Deserts can be created by overgrazing, burning of the ground cover, and poor cultivation practices. The most dramatic recent example of desertification has been the Sahel. It has been estimated that 250,000 square miles of agricultural or grazing land in this region has been added to the Sahara during the last fifty years (Eckholm, 1976: 61). Also threatened is much of East Africa, including parts of the Sudan which have the potential to become a breadbasket for North Africa and the Middle East.

Desertification can be halted through a reduction in livestock numbers, a ban on the cultivation of marginal lands during periods of good rainfall,[13] and tree planting to reduce wind erosion. Income from live-

---

13. The cultivation of wheat on marginal lands was largely responsible for the "Dust Bowl" conditions in the U.S. Great Plains during the 1930s and in the Virgin Lands, which the Soviet Union attempted to bring into production in the late 1950s and early 1960s (Eckholm, 1976: ch. 3).

stock operations can be increased significantly if herd sizes are drastically reduced so that the remaining animals obtain sufficient forage (through proper range management) to have higher reproduction rates, higher milk yields, and greater weight. If smaller herds will yield higher incomes, why do farmers insist on keeping large numbers of animals? Ignorance is part of the problem, but perhaps not the most important part. Overgrazing can be rational *individual* behavior where rangelands are common property resources. Individuals can try to capture economic rents by increasing grazing intensity up to the point where marginal private cost equals the average product of grazing activity. This may push grazing intensity beyond its renewable limit, causing forage production to decline in subsequent periods and creating external costs in the form of rainwater runoff and erosion.[14] Other factors possibly contributing to overgrazing include (1) the fact that social status in some societies has long been measured by numbers of animals, (2) lack of credit for improved breeds and better range management, and (3) lack of markets for the increased production of milk and meat that smaller herds make possible. Overcoming these obstacles and introducing better range managment is no easy task, as years of determined but disappointing efforts in Bolivia have demonstrated. As with reforestation, a high degree of farmer cooperation is required.

Salination

A potentially serious problem associated with many irrigation systems is the progressive salination of groundwater. The salts present in all water can be filtered down to the water table, carried by irrigation waters which are not absorbed by plants or by the air through evaporation. Seepage from irrigation canals and floodwaters will also filter down to the water table, which will rise over time unless a natural or artificial drainage system is present. When the groundwater reaches the root zones, it begins to affect crop yields adversely. Eventually it will force the substitution of salt-resistant crops such as barley or cotton for wheat and other high-value crops with less tolerance to salt. Finally, capillary action will bring the salty water to the surface, where its accumulation can prevent the growing of any crops. Perhaps 20 to 30 percent of Iraq's once irrigable land has been lost through this process (Eckholm, 1976: 15), and a similarly large-scale problem was developing in Pakistan before the process was halted by action taken during the 1960s.

14. See Morris D. Whitaker and E. Boyd Wennergren, *Common-Property Rangeland and Induced Neighborhood Effects: Resource Misallocation in Bolivian Agriculture,* CID Technical Report 001/76 (La Paz, Bolivia: Consortium for International Development, 1976).

Salination can be prevented through the construction of drainage facilities and the installation of tubewells to tap underground water for irrigation purposes. But these investments will have a favorable rate of return only when accompanied by proper management of pumping and irrigation practices. This requires not only skilled centralized direction of an entire irrigation system but also the cooperation of farmers whose improper use of water, while sometimes constituting rational short-run individual behavior, can be detrimental to all in the long run.

Conserving Food Production Capability

It has been evident from our discussion of deforestation, desertification, and salination that many of the farming practices giving rise to environmental destruction represent rational survival behavior by individuals whose limited access to new technology and productive resources gives them little choice. A solution to these problems requires not only well-planned and well-financed efforts at the national level but also cooperation among farmers who—contrary to popular belief—do not always have strong cooperative or communal traditions. Another important lesson from soil conservation efforts throughout the world is that farmers must have land tenure security if they are to make the investments and undertake the maintenance expenditures required. This often will require radical agrarian reform measures which many governments seem unwilling to take.

The destruction of the earth's food supply capability has extended beyond the land into the sea. In addition to the damage caused by pollution, overfishing has become a very real threat. Indeed, overfishing contributed to a three-year sustained decline in the world's fish catch during the early 1970s. Again, cooperation is required—this time on an international level—to regulate behavior that is rational for individual boat operators or countries in the short run, but ultimately harmful to all. The difficulties in achieving such cooperation are illustrated by the fact that the United Nations Law of the Sea Conference, convened in 1973, is still trying to produce an international treaty.

A NEW INTERNATIONAL ORDER

In May 1974 the Sixth Special Session of the United Nations General Assembly, acting upon an initiative taken by Algeria and supported by the Group of Non-Aligned Countries, adopted a resolution which expressed the member states' desire to work toward the establishment of a "New International Economic Order" (NIEO) governing relations among them. Also adopted at this session was a Program of Action outlining the profound changes in political and economic relationships among nations deemed necessary to establish the NIEO.

The call for a NIEO was not a bolt from the blue. Rather, it was the culmination of a series of events that already had altered significantly the relationships between developed and developing countries in the post-World War II period. At a high level of generalization, we may identify four events that played an important role in bringing about this change: (1) the decolonialization movement, which brought political (but not always economic) independence to scores of nations and, later, significantly altered the balance of power in the United Nations and other international forums; (2) the quadrennial UNCTAD meetings, beginning in 1964, which at first produced few changes in international trade and finance but later resulted indirectly in more change than is commonly assumed (see chapter 15); (3) the collapse of the Bretton Woods exchange-rate system in 1971, an event that particularly weakened the international economic and political power of the United States, one of the major foot-draggers in the movement toward what has come to be called the NIEO; and (4) the petroleum embargo and, later, the price increases implemented by the OPEC nations, which demonstrated clearly that developing nations had the power to take effective unilateral action in matters affecting international economic relationships.

The passage of time should make clear that economic relationships between developed and developing countries are very different now from what they were in 1945. On the other hand, international inequalities have widened, and the changes that have taken place in trade and finance have fallen far short of the developing countries' aspirations. The call for a "new" international economic order demonstrates that the old order, while weakened, has far from vanished. Furthermore, the fact that the resolutions on the NIEO and the Program of Action were adopted without a vote—and with some developed countries placing on the record their reservations and objections to certain principles—signifies that the developed countries as a group remain reluctant to quicken significantly the pace of change.

The NIEO resolution contains twenty principles, among which are statements concerning respect for the sovereign equality of states: accelerated development of the developing countries; freedom of nations to choose their own economic and social systems; regulation of transnational corporations; the formation of producer associations; conservation of natural resources (including food); greater transfer of technology; and the various reforms in international trade and finance which developing countries have been seeking in the UNCTAD negotiations. The Program of Action calls for measures in the following areas:

1. Production and trade of raw materials
2. Changes in the international monetary system
3. Industrialization of the developing countries
4. Transfer of technology
5. Regulation of transnational corporations
6. Adoption of the proposed U.N. Charter of Economic Rights and Duties of States[15]
7. Cooperation among developing countries
8. National sovereignty over natural resources
9. A stronger role for the United Nations in international economic cooperation
10. Special programs to assist least-developed and land-locked countries.

Many of the NIEO principles and action programs are included in the recommendations of a study sponsored by the Club of Rome and prepared by a group of twenty-one individuals representing a variety of countries, social systems, and fields of specialization. This group, headed by Jan Tinbergen of the Netherlands, presented its interim report to the Seventh Special Session of the U.N. General Assembly in 1975; the final report was published the following year as *Reshaping the International Order* (Tinbergen, 1976). The title reflects the group's insistence that the changes needed require far more than new economic relationships; thus "NIEO" becomes "NIO." The international order is defined loosely *"as comprising all relations and institutions, both formal and informal, which link persons living in different nations"* (p. 7). Under the NIO "a life of dignity and well-being becomes the inalienable right to all" (p. 4).

Like the two other Club of Rome studies discussed above, *RIO* stresses the importance of international cooperation for solving the pressing problems facing humankind: "Few of [these] problems have purely national solutions. They call for cooperative solutions: actions organized multilaterally and globally. That they require united action demonstrates

15. The charter was adopted by the U.N. General Assembly in December 1974. Among the Western developed countries, only Sweden voted for its acceptance; countries voting for rejection included West Germany, Japan, the United Kingdom, and the United States. The charter is based on fifteen "fundamentals of international economic relations": (1) sovereign territorial integrity and political independence of states; (2) sovereign equality of all states; (3) nonaggression; (4) nonintervention; (5) mutual and equitable benefit; (6) peaceful coexistence; (7) equal rights and self-determination of peoples; (8) peaceful settlement of disputes; (9) remedying the injustices which have been brought about by force and which deprive a nation of the natural means necessary for its normal development; (10) fulfillment in good faith of international obligations; (11) respect for human rights and fundamental freedoms; (12) no attempt to seek hegemony and spheres of influence; (13) promotion of international social justice; (14) international cooperation for development; and (15) free access to and from the sea by land-locked countries within the framework of the above principles.

the fact that nations, in addition to being economically, technologically, and ecologically interdependent, are also politically interdependent" (pp. 44–45). In the authors' view, the fact of political interdependence requires that solutions to problems be sought within the framework of the United Nations: "it may be weak and imperfect yet it remains the only machinery with the potential for constructing a fairer world" (p. 43). This writer supports their judgment, for if nations cannot resolve their differences through an existing organization, they are unlikely to resolve them at all.

The authors of the *RIO* report argue that achievement of the NIO will require more than the strengthening of existing U.N. agencies; new agencies, they believe, must be created. Among those recommended for the medium term are a World Trade and Development Organization, with the power to regulate export prices and "continually improve" the terms of trade, and a World Energy Research Authority, partially financed by a tax on kilowatt-hours of energy generated by nuclear fission. Over the long run, the *RIO* report calls for the establishment of a World Technological Development Authority, supported by an International Bank for Technological Development and based on the principle that science and technology are the common heritage of all humankind; an International Authority on Transnational Enterprises, with powers to tax the profits of these enterprises; and a World Treasury, with revenues derived from international taxes[16] and from the world community's ownership of productive resources.

These recommendations should make clear—without having to list all of *RIO*'s eighty-three medium-range proposals and several dozen long-range proposals[17]—that what is being called for is a radical change implying not only a more equitable sharing of resources among and within nations but also the surrender of considerable national sovereignty to a world organization(s). Such a transfer of sovereignty would not be accomplished easily. Even the EEC nations—whose economic, social, and political institutions are broadly similar—have found it difficult to give much power to the Communitywide political organizations established by the 1957 Treaty of Rome. Where even greater differences among nations must be reconciled, the creation of a strong supranational authority becomes even more difficult. The authors of the *RIO* report are well aware

---

16. It is recommended that a system of world taxation replace national taxes on minerals, resources which would be viewed as the common heritage of all humankind.

17. Proposals are made in the following specific areas: (1) international monetary arrangements; (2) income redistribution and development finance; (3) food production; (4) industrialization, trade, and the international division of labor; (5) energy, ores, and minerals; (6) scientific research and technological development; (7) transnational enterprises; (8) the human environment; (9) arms reduction; and (10) ocean management.

that acceptance of interdependence and supranationalism will be strongly resisted, but they warn that "excessive insistence on national sovereignty that exists in theory but barely in practice carries the seeds of confrontation, antagonism and, ultimately, war" (p. 45). Elsewhere, they argue that "the arms race is incompatible with the quest for a new international order" (p. 166) and inevitably will lead to nuclear war (p. 26). In brief, their message to the world's nations, like that of the first two reports to the Club of Rome, is "cooperate or perish."

The concluding chapter of the *RIO* report calls for developed and developing nations to negotiate comprehensive "packages" of institutional and policy measures. Under present conditions, the authors argue, negotiations must continue to be carried out through a "collective bargaining" approach in which the element of confrontation is still present. The danger of this approach, they note, is that the unequal strength of the two parties will result only in reformist tinkering with the existing international order. Accordingly, it is recommended that the developed countries recognize the right of the developing countries to have a more equal role in the bargaining process—e.g., through the formation of producer associations and regional associations, the greater use of the United Nations as a forum, and a realignment of voting strength in the IMF and World Bank. The authors recommend that priority be given to the negotiation of packages that would (1) remove gross inequalities in world income and economic opportunity, (2) ensure more harmonious growth of the world economy, and (3) lay the groundwork for a global planning system. In all three cases, they argue, long-term success will require that negotiations involve the centrally planned economies (principally the Soviet Union and China) as well as the developed Western nations and the developing countries.

Some progress toward achieving international agreements in these areas has been made, but the pace has been slower than what the authors of *RIO* would deem necessary. The desirability of narrowing world inequalities is increasingly being accepted in the developed countries, though the measures adopted to help bring this about have been rather weak. With regard to the second package, the developed countries still have some disagreements among themselves over "harmonious growth," and difficult decisions regarding the future of the international monetary system continue to be postponed. OPEC, on the other hand, has in the past few years followed policies supportive of harmonious growth. The least progress has been made in negotiating the third package.

If the authors of *RIO* are right about the need for greater international cooperation to prevent some kind of global catastrophe—and this writer believes they are—does this mean that the present "reformist tinkering" will prove to be too little, too late? Not necessarily. It is possible, for example, to envision a scenario in which the developed countries acquiesce to a series of dramatic actions, comparable to the OPEC price increases of 1973–1974, initiated by the developing countries. The developed countries, while finding such actions painful, would regard the consequences of acquiescence to be preferable to those likely to result from retaliation against the developing countries. The danger with this scenario is that it would perpetuate a climate of hostility; eventually one party or another very likely would resort to violence to achieve its ends. To create a climate of cooperation and to reduce the chances of armed conflict, the developed countries will need to take more of an initiative in helping to create a new international order.

A CONCLUDING NOTE

One does not have to accept the doomsday predictions of the Meadows model to recognize that there are in fact limits to economic growth in a world where increasing numbers of people are pressing on resources whose supply is either fixed or unlikely to grow as fast as demand. While technology can create additional resources, or find ways to use existing ones more efficiently, the serious problems confronting humankind are not going to be solved simply through faith in technology. Neither are they going to be solved if the developed countries adopt a "zero-growth" strategy, for this would have negative consequences for the developing countries, where more rapid growth (and development) is becoming an imperative if the world political order is to be relatively peaceful.

An appropriate strategy for governments of both developed and developing countries would be to attempt to change attitudes toward growth (with the aid of the price mechanism) away from its quantitative dimensions. Economic growth need not be sacrificed if it is increasingly based on the production of goods and services using renewable resources and yielding recyclable wastes. How to change patterns of demand in this direction will be one of the major political problems facing developed country governments in the not-too-distant future. If the change cannot be brought about by market forces and exhortations to act responsibly in the interest of all humankind, then mandatory controls will be difficult to escape.

It should be clear that a solution to global economic problems will require a high degree of cooperation among all the world's nations. Such cooperation will be difficult to achieve given present political divisions, and a lack of understanding of the nature of the problems—in developed and developing countries alike—only makes matters worse. But without international cooperation, prospects for serious strife—with the use of nuclear weapons a growing threat—will be great.

Suggested Readings

Eckholm, Erik P. *Losing Ground: Environmental Stress and World Food Prospects.* Foreword by Maurice F. Strong. New York: W. W. Norton & Company, Inc. for the Worldwatch Institute, with the Support and Cooperation of the United Nations Environment Program, 1976.
    This worldwide survey describes how agricultural land is losing its fertility because of erosion, salinity, and other problems traceable ultimately to population pressures in countries with rigid socioeconomic structures. There is also a chapter on the declining "fertility" of the oceans, attributable to both pollution and overfishing.

Leontief, Wassily, Anne P. Carter, and Peter Petri. *The Future of the World Economy.* New York: Oxford University Press, 1977.
    This report, prepared for the United Nations, utilizes an economic model which divides the world into fifteen regions. It examines such problems as agricultural production, environmental pollution, natural resource scarcities, capital flows, changes in international relations, and the income gap between developed and developing countries. The model shows that the U.N.'s target growth rate for developing countries in the 1970s (6.0 percent annually, or about 3.5 percent per capita) would fail to narrow the relative gap between developed and developing countries' per capita incomes even by the year 2000. The authors argue that accelerated growth and development in the developing world requires both a new international economic order and fundamental social, political, and institutional changes in the *developing* countries.

Meadows, Donnella H., et al. *The Limits to Growth.* A Report for the Club of Rome's Project on the Predicament of Mankind. New York: Universe Books, 1972. (Paper ed. published by New American Library, Signet Books, New York, 1972), 2nd ed. 1974.
    The "doomsday" predictions generated by this study's computerized model have served as a needed antidote to the "growth optimism" of the 1950s and 1960s, which paid little attention to such issues as resource scarcities and environmental pollution. The usefulness of the model is weakened, however, by its unrealistic assumptions regarding the interrelationships and behavior over time of several key variables.

Mesarovic, Mihajlo, and Eduard Pestel. *Mankind at the Turning Point.* The Second Report to the Club of Rome. New York: E. P. Dutton and Company, Inc., 1974. (Paper ed. published by New American Library, Signet Books, 1976.)
    The Mesarovic-Pestel model, more complex than and conceptually superior to the *Limits of Growth* model, divides the world into ten interdependent regions and includes social and political variables. Curiously, it has received relatively little attention, despite the fact that its basic structure is easily comprehensible to the general reader.

Tinbergen, Jan, coord. *Reshaping the International Order.* A Report to the Club of Rome. New York: E. P. Dutton and Company, Inc., 1976.

The authors argue that "the present system of relationships between nations fails to serve the common interests of mankind as a whole and that only through the establishment of a new international order can existing injustices be rectified and the basis established for a more just and peaceful world." Ultimately, it is argued, considerable national sovereignty should be surrendered to a supranational authority.

Vernon, Raymond, ed. *The Oil Crisis.* New York: W. W. Norton & Company, Inc., 1976.

The sixteen essays in this book, written by specialists representing various disciplines and viewpoints, discuss the origins of the 1973 oil crisis and its political and economic impact on both oil-exporting and oil-importing nations.

Index

---

* Note: Asterisks refer to bibliographic entries; italics indicate figures.